D0765583

Persuasive Communication and
Drug Abuse Prevention

COMMUNICATION

A series of volumes edited by
Dolf Zillmann and Jennings Bryant

Persuasive Communication and Drug Abuse Prevention

Edited by

Lewis Donohew
University of Kentucky

Howard E. Sypher
University of Kansas

William J. Bukoski
National Institute on Drug Abuse

LEA LAWRENCE ERLBAUM ASSOCIATES, PUBLISHERS
1991 Hillsdale, New Jersey   Hove and London

Lawrence Erlbaum Associates, Inc., Publishers
365 Broadway
Hillsdale, New Jersey 07642

Library of Congress Cataloging-in-Publication Data

Persuasive communication and drug abuse prevention / edited by Lewis
Donohew, Howard E. Sypher, William J. Bukoski.
    p.   cm. — (Communication)
    Papers delivered at a symposium sponsored by the National
Institute on Drug Abuse and University of Kentucky's Center for
Prevention Research ; held in the spring of 1989.
    Includes bibliographical references and index.
    ISBN 0-8058-0693-8 (c)
    1. Drug abuse—United States—Prevention—Congresses. 2. Drugs
and mass media—United States—Congresses. 3. Narcotics, Control
of—United States—Congresses. I. Donohew, Lewis. II. Sypher,
Howard E. III. Bukoski, William J. IV. National Institute on Drug
Abuse. V. University of Kentucky. Center for Prevention Research.
VI. Series: Communication (Hillsdale, N.J.)
HV5825.P375 1991
362.29′ 17′ 0973—dc20   90-14017
                                            CIP

Printed in the United States of America
10 9 8 7 6 5 4 3 2 1

Contents

Contributors

Jerald G. Bachman • Institute for Social Research, Survey Research Center, University of Michigan, Ann Arbor, MI 48106.

Sara M. Baker • Department of Psychology, The Ohio State University, 142 Townsend Hall, Columbus, OH 43210.

James Banning • Department of Psychology, Colorado State University, Fort Collins, CO 80523.

Michael T. Bardo • Department of Psychology, University of Kentucky, 121C, Kastle Hall, Lexington, KY 40506.

Fred Beauvais • Western Behavioral Studies, Colorado State University, Fort Collins, CO 80523.

Analee E. Beisecker • Center on Aging, University of Kansas Medical Center, 39th and Rainbow Blvd., Kansas City, KS 66103.

Gordon S. Black • Gordon S. Black Corporation, 1661 Penfield Rd, Rochester, NY 14625.

William J. Bukoski • William J. Bukoski, Ph.D., Prevention Research Branch, National Institute on Drug Abuse, 5600 Fishers Lane, Room 10-A-38, Rockville, MD 20857.

Richard F. Catalano • Social Development Research Group, University of Washington School of Social Work, 146 North Canal Street, Suite 211, Seattle, WA 98103.

Anne Cattarello • Center for Prevention Research, University of Kentucky, 147 Washington Avenue, Lexington, KY 40506.

Richard Clayton • Department of Sociology and Center for Prevention Research, University of Kentucky, 147 Washington Avenue, Lexington, KY 40506.

Louis P. Cusella • Department of Communication, University of Dayton, 300 College Park, Dayton, OH 45469.

L. Edward Day • School of Social Work, Social Development Group, University of Washington, DK-40, Seattle, WA 98195.

Lewis Donohew • Department of Communication and Center for Prevention Research, University of Kentucky, 147 Washington Avenue, Lexington, KY 40506.

Susan Foreman • Office of the Executive Vice President for Academic Affairs and Provost, University of South Carolina, Columbia, SC 29208.

Faith Gleicher • Department of Psychology, The Ohio State University, 142 Townsend Hall, Columbus, OH 43210-1222.

J. David Hawkins • Social Development Research Group, University of Washington, 4101 15th Avenue N.E., JH-30, Seattle, WA 98195.

Lloyd Johnston • Institute for Social Research, Survey Research Center, University of Michigan, Ann Arbor, MI 48106.

Lori Kent • Social Development Research Group, University of Washington, 4101 15th Avenue, N.E., JH-30, Seattle, WA 98195.

Carl Leukefeld • Center for Alcohol and Drug Research, 206 Medical Center, Annex 2, University of Kentucky, Lexington, KY 40506.

Jean Ann Linney • Department of Psychology, University of South Carolina, Columbia, SC 29208.

Elizabeth P. Lorch • Department of Psychology, University of Kentucky, 220C Kastle Hall, Lexington, KY 40506-00442.

Susan Middlestadt • Centers for Disease Control, 1600 Clifton Road, N.E. 1-B413, Atlanta, GA 30333

Charles W. Mueller • School of Social Work, University of Hawaii, Hawaii Hall, Rm. 217, 2500 Campus Road, Honolulu, HI 96822.

Eugene R. Oetting • Department of Psychology, Colorado State University, Fort Collins, CO 80523.

Patrick O'Malley • Institute for Social Research, Survey Research Center, University of Michigan, Ann Arbor, MI 48106.

Philip Palmgreen • Department of Communication, University of Kentucky, 147 Washington Avenue, Lexington, KY 40506.

Richard E. Petty • Department of Psychology, The Ohio State University, 142 Townsend Hall, Columbus, OH 43210-1222.

Roy W. Pickens • Addiction Research Center, Baltimore, MD 21214.

Charles R. Schuster • National Institute on Drug Abuse, 5600 Fishers Lane, Room 10-A-38, Rockville, MD 20857.

Susan Spooner • Associate Professor of College Student Personnel Administration, University of Northern Colorado, Greeley, CO 80639.

Dace S. Svikis • Department of Psychiatry and the Behavioral Sciences, The Johns Hopkins University, Baltimore, MD 21205.

Howard Sypher • Department of Communications Studies, University of Kansas, Lawrence, KS 66045.

Teresa L. Thompson • Department of Communication, University of Dayton, 300 College Park, Dayton, OH 45469

Katherine F. Walden • Center for Prevention Research, University of Kentucky, 147 Washington Avenue, Lexington, KY 40506.

Ellen Wartella • Department of Communications, University of Illinois at Urbana Champaign, 103 Gregory Hall, Urbana, IL 61801.

Foreword

Charles R. Schuster
Director, National Institute on Drug Abuse

This book is an important event for the National Institute on Drug Abuse (NIDA), representing a collective effort by NIDA and the researchers interested in drug abuse prevention.It grows out of an historic scientific meeting on the role of persuasive communication and drug abuse prevention sponsored by the Center for Prevention Research at the University of Kentucky, which brought together some of the outstanding researchers on drug prevention from throughout the country.

NIDA was pleased to found the Center in 1987, and looks forward to a continuing, fruitful relationship with it and to the establishment of centers modeled after this one in other communities. The Center provides an opportunity for researchers from various specialty areas to work together with people in the community who are involved in various aspects of drug abuse prevention. The Center, with its cross-department and cross-college structure, serves to facilitate interdisciplinary research and communication by linking social and life science perspectives on substance abuse.

Furthermore, by linking research programs with the efforts of community practitioners, who generally hold a more pragmatic view of drug abuse problems, the Center works to broaden the perspective of the academic-based researcher and maximize opportunities to develop prevention programs that will be both effective and politically and economically feasible. The funding of the Center demonstrated a recognition at the federal level that prevention sciences had come of age and represented an area of inquiry that demanded integration throughout the establishment of and support of university-based center projects. The maturation of the Prevention Research Center at the University of Kentucky and the establishment of other centers modeled after it, has the potential to move prevention sciences forward at an unparalleled pace.

My view of drug abuse prevention research encompasses scientific research related to drugs, per se, the individual, his or her environment, and the interaction of these three classes of variables. If a drug-free society is to become a national reality, not just a goal of the federal government, a fundamental change will have to occur in the lifestyle of vast numbers of people.

The linear decline we have seen in cigarette smoking in the United States since 1974, a period during which 48 million Americans, 20 years of age and over, became former smokers, gives us proof that large-scale lifestyle changes can occur in the way harmful substances are self-administered. Prevention researchers and practitioners can take pride in the fact that smoking initiation has decreased across races and gender. However, analyses of 25 years of smoking data have highlighted the fact that not all groups respond similarly to messages about smoking's harmful effects.

Analyses of the trends show that education has replaced gender as the major sociodemographic predictor of smoking status, with more highly educated persons becoming ex or nonsmokers at five times the rate of less-educated persons. It is estimated that by the year 2000 at least 30% of those who have not entered college will be smokers, whereas less than 10% of college graduates will smoke. Rates along gender/race lines will be almost equal with 23% of women smoking to 20% of men and 25% of Blacks smoking versus 21% of Whites.

NIDA also has been receiving good news from its annual national surveys of drug use among high school seniors, directed by some of the chapter authors in this book. These surveys have shown declines in the use of many illicit drugs and increases in the percent of seniors concerned about adverse effects of marijuana, PCP, and cocaine. Researchers working in prevention of both illicit and licit drug initiation and use have reason to be optimistic that carefully planned programs can influence young people's understanding of the potential adverse effects of drugs and their use of them.

The trends we have seen in smoking behavior in the general population and illicit drug use in those young people who reach their senior year in high school can be conceptualized as resulting from four major factors: (a) accurate information, (b) adequate motivation to become or remain drug-free, (c) ongoing social support systems, and (d) reinforcement for drug-free behaviors.

The provision of accurate information begins with an understanding of a drug's properties and its reinforcing effects. Since its inception in 1972, NIDA has funded the work of psychopharmacologists who, using animal models of self-administration and drug discrimination, have characterized the abuse liability and reinforcing properties of new psychoactive drugs. Although it is often overlooked when prevention efforts are examined, testing that provides clear information about the probability that a drug will be abused is a first stage of drug abuse prevention.

Those of you who work in persuasive communications are acutely aware that accurate information is not in itself adequate to guarantee changes in drug use behavior or any other behavior, for that matter. In a review of the role of mass media in preventing adolescent substance abuse, Brian Flay and Judith Sobel note that information-based programs do change knowledge. However, they caution that knowledge is only one of the factors in a chain of events that determine a final behavioral outcome. We know, for example, that who imparts information and how it is imparted are important determinants of whether or not a person acts on that information. In a paper published in 1986, Nancy Tobler[1] presented a meta-analysis of 143 adolescent drug prevention programs to identify the relative success of program variables in influencing knowledge, attitudes, use, skill and behavior measures. She evaluated five modalities of programs:

- those that utilized only knowledge about drugs,
- those concentrating on knowledge about affective psychological features that place people at risk for drug use,
- those combining drug and affective education,
- those utilizing peer influence to provide a social inoculation against vulnerability to drug use, and
- those concentrating on teaching not directly focused on drug abuse.

Tobler's analysis showed that those programs using peers in a instructional or counseling role to teach refusal skills, interpersonal communication, or affective awareness were clearly superior to all others in decreasing alcohol, tobacco, and illicit drug use. With the support of funding from NIDA, Dr. Tobler has been able to increase the number of studies covered in the meta-analysis and to assess more fully the role of the various persons who deliver information about drugs to teenagers. Clearly, information about the relative success of various program modalities and service delivery personnel will help to improve future programs.

Richard I. Evans of the University of Houston whose research program is responsible for much of our current knowledge about social inoculation techniques believes that in spite of our current progress, use of licit and illicit drugs will remain a significant social problem until we have a clearer

---

[1]From Tobler, N. (1986). Meta-analysis of 143 adolescent drug prevention programs. *The Journal of Drug Issues, 16*(4), 537–567.

idea of numerous variables related to initiation, escalation, and maintenance of drug use. More research is needed to clarify the factors that account for the variance in drug abuse patterns in minority populations, lower socioeconomic groups, the less-educated segments of our population, between the sexes, and among the very young. This information will allow us to target prevention programs for those who are at greatest risk for drug abuse.

In discussing the role of federal research in drug abuse prevention in his chapter in this book, Dr. Carl Leukefeld describes NIDA's broad portfolio of sponsored programs designed to provide information on the etiology of drug abuse, the characteristics that constitute vulnerability to initial drug use and its escalation, and the socioeconomic and other demographic factors that act to modify drug use. We view these prevention research efforts as synergistic with intervention research designed to identify strategies, including the use of communications, that can prevent or reduce drug taking.

Preface

The history of drug abuse prevention campaigns suggests significant limitations in producing measurable changes in behavior. Carl Leukefeld points out in his chapter of this book that a moratorium on drug information dissemination by the Federal government was imposed during the Nixon Administration because of a concern that these publications may encourage interest in drug use rather than prevent it. Although scant scientifically sound empirical evidence exists to support these opinions, a number of textbooks in the social sciences still reference these early reports as evidence against persuasive campaigns, particularly those employing the mass media. Reviews of early drug abuse prevention campaign research appears to indicate that many studies suffered from a lack of rigor in theory testing and inadequate research methods. Political sensitivities to the drug-crime nexus current during the middle and late 1960s also complicates objective interpretation of the efficacy of drug information activities implemented during this era.

In recent years, however, research in communication and in its uses in drug abuse prevention have become considerably more sophisticated, underlying assumptions have changed, and communication is being used far more effectively (see e.g., Shoemaker, 1989[1]). For one thing, persuasive messages are not expected to carry the entire burden of persuasion, but are paired with other activities in both mass and interpersonal campaigns.

One fundamental change is in the assumptions made about audiences themselves. Early work assumed direct effects of media on reactive au-

---

[1]Shoemaker, P. J. (Ed.). (1989). *Communication campaigns about drugs: Government, media, and public.* Hillsdale, NJ: Lawrence Erlbaum Associates.

diences, an overly simplistic approach. When evidence was found in the early voting and influence studies that this was not true, a limited effects model was developed, assuming people were more pro-active and that peers were the predominant sources of influence. Models developed during this period drew upon the failure of early public communication campaigns for empirical support. The models tended to be guided by the "rational human beings" social science theories of the time, which assumed that individuals are fully conscious of the elements involved in their information processing and decision making.

More recent research indicates far more complex processes, with information exposure and processing guided by both cognition and affect, which can vary greatly across individuals. This research has led to more careful selection of audiences to be targeted and more precise design of messages to reach them. Approaches in which messages are prepared for a single mass audience are giving way to approaches involving formative research in which samples of the target audiences are used in evaluating and painstakingly revising message designs before they are brought forth for presentation to the public.

More recent mass media campaigns against drug abuse, smoking, or other areas of health and behavior concerns have been found to have one or more of the following effects:

1. Substantial changes in the general climate of public opinion have been brought about through campaigns that involve extensive use of the media and are targeted at general audiences over extended periods of time.
2. More direct changes in individual attitudes and behavioral intentions, on the other hand, may be brought about through mass media messages which employ formative research in their design and that are more precisely targeted to at-risk individuals.

In both these instances, there is a somewhat more modest expectation of the media than in older studies. In the more recent studies, the media are used primarily to motivate individuals to contact other persons for interpersonal instruction or assistance.

In this book, we bring together some of the most successful drug abuse prevention researchers in the country—along with others with particular expertise in either persuasive communication or drug abuse prevention—to address use and effects of both mass media and interpersonal strategies.

Chapters in this book were written by participants in a conference at the University of Kentucky in the Spring of 1989 under sponsorship of the National Institute on Drug Abuse and the University's Center for Prevention Research. The initial impetus for the conference came from one of the editors of this book, Dr. William Bukoski, Program Director, Intervention Research, of the Prevention Research Branch of the National Institute on Drug Abuse, who suggested that a conference on communication and drug abuse prevention might be a good project for the newly established Center. He suggested that it be modeled after an earlier conference at the University on communication, social cognition, and affect, which brought together many of the leading scholars in these areas for a conference and book.

At this point, we express appreciation to a number of persons who have been involved in our labors. Lewis Donohew would first like to thank Bill Bukoski, who has been the project officer for each of his studies since he began studying drug abuse prevention in the middle of the past decade, for Bill's penetrating criticisms and sound advice on the projects during this period. He also thanks Nancy Grant for her enthusiasm, energy, and exceptional attention to detail in helping carry out a highly successful conference; David Helm, hard-working research analyst and gadfly, who has been with him from the beginning; Patricia Lawrence, self-starting and innovative project manager for the first study; Mary Rogus, jack of all trades and master of all of them; Margaret Dsilva, who is both a quick learner and conscientious researcher; Stacy Baer, who has kept the subjects moving and their attention scores coded; and Michael Kilbourne, the talented and cooperative producer of our public service announcements used in the research. Finally, he thanks his co-editor on a number of projects, Howard Sypher, his co-principal investigators, Philip Palmgreen and Betty Lorch on the PSA project, and Dick Clayton, whose DARE evaluation project is providing a piggy-back ride for a longitudinal study of sensation-seeking, peer influences, and drug use, for being the knowledgable and cooperative colleagues that they are, and Jim Applegate, Marlyne Kilbey, Mark Prather, David Ben-Nahum, Reggie Boerschinger, and Karen Lindeman for filling in all the rest of the blanks.

I

DRUG ABUSE PREVENTION:
HISTORY AND PERSPECTIVES

1

A Definition of Drug Abuse Prevention Research

William J. Bukoski
National Institute on Drug Abuse

My task in this chapter is to provide a definition of *drug abuse prevention research*. The assignment is challenging because two definitions are necessary. First, one needs to define the term *drug abuse prevention* and, second, provide a framework for understanding and defining research focused on the etiology of drug use onset and progression and on the assessment of the effectiveness of preventive interventions. I limit this discussion to the development of a research model most appropriate for defining and guiding the research.

A DEFINITION OF DRUG ABUSE PREVENTION

There have been a number of diverse definitions and perspectives in the research literature describing the term *drug abuse prevention*.

The Public Health Model

For example, the public health model, which encompasses the concepts of primary, secondary, and tertiary prevention (Last, 1980), has been applied as a framework for defining drug abuse prevention. According to this model, primary prevention activities are designed to prevent the onset of a disease. Prevention of the initial use of drugs, including alcohol, tobac co, marijuana, cocaine, and other illicit substances, has been defined as primary prevention of drug abuse.

Secondary prevention has traditionally included early identification and corrective actions or treatments to halt the progression of the disease and its sequelae after inception (Clark & MacMahon, 1981; Sheridan & Winogrand, 1987). Tertiary prevention refers to those health strategies designed to restore functioning through rehabilitation, prevent disability, and maintain sobriety through relapse prevention programs.

The problem with the public health model is that the dividing lines between primary, secondary, and tertiary prevention are not clear and have not been firmly agreed upon by experts in the public health and mental health fields (Clark & MacMahon, 1981). In response to the differences in point of view, Albee and Gullota (1986) suggested dropping the terms *primary, secondary,* and *tertiary* altogether and simply using the terms *prevention, treatment,* and *rehabilitation* to describe the three functional levels of the model.

The Communicable Disease Model

A second prevention model adapted from the study of communicable diseases focuses on prevention and treatment of three elements: the agent, the host, and the environment (Wilner, Walkley, & O'Neil, 1978). The agent is that entity that by its presence (e.g., bacteria or virus) or by its absence (e.g., Vitamin C), is the cause of the disease. Agents can be physical (sources of injury), chemical (dust, vapors), nutrient (vitamins, minerals), or biologic (bacteria, viruses, etc.). The host relates to human susceptibility or resistance to the disease that can be influenced by a number of factors including heredity and lifestyle behaviors, for example, social attitudes/beliefs/norms, quality of living conditions (crowding, deprivation), social discrimination, or lack of economic mobility can influence the spread of a disease and the health of the community.

The agent–host–environment communicable disease model has been applied to chronic diseases such as alcohol and drug abuse. For example, Haddon, Suchman, and Klein (1964) found that death and injury resulting from auto crashes are due to the interaction of three factors: availability and exposure to alcohol (agent), the consumption of alcohol and intoxication by the driver (host), and excessive speeds on dangerous roadways (environment).

The communicable disease model can guide the development of appropriate prevention strategies. For example, Arnold, Kuller, and Greenlick (1981) suggested four categories of action (the drug examples are the author's):

1. increasing individual resistance to the agent (smoking cessation, dietary supplements, peer resistance training);
2. protecting the individual from the agent (seatbelt restraints, minimum drinking age laws, awareness education, and promotion of abstinence);
3. isolating the agents from the host (elimination of asbestos from the environment, smoke-free workplace rules and regulation, drug-free school/community zones); and
4. modifying the agent to reduce risk of harm (lowering food cholesterol and fat content, lowering the alcohol content of the beverage).

The Risk-Factor Model

A third model is the risk-factor model that focuses on the identification of those psychological, social, biological, and behavioral factors that appear to be correlated with the emergence of a health problem. The term *risk factor* was used initially by Stamler in 1958 (Arnold et al., 1981, p. 5) and was applied to cardiovascular disease prevention (Stamler, 1978). The concept has quickly become a valuable and popular approach in public health and specifically in drug abuse prevention.

Guided by the risk-factor model, specific factors that place an individual at risk of heart disease, cancer, stroke, or alcohol and drug abuse are identified by epidiological research and targeted for corrective action (Matarazzo, Weiss, Herd, Miller, & Weiss, 1984). Disease prevention and health promotion strategies are designed to either remove or reduce the extent of adverse effects produced by relevant risk factors.

In the late 1970s, the U.S. Public Health Service devoted increased attention to disease prevention and health promotion by utilizing the risk-factor model. For example, in 1979, then Secretary of Health Education and Welfare, Joseph Califano, in his report to Congress, indicated that of the 10 major causes of death in the United States (heart disease, cancer, stroke, all accidents except motor vehicle, infectious diseases, motor vehicle accidents, diabetes, cirrhosis of the liver, arteriosclerosis, and suicide), 7 could be substantially reduced by changes in five health behaviors including diet, smoking, lack of exercise, alcohol abuse, and the use of hypertension medication (Califano, 1979).

Since that time, the risk-factor approach to disease prevention and health promotion has been the basis for a number of prevention initiatives conducted by the office of the Assistant Secretary for Health, Office of Disease Prevention and Health Promotion; Department of Health and Human Services, including the 1990 Health Objectives for the Nation (DHHS, U.S. Public Health Service, 1980); and more recently, the Year 2000 Health Objectives currently under development by the U.S. Public Health Service.

Etiological research helps identify significant psychological, behavioral, social, environmental, and biological risk factors that correlate with drug abuse. Since the 1970s, a large number of research studies have examined these factors. Research by Gorsuch and Butler (1976); Bry (1983); Hawkins; Lishner, Catalano, and Howard (1986); Newcomb (1988); Cloninger (1988); Schuckit (1987); Pickens and Svikis (1988); and numerous other scientists provide a theoretical basis and empirical structure toward our understanding of the causes of drug abuse and what preventive interventions can be designed and tested.

Although this research is still in progress, the picture of who is at risk of taking drugs is becoming clearer. Research has identified a number of categories of risk factors including factors that pertain to the individual, the family, peer structure, the community, the school, the workplace, and the neighborhood (NIDA, 1987).

A number of individual risk factors have been reported in the literature, including early use of alcohol and cigarettes; nonconventionality, inadequate social bonding, and deviant behavior; adult, parental, or older sibling role models who use drugs; novelty or sensation seeking; personality factors such as early signs of aggressive or noncompliant behavior; low religiosity; low academic achievement; psychological distress or depression; and low self-efficacy or self-acceptance (Jones & Battjes, 1985; Newcomb, Maddahian, & Bentler, 1986).

Family factors include history of alcoholism and antisocial behavior, parental and older sibling drug using role models, ineffective parenting practices (NIDA, 1987), and lack of mutual parent–child attachment and warmth (Brook, Whiteman, Gordon, Brook, & Cohen, in press).

Peer factors include use of drugs by peers (Newcomb et al., 1986), peer cluster influence through social interaction (Oetting & Beauvais, 1987), and peer social pressure (Brown, Stetson, & Beatty, 1989).

Community factors include availability of alcohol (Rush, Gliksman, & Brook, 1986), drinking and driving laws and their enforcement, price of alcohol, minimum drinking age laws (NIAAA, 1987), social/cultural norms and mores relevant to use, social stress (Linsky & Straus, 1986), poverty, and lack of economic mobility and social supports (Auslander, 1988).

Although traditionally not viewed as an etiological risk factor to drug use, survey research indicates that an important risk factor is a youth's perception of harmful consequences and social disapproval of using drugs (Johnston, 1985). Bachman, Johnston, O'Malley, and Humphrey (1988) reported that analyses of the downward trend in marijuana use from 1978 to early 1990 can best be explained by positive changes in these two variables since the late 1970s. They summarize the research by saying, "the analysis suggests that if perceived risks and disapproval associated with regular marijuana use had not risen substantially in recent years, the decline in actual use would not have occurred" (Bachman et al., 1988, p. 92)

A press conference announcing the release of findings from the 1988 High School Senior Survey of Drug Abuse, indicates that positive changes in these same two variables may also help explain the recent and rather dramatic downturn in cocaine use reported by high school seniors from 1986 to the present (ADAMHA Press Conference, 1989).

These findings are important to our understanding and definition of drug use at the individual and peer-cluster level, gleaned from a variety of information sources including the media, prevention education, and perhaps most importantly, personal of friends' experiences with drugs, and the establishment of a drug-free social norm at the peer-cluster and social level, may help reduce the use of drugs by adolescents over the course of time.

Etiological research indicates that drug abuse involves the presence and interaction of multiple risk factors. For example, Bry, McKeon, and Pandina (1982) and Newcomb et al. (1986) reported that the number of risk factors present is linearly related to increased percentage of users, frequency of use, and heavy use. According to Newcomb et al. (1986) "Those with zero risk factors were one-fifth less likely to use cannabis on a daily basis than the total sample, whereas those with seven or more risk factors were almost seven times more likely to be heavy users of cannabis compared to the sample in general" (p. 528).

The vast number of etiological research studies conducted to date supports the view that there are many different pathways to drug abuse and there is no one simple reason why youth must be vulnerable to it. Likewise, this literature suggests that less exposure to salient risk factors may serve to protect or inoculate youth against the subsequent abuse of drug (Simons, Conger, & Whitbeck, 1988).

The prevention intervention research literature suggests that given the multiple pathways to drug abuse, the most effective prevention approach would be to use multiple components that address a number of salient risk factors within the same program (Schaps, DiBartolo, Moskowitz, Palley, & Churgin, 1981).

These programs could focus on the prevention of the precursors to drug use such as aggression (Lochman & Curry, 1986), early problems with interpersonal relationships (Yu, Harris, Solovitz & Franklin, 1986), and oppositional behavior (Gard & Berry, 1986) as well as those risk factors that emerge after drug use has first appeared and has become more frequent, intense, and problematic. In addition, Hawkins suggested building stronger social bonds to the schooling process at the elementary grade level through expansion of opportunities to learn and succeed in school, development of academic skills needed for mastery learning, and positive and consistent reinforcement for learning gains (Hawkins, Doeck, & Lishner, 1988).

Because drug abuse is a progressive and chronic health problem with multiple pathways, it may be necessary to target different preventive strate gies at different stages of the emerging problem. It also appears that one should simultaneously focus preventive strategies of the individual, the family, and the community, including the school, workplace, and neighborhood.

A Comprehensive Definition
of Drug Abuse Prevention

A comprehensive approach to drug abuse prevention would offer a combination of prevention strategies consistent with the needs and developmental level of the individual, while sequencing these interventions to be appropriate to each stage of drug use behavior.

This definition of drug abuse prevention recognizes that drug abuse encompasses behaviors covering the spectrum from nonuse to dependency and includes a comparable range of theoretically based prevention strategies appropriate to different points along this continuum of drug use.

Stages of Drug Use.   Addiction to drugs and drug dependency is, for most drugs, a progressive health and social problem that takes a person from a point of being categorized as a nonuser through being drug dependent. The first stage is that of nonuse, followed by a series of initial drug experiences comparable to having that first, second, third cigarette, drink, and so forth. Some view prevention (or primary prevention) as involving only these two stages: transition from nonuse to initial or first time use. An alternate position is that these two stages are only the first two of six stages of drug abuse development and that all six stages are within the purview of drug and alcohol prevention programs.

Drug prevention programming as practiced today at the state and local levels does go beyond the more restricted concept of primary prevention and includes prevention program activities aimed at youth and young adults who are moving through the stages of drug experimentation, occasional/frequent use, making drugs an integral part of their lifestyle to the point of a medically diagnosed drug abuse program.

At that point, prevention as a health program concept ends and drug treatment, with its many therapeutic approaches begins. Optimistically, treatment will eventually lead to recovery that can be maintained through rehabilitation and relapse prevention activities that an individual needs to pursue after leaving a treatment program.

Multiple Prevention Program Components.   The recognition of the variety and complexity of individual, family, peer, and community risk factors of drug abuse have led to the development of at least four types of prevention programs.

Information programs attempt to describe the harmful physical and psychological consequences of drug consumption. Information programs include media campaigns, drug education lectures, films, pamphlets, flyers, bumper stickers, and media coverage of drug-related events (Shoemaker, 1989). *Education programs* are designed to remedy deficiencies in social and psychological skills in order to improve interpersonal communication, promote self-understanding and acceptance, and master refusal training to counter a variety of social influences to use drugs. Given that research indicates that academic success and achievement may serve as a protective factor against drug abuse (Brook, Gordon, Whiteman, & Cohen, 1986; Hawkins et al., 1988), comprehensive drug prevention programs include educational activities to improve educational attainment through techniques such as mastery learning (Kellam et al., in press).

Alternative programs provide opportunities to youth who may be at risk of drug use because of an unsatisfied need for excitement or sensation and need a socially acceptable and authentic way of offsetting boredom or dissatisfaction with their lives. Positive alternatives to drug use have included outward bound or wilderness experiences, cooperative community service or restoration projects, sky diving, volunteering one's time or talents to help less fortunate persons (Cook, 1985; Cook, Lawrence, Morse, & Roehl, 1984; "Federal grant aids," 1989; Tobler, 1986).

Finally, for those individuals who need special assistance to recognize the signs and symptoms of initial drug and alcohol dependency, comprehensive prevention includes *intervention programs* that may take the form of crisis intervention or drug hotlines, peer counseling, peer leadership programs, parent–peer groups, psychological counseling at the individual or family level, and the use of physiological testing to detect or confirm a drug use episode that includes rapid eye testing, breath analyzers or urine screens (Manatt, 1983; Morehouse, 1979; Myrick & Erney, 1979; Telesis II, 1989; Tobler, 1986). Prevention intervention of this type represents the last program activity that attempts to deal with an emerging drug use problem, prior to medical diagnosis of addiction or dependency.

This type of comprehensive prevention model has flexibility and can be expanded to focus preventive activities at four levels: the individual, the family, the peer group, and the community at large, including the school, workplace, and neighborhood. One can target information, education, alternatives, and intervention programs from the individual through all levels of the community. Given the complexity of the drug abuse problem, its pervasive negative influence on society, and the multiple pathways that can lead to drug use onset and progression, it appears that comprehensive prevention programming may be the most appropriate public health approach to the drug abuse problem.

A DEFINITION OF DRUG ABUSE RESEARCH

The next question becomes: How does one research the effectiveness of comprehensive prevention programming?

A Drug Abuse Prevention Research Model

A major question facing the prevention field is: Do drug prevention programs work? Addressing this question requires a comprehensive approach to prevention intervention research that encompasses three levels of investigation: process research, outcome research, and impact research (French & Kaufman, 1984).

Process Research. In experimental research terms, *process research* is the equivalent of measuring the "independent variable" (Schuerman, 1983). Verification of the independent variable is important for three reasons (Shaver, 1983). First, researchers should not draw conclusions concerning the efficacy of an intervention without first confirming that the independent variables was actually implemented. Second, accurate replication of research requires a thorough knowledge of the experimental conditions and setting. Third, synthesis of research findings is facilitated because data drawn from research studies that include accurate and well-defined interventions can be more accurately and comprehensively.

On the surface, the task would seem to be straightforward. One would simply ask: Did the client receive the intervention or not? The issue is, in reality, far more complex particularly given that prevention programs include multiple components. Process research attempts to answer a number of salient questions.

1. What was the theoretical basis, scope, and quality of the intervention?
2. Was the intervention implemented as planned? Did the intervention instructor modify elements of the program to meet his or her unique teaching styles or the perceived learning needs of the subjects? Did the client or subject attend all sessions of the program? Did the subject actively participate in all sessions of the program? What was the actual content of the program as delivered in the test site? Was the content varied either in terms of sequencing or extent of coverage?
3. Was the intervention relevant and appropriate to the target audience?
4. Was the program fiscally accountable and efficiently operated?

Unlike the laboratory studies in the physical sciences, where the quantity and quality of the independent variable is usually well-controlled, the prevention intervention trial is conducted in laboratory and applied settings such as in the school, community, and workplace that may effect the independent variable. Process research needs to identify the source, magnitude, and potential consequences of these influences on this variable.

Process research provides a systematic method of collecting information about the program. Weiss (1972) indicated that it is important to describe the black box for several reasons. First, process research provides the meaning of the intervention by delineating the individual activities involved and their range. Second, process research contributes to our knowledge of which elements in the intervention were working and which elements did not contribute to the intended effects.

Weiss recommended the inclusion of information on the output and intervening variables in evaluation research. Input variables include purpose, principles, methods, staffing, demographics of target audience, length of program, location, and management system. Intervening variables are of two types: program operation and bridging variables. Program operation variables include the frequency and type of program activities provided to the clients, coordination of program components, and client receptivity to the program. Bridging variables include those mediating factors thought to facilitate the attainment of program outcomes, such as changes in drug use. For example, the program may posit that improved resistance or assertiveness skill training will lead to reductions in drug use. Process research reveals the extent to which these theoretically relevant and predicted changes in bridging variables occurred as the result of exposure to intervention.

But process research is more than just head counting of clients in a session or monitoring the flow of events.

Process research captures in still-frame fashion the operational features and dynamics of a prevention program through qualitative analysis. Process research details the theoretical basis for the intervention and describes in comprehensive fashion the program activities planned and implemented to achieve the desired changes in drug-related attitudes, knowledge, and behaviors. Also, process research identifies and measures unanticipated or unplanned events and assesses their effects on planned program operations.

Process research captures the heart, soul, spirit, emotion, and goal-directed action of a prevention program in a clear, objective, and insightful fashion. Process research tells the field what the program did in the name of prevention, provides a theoretical rationale for the actions taken, describes for whom the program was actually designed, delineates the operation of the program, depicts the type of professional staff used, and provides a fiscal accounting of the resources expended to operate the program.

Process research provides a measure of the integrity of the preventive intervention. Through process research, the intervention is thoroughly described in terms of its theory, objectives, and implementation, making it possible to determine why a program's intended outcomes were or were not achieved. In essence, the purpose of process research is to discover the reality of the intervention rather than its illusion.

This detailed accounting has two other valuable uses. First, process research can be used by those who wish to accurately replicate the intervention research in a different setting or with a different population. Second, if the program were judged successful and a decision was made to include the intervention in the regular prevention service system, the process research would help identify which program components were essential and should be retained in the broad scale implementation, and which program elements appeared incidental to achieving the positive effects (Jason, Thompson, & Rose, 1986).

A number of process research techniques have been developed and described in the literature (French & Kaufman, 1984; Hawkins & Nederhood, 1987). Process research methods include management case study, participant observation and key informant approaches drawn from ethnography, qualitative methods, quality assurance techniques, and quality circles that serve as a management tool, and also doubles as an excellent source of "insider" concerning the actual operation of a program.

Several good guidebooks have described process research from how-to-do-it handbooks to research texts. For example, Herman and colleagues (Herman, Morris, & Fitz-Gibbon, 1987) provided a convenient step-by-step set of guidelines for planning and implementing process research or what they term *formulative evaluation*. Their four-phase process includes setting the boundaries for the evaluation, selecting appropriate evaluation methods, collecting and analyzing the information, and reporting findings.

Rossi and Freeman (1982) provided an excellent discussion and examples of process research techniques to monitor program implementation and measure its accountability. Questions addressed by accountability assessment include:

Coverage accountability: Are the persons served those who are designated as targets? *Service delivery accountability:* Are the treatments delivered to those the program is supposed to be delivering? *Fiscal Accountability:* Are relevant laws being observed by the program, including those concerning affirmative action, occupational safety and health, and privacy of individual records. (Rossi & Freeman, 1982, p. 127)

Qualitative research techniques developed by Patton (1987) have direct relevance for process research. These include the use of intensive, open-ended interviews of participants, staff, and relevant observers of program implementation, direct observations of program implementation within the school and classroom (if possible), and archival or written program documentation consisting of excerpts from training manuals or policy statements, official reports, program relevant correspondence, and budgetary documents.

Process research provides scientifically sound data on the program theory, objectives, operation, and management. Results from process research should provide a complete description of all elements of the intervention including a theoretical basis, content, sequencing of activities, scope and intensity of intervention components, requisite staffing patterns, physical and fiscal resource needs, operational relationship between program components, and the salience of intervention for the target audience. The description should provide a narrative of all facets of the program operation as seen from the perspective of both the provider and the program recipient and should include a fiscal account of costs and expenditures associated with program operations.

Process research serves as the basis for asking the second research question: What is the efficacy of the tested intervention?

Outcome Research. The purpose of outcome research is to assess the efficacy of the intervention to effect changes in program specific dependent variables. Variables of interest may include drug-related knowledge; attitudes; beliefs; perception of harmful consequences; perception of social disapproval; drug use; and drug-related behaviors such as truancy, school achievement, or delinquent acts. We look to the findings of outcome research to determine the extent to which we can attribute changes in the measured dependent variables to the intervention and not to other extraneous or unmeasured influences (French & Kaufman, 1984; Hawkins & Nederhood, 1987).

The design and implementation of scientifically sound outcome research focuses on two research issues: internal and external research validity. *Internal validity* refers to the capacity of the outcome research to directly link changes in relevant dependent measures (drug measures) to participation in the experimental intervention, rather than to unmeasured variables or extraneous events. Threats to internal validity have been identified by Cambell and Stanley (1963) and others (Bernstein, 1976) and include history, maturation, testing, instrumentation, statistical regression, selection bias, selection-maturation interactions.

In addition, outcome research needs to address, but perhaps to a lesser extent, threats due to the external validity of the research. *External validity* refers to the capacity of the experimental research design to generalize to other populations, settings, times, and other treatment variables (Campbell & Stanley, 1963). Factors that threaten external validity or the representativeness of the research include reactive effects of testing that may increase or decrease the participant's response to the intervention, interaction effects of selection bias and the experimental variable, reactive effects due to the experimental environment that would not carry over to the implementation of the intervention in nonexperimental settings, and the effects of multiple treatments administered to the same respondents.

The classic approach to outcome research is the well-controlled randomized study that compares and contrasts the effects of intervention on individuals randomly assigned to the treatment condition with individuals randomly assigned to either a placebo or an alternative condition. In many clinical trials, this model of outcome research can be enhanced by the use of double-blind procedures where neither the subject nor the provider is aware of the treatment conditions. Although drug prevention research has employed randomized controlled experiments with randomization occurring with the individual or school class as the unit of assignment, few if any drug prevention studies have employed double-blind procedures.

As an alternative to the experimental design, quasi-experimental study designs have been effectively used when randomization if either individuals or classes is not possible. In these instances, it has been proposed by Campbell and Stanley (1963) that a variety of quasi-experiments can be designed including time-series designs, nonequivalent control groups, and a variety of separate sample pre-post designs. Each has individual strengths and weaknesses relevant to the threats to internal and external validity.

Flay (1986) suggested that outcome research that he called ''efficacy'' trials, could also use a ''historical control'' design when randomized control studies are not possible and the comparison groups are one or more conditions from a previous trial and not randomly assigned.

Of importance to note is that both process and outcome research focus on specific program specific effects. Also, both process and outcome research findings are essential and should be included within the same study design. Although outcome research provides the quantitative measure of program effects, process research provides a rich and deep description of the program's content, operation, and community context drawing from both quantitative and qualitative types of data, to help explain why some elements of the program may have worked and other elements may have failed to achieve the predicted changes.

Impact Research. The third level of research, impact research, is distinctly different from process and outcome research in that it is not program specific. Rather, impact research assesses the cumulative or aggregate effects of a number of (hopefully) validated prevention programs operating within a geographic area and over a specified time period (French &

Kaufman, 1984). The geographic area could be a school or school system, county, city, state, region, or the nation as a whole.

The major indicators for impact research include the assessment of trends over time in the incidence and prevalence of drug abuse (e.g., community epidemiologic drug surveys, national epidemiologic drug surveys—National Household Survey, the National High School Senior Survey on Drug Abuse); in drug-related morbidity (e.g., DAWN data from hospital emergency rooms); in drug-related mortality (e.g., Medical examiner reports); in drug-related accidents; in drug-related child abuse, and so on.

The purpose of impact research is to measure significant changes in drug-related indicators at the community level and to link those changes to prior process and outcome research activities. In contrast to process and outcome research, impact research attempts to assess the global, cumulative, aggregate, and interactive effects of validated drug prevention programming operating or possibly effecting the use of drugs in a predetermined geographic area. Ideally, all prevention programs operating within a community would have been tested and validated to determine their level of efficacy through outcome and process research.

In essence, impact research attempts to determine how "effective" each and every preventive intervention tested within a well-controlled outcome research setting is when implemented under real-world conditions by health educators, public health specialists, or the medical community.

Impact research should consider a number of issues. First, one must be confident that the measurement of drug-use trend data has been done repeatedly in the same community with a high degree of scientific competence and consistency in content, sampling frame, intervals between data collection, and administrative procedures and that the measurements are reliable and valid from a psychometric perspective.

Second, impact research should establish the extent to which process and outcome research studies have been completed for preventive interventions within the community being assessed, and the degree to which these studies document the standardization of the program and establish at some confidence level the efficacy of the interventions.

Finally, impact research should focus on determining how effectively the various programs were implemented within the community by the health-care and educational system.

Flay (1986) suggested that effectiveness research should consider three major questions: first, was the validated prevention program(s) implemented in the community in a comparable fashion as documented by the original process evaluation? Asked in another way, what was the fidelity or match between the program standardized and tested by the process/outcome research and that program implemented in the community?

Second, was the program implemented in the community in such a way so that it was available to the target audience?

Third, was the standardized/validated program sufficiently acceptable to the target audiences that it was receptive to it, participated in its activities, and tended to comply with its recommendations?

A number of epidemiological research methods have applicability to impact research. Although the use of randomized clinical trial consisting of multiple treatment and control conditions is desired, it may not be possible because of the difficulties raised by real world constraints. As a result, quasi-experimental techniques may have to be employed (Flay, 1986). Other epidemiological research designs that have potential for impact research include cross-sectional field surveys, cohort studies of which the Framingham Study serves as the best example, and case-control studies (Susser, 1987).

For a detailed discussion of each of these techniques including experimental intervention trials at the community level, the reader is referred to the technical papers of Abramson (1985) on cross-sectional studies, Feinleib and Detels (1985) on cohort studies, Puska (1985) on intervention and experimental studies, and Greenburg and Ibrahim (1985) on case-control studies in a recent anthology of epidemiological research methods edited by Holland, Detels and Knox (1985).

For an excellent discussion of cost-effectiveness and cost-benefit study designs for impact research the reader is referred to the review of the cost effectiveness of preventive care by Russell (1987) and to Drummond, Stoddart, and Torrance (1987) on economic methods for evaluating health-care programs.

In summary, intervention research requires a multiple component comprehensive model that yields scientifically sound data that describes the theory, content, and implementation features of the tested intervention, that provides in an uncompromising fashion a detailed assessment of the efficacy of the intervention, and finally, provides substantive research data at the community level of effectiveness of preventive interventions measured individually and in the aggregate. This chapter proposed that a prevention research model focused on process, outcome, and impact research provides a good test of comprehensive prevention programming when implemented at the individual, school, or community level.

REFERENCES

Abramson, J. H. (1985). Cross-sectional studies. In W. W. Holland, R. Detels, & G. Knox (Eds.), *Oxford textbook of public health* (Vol. 3, pp. 89–100). Oxford: Oxford University Press.

ADAMHA Press Conference. (1985). Washington, DC.

Albee, G. & Gullota, T. (1986). Facts and failures about primary prevention. *Journal of Primary Prevention, 6(4)*, 207–208.

Arnold, C., Kuller, L., & Greenlick, M. (Eds.). (1981). *Advances in disease prevention* (Vol. 1). New York: Springer.

Auslander, G. (1988). Social networks and the functional health status of the poor. *Journal of Community Health, 13*(4), 197–209.

Bachman, J., Johnston, L., O'Malley, P. & Humphrey, R. (1988). Explaining the recent decline in marijuana use-differentiating the effects of perceived risks, disapproval, and general lifestyle factors. *Journal of Health and Social Behavior, 29*(1), 92–112.

Bernstein, I. (Ed.). (1976). *Validity issues in evaluative research.* Beverly Hills: Sage.

Brook, J., Gordon, A., Whiteman, M., & Cohen, P. (1986). Dynamics of childhood and adolescent personality traits and adolescent drug use. *Developmental Psychology, 22*(3), 403–414.

Brook, J. Whiteman, M., Gordon, A., Brook, D., & Cohen, P. (in press). the psychosocial etiology of adolescent drug use: A family interactional approach. In *Genetic, social and general psychology monographs.* Washington, DC: Heldref Publications.

Brown, S., Stetson, B., & Beatty, P. (1989). Cognitive and behavioral features of adolescent coping in high-risk drinking situations. *Addictive Behaviors, 14,* 43–52.

Bry, B., McKeon, P., & Pandina, R. (1982). Extent of drug use as a function of number of risk factors. *Journal of Abnormal Psychology, 91,* 273–279.

Bry, S. (1983). Predicting drug abuse: Review and reformulation. *International Journal of the Addictions, 18*(2), 223–233.

Califano, J. (1979). *Healthy people: The Surgeon General's Report on health promotion and disease prevention.* Washington, DC: U.S. Government Printing Office (Stock No. 017-001-00416-2).

Campbell, D., & Stanley, J. (1963). *Experimental and quasi-experimental designs for research.* Chicago: Rand McNally College Publishing.

Clark, P. W., & MacMahon, B. (Eds.). (1981). *Preventive and Community Medicine* (2nd ed.). Boston: Little-Brown.

Cloninger, C. (1988). Etiologic factors in substance abuse: An adoption study perspective. In R. Pickens & D. Svikis (Eds.), *Biological vulnerability to drug abuse* (DHHS Pub. No. ADM 88-1590, pp. 52–72). Washington, DC: U.S. Government Printing Office.

Cook, R. (1985). The alternatives approach revisited: A biopsychological model and guidelines for application. *The International Journal of the Addictions, 20*(9), 1399–1419.

Cook, R., Lawrence, H., Morse, C., & Roehl, J. (1984). An evaluation of the alternatives approach to drug abuse prevention. *The International Journal of the Addictions, 19*(7), 767–787.

Department of Health and Human Services, U.S. Public Health Service. (1980). *Promoting health/preventing disease: Objectives for the nation.* Washington, DC: U.S. Government Printing Office.

Drummond, M., Stoddart, G., & Torrance, G. (1987). *Methods for the economic evaluation of health care programmes.* Oxford: Oxford University Press.

Federal grant aids MAD in fighting drug use. (February 23, 1989). *The Times,* pp. 00

Feinlieb, M., & Detels, R. (1985). Cohort studies. In W. W. Holland, R. Detels, & G. Knox (Eds.), *Oxford textbook of public health* (Vol. 3, pp. 101–112). Oxford: Oxford University Press.

Flay, B. (1986). Efficacy and effectiveness trials (and other phases of research) in the development of health promotion programs. *Preventive Medicine, 15,* 451–474.

French, J., & Kaufman, N. (1984). *Handbook for prevention evaluation* (DHHS Publication No. ADM 84-1145). Washington, DC: U.S. Government Printing Office.

Gard, G., & Berry K. (1986). Oppositional children: Taming tyrants. *Journal of Clinical Child Psychology, 15*(2), 147–158.

Gorsuch, R., & Butler, M. (1976). Initial drug abuse: A review of predisposing social psychological factors. *Psychological Bulletin, 83*(1), 120–137.

Greenberg, R., & Ibrahim, M. I. (1985). The case control study. In W. W. Holland, R. Detels, & G. Knox (Eds.), *Oxford textbook of public health* (Vol. 3, pp. 123–143). Oxford: Oxford University Press.

Haddon, W., Suchman, E., & Klein, D. (1964). *Accident research: Methods and approaches.* New York: Harper & Row.

Hawkins, D., Doeck, H., & Lishner, D. (1988). Changing teaching practices in mainstream classrooms to improve bonding and behavior of low achievers. *American Educational Research Journal,* 25(1), 31–50.

Hawkins, J., Lishner, D., Catalano, R., & Howard, M. (1986). Childhood predictors of adolescent substance abuse: Toward an empirically grounded theory. In S. Griswold-Ezekoye, K. Kumpfer, W. Bukoski (Eds.), *Childhood and chemical abuse: Prevention and intervention* (pp. 11–48). New York: Haworth.

Hawkins, J., & Nederhood, B. (1987). *Handbook for evaluating drug and alcohol prevention programs* (DHHS Publication No. ADM 87-1512). Washington, DC: U.S. Government Printing Office.

Herman, J., Morris, L., and Fitz-Gibbon, C. (1987). *Evaluator's handbook.* Beverly Hills: Sage.

Holland, W., Detels, R., & Knox, G. (Eds.). (1985). *Oxford textbook of public health* (Vol. 3). Oxford: Oxford University Press.

Jason, L., Thompson, D., & Rose, T. (1986). Methodological issues in prevention. In B. Edelstein & L. Michelson (Eds.), *Handbook of prevention* (pp. 1–19). New York: Plenum Press.

Johnston, L. (1985). The etiology and prevention of substance use: What can we learn from recent historical changes. In C. Jones & R. Battjes (Eds.), *Etiology of drug abuse: Implications for prevention* (DHHS Publication No. ADM 85-1335, pp. 155–177). Washington, DC: U.S. Government Printing Office.

Jones, C., & Battjes, R. (Eds.). (1985). *Etiology of drug abuse: Implications for prevention* (DHHS Publication No. ADM 85-1335). Washington, DC: U.S. Government Printing Office.

Kellam, S., Werthemer-Larsson, L., Dolan, L., Brown, C., Laudolff, J., Anthony, J., Wilson, R., Edelsohn, G., & Spencer, P. (in press). Developmental epidemiologically-based preventive trials: Baseline modeling of early target behaviors and depressive symptoms. *Journal of Community Psychology.*

Last, J. (1980). *Public health and preventive medicine* (11th ed.). New York: Appleton-Century-Crofts.

Linsky, A. D., & Strauss, A. (1986). *Social stress in the United States: Links to regional patterns in crime and illness.* Dover, MA: Auburn House.

Lochman, J., & Curry, J. (1986). Effects of social problem solving training and self-instruction training with aggressive boys. *Journal of Clinical Child Psychology,* 15(2), 159–164.

Manatt, M. (1983). *Parents, peer, and pot II* (DHHS Publication No. ADM 83-1290). Washington, DC: U.S. Government Printing Office.

Matarazzo, J., Weiss, S., Herd, J., Miller, N., & Weiss, S. (1984). *Behavioral health: A handbook for health enhancement and disease prevention.* New York: Wiley.

Morehouse, E. (1979). Working in the schools with children of alcoholic parents. *Health and Social Work,* 4(4), 145–162.

Myrick, R., & Erney, T. (1979). *Youth helping youth: A handbook for training peer facilitators.* Minneapolis: Educational Media.

NIAAA. (1987). *Alcohol and health* (DHHS Publication No. ADM 87-1519). Washington, DC: U.S. Government Printing Office.

National Institute on Drug Abuse. (1987). Prevention research. *In drug abuse and drug abuse research: The second triennial report to congress* (DHHS Publication No. ADM 87-1486, pp. 33–58). Washington, DC: U.S. Government Printing Office.

Newcomb, M. (1988). *Drug use in the workplace: Risk factors for disruptive substance use among young adults.* Dover, MA: Auburn House.

Newcomb, M., Maddahian, E., & Bentler, P. (1986). Risk factors for drug use among adolescents: Concurrent and longitudinal analysis. *American Journal of Public Health, 76*(5), 525–531.

Oetting, E., & Beauvais, F. (1987). Peer cluster theory, socialization characteristics, and adolescent drug use: A path analysis. *Journal of Counseling Psychology, 34*(2), 205–213.

Patton, M. (1987). *How to use qualitative methods in evaluation.* Beverly Hills: Sage.

Pickens, R., & Svikis, D. (Eds.). (1988). *Biological vulnerability to drug abuse* (DHHS Publication No. ADM 88–1590). Washington, DC: U.S. Government Printing Office.

Puska, P. (1985). Intervention and experimental studies. In W. W. Holland, R. Detels, & G. Knox (Eds.), *Oxford textbook of public health* (Vol. 3, pp. 113–122). Oxford: Oxford University Press.

Rossi, P., & Freeman, H. (1982). *Evaluation: A systematic approach.* Beverly Hills: Sage.

Rush, B., Gliksman, L., & Brook, R. (1986). Alcohol availability, alcohol consumption and alcohol-related damage. I. The distribution of consumption model. *Journal of Studies on Alcohol, 47*(1), 1–10.

Russell, L. (1987). *Evaluating preventive care.* Washington, DC: The Brookings Institution.

Schaps, E., DiBartolo, R., Moskowitz, J., Palley, C., & Churgin, S. (1981). Primary prevention evaluation research: A review of 127 impact studies. *Journal of Drug Issues, 11,* 17–43.

Schuckit, M. (1987). Biological vulnerability to alcoholism. *Journal of Consulting and Clinical Psychology, 55*(3), 301–309.

Schuerman, J. (1983). *Research and evaluation in the human services.* New York: The Free Press.

Shaver, J. (1983, October). The verification of independent variables in teaching methods research. *Educational Researcher,* pp. 3–9.

Sheridan, D., & Winogrand, I. (1987). *The preventative approach to patient care.* New York: Elsevier.

Shoemaker, P. (Ed.). (1989). *Communication campaigns about drugs: Government, media, and the public.* Hillsdale, NJ: Lawrence Erlbaum Associates.

Simons, R., Conger, R., & Whitbeck, K. (1988). A multistage social learning model of the influences of family and peers upon adolescent substance abuse. *Journal of Drug Issues, 6,* 293–315.

Stamler, J. (1978). Lifestyles, major risk factors, proof, and public policy. *Circulation, 58,* 3–19.

Susser, M. (1987). Epidemiology in the United States after World War II: The evolution of technique. In M. Susser (Ed.), *Epidemiology, health, and society* (pp. 22–49). New York: Oxford University Press.

Telesis II. (1989). *Senior peers assistance program and the student peer counseling program.* San Diego: Author.

Tobler, N. (1986). Meta-analysis of 143 adolescent drug prevention programs. *The Journal of Drug Issues, 16*(4), 537–567.

Weiss, C. (1972). *Evaluation research.* Englewood Cliffs, NJ: Prentice-Hall.

Wilner, D., Walkley, R., & O'Neil, E. (1978). *Introduction to public health* (7th ed.). New York: MacMillan.

Yu, P., Harris, G., Solovitz, B., & Franklin, J. (1986). A social problem-solving intervention for children at high risk for later psychopathology. *Journal of Clinical Child Psychology, 15*(1), 30–40.

2

The Role of the National Institute on Drug Abuse in Drug Abuse Prevention Research

Carl G. Leukefeld
University of Kentucky

Prevention research supported by the National Institute on Drug Abuse (NIDA) has been described in different ways. On the one hand, it has been described as knowledge development activities focused on etiology, human development, vulnerability and evaluation research. On the other hand, drug abuse prevention research has been depicted as lightning rod research which has repeatedly attracted negatively grounded evaluation findings. Perhaps this chapter will add to further understanding of the institute's role in promoting high quality research. In order to explore NIDA's prevention research it should be examined within the Institute's overall goals, which include knowledge development through both intramurally and extramurally funded research, leadership activities, research training, and initiatives designed to transfer knowledge to various publics and groups.

NIDA's prevention research has an interesting history. The National Institute on Drug Abuse (NIDA) was established in September 1972, and given statutory authority in 1973. It seems important to remind ourselves that drug abuse prevention research is not very different from other areas of prevention research in the public health arena. More specifically, it seems that there is a need to bring together the scientific method with the practice and art of prevention intervention. Perhaps mutual and sustained interaction may be a theme. That theme has been influenced by science, politics, pressure groups, and by "the times."

Drug abuse prevention has been controversial since it was highlighted in the late 1960s (DeLone, 1972; Halleck, 1970; Swisher, 1979). Swisher (1979) for example, suggested that drug abuse prevention was questioned externally as well as from its own ranks. He identified the following areas of controversy: evidence that prevention makes a difference; difficulty in agreeing on how to demonstrate the effectiveness of prevention strategies; confusion regarding the differences among treatment, intervention, and prevention efforts; and concern about the purpose of prevention—reduction of drug use or its total elimination in the target population.

It is also interesting to note that little seems to change even as change takes place. For example, the *White Paper on Drug Abuse in 1975* recommended" . . . that priorities in research be established . . . to determine relative effectiveness of different prevention . . . approaches" (pp. 103–104). In 1984 the *National Strategy for Prevention of Drug Abuse and Drug Trafficking* included the following research objective: "Studying the effectiveness of prevention . . . approaches" (p. 98). And in 1989 the evolving Prevention Plan includes the same priority on effectiveness research. It is clear, however, that a major goal of the Institute's prevention research program for the past 15 years has been to identify effective prevention strategies using the findings from peer-reviewed research. Unfortunately, research studies funded by NIDA have been able to tell us more about what does not work than about what does. Moreover, at this time, no drug prevention strategy has been consistently effective. However, promising prevention approaches have been evaluated by the institute within the research context (Leukefeld, 1990).

APPROACHES AND INFLUENCES
OF KNOWLEDGE DEVELOPMENT

This chapter is organized around approaches and influences related to knowledge development. These areas were selected in order to capture important trends that give the reader a sense of historical development and a brief glimpse at the future from one point of view. The selected approaches and influences are: information as prevention, evaluating prevention without control groups, correlation research, public health influence, smoking research influence, and controlled/comparative evaluation.

Information as Prevention

Evaluations of early prevention programs were limited. Providing information was considered drug education and was called *drug abuse prevention*. In fact, drug abuse prevention information included descriptions of using drugs and drug paraphernalia that were so detailed that they probably helped teach a number of persons how to use drugs. This information could have encouraged drug abuse by reinforcing curiosity. In response to this concern, and based on anecdotal as well as prevalence data, the federal government declared a moratorium on the production of drug information and issued new guidelines for federal agencies regarding the publishing of drug abuse information. These guidelines were imposed on contractors and grantees as well. This moratorium was effective until February 1974, when it was lifted and replaced with guidelines that, among other things, ensured audience identification, pretested materials, excluded fear messages, stressed the complexity of the drug problem, and stressed alternatives and positive role models for young people (*Recommendations for Future Federal Activities in Drug Abuse Prevention*, 1977). The new guidelines also redirected the thrust away from concentrating on specific drugs or methods of use. Instead of that emphasis, nonspecific drug programs, which taught approaches to values clarification and decision making in the broadest sense, were encouraged.

The bulk of prevention studies funded by the Institute has focused on evaluating the effects of prevention interventions—largely in school settings. Initial prevention evaluation studies funded in the mid-1970s were at best quasi-experimental and often lacked control or adequate comparison groups. It is important to mention that at the same time the institute, in keeping with the existent legislation, developed various prevention technology transfer activities aimed at facilitating and assisting drug abuse prevention efforts.

Two of these activities were: The Multicultural Resource Center, which focused on developing information to prevent drug abuse in five minority groups; and The Pyramid Project, which provided technical assistance and consultant resources to communities and schools. The Multicultural Resource Center was short-lived but Pyramid was very popular and provided the early resources to help initiate multiple prevention activities, including community parents groups. It must also be kept in mind that, during that period of time, such activities were not exclusively associated with prevention efforts but also characterized other institute activities that included the legislatively mandated National Drug Abuse Training Center. In addition, NIDA also funded a prevention coordinator in each state and territory. The prevention coordinator helped establish prevention programs even before drug abuse prevention service monies were granted to states by the Institute and before drug abuse prevention approaches were evaluated.

About that time, parent groups were forming throughout the country. Atlanta, Georgia became a central point for parent group activities. The National Federation of Parents was formed to support local parent groups and to put pressure in order to change policies related to drug laws and closing "head shops" (stores that sell drug paraphernalia to juveniles). In addition, Marsha Manatt's (1979, 1983) books, often referred to as "the bibles" of the parents movement, were used by parents to develop local parent groups. These volumes were edited and published by NIDA and were widely distributed by the Institute's clearinghouse.

What these activities point out is that the Institute's early prevention efforts were not solely focused on research but included evaluative research; technical assistance; efforts to conceptualize and define drug abuse prevention; activities to describe process, outcome, and impact research; and efforts to develop drug abuse prevention as a profession. Each of these areas are worthy of discussion. However, the goal here is to merely set the stage.

Evaluating Prevention Without Control Groups

Initial prevention activities were funded by both the National Institute on Mental Health (NIMH); the Division of Narcotic Addiction and Drug Abuse, which later became NIDA; and the Office of Education, which formed the organizational base for the Department of Education. Early prevention efforts did not include evaluation. Attempts were later made to obtain data from these prevention grants, but they provided limited and weak results, for obvious reasons.

From the outset it was suggested that drug abuse prevention evaluation research and, for that matter, prevention evaluation in general, had limited methodology to adequately measure the impact and outcome of prevention interventions. From my point of view, the situation has not changed drastically, and new methodologies can be developed. Perhaps, the organizational placement by NIDA of prevention activities in the Division of Resource Development, which emphasized evaluation, rather than in the Division of Research, which was responsible for the Institute's research portfolio, was a contributing factor.

The results of the Institute's early prevention evaluation studies can be summarized in one statement: Drug abuse prevention evaluations did not show significant changes in drug use as a result of prevention programs. Reviews by Bracht, Follingstad, Brakarsh & Berry, (1973); Goodstat (1974); and Berberian, Gross, Lovejoy, & Paparella (1976) showed the weakness and immaturity of early prevention evaluation efforts.

The situation had not changed by 1977, when the Institute's Prevention Branch published an annotated guide to prevention literature (*Primary Prevention in Drug Abuse: An Annotated Guide to the Literature*, 1977). This publication included the prevention literature and evaluation studies available at that time. However, only 3 of the 44 evaluative studies cited were published in peer-reviewed journals (see pp. 111–114). Drug abuse prevention research had clearly not matured.

However, the institute did develop activities to help prevention research mature. Most noteworthy was the National Prevention Evaluation Research Network (NPERN). NPERN was developed by William J. Bukoski with the New Jersey Single State Agency for Alcohol and Drug Abuse in 1978. NPERN was designed to improve the number and quality of drug abuse prevention evaluations by providing on-site technical assistance to prevention programs (French, Fisher, & Costa, 1983). Two major NPERN publications were developed: *A Handbook for Prevention Evaluation* and *Working With Evaluators*. The handbook provided a summary of evaluation techniques and was primarily written for evaluators, whereas the second volume was designed for prevention program managers as a companion to the handbook. In the latter phases of NPERN, the National Institute on Alcohol Abuse and Alcoholism joined NIDA with the sponsorship of NPERN. One NPERN publication was updated by the Office of Substance Abuse Prevention in 1987, edited by Hawkins and Nederhood and published under the title *Handbook for Evaluating Drug and Alcohol Prevention Programs: Staff/Team Evaluation of Prevention Programs (STEPP)*.

The definition of drug abuse prevention that guided the Institute at that time included four modalities (NIDA, 1978):

1. *Information* that involved the distribution of accurate and objective data about all types of drugs and the effects of those drugs on the human systems;
2. *Education* that involved a well-defined and structured learning process that helps individuals develop the affective skills they need to help themselves;
3. *Alternatives* providing challenging, growth-filled community experiences through which people develop; and
4. *Intervention* that gave assistance and support to young people during critical periods of their life when person-to-person, sharing of experiences and empathetic listening would contribute to successful adjustment.

At that same time, and while redefining drug abuse prevention, the institute was focusing on a prevention evaluation research model (Bukoski, 1979). The model included three levels of evaluation:

1. Process evaluation that assesses the service operation of a prevention program and includes descriptions of the programs prevention services, resources use, and costs;
2. Outcome evaluation to determine if a prevention program's objectives were met by the participants; and

3. Impact evaluation that assesses macro-indicators of drug abuse at the community level.

As noted by Bukoski elsewhere in this volume, this model is relevant today because it can be used as a framework for comprehensive intervention research.

Correlation Research

During the 1970s, a number of correlation studies were initiated to better understand factors leading to drug use and drug dependence among adolescents. Bukoski (1979) suggested that correlate research focus attention on potential causal factors that promote or precipitate drug use. The correlation literature is extensive and in the 1970s was used as a research foundation to develop drug abuse prevention programs.

The following selected correlates were frequently cited as associated with drug abuse and dependency: lower cognitive development (Spivack, Platt, & Shure, 1976); lower educational aspiration and greater heterosexual activity (Milman & Wen-Huey, 1973); lower religiosity and premarital intercourse (Jessor & Jessor, 1977); higher life stress scores (Duncan, 1977); frequency of school absenteeism and lack of success in attaining school goals (Cooper, Olson & Fournier, 1977); low self-esteem (Smith & Fogg, 1975); and higher alienation (Block, 1975).

The purpose here is to provide a sense of what many prevention practitioners used in the late 1970s and early 1980s to support prevention programs. When prevention interventions were evaluated using these behaviors and others as dependent variables, there were either no changes or very limited ones in these outcomes and little or no effect on drug using behavior. No considerable effects were discovered even when intervention groups were compared with control or comparison groups. These results were noted by Schaps, DiBartolo, Moskowitz, Palley, and Churgin (1981) in a review of 127 evaluations of prevention programs that was commissioned and funded by the Institute. That should have been expected because many prevention programs did not target specific behaviors but focused more broadly on clarifying values and on decision making. There was a shift away from relying only on correlate research. Although a major contributing factor for this change was probably the scientific development of the field, another one was the influence of public health activities.

Influence of Public Health

At least two events in the late 1970s initiated by the U.S. Public Health Service and the Surgeon General, influenced the overall direction of drug abuse prevention research. The first major event was the first Surgeon

General's Report in 1979 on health promotion and disease prevention, titled *Healthy People*. The report was intended to encourage a second public
health revolution in the United States. The second revolution emphasized
the role of prevention and suggested that prevention was an idea whose
time had come, whereas the first revolution had been the nation's strug-
gle against infectious diseases.

Healthy People was structured conceptually in a way that paralleled the
Canadian Government's report of 1974 titled *A New Perspective on the Health
of Canadians*. The Canadian report introduced four elements as causes of
death and disease:

1. inadequacies of the existing health-care system;
2. behavioral factors or unhealthy lifestyles;
3. environmental factors; and
4. human biological factors.

Using the Canadian framework, a group of Americans analyzed the Nation's causes of death and concluded that there were three reasons for emphasizing prevention:

1. prevention saves lives;
2. prevention improves the quality of life; and
3. prevention can save money (*Healthy People*, 1979, p. 9).

Alcohol and drug abuse prevention were identified as challenges for
prevention and became a subgoal by pointing to the high prevalence of
alcohol and drug abuse among the nation's youth. The report also established five major goals that focused on lifecycle stages: healthy infants,
healthy children, healthy adolescents and young adults, healthy adults,
and healthy older adults.

The second major event was the establishment of priority objectives that
are described in the 1980 report titled *Health/Promotion and Disease Prevention*. Fifteen priority areas were selected and measurable objectives were
developed during a one year effort that involved a number of groups and
individuals. Abuse of alcohol and drugs was one of the priority areas and
measurable objectives were developed for 1990 (pp. 67–72). Thus, alcohol
and drug abuse became part of public health prevention activities and
moved into a position which facilitated recognition of the importance of
prevention.

During the late 1970s the Institute was attempting to accomplish the
goal of ''mainstreaming'' drug abuse prevention with a 1977 report titled
Recommendations for Future Federal Activities in Drug Abuse Prevention. This

report was developed at the conclusion of a review of the federal government's drug abuse prevention efforts that was called for by the 1975 *White Paper on Drug Abuse*. Along with specific recommendations to increase prevention research funding, the report stressed the compelling reasons to emphasize prevention activities. One of the eight themes selected was research. More specifically, "Knowledge development must receive high priority so that we can better target populations . . . through careful evaluation of new applied research efforts" (p. 10). Not only was there a call for evaluation research, as before, but research initiatives and funding needs were also identified (i.e. formative research, impact research, and community services evaluation).

Smoking Research Influence

With the organizational emphasis on prevention, the Institute was eager to explore smoking studies initiated by Evans and his associates (Evans et al., 1978; Evans et al., 1981) at the University of Houston. This research identified two approaches, social inoculation/pressures training (Flay, 1985a) and social skills training (Botvin & Wills, 1985; Schinke, Gilchrist, & Snow, 1985) that were promising for alcohol and drug abuse prevention. Evans' studies were replicated by McAlister, Perry, and Maccoby (1979) and others (Perry, Killen, Slinkard, & McAlister, 1980; Perry, Maccoby, McAlister, 1980; Perry, Telch, Killen, Dass, & Maccoby, 1983) who reported that psychological inoculation ("Just Say No") combined with social skills training reduced tobacco use by school-age children.

Funding these types of studies "fit well" with the Institute's efforts to identify effective prevention interventions (Battjes, 1985). And almost immediately "Just Say No" interventions were readily accepted as an approach to reducing drug and tobacco use. Suddenly "Just Say No" had developed and matured while data were still coming in. Although there have been methodological analyses pointing out the weaknesses of these school-based studies, evaluations of the two approaches were generally positive (Biglan & Ary, 1985; Biglan et al., 1987; Flay, 1985b; Gilchrist, in press; McCaul & Glasgow, 1985). However, reports of results were less clear with regard to school-only programs that focus on drugs rather than on smoking (Gilchrist, 1990; Goodstadt, 1986; Moskowitz, 1983; Schaps et al., 1981; Tobler, 1986). Finally, most recent findings by Pentz et al. (1990) at the University of Southern California add to the research that reports the positive impact of multiple component (i.e., peer, parents, and community) prevention interventions and is reviewed by Bukoski elsewhere in this volume.

Controlled/Comparative Research

With the passage of legislation in 1986, the Office Of Substance Abuse (OSAP) was established in order to focus on prevention and, among other things, to fund demonstrations, (i.e., field studies carried out after controlled studies for validation). It directs its efforts to prevention process research and evaluation of prevention interventions. OSAP is focused only on prevention, and the prevention drug and alcohol abuse now has a bureaucratic identity. In addition, OSAP is concentrating activities on technology transfer and is rebuilding and adding to early prevention technology transfer activities.

NIDA is now sharply focusing on prevention research. A first step in redirecting drug abuse prevention research is a study that the Institute has commissioned and funded with the National Academy of Sciences. The purpose of this study is to conduct an expert review of drug abuse prevention research, including the effectiveness of existing prevention strategies, a discussion of relevant methodological issues, and some discussion of the future of prevention research. In other words, the study has been designed by the Institute to examine drug abuse prevention and develop a report, based on a 2-year review that addresses the questions of what works, what does not work, and what is harmful or has the potential for being harmful. Future prevention research at NIDA will most probably incorporate controlled and comparative research that emphasizes tightly structured studies, and include the areas that follow here.

Effectiveness Research and Developing New Interventions. It is expected that a primary focus will be research on how to prevent initial drug abuse and interrupt the progression to more intense use of multiple substances. Primary prevention research studies might also better distinguish between factors that contribute to initial drug dependency. Studies concerning initial use could focus on incorporating larger societal units into the intervention. Studies of dependence could incorporate interventions for those for whom "Just Say No" is not effective. Prevention intervention studies could also focus on the strength of the intervention's effects over time.

Methodological Issues. Design limitations, attrition, sample size, unit of analysis, definition of outcome variables, and related issues might be examined in prevention intervention studies. As a beginning the institute is planning a technical review focusing on methodological issues related to prevention intervention research. The review will examine the state-of-the-art of drug abuse prevention research methodology, make suggestions for refining current approaches, and develop an agenda for future research applications. A prime example is the choice of outcome measures (i.e., no drug use as contrasted with occasional drug use). The choice obviously has a significant effect on the findings and importance of studies in this area.

Preventing Intravenous Drug Use.   Only a limited number of research studies now focus on preventing the initiation of intravenous drug use, although this practice has been identified as a major factor in the spread of AIDS. Furthermore, existing research suggests that the lives of many intravenous drug users are dominated by drugs. The public health approach is directed to eliminating drug use, but when eliminating use fails, emphasis can be placed on reducing the harmful consequences of drug use. It is suggested that prevention studies capitalize on developing and refining specific interventions.

Environmental Studies.   Research suggests that environmental factors can influence behaviors. Research is needed to assess single and aggregate effects of prevention initiatives focused on environmental changes. Specific studies might focus on institutional settings such as colleges, schools, or social organizations. Tightly controlled studies might be directed to policy changes, changes in regulations, more controlled enforcement of existing policies, and the effects of user accountability.

Early Intervention.   A number of primary prevention programs focus on preventing drug use and progression from use to dependency. These prevention activities are frequently focused on youth in school settings. There has been discussion about the difference between treatment efforts aimed at delaying or reducing drug use progression and primary prevention efforts. This chapter will not enter into that debate but rather suggests that additional research might focus on studies to better understand the characteristics of successful early intervention approaches.

Etiological Issues and Risk-Factors (Vulnerability) Research.   Research might be directed toward better understanding of the causes of drug abuse and dependence. Research suggests that drug abusers progress through stages starting with cigarettes and alcohol to intravenous drug abuse for a limited number of individuals (Kandel, Logan, 1984; Kandel & Yammaguchi, 1985). Research could focus on better understanding this drug progression.

Vulnerability is often described as factors contributing to placing individuals at differential risk for engaging in drug use and for developing drug dependence (Jessor & Jessor, 1977). A goal of prevention research is to develop the necessary information, theories, and methodologies to identify individuals who are at high risk for drug abuse. Vulnerability research could involve understanding factors predisposing to drug abuse. Studies might focus on identifying individuals and groups at risk, in order to target interventions, family history and early social and behavioral problems related to drug use and dependence, and factors that protect an individual from drug abuse.

Additional research could examine the differential effects of prevention programs and prevention interventions on high risk individuals with identifiable personality or social characteristics. Prospective studies might identify and monitor the development of multiple high risk behaviors from childhood through adulthood. Early biological, behavioral, and social makers could be identified for use as validated diagnostic measures for clinical use.

CONCLUDING REMARKS

This chapter suggests that drug abuse prevention research is alive and well at the National Institute on Drug Abuse. When drug abuse prevention research is examined at the National Institute on Drug Abuse, it is important to keep in mind that the institute initially funded multiple prevention activities including evaluative research, technical assistance efforts, prevention services, state prevention coordinators, evaluation technical assistance, and other activities designed to develop drug abuse prevention as a profession. Two major influences on drug abuse prevention research (public health and smoking research) are also presented to provide a flavor of activities that helped drug abuse prevention research mature.

It must be noted that we still know more about what does not work than about what does work in preventing drug abuse. However, promising approaches have been developed and are being examined, and we can expect advances in our knowledge from that research and from researchers like those who contributed to this volume.

The drug abuse prevention field is maturing with more energy being directed to practice by the Office of Substance Abuse Prevention and to research by the National Institute on Drug Abuse. A number of practitioners believe that prevention is effective. Many of them suggest that existing research methodology is not sensitive enough to capture changes resulting from drug abuse prevention interventions. Perhaps these are the people who should help design prevention interventions and develop research methodology.

REFERENCES

A new perspective on the health of Canadians. (1974). Ministry of Health, Canada, Ontario.
Battjes, R. J. (1985). Prevention of adolescent drug abuse. The International Journal of The Addictions, 20(6&7), 1113–1134.

Berberian, R. M., Gross, C., Lovejoy, J., & Paparella, C. (1976). The effectiveness of drug education programs: A critical review. *Health Education Monograph, 4,* 377–398.

Biglan, A., & Ary, D. V. (1985). Methodological issues in research on smoking prevention. In C. S. Bell & R. J. Battjes (Eds.). *Prevention research: Deterring drug abuse among children and adolescents* (pp. 180–195). Washington, DC: U.S. Government Printing Office.

Biglan, A., Severson, H., Ary, D., Faller, C., Gallison, C., Thompson, R., Glasgow, R., & Lichtenstein, E. (1987). Do smoking prevention programs really work? Attrition and the internal and external validity of an evaluation of a refusal skills training program. *Journal of Behavioral Medicine, 10,* 159–171.

Block, J. R. (1975). Behavioral and demographic correlates of drug use among students in grades 7–12. In D. Lettieri (Ed.), *Predicting adolescent drug abuse: A review of issues, methods and correlates* (Pp. 265–276). Rockville, MD: National Institute on Drug Abuse.

Botvin, G. J., & Wills, T. A. (1985). Personal and social skills training: Cognitive-behavioral approaches to substance abuse prevention. In C. S. Bell, & R. J. Battjes (Eds.), *Prevention research: Deterring drug abuse among children and adolescents* (pp. 3–49). Washington, DC: U.S. Government Printing Office.

Bracht, G. N., Follingstad, D., Brakarsh, D., & Berry, K. L. (1973). Drug education: A review of goals, approaches, and effectiveness, and a paradigm for evaluation. *Quarterly Journal of Studies on Alcohol, 34,* 1279–1292.

Bukoski, W. J. (1979, November). *Drug abuse prevention evaluation: A meta-evaluation process.* Paper present at the annual conference of the American Public Health Association, New York.

Cooper, D. M., Olson, D., & Fournier, D. (1977, Spring) Adolescent drug use related to family support, self-esteem, and school behavior. *Center Quarterly Focus,* 121–134.

DeLone, R. J. (1972, November) The ups and downs of drug abuse education. *Saturday Review of Education, 11,* 27–32.

Duncan, D. F. (1977) Life stress as a precursor to adolescent drug dependence. *International Journal of the Addictions, 12*(8), 1047–1056.

Evans, R. I., Rozelle, R. M., Maxwell, S. E., Raines, B. E., Dill, C. A., & Guthrie, T. J. (1981). Social modeling films to deter smoking in adolescents: Results of a three-year field investigation. *Journal of Applied Psychology, 66,* 399–414.

Evans, R. I., Rozelle, R. M., Mittelmark, M. B., Hansen, W. B., Bane, A. L., & Havis, J. (1978) Deterring the onset of smoking in children: Knowledge of immediate physiological peer pressure, media pressure, and parent modeling. *Journal of Applied Social Psychology, 8,* 126–135.

Flay, B. R. (1985a). Psychosocial approaches to smoking prevention: A review of findings. *Health Psychology, 4,* 449–488.

Flay, B. R. (1985b). What do we know about the social influences approach to smoking prevention: Review and recommendations. In C. S. Bell & R. Battjes (Eds.), *Prevention research: Deterring drug abuse among children and adolescents* (pp. 67–112). Washington, DC: U.S. Government Printing Office.

French, J. F., Fisher, C. C., Costa, S. J. (Eds.). (1983). *Working with evaluators: A guide for drug abuse prevention program managers.* Rockville, MD: Alcohol, Drug Abuse, Mental Health Administration.

Gilchrist, L. D. (1990). Selected community groups: Schools. In C. G. Leukefeld, R. J. Battjes, & Z. Amsel (Eds.), *AIDS and intravenous drug use: Future directions for community-based prevention research* (pp. 150–166). Washington, DC: U.S. Government Printing Office.

Goodstadt, M. S. (1974). Myths & methodology in drug education: A critical review of research evidence. In M. S. Goodstadt (Ed.), *Research on methods and programs of drug education.* Toronto, Canada: Addiction Research Foundation.

Goodstadt, M. S. (1986). School-based drug education in North America: What is wrong? What can be done? *Journal of School Health, 56,* 278–281.

Halleck, S. (1970). The great drug education hoax. *The Progressive, 34,* 1–7.

Hawkins, J. D., & Nederhood, (Eds.). B. (1987). *Handbook for evaluating drug and alcohol prevention programs (STEPP).* Washington, DC: U.S. Government Printing Office.

Health promotion and disease prevention: Objectives for the nation. (1980). Washington, DC: U.S. Government Printing Office.

Healthy People: The Surgeon General's report on health promotion and disease prevention. (1979). Washington, DC: U.S. Government Printing Office.

Jessor, R., & Jessor, S. L. (1977). *Problem behavior and psychosocial development: A longitudinal study of youth.* New York: Academic Press.

Kandel, D. B., & Logan, J. A. (1984). Patterns of drug use from adolescence to young adulthood: I. Periods of risk for initiation, continued use, and discontinuation. *American Journal of Public Health, 74,* 660–666.

Kandel, D. B., & Yammaguchi, K. (1985). Developmental patterns of the use of legal, illegal, and medically prescribed drugs from adolescence to young adulthood. In C. S. Bell and R. J. Battjes (Eds.), *Prevention research: Deterring drug abuse among children and adolescents* (National Institute on Drug Abuse Research Monograph 63, pp. 193–235). Washington, DC: U.S. Government Printing Office.

Leukefeld, C. (1990). Drug abuse prevention: research needs. In K. H. Rey, C. L. Faegre, & P. Lowry (Eds.), *Prevention research findings: 1988* (pp. 46–52). Washington DC: U.S. Government Printing Office.

Manatt, M. (1979) *Parents, peers, and pot* (DHEW Publication No. 79–812). Rockville, MD: Department of Health, Education and Welfare.

Manatt, M. (1983). *Parents, peers, and pot II: Parents in action.* Washington, DC: U.S. Government Printing Office.

McAlister, A. L., Perry, C., & Maccoby, N. (1979). Adolescent smoking: onset and prevention. *Pediatrics, 63,* 650–657.

McCaul, K. D., & Glasgow, R. E. (1985). Preventing adolescent smoking: What we learned about treatment construct validity? *Health Psychology, 4,* 361–387.

Milman, D. H., & Wen-Huey, S. (1973). Patterns of illicit drug use among secondary school students. *Journal of Pediatrics, 83*(2), 314–320.

Moskowitz, J. M. (1983). Preventing adolescent substance abuse through drug education. In T. J. Glynn, C. G. Leukefeld, & J. P. Ludford (Eds.), *Preventing adolescent drug abuse: Intervention strategies* (pp. 233–249). Washington, DC: U.S. Government Printing Office.

National Institute on Drug Abuse. (1978). *It starts with people.* Washington, DC: DHEW.

National strategy for prevention of drug abuse and drug trafficking (1984). Washington, DC: U.S. Government Printing Office.

Pentz, M. A., Dwyer, J. H., MacKinnon, D. P., Flay, B. R., Hansen, W. B., Wang, E. Y., & Johnson, C. A. (1990). A multi-community trial for primary prevention of adolescent drug abuse: Effects on drug abuse prevalence. *Journal of The American Medical Association, 261*(22), 3259–3266.

Perry, C. L., Killen, J., Slinkard, L. A., & McAlister, A. L. (1980). Peer training and smoking prevention among junior high students. *Adolescence, 15,* 277–281.

Perry, C. L., Maccoby N., & McAlister, A. L. (1980). Adolescent smoking prevention: a third year follow-up. *World Smoking and Health, 5,* 40–45.

Perry, C. L., Telch, M. J., Killen, J., Dass, R., & Maccoby, N. (1983). High school smoking prevention: The relative efficacy of varied treatments and instructors. *Adolescence, 18,* 561–566.

Primary prevention in drug abuse: An annotated guide to the literature. (1977). Washington, DC: U.S. Government Printing Office.

Recommendations for the future federal activities in drug abuse prevention. (1977). Washington, DC: U.S. Government Printing Office.

Schaps, E., DiBartolo, R. D., Moskowitz, J., Palley, C. S., & Churgin, S. (1981). A review of 127 drug abuse prevention program evaluations. *Journal of Drug Issues, 11*, 17–43.

Schinke, S. P., Gilchrist, L. D., & Snow, W. H. (1985). Skills intervention to prevent cigarette smoking among adolescents. *American Journal of Public Health, 75*, 665–667.

Smith, G., & Fogg, C. (1975). Teenage drug use: a search for cause and consequences. In D. Lettieri (Ed.), *Predicting adolescent drug abuse: A review of issues, methods and correlates*. (pp. 279–282). Rockville, MD: National Institute on Drug Abuse.

Spivack, G., Platt, J. J., & Shure, M. B. (1976). *The problem-solving approach to adjustment*. San Francisco: Jossey-Bass.

Swisher, J. D. (1979). Prevention issues. In R. L. Dupont, A. Goldstein, & J. O'Donnell (Eds.), *Handbook on drug abuse* (pp. 00). Washington, DC: U.S. Government Printing Office.

Tobler, N. S. (1986). Meta-analysis of 143 adolescent drug prevention programs: Quantitative outcome results of program participants compared to control or comparison group. *Journal of Drug Issues, 16*, 537–567.

White Paper on Drug Abuse. (1975). Washington, DC: U.S. Government Printing Office.

ɟ

3

Prevention of Drug Abuse: Targeting Risk Factors

Roy W. Pickens
National Institute on Drug Abuse

Dace S. Svikis
Johns Hopkins University

Preventing drug abuse is a priority in our national effort to reduce the demand for illicit drugs. The possibility that external events can influence drug use is suggested by changes in substance use that have occurred over the past several decades. Rather than remaining constant, per capita consumption of alcohol and tobacco has fluctuated over time, seemingly in response to environmental influences (Cloninger, Reich, Sigvardsson, von Knorring, & Bohman, 1988; Warner, 1986). For example, tobacco use increased significantly during World War II, but declined during the 1950s immediately after publication of the Surgeon General's report on the harmful effects of smoking (Warner, 1986). Because these associations are only correlational, however, they do not prove that the observed changes in substance use were caused by the environmental events. Nevertheless, they do suggest that environmental events may influence drug use, and therefore that the prevention of drug abuse is possible.

The influence of environmental events on substance use has been more convincingly demonstrated by controlled studies evaluating the effectiveness of specific interventions. These studies compare drug use of subjects receiving and not receiving an intervention to determine if the intervention is effective in reducing drug use. Unfortunately, over the relatively short history of prevention research, not all strategies have been found to be effective. Particularly in the early years, prevention efforts often failed to reduce drug use. In recent years, however, prevention efforts have become more successful (e.g., Flay, 1985). To date, strategies that involve teaching adolescents to resist social pressures to smoke have been relatively successful in preventing tobacco use. Compared with subjects not receiving the interventions, reductions of 25% to 50% in new cases of self-reported smoking have been obtained (Botvin, 1983). At present, these same strategies are being applied in order to reduce other types of drug use and hopefully the results will be as successful.

IMPLICATIONS OF FINDINGS

Obviously these findings suggest that prevention of drug use is both possible and practical, and that we should continue to invest in this important demand-reduction strategy. What might not be as apparent is the important role played by an expanding science base in the development of effective interventions. Such interventions did not develop by chance, but rather were the product of a steadily expanding science base that eventually made the prevention of tobacco use possible. This science base included findings about the effectiveness of previous interventions, as well as improvements in our understanding of the nature of drug use and factors controlling human behavior. In cigarette smoking, for example, effective interventions were based on knowledge about the effectiveness of previous attempts to prevent smoking, peer pressure as a contributing factor in smoking, and age factors in onset of adolescent cigarette use (Flay, 1985).

ETIOLOGY OF DRUG USE

Etiological studies play an important role in the science base supporting the development of effective interventions. Although we are all capable of drug use, only some people ever use drugs. Differences in the tendency to use drugs have been attributed to risk factors, which are biological, behavioral, social, psychiatric, and cultural influences that increase an individual's tendency to use drugs. Risk factors appear to be additive, with increasing numbers of risk factors being associated with an increased tendency to use drugs (Newcomb, Maddahian, & Bentler, 1986).

Identification of risk factors often begins with identification of risk groups, which are clusters of individuals showing high rates of drug use. Unfortunately, risk groups are often too broadly defined to be useful in either understanding or predicting drug use. Males, for example, may be considered a risk group because they have higher rates of drug use than females. However, such knowledge lacks specificity and does not significantly enhance our understanding of the etiology of drug use. As knowledge improves, broadly defined risk groups typically yield to increasingly narrowly defined risk groups, which greatly improves our understanding of factors contributing to drug use. Very narrowly defined risk groups may lead to identification of the basic biological, behavioral, and social mechanisms that underlie an individual's predisposition to use drugs.

Both risk groups and basic mechanisms that underlie drug use play important roles in etiological research. Risk groups permit identification of individuals who are at high risk for drug use and thus allow targeting of interventions. Care must be taken in labeling a person as a member of a risk group, however, as labeling can be stigmatizing and thus potentially harmful. Knowledge of risk mechanisms, on the other hand, allows the drug-use tendencies of a given individual to be understood, with the identification of mechanisms that underlie drug use being the ultimate goal of etiological research. The process of identifying risk factors can be illustrated in the AIDS area where homosexual men were initially identified as a risk group for HIV infection. As knowledge about AIDS increased, unprotected sexual contact with an infected person was eventually identified as the specific factor responsible for homosexual HIV transmission. This discovery shifted attention away from the risk group and toward avoiding unprotected sexual contact in HIV prevention efforts.

RISK FACTORS IN DRUG USE

A number of risk factors have been implicated in drug use, including familial alcohol and drug abuse, poor achievement in school, peer pressure, poor relationship with parents, low self-esteem, premorbid antisocial personality disorder, depression, low religiosity, and cultural and ethnic influences (Newcomb et al., 1986; Vaillant & Milofsky, 1982; Zucker & Gomberg, 1986). Most of these risk factors describe quite narrowly defined risk groups. For example, the risk factor of familial alcohol and drug abuse identifies individuals within families of alcohol and drug abusers as having high rates of drug use, whereas the risk factor of depression indicates that depressed people have higher rates of drug use. Neither risk factor, however, identifies the basic mechanisms that are responsible for the increased risk. Of these risk factors, peer pressure comes closest to identifying a basic mechanism that controls drug use, as it indicates that social reinforcement by peers will contribute to drug use by adolescents.

Within a given individual, risk factors have been shown to be additive in determining probability of drug use (Newcomb et al., 1986). Because multiple risk factors are involved in drug use, it seems logical that to prevent drug use we must identify and develop interventions dealing with each factor. Obviously, this will be a complex and difficult task due to the large

number of risk factors that may be involved. The task is further complicated by the fact that risk factors may interact, and certain risk factors may
be active only at certain times during development. Hopefully, however,
the task will be simplified by identification of only a few major risk factors, which can then be the primary focus of intervention efforts.

Risk factors not only require different types of interventions, but they
also require different strategies for delivering interventions to affected persons. Some risk factors affect primarily individuals, whereas others influence predominantly small groups or entire populations. Low self-esteem,
for example, may touch only a single individual and not be a risk factor
for other relatives or peers. A substance-abusing parent, on the other hand,
may have a profound effect on several people, namely his or her spouse
and children, but will have less influence on those outside of the immediate family. Finally, peer influences affect relatively large numbers of persons of the same age, and cultural influences have widespread and pervasive effects on members of entire populations.

For peer and ethnic influences, community-wide interventions may be
most appropriate, as these risk factors affect large numbers of people. For
risk factors that affect only individuals or small groups, community-wide
interventions may be less appropriate. For these risk factors, identification and delivery of interventions to at-risk individuals will be more difficult.
This is particularly the case for risk factors that require intensive intervention. For example, depression as a risk factor for drug use may require
intensive therapy and may not be responsive to educational interventions
delivered through the media. Developing interventions that affect risk factors that occur in individuals or in small groups and developing strategies
for delivering the interventions to at-risk populations will be among our
greatest challenges in prevention research. Community-wide programs are
expected to play a role in this process, however, by assisting in the identification and delivery of interventions to at-risk individuals.

ALLEVIATING RISK FACTORS

There is no question about the importance of peer influences in the etiology of initial drug use. Studies have repeatedly shown that use of drugs by
peers is one of the best predictors of drug use by individuals (Battjes, 1984;
Hawkins, Lishner, & Catalano, 1985). Because our most successful interventions in reducing tobacco use are based on increasing resistance to peer
pressure to smoke, it is logical to expect that such interventions would be
effective in reducing new cases of other drug use as well. However, a large
number of other risk factors are also involved in the initiation of drug use

and attention must be paid to these factors as well if we are to achieve our overall goal of preventing drug use.

Because considerable attention has been paid to the role of peer influences in the initiation of drug use, this chapter focuses on other etiological influences that are involved in drug use. Lack of attention to these other influences may at least partly explain the ineffectiveness of peer resistance strategies for some individuals. For example, studies typically show that peer resistance strategies are effective in reducing new cases of drug use by 25% to 50%, indicating that such strategies are ineffective for a substantial number of the adolescents tested (Flay, 1985). Also, some adolescents initiate drug use prior to substantial involvement with drugs by their peers, and thus peer resistance is not likely to be a significant influence on their initiation of drug use (Kandel, 1980).

The influence of other etiological factors will be greatest in areas where such factors predominate. In inner-city areas, for example, peer influence may play a less significant role than in other areas. This is not because peer influences are weaker in those areas, but because other influences are more likely to be present. Inner-city areas typically have higher rates of familial substance abuse, sociopathy and depression, greater drug availability, and more individuals living in impoverished conditions, which have all been considered as etiological influences in drug use (Chein, Gerard, Lee, & Rosenfeld, 1964; Sykes, 1978). Thus, such influences can be expected to play a greater role in the development of drug use in inner-city areas than would be the case in other areas where they are less prevalent.

At present, strategies for dealing with other etiological influences in drug use are less advanced than strategies for mitigating peer influences. Although continuing research is needed to improve the effectiveness of peer-resistance strategies, research on other etiological influences is also needed if we are to improve the overall effectiveness of prevention interventions.

RISK FACTORS FOR DRUG USE
VERSUS DEPENDENCE

Drug use can be described as a continuum ranging from no use to drug dependence. Not everyone who initially experiments with drugs will become drug dependent. Some people experiment with drugs and then discontinue use. Others, however, will become regular users and some of those will progress to drug dependence. Identification of risk groups and risk factors for initial use, regular use, and drug dependence is an important goal in etiological research. Risk factors for initiation of drug use may be different from risk factors for regular use or dependence. Also, it is not clear whether the same risk factors are involved in initial use, regular use, or dependence on different types of drugs (e.g., marijuana vs. heroin), or different groups (e.g., males vs. females, adolescents vs. the elderly).

Relatively little attention has been paid to risk factors contributing to drug dependence. Initial drug use is obviously a necessary (but not sufficient) risk factor for drug dependence, because a person must use drugs in order to develop drug dependence. Early use of licit drugs may be a risk factor for later use of illicit drugs, which may have a greater dependence potential (Kandel, 1978). Also, age of onset of drug use is related to later development of drug disorders. In a population-based study, Robins and Przybeck (1985) found that when drug use (defined as drug use on five or more occasions) was started before the age of 15, about half of the men and two-fifths of the women eventually developed a DSM-III diagnosed drug-abuse disorder. The longer that first use was delayed, the lower was the risk for developing a disorder. Developing severe dependency was also somewhat higher for those who began drug use before the age of 15.

The importance of these other etiological influences in the maintenance of drug use is illustrated in a recent study by Kandel and Raveis (1989), who examined factors related to cessation of drug use by young adults. They found that those who initially used drugs in response to social influences during adolescence were more likely to stop using drugs as adults than those who began drug use for personal enjoyment or for psychological reasons.

FAMILIAL INFLUENCES IN SUBSTANCE ABUSE

Of the large number of etiological influences in drug abuse, several deserve special attention. One of these is premorbid antisocial personality disorder, which has been closely associated with drug use (Cadoret, Troughton & Widmer, 1984; Robins, 1978; Zucker & Gomberg, 1986). Another is depression and anxiety disorders in young adults, which was found to double the risk for later drug abuse or dependence (Christie et al., 1988). A third is childhood adjustment problems, such as aggressiveness, shyness, and learning difficulties (Kellam, Brown, Rubin & Ensminger, 1983; West & Prinz, 1987). A fourth is familial substance abuse, the abuse of alcohol and drugs by parents and other family members (Cotton, 1979). Because it is not possible to review all three areas, this chapter focuses on familial substance abuse to illustrate its influence on alcoholism and drug dependence, as well as to illustrate the limitation of such influence in explaining those dependencies.

Familial Factors in Alcoholism. Alcoholism has long been known to run in families. Within families, it appears both in members of different generations and in members of the same generation. Studies have consistently shown alcoholics to be more likely than nonalcoholics to have at least one alcoholic parent. Among first-degree relatives of alcoholics, as among alcoholics themselves, alcoholism tends to run primarily on the male side of the family. Thus, it is more common for fathers, brothers, and sons of alcoholics to be alcoholic than for mothers, sisters, and daughters. However, female alcoholics are at least as likely as male alcoholics to have alcoholic relatives (with several studies suggesting that females may be more likely than males to have alcoholic relatives).

In reviewing studies of familial alcoholism, alcoholism rates in families of alcoholics are typically compared to alcoholism rates in families of nonalcoholic controls. Rather than focusing on absolute rates of alcoholism in these two groups, however, it is more important to focus on relative rates of alcoholism, as absolute rates are influenced largely by diagnostic criteria employed.

In determining the prevalence of alcoholism in parents of alcoholics, Cotton (1979) conducted a comprehensive review of the literature in 1979 and summarized data from 39 studies of families of 6,251 alcoholics and 4,083 nonalcoholics (Table 3.1). Various criteria were used for diagnosing alcoholism, and alcoholics were recruited predominantly from inpatient treatment programs. Across the studies, 31% of the alcoholics were found to have at least one parent who was alcoholic. In contrast, alcoholism was found in only 5% of parents of controls (typically nonpsychiatric inpatients). Thus, the rate of alcoholism in one or both parents of alcoholics was found to be over six times that found in parents of controls.

Table 3.1
Alcoholism in Parents of Alcoholics
(From Cotton, 1979)

Probands	Father Alcoholic	Mother Alcoholic	Either/Both Alcoholic
Alcoholic	27%	5%	31%
Nonpsychiatric controls	5%	1%	5%

In a more recent study, Hesselbrock, Stabenau and Hall (1985) used DSM-III criteria to diagnose alcoholism in hospitalized probands and Family History-Research Diagnostic Criteria to diagnose alcoholism in their parents (Table 3.2). They found that 37% of fathers of male alcoholic probands were alcoholic, compared to only 10% of fathers of controls (dental patients). Alcoholism was present in 11% of the mothers of male alcoholic

Table 3.2
Lifetime Risk for Alcoholism in Parent of Alcoholic Probands*
(From Hesselbrock et al., 1985)

Probands	Father Alcoholic	Mother Alcoholic
Males		
Alcoholic (N = 212)	37%	11%
Control (N = 29)	10%	0%
Females		
Alcoholic (N = 79)	38%	20%
Control (N = 42)	19%	7%

*Using DSM-III criteria to diagnose probands and FH-RDC criteria to diagnose family members.

probands, compared to 0% in mothers of male controls. For female alcoholic probands, 38% of their fathers were alcoholic, compared to 19% of fathers of controls. Alcoholism was present in 20% of mothers of female alcoholic probands, compared to 7% in mothers of female controls. Thus, for male alcoholics, alcoholism rates in their fathers were almost 4 times higher than controls, and in their mothers approximately 10 times higher than controls. For females, alcoholism rates were twice as high in the fathers of alcoholics than controls, and almost three times higher in the mothers of alcoholics than controls.

Cloninger et al. (1988) examined prevalence of alcoholism among first-degree relatives of 286 hospitalized alcoholics (Table 3.3). Feighner criteria were used to diagnose alcoholism in both probands and their relatives. Alcoholism rates were higher in the male than in the female relatives of both male and female alcoholic probands. For male alcoholic probands,

TABLE 3.3
Lifetime Risk for Alcoholism in Adult First-Degree
Relatives of Alcoholic Probands*
(From Clininger et al. 1988)

Probands	Male Relatives	Female Relatives	Population Baserates**
Male alcoholics	63%	21%	29%
(N = 132)	(N = 319)	(N = 319)	(N = 1202)
Female alcoholics	61%	21%	4%
(N = 52)	(N = 67)	(N = 91)	(N = 1802)

*using Feighner et al. criteria for definite or probable alcoholism
**from ECA data for St. Louis, 1983

63% of male relatives and 21% of female relatives were alcoholic, whereas for female alcoholic probands, 61% of male relatives and 21% of female relatives were alcoholic. In contrast, Epidemiological Catchment Area survey data from the general population in the same geographical area (St. Louis) found alcoholism baserates to be 29% for males and 4% for females. Thus, male relatives of both male and female alcoholics had alcoholism rates approximately twice as high as controls, whereas female relatives of both male and female alcoholics had alcoholism rates approximately five times higher than controls.

Number of alcoholic parents is also related to alcoholism in probands. Cloninger et al. (1988) found higher alcoholism rates in children when both of their parents were alcoholic than when only one parent was alcoholic or neither parent was alcoholic. McKenna and Pickens (1981) reported that children of two alcoholic parents were more likely than children of one alcoholic parent, who were more likely than children of nonalcoholics, to be younger when first intoxicated, to have more pretreatment behavioral problems, and to proceed more rapidly from first intoxication to treatment. Similar findings have also been reported by Schuckit (1984).

The studies just cited concerned alcoholism rates in relatives of alcoholics in treatment populations. Similar findings have been reported for alcoholics in the general population. Midanik (1983) used a stratified area-probability sample of adults living in households in the United States to examine prevalence of alcoholism and problem drinking in relatives of alcoholic respondents (Table 3.4). Respondents with alcohol problems were more likely to report alcoholism or problem drinking in their first-degree relatives than were respondents without alcohol problems. Women with alcohol problems were more likely to have alcoholic or problem drinking parents than were men. Schuckit and Sweeney (1987) examined alcohol-related problems in male college students, and found the number of alcohol-

TABLE 3.4
Alcoholism in First-Degree Relatives
of Alcohol Abusers in the General Population
(From Midanik, 1983)

	Father	Mother	Brother	Sister
Males				
Alcoholic/problem drinkers	14%	4%	15%	2%
Nonabusers	8%	2%	11%	2%
Females				
Alcoholic/problem drinkers	24%	17%	15%	10%
Nonabusers	12%	3%	14%	4%

related problems to be related to family density of alcoholism (alcoholism in no relatives, second-degree relatives only, first-degree relatives only, both first- and second-degree relatives).

Limitation of Familial Factors in Explaining Alcoholism. Although familial alcoholism is clearly a significant risk factor in alcoholism, it is also important to recognize its limitation in explaining alcoholism. This is illustrated by the fact that not all alcoholics have alcoholic parents or other first-degree relatives. Cotton (1979), in her review of 39 family alcoholism studies, found that 47%–82% of alcoholics in the reviewed studies did not have alcoholic parents. Similarly, Hesselbrock et al. (1985) found that 42% of their alcoholic probands did not have a parent who was a problem drinker. Schuckit (1983) found 56% of a sample of male alcoholics reporting no history of alcoholism in first-degree relatives. However, this percentage decreased to 41% when data from another resource person was added, and when second-degree relatives were included, the percentage of alcoholics with no alcoholism in either a first- or second-degree relative decreased to only 31%.

Although not all alcoholics have alcoholic parents, not all persons with alcoholic parents develop alcoholism. In studies of alcoholism in the children of alcoholics, Winokur, Reich, Rimmer, and Pitts (1970) found alcoholism rates of 30% in the sons of male alcoholics and 33% in the sons of female alcoholics, and alcoholism rates of 0% in the daughters of male alcoholics and 5% in the daughters of female alcoholics. These findings suggest that a significant majority of children of alcoholics do not develop alcoholism. However, because children of alcoholics may not have passed the age of risk for alcoholism at the time of parental ascertainment, the actual rate of alcoholism in this group may increase over time. In addition to alcoholics not always having alcoholic parents, it is also clear that not all moderate drinkers come from moderate drinking or abstaining parents. Hesselbrock et al. (1985), for example, found that 27% of their nonalcoholic control probands had a problem-drinking parent.

Although these data indicate that not all alcoholism can be attributed to familial influences, it is important to recognize that these data may represent an overestimate of the actual rates of nonfamilial alcoholism. Such rates tend to decrease when both first- and second-degree relatives are included as family members, and when interviews involve other family members in addition to the proband. Also, many children of alcoholics have not yet passed the age of risk for alcoholism at the time of parental ascertainment, suggesting that a number of these children may develop alcoholism in the future. Thus, familial influences on development of alcoholism may be even greater than suggested by these data.

Familial Studies of Other Drug Use. The study of familial transmission of other types of drug use is not as advanced as the study of familial transmission of alcoholism. However, because families of alcoholics and drug abusers are similar in many ways, findings regarding alcoholics may apply in large measure to other types of drug use as well (Kaufman, 1984). Children of alcoholics are at high risk for use of other drugs. In a study of men with primary alcoholism, Schuckit (1984) found higher rates of marijuana, barbiturate, and amphetamine use in subjects with alcoholic parents. Similar findings have been reported by others (McGlothlin, 1975; Smart & Fejer, 1972). Schuckit and Sweeney (1987) found use of cocaine, amphetamines, and hallucinogens in a group of college students to be related to familial density of alcoholism in first- and second-degree relatives.

Use of both licit and illicit drugs by adolescents is correlated with their parents' use of psychoactive drugs, including prescribed medications (Smart, Fejer, & Alexander, 1970; Smart, Fejer, & White, 1971). Use of similar drugs by different members of the same family has been reported by others, as when pain-killers are used both by parents and their children (Annis, 1974), and marijuana use by youth is highly correlated with maternal marijuana use (Gfroerer, 1987). For illicit opiates, establishing familial patterns of dependence has been difficult because of the low rate of opioid dependence in the general population. Nevertheless, Maddux and Desmond (1989) recently reported that lifetime prevalence of opioid dependence in first-degree relatives of opioid addicts was 8.4%, which greatly exceeds the estimated U.S. population prevalence (0.9%). Rates of opioid dependence were highest in the brothers of opioid addicts (20%) and lowest in their mothers (0%). Overall, rate of opioid dependence in first-degree relatives of opioid addicts was over nine times that estimated for the general population (Table 3.5).

Whether abusers of other drugs have higher rates of parental alcoholism is not clear. Earlier studies reported a disproportionate number of alcoholics among the fathers of heroin addicts (Ellinwood, Smith & Vaillant, 1966). In contrast, later studies have produced conflicting results (Kosten, Rounsaville, & Kleber, 1985; Maddux & Desmond, 1989). Heroin addicts

TABLE 3.5
Heroin Addiction in First-Degree Relatives of Heroin-Dependent Probands[*]
(From Maddux & Desmond, 1989)

Probands	Fathers (N = 235)	Mothers (N = 235)	Brothers (N = 573)	Sisters (N = 540)	All[**] (N = 1538)
Opioid dependence only	0.4%	0%	16.6%	2.2%	6.8%
Opioid dependence and alcoholism	1.7%	0%	3.4%	0.2%	1.6%
Total	2.1%	0%	20.0%	2.4%	8.4%

[*]using DSM-III-R criteria
[**]estimated U.S. prevalence of opioid dependence = 0.9%

with parental alcoholism, however, were more likely to be alcoholics themselves than heroin addicts without parental alcoholism, suggesting specificity of alcoholism transmission (Kosten et al., 1985).

SUMMARY

The purpose of this chapter has been to call attention to the importance of etiological research in the prevention of drug use. Because multiple risk factors appear to be involved in drug use, interventions must be developed to confront each of these risk factors if we are to be effective in our overall goal of preventing drug use. However, it is recognized that knowledge about etiology alone will not be sufficient. Other knowledge is also needed, including knowledge about the nature and characteristics of drug use, the adverse consequences of drug use, and methods for effective delivery of prevention materials. Taken together, this research provides the foundation on which new prevention interventions are developed. Thus, rather than focusing on evaluation of the effectiveness of interventions, prevention research is a broad-based area of study, encompassing many research fields.

Particular attention was paid to familial alcohol and drug use as a risk factor for development of alcohol and drug dependence. First-degree relatives of substance abusers have significantly higher rates of substance abuse than is seen in the general population, making them an important target for prevention efforts. Compared to other family members, children of alcoholics and drug abusers offer the most promising targets for intervention, since they are younger and therefore more likely to be ascertained prior to substantial involvement with alcohol or drugs (Svikis & Pickens, 1988). This group has received a considerable amount of attention recently, with specific points for intervention identified (Burk & Sher, 1988). A number of prevention studies focusing on children of alcoholics as a high risk group for substance abuse are currently underway (e.g., Kumpfer, 1989). However, because familial transmission alone cannot explain all substance abuse, attention should not be focused solely on this risk factor. Interventions for affecting multiple risk factors should be developed and tested.

Unlike social pressure that has a widespread influence, familial substance abuse is clustered in small groups (i.e., families of substance abusers). Thus, compared to social pressure, the number of people affected by this risk factor is relatively small. However, within families of substance abusers, having an alcoholic or drug abusing parent can be a significant risk factor for drug use, and possibly a major determinant of alcoholism or drug dependence as well. Because of its clustering in the general population, developing strategies for confronting familial substance abuse and for delivering interventions to affected families will be difficult.

In future etiological research, increased attention should be paid to familial transmission of both drug use and dependence, and to possible mechanisms (both genetic and environmental) that may underlie familial influences (Tarter, 1988). Because most children of alcoholics and drug abusers do not become alcoholics or drug abusers themselves, identification of mechanisms that underlie drug use may allow individuals in this group to be identified on the basis of some characteristics other than group membership, thus avoiding the negative effects of labeling. In future studies of familial transmission, particular attention should be paid to members of high-density alcoholic families who do not develop alcoholism, as such studies may identify protective influences.

REFERENCES

Annis, H. M. (1974). Patterns of intra-familial drug use. *British Journal of the Addictions, 69,* 361–369.

Battjes, R. J. (1984). Symbolic interaction theory: A perspective on drug abuse and its treatment. *International Journal of Addictions, 19,* 675–688.

Botvin, G. J. (1983). Prevention of adolescent substance abuse through the development of personal and social competence. In T. J. Glynn, C. G. Leukefeld, & J. P. Ludford (Eds.), *Preventing adolescent drug abuse: Intervention strategies* (NIDA Research Monograph 47, DHHS Publication No. (ADM) 83–1280, pp. 115–140). Washington DC: U.S. Government Printing Office.

Burk, J. P., & Sher, K. J. (1988). "Forgotten children" revisited: Neglected areas of COA research. *Clinical Psychology Review, 8,* 285–302.

Cadoret, R., Troughton, E., & Widmer, R. (1984). Clinical differences between antisocial and primary alcoholics. *Comprehensive Psychiatry, 25,* 1–8.

Chein, I., Gerard, D. L., Lee, R. S., & Rosenfeld, E. (1964). *The Road to H.* New York: Basic Books.

Christie, K. A., Burke, J. D., Regier, D. A., Rae, D. S., Boyd, J. H., & Locke, B. Z. (1988). Epidemiologic evidence for early onset of mental disorders and higher risk of drug abuse in young adults. *American Journal of Psychiatry, 145,* 971–975.

Cloninger, C. R., Reich, T., Sigvardsson, S., von Knorring, A. L. & Bohman, M. (1988). Effects of changes in alcohol use between generations on inheritance of alcohol abuse. In R. M. Rose & J. Barrett (Eds.), *Alcoholism: Origins and outcomes* (pp. 49–73). New York: Raven Press.

Cotton, N. S. (1979). The familial incidence of alcoholism: A review. *Journal of Studies on Alcohol, 40,* 89–116.

Ellinwood, E. H., Smith, W. G., & Vaillant, G. E. (1966). Narcotic addiction in males and females: A comparison. *International Journal of the Addictions, 1,* 33–45.

Flay, B. R. (1985). What we know about the social influences approach to smoking prevention: Review and recommendations. In C. S. Bell & R. Battjes (Eds.), *Prevention research: Deterring drug abuse among children and adolescents* (NIDA Research Monograph 63, DHHS Publication No. (ADM) 85–1334, pp. 67–192). Washington, DC: U.S. Government Printing Office.

Gfroerer, J. (1987). Correlation between drug use by teenagers and drug use by older family members. *American Journal of Drug and Alcohol Use, 13,* 95–108.

Hawkins, J. D., Lishner, D. M., & Catalano, R. F. (1985). Childhood predictors and the prevention of adolescent substance abuse. In C. L. Jones & R. J. Battjes (Eds.), *Etiology of Drug Abuse: Implications for Prevention* (NIDA Research Monograph 56, DHHS Publication No. (ADM) 85–1334, pp. 75–126). Washington, DC: U.S. Government Printing Office.

Hesselbrock, V. M., Stabenau, J. R., & Hall, R. (1985). Drinking style of parents of alcoholic and control probands. *Alcohol, 2,* 525–528.

Kandel, D. B. (1978), *Longitudinal research on drug use: Empirical findings and methodological issues.* Washington, DC: Hemisphere-Wiley. Kandel, D. B. (1980). Drug and drinking behavior among youth. *Annual Review of Sociology, 6,* 235–285.

Kandel, D. B., & Raveis, V. H. (1989). Cessation of illicit drug use in young adulthood. *Archives of General Psychiatry, 46,* 109–116.

Kaufman, E. (1984). Family systems variables in alcoholism. *Alcoholism: Clinical and Experimental Research, 8,* 4–8.

Kellam, S. G., Brown, C. H., Rubin, B. R., & Ensminger, M. E. (1983). Paths leading to teenage psychiatric symptoms and substance use: Developmental epidemiological studies in Woodlawn. In S. B. Guze, F. J. Earls, & J. E. Barrett (Eds.), *Childhood psychopathology and development* (pp. 17–47). New York: Raven Press.

Kosten, T. R., Rounsaville, B. J., & Kleber, H. D. (1985). Parental alcoholism in opioid addicts. *Journal of Nervous and Mental Diseases, 173,* 461–469.

Kumpfer, K. (1989). Promising prevention strategies for children of substance abusers. *OSAP High Risk Youth Update, 2,* (Whole No. 1).

Maddux, J. F., & Desmond, D. P. (1989). Family and environment in the choice of opioid dependence or alcoholism. *American Journal of Drug and Alcohol Abuse, 15,* 117–134.

McGlothlin, W. H. (1975). Drug use and abuse. *Annual Review of Psychology, 26,* 45–64.

McKenna, T., & Pickens, R. (1981). Alcoholic children of alcoholics. *Journal of Studies on Alcohol, 42,* 1021–1029.

Midanik, L. (1983). Familial alcoholism and problem drinking in a national drinking practices survey. *Addictive Behaviors, 8,* 133–141.

Newcomb, M. D., Maddahian, E., & Bentler, P. M. (1986). Risk factors for drug use among adolescents: Concurrent and longitudinal analyses. *American Journal of Public Health, 76,* 525–531.

Robins, L. N. (1978). Sturdy childhood predictors of adult antisocial behaviour: Replications from longitudinal studies. *Psychological Medicine, 8,* 611–622.

Robins, L. N., & Przybeck, T. R. (1985). Age of onset of drug use as a factor in drug and other disorders. In C. L. Jones & R. J. Battjes (Eds.), *Etiology of drug abuse: Implications for prevention* (NIDA Research Monograph 56, DHHS Publication No. (ADM) 85–1334, pp. 178–192). Washington, DC: U.S. Government Printing Office.

Schuckit, M. A. (1983). Alcoholic men with no alcoholic first-degree relatives. *American Journal of Psychiatry, 140,* 439–443.

Schuckit, M. A. (1984). Relationship between the course of primary alcoholism in men and family history. *Journal of Studies on Alcohol, 45,* 334–338.

Schuckit, M. A., & Sweeney, S. (1987). Substance use and mental health problems among sons of alcoholics and controls. *Journal of Studies on Alcohol, 48,* 528–534.

Smart, R. G., & Fejer, D. (1972). Drug use among adolescents and their parents: Using the generation gap in mood modification. *Journal of Abnormal Psychology, 70,* 153–166.

Smart, R. G., Fejer, D., & Alexander, E. (1970). *Drug use among high school students and their parents in Lincoln and Welland Counties.* Toronto: Addiction Research Foundation. Smart, R. G., Fejer, D., & White, J. (1971). The extent of drug use in metropolitan Toronto schools: A study of changes from 1968 to 1970. *Addictions, 18,* 1–17.

Svikis, D. S., & Pickens, R. W. (1988). Children of alcoholics: A target for prevention efforts. In *Physical medicine and rehabilitation: State of the art reviews* (pp. 203–211). Philadelphia: Hanley & Belfus.

Sykes, G. M. (1978). *Criminology.* New York: Harcourt Brace Jovanovich. Tarter, R. E. (1988). Are there inherited behavioral traits that predispose to substance abuse. *Journal of Consulting and Clinical Psychology, 56,* 189–196.

Tarter, R. E. (1988). Are there inherited behavioral traits that predispose to substance abuse. *Journal of Consulting and Clinical Psychology, 56,* 189–196.

Vaillant, G. E., & Milofsky, E. S. (1982). The etiology of alcoholism: A prospective viewpoint. *American Psychologist, 37,* 494–503.

Warner, K. E. (1986). *Selling smoke.* Washington, DC: American Public Health Association.

West, M., & Prinz, R. J. (1987). Parental alcoholism and childhood psychopathology. *Psychological Bulletin, 102,* 204–218.

Winokur, G., Reich, T., Rimmer, J., & Pitts, F. (1970). Alcoholism: III. Diagnosis and familial psychiatric illness in 259 alcoholic probands. *Archives of General Psychiatry, 23,* 104–111.

Zucker, R. A., & Gomberg, E. S. L. (1986). Etiology of alcoholism reconsidered: The case for a biopsychosocial process. *American Psychologist, 41,* 783–793.

II

COMMUNICATION: PAST AND POTENTIAL ROLES

4

Mass Communication and Persuasion: The Evolution of Direct Effects, Limited Effects, Information Processing, and Affect and Arousal Models

Ellen Wartella
Susan Middlestadt
University of Illinois at Urbana–Champaign

This chapter offers a review of American research on mass communication and persuasion. Most reviews of this type begin with the study of mass media persuasive effects on audiences with the rise of movies and radio in the 20th century. Although the scientific study of mass media effects did indeed begin then, public communication campaigns did not. Long before the advent of broadcasting and other electronic forms of communication, there were intentional attempts to influence someone else's beliefs or behavior through communicated appeals (Paisley, 1981). McGuire (1985) harkened back to the rhetorical strategies of the Greeks for the roots of contemporary persuasive strategies. Paisley (1981) provided an example within the American context, the publication of the *Federalist Papers* in 1787. The motive for publication of the 85 installments of the *Papers* was clearly persuasion: Each separate publication addressed a different criticism of the proposed constitution, and the *Papers* were clearly public in "their patient reasoning and their respectful acknowledgement of opposing points of view" (Paisley, 1981, p. 17). Moreover, the social contract underlying the American constitution is based on persuasive communication as a central mechanism of governance, as de Tocqueville noted in 1835:

> When men are no longer united amongst themselves by firm and lasting ties, it is impossible to obtain the concurrence of any great number of them, unless you can persuade every man whose concurrence you require that his private interest obliges him voluntarily to unite his exertions to the exertions

of all the rest. This can only be habitually and conveniently effected by means of a newspaper: nothing but a newspaper can drop the same thought into a thousand minds at the same moment. (de Tocqueville, 1900, p. 119)

Indeed, de Tocqueville's faith in the role of newspapers and the mass media represents a libertarian philosophy of media performance, one current during the rise of the scientific study of the mass media at the turn of the 20th century (Siebert, Peterson, & Schramm, 1956). The libertarian philosophy supported the notion that in order for citizens to participate effectively in the marketplace of ideas, they must have access to contrasting ideas, and thus what society needs is many competing voices in the mass media.

This faith in the essential role of the media in maintaining our democratic state was elaborated by early American sociologists of the Chicago School (Bramson, 1961). As proponents of an American brand of ''mass society'' theory, they developed both a theoretical and an empirical program of study in the first three decades of this century, to examine the nature of the media's influence as a means of public communication.

The mass society theory promoted by the Chicago School was originally a far more optimistic version of a European theory with roots in late 19th-century France, Germany and England (Bramson, 1961). George Herbert Mead and John Dewey, in particular, argued for the role of the mass media in taking the place of small towns and helping to create a sense of community that might be lost with urbanization and industrialization (Bramson, 1961). For these early Chicago School theorists, the rise of a mass society and new forms of collective behavior had a constructive side (as well as the more destructive side stressed in 19th-century European writings about the crowd and mob). For the first generation of Chicago School theorists in the last two decades of the 19th century and first few years of the 20th century, collective behavior could bring about a new social order with new institutions (Bramson, 1961). These social theorists, according to Bramson, ''conceived of social behavior and society as constituted of individual behavior, and particularly emphasized the motivations of individuals in association'' (p. 85) The extent to which the individual was integrated into the community or became atomized and isolated was a focal point in their theories.

Concern about the disorganization of American life brought about by rising urbanization, industrialization, and huge waves of immigration at the turn of the century, led a second generation of Chicago School social scientists in the first 30 years of the 1900s to focus on the negative consequences of the mass society and modern life. They examined the growth of gangs and delinquency, the conflict of different races living together, the difficult adjustment of immigrants to American life, and the impact of new technologies such as movies and radio on individuals. Thus, theorizing about mass society became central to theorizing about the mass media.

Although some theorists within the Chicago School, such as Dewey, had faith that the mass media could help create a common culture and bring to public life a forum for rational public discourse, others within the Chicago School circle were more pessimistic (Bramson, 1961). Gradually, the dislocations of the first few decades of this century brought a harsher view of the mass society and the atomized individuals who resided within it and of the seeming failure of the mass media to provide a sense of community or democratic communication. In particular, the effectiveness of the propaganda campaigns of World War I, the rise of public relations during the early 1900s, which could effectively change the image of the rich from miserly to philanthropic, and the ability of the media to create the "pictures in our heads," as Lippmann (1922) put it, gave rise to the belief that the mass media were enormously powerful in shaping directly their audiences' knowledge, attitudes and social behavior.

During the first third of this century, then, the earliest theorizing about the mass media argued for the enormous power of public communication in influencing the atomized and isolated individuals living in the mass society. This period in American communication research is often referred to as the period of *direct effects* or *mass society theory* or the era of the belief in the *hypodermic needle model* (articulated by Harold Lasswell in 1927) of the media's influence. We eschew all of these terms because in many ways they are more misleading than clarifying. They suggest that scholars of the mass media in this period did not recognize individual differences in responses to mass communication campaigns. This was not the case. In order to elaborate in a clearer way on this early period of American media research, we need to shift our focus to the empirical literature on mass communication and persuasion, published during the era that McGuire (1985) referred to as the first stage of research on attitudes and persuasion (i.e., from the turn of the century to the mid-1930s).

EARLY RESEARCH ON MEDIA
AND PERSUASION: 1900–1930s

Some of the earliest research on American mass media effects on audiences was conducted at the University of Chicago in the first decades of this century. As early as 1909, a Chicago School dissertation by Frances Fenton was devoted to studying the effects of newspaper coverage of crime on fostering juvenile delinquency. In 1922, Alice Miller Mitchell's study of

the movie-going behavior of children and adolescents employed both surveys and observational study. One of the classic studies utilizing life history methods, a mainstay of qualitative sociological methodology, was
Thrasher's (1933) study, *The Gang: A Study of 1,313 Gangs in Chicago*, which
included a detailed analysis of the influence of movies and dime store novels
on the boys in the gang in providing both cheap entertainment and patterns for play and social behavior. Most important for the study of mass
communication and persuasion, however, were the Payne Fund studies
of 1929–1932 on the effects of movies on American youth.

An elaborate discussion of the importance of the Payne Fund studies
in American research on children and media has been offered elsewhere
(Wartella & Reeves, 1985); equally important, however, and not often mentioned is the role of the Payne Fund research in studies of American public communication campaigns. Notably, 1 of the 12 Payne Fund volumes
is the elaborate series of studies of attitude change through movies by social psychologists Ruth C. Peterson and L. L. Thurstone (1933). This work
is illustrative both of the more complicated view of media effects on audiences that was current by the 1930s and the empirical paradigm to be
followed in succeeding generations of studies of media's influence on audience attitudes and behaviors. The intent of these studies was twofold:
first, to study the effects of movies on producing attitude change among
audience members, and second, to develop and elaborate the methodology underlying Thurstone's Equal Appearing Interval Scale for measuring
attitudes. Peterson and Thurstone designed a series of pretest-posttest only
experiments with children and adolescents utilizing a variety of Hollywood-
made motion pictures that were thought to influence children's attitudes
toward various ethnic groups, racial groups and social classes. Notable
among the stimuli was the film *Birth of a Nation*, which had been implicated in a major public debate when it was first issued, shortly before World
War I, for its alleged anti-Black portrayals of slavery in the Civil War South.
Another stimulus was the anti-war film *All Quiet on the Western Front*. The
experimental design called for testing the youthful audiences in their school-
rooms 2 weeks before the children were given tickets to go to a local movie
house to see a particular film. The day after the film, postviewing measures of attitudes were taken, once again in their classrooms. Overall, two
dozen studies were completed, some of them on the effect of a single film,
other studies of the cumulative effects of two or three pictures on the same
theme. Peterson and Thurstone also examined the persistence of attitude
changes produced 2 to 19 months after moviegoing.

The results of these studies demonstrated that the mass medium of movies could produce attitude change in children. The results were greater
for younger children than for older ones, and seeing two or three movies

treating the same topic in the same way achieved greater results than seeing only one film. Peterson and Thurstone found that the effects of the
movies on attitudes were more likely to appear when the children had no
firsthand knowledge about the people or ideas presented; that is, when
the media do not have to compete with the children's already formed opinions on the topic, media's influence is greatest. Most importantly, the
authors concluded that attitude change can persist over time; in one case,
60% of the original attitude change was retained 19 months later (Peterson & Thurstone, 1933, p. 63).

Thus, as early as 1933, the Peterson and Thurstone study represented
a model for studying media effects on audience attitudes. It was an important illustration of the use of an experimental method for studying media
effects; it demonstrated relatively sophisticated theorizing about media's
influence which was in no way direct and uniformly effective for all members of the audience; and its methodology for studying attitudes, the Thurstone Equal Appearing Interval scale, premised on the Law of Comparative Judgment, supplied the rationale for attitude measurement today. Like
the other Payne Fund volumes, this work was in no way illustrative of a
"direct effects" theory of media. Rather, as in other studies on the effects
of mass media and youth coming from the University of Chicago, and much
like contemporary studies of children and television, the Payne Fund
researches demonstrated that the same film would affect children differently depending on each child's age, gender, predispositions, perceptions,
social environment, past experiences, and parental influences (Wartella &
Reeves, 1985).

However, it took another 10 to 15 years of research on the mass media
for a well-articulated theory of the *relative inability* of the mass media to
change audience beliefs and behaviors to develop. The era of so-called "indirect effects" of persuasive media campaigns on audiences was promoted not by researchers at the University of Chicago (even though their
research demonstrated more limited media effects than the mass society
theorizing at the turn of the century suggested), but rather by psychologists and sociologists on the East Coast, studying media's influence from
World War II through the 1950s. This second period of theorizing about
media's influence is referred to in many basic mass media texts as the period
of "limited" or "indirect" effects of the media. This period also corresponds to McGuire's (1985) third stage of attitude change research during the 1950s and early 1960s. During this stage, attitude research was at
the center stage of social psychology. There was particular emphasis on
the development of theory-based empirical demonstrations of attitude
change and many of these demonstrations were studies of mass media persuasive communications.

THE INDIRECT EFFECTS ERA
OF MEDIA STUDY: 1940s–1960s

The eclectic nature of the empirical study of mass media effects, which characterized mass media research in the early decades of the 20th century, changed rather dramatically with the advent of the 1940s. Most important in bringing about a "paradigm shift," more in cohesive research practices than in theorizing perhaps, was the rise in prominence of the field survey research on mass communication carried out at the Bureau of Applied Social Research at Columbia University by Paul Lazarsfeld and his colleagues. From 1939 through the 1960s, the Bureau's research programs became central in the development of the belief in the "limited" role of the mass media in any intentional public communication campaign.

A number of brief historical accounts of the development of American mass communication research (such as the basic text *Theories of Mass Communication* by Melvin DeFleur and Sandra Ball-Rokeach, 1982; the introduction to *Personal Influence* by Elihu Katz and Paul Lazarsfeld in 1955; and the first chapter of the 1960 *Effects of Mass Communication* by Joseph Klapper) refer to Paul Lazarsfeld's 1940s research as offering the first empirical demonstrations of the qualified nature of media effects. The two volumes, *The People's Choice* (Lazarsfeld, Berelson, & Gaudet, 1948), a study of the effects of radio and newspapers on voting patterns among residents ot Erie County, Ohio, in the presidential campaign of 1940, and Katz and Lazarsfeld's (1955) *Personal Influence*, a study of the role of interpersonal opinion leaders relative to the mass media in shaping the preferences of a sample of Decatur, Illinois, women in moviegoing, fashion, grocery shopping, and public affairs issues, are frequently considered the major challenges of the direct effects model of media influence. However, as attention to earlier work at Chicago demonstrates, there are earlier qualifications of media's powerful direct influence on audiences. What the Lazarsfeld studies do offer is a sharply focused research paradigm that colonized thinking about mass media campaign effects from the end of World War II through the 1960s.

In short, these studies, all major field surveys, based on self-reports of media's influence on their audiences, questioned the ability of radio and print media to influence directly important political or consumer decisions and found that the media had "limited persuasive power." What little influence existed operated through opinion leaders in the community who, in turn, influenced their followers. Thus, the "two-step flow" theory of media's influence arose and was elaborated on particularly in the volume *Personal Influence*. According to these studies, media are not often involved in converting people's attitudes. Rather, media tend to be better at reinforcing people's already held beliefs. Reinforcement results from a combination of audiences selectively attending to material in the mass media with which they already agree, and selectively retaining what they attend to, such that the audience's memory of the material is consistent with its attitudes toward the subject matter. This became virtual canon in Joseph Klapper's influential work *The Effects of Mass Communication* (1960).

These large-scale sociological studies of media's "limited" influence were reinforced by the publication of *Experiments in Mass Communication* by Hovland, Lumsdaine, and Sheffield (in 1949). This book reported a series of social psychological studies, carried out during World War II, of the effects of the *Why We fight* series of films on soldiers' attitudes toward the war (Hovland, Lumsdaine, & Sheffield, 1950). These studies are considered landmarks because of their sophisticated experimental design (pretest-posttest design with control group) and their conceptualization of communication campaigns in terms of variables of the source (such as credibility), the message (one-sided vs. two-sided appeals, effects of fear appeals) and the receiver (intellectual ability of audience members). Hovland et al. found few effects of the training films on the recruits' attitudes toward the war in general and on their motivation to serve as soldiers, the ultimate objective of the films. However, the films did have marked effects on the men's knowledge of the factual material in them, such as the events leading up to the war, and the films had some effect on opinion where the film specifically covered the factors involved in a particular interpretation of the facts it presented. Moreover, Hovland et al. found evidence of a "sleeper effect": Nine weeks after initially seeing the films, soldiers forgot much of the information in the films but their opinions changed even more compared to the changes that were observed immediately after having seeing the films.

The publication of these major empirical tests of the effects of mass communication during political campaigns and through wartime indoctrination films seemed to suggest that mass media were not influential in changing audiences' attitudes directly. These studies, when coupled with the often-cited Hyman and Sheatsley (1947) review of "Some Reasons Why Information Campaigns Fail," and Star and Hughes' (1950) demonstration of the failure of an information campaign about the United Nations in Cincinnati, crystallized the view that mass media alone cannot affect attitude change. And attitude change until the late 1960s was the criterion variable for demonstrating an "effect" of public communication campaigns. Scholars questioned the efficacy of using the mass media in persuasive communication campaigns. For this reason, among others, mass communication researchers began to cast about for evidence of "media influence" other than demonstrations of attitude change. Many researchers, including Hovland et al., demonstrated that the mass media seemed more successful in changing people's knowledge about issues and events than in changing their attitudes toward them. By the early 1970s, much media research shifted attention from concern with persuasive communication effects on attitude change to the examination of mass media's ability to change the audience's level of information and knowledge about issues and events. Thus, there was a shift in media effects research away from "attitude" as the focal variable of interest and towards the demonstration of media produced "knowledge change" (see e.g., Gerbner, Gross, & Signorielli, 1986). During the same period of the 1950s and 1960s, according to McGuire (1985), the social psychologists theorizing about persuasion and attitude change also became frustrated primarily over the difficulty of demonstrating that attitude measures could predict behavior change (Wicker, 1969). This led many researchers to move away from the attitude and persuasion models in the 1960s and early 1970s.

Consequently, by the early 1970s, both the larger literature of mass media and public communication campaigns and the more specific social psychological literature on attitude change and persuasion had undergone a paradigm shift. Scholars of mass media moved away from conceptualizing public communication campaign effects in terms of the ability to produce attitude changes. Meanwhile, many social psychologists also moved away from the study of attitudes. Moreover, although for the first half of the century, the literature on mass media effects and the literature on the social psychological study of persuasion overlapped considerably (such as in the work of L. L. Thurstone or Carl Hovland), these two trends became increasingly distinct after 1970. By the early to mid-1970s, the literature on mass communication and persuasion became fragmented with a variety of different theoretical approaches to the study of the persuasive impact of communication, and it became disconnected, by and large, from the social psychological literature. It is difficult, if not impossible, to offer a coherent historical narrative combining the mass communication effects literature with the social psychological literature on attitudes and persuasion from 1970 on. And even to offer a coherent narrative of the media effects literature itself is not easy.

CONTEMPORARY APPROACHES
TO COMMUNICATION AND PERSUASION

The problem faced by researchers interested in the role of mass communication in persuasion or public communication campaigns from the early 1970s on can be stated succinctly: How could media researchers demonstrate the seemingly obvious power of the mass media, in the face of the equally well-demonstrated "obstinate audience"? Attempts to grapple with this conundrum resulted in several very disparate lines of research. For the purposes of this chapter, we try to summarize three such areas of research: (a) studies of media effects on the audience's social knowledge; (b) research on limited, circumscribed public information campaigns developed to induce behavior change—such as seat belt campaigns or other health campaigns; and (c) the eclectic and varied models currently available describing the role of persuasive messages (either through the mass media or through some other form of intervention) in changing people's attitudes or behaviors.

Media Effects on Knowledge. Several rather distinct lines of research have developed over the past 20 years or so, examining the effects of mass media on the audience's knowledge about the world. First, in the area of mass communication and public opinion research, there is work on the "agenda-setting hypothesis." Rooted in political science theories of public opinion, the agenda-setting research argues that the amount of media coverage devoted to political or social issues influences audience perceptions of the importance of those issues in American life.

A second area of research on media influences on social knowledge is examining the influence of television entertainment programming on audiences' beliefs about social reality (Gerbner et al., 1986). Gerbner's argument is that the social world presented on fictional television programs is a very biased and constructed view of American life, (e.g., too few minority groups, too few women, too much violence, etc.). Consequently, heavy television viewers who are saturated in this fictional world come to view the "real world" as similar to the "TV world." In this way, television is said to cultivate the audience's beliefs about social reality. There has been some dispute over the specific "scary world hypothesis" proposed by Gerbner and his colleagues. This is the notion that television viewers tend to see the world as more violent than it really is because of watching heavy amounts of violence on television. However, cultivation research across a variety of knowledge domains has generally supported the argument of television's cultivation of the audience's social beliefs (see Gerbner et al., 1986, for a review).

Communication Campaigns. Since the early 1970s there have been a variety of communication campaign studies (see Rogers & Storey, 1987, for a major review). These studies differ from the earlier 1940s and 1950s research in that they look at much more focused and directed communication activities. According to Rogers and Storey (1987) a communication campaign is a set of communication activities that is purposive with specific intended outcomes, it is aimed at large audiences, and it has a more or less specifically defined time limit. Several guidelines have been developed for successful media campaigns. To be successful, communication cam-

paigns should adopt a strategic approach that involves considerable formative research, in order to design appropriate campaign messages for the
intended audience, target the messages to specific audience members (what
is known in marketing as *market segmentation*) and set realistic goals (e.g.,
not expect short-term behavioral change outcomes). Moreover, media campaigns should be viewed as complementary to interpersonal or community-
based intervention efforts. Unlike the dire claims of the failure of information campaigns in the literature of the 1950s and 1960s, the contemporary literature on public communication campaigns suggests that well-
crafted media campaigns can succeed under the right circumstances. According to Rogers and Storey (1987) this occurs when there is widespread
acceptance of the campaign by the target audience; when media are used
to create awareness and knowledge of the issue, to stimulate interpersonal
communication and to recruit individuals to participate in campaign activities; and when interpersonal communication channels such as peer networks are used to encourage and maintain behavior change among the
target audience. As noted earlier, media communication campaigns must
be constructed carefully. Researchers have noted, for instance, that the
perceived credibility of a communication source or channel enhances the
effectiveness of media messages; that well-targeted media messages improve the success rate; that message appeals must be socially near rather
than distant; and that media campaigns promoting prevention are typically less successful than those with immediate consequences (Rogers &
Storey, 1987).

Persuasive Communication Research. The research on persuasive
communication per se is rooted largely in social psychological theorizing
about the relationship between attitudes and behavior. This research has
influenced media research largely in advertising, marketing, and consumer
research. The research here focuses on theory-based models of how persuasion operates to produce changes in cognition, affect, and behavior
(McGuire, 1985, offered a thorough review). This literature is enormous
(McGuire found over 7,000 citations relevant to the study of persuasive
communication). In this chapter, we briefly identify some of the major theoretical approaches to persuasive communication that are important in suggesting ways to develop effective, persuasive mass media communication
campaigns.

Beginning in the 1960s and for many years since, contemporary social
psychological approaches to attitude change and persuasive communication have been expectancy-value formulations of attitudes and behavior.
According to this approach, attitudes are based on a cognitive algebra involving beliefs about associated characteristics, and evaluations of these
characteristics. Most importantly, these theories suggest that in order to

change behavior one needs to change these underlying expectations and values. The *theory of reasoned action* is one of the most influential, widely used, and strongly supported expectancy-value models, which is of importance to contemporary discussions of persuasion (Ajzen & Fishbein, 1980; Fishbein & Ajzen, 1975). In fact, it has been used successfully to understand behaviors in a variety of domains, including a number of behaviors in the health domain (Fishbein & Middlestadt, 1987; Middlestadt, 1990). Proponents of this theory argue that it is useful in designing communication aimed at encouraging people to perform a behavior.

According to the theory, the best predictor of whether or not a person will engage in a behavior is the person's intention to engage in the behavior. A person's intention is, in turn, determined by two components, one personal (the person's attitude toward the behavior) and the other social in nature (the subjective norm—the person's perception that people who are important to him or her think they should engage in the behavior). The attitude toward the behavior and the subjective norm jointly determine the intention to engage in the behavior. The importance of the two factors differs from situation to situation depending on a number of factors, such as the behavior and the population being studied.

Because this theory assumes that most behavior is ultimately determined by sets of underlying beliefs, it follows that behavior change is accomplished by changing these beliefs. Changes in underlying beliefs lead to changes in attitudes and norms that, in turn, lead to changes in intention and behavior. Thus, a key tenet of the theory of reasoned action is that media messages intended to change behavior must be designed and aimed at the underlying beliefs that are associated with behavioral intentions in the population under study.

Attempts to understand how to change these underlying beliefs have led to considerable research utilizing information-processing models of the persuasion process. According to the information-processing approach to persuasion it is necessary to determine how an individual processes a communicated message, how initial knowledge relevant to the message is represented and it influences the information processed from the message, and how the individual is transformed or changed in response to the message, from an initial to a final knowledge state. Information-processing researchers pay particular attention to the relationship between attitudes and cognitive processes, to the influence of prior attitudes on the selection and processing of the information in communicated messages, and to the relationship of the recollection of a message to attitudes and behavior toward the objects of interest. The emphasis is on how the message is processed rather than on the content of the message.

The cognitive response approach has been a major representative of an information-processing perspective in the field of advertising and persuasive communication. This model (Greenwald, 1968) suggests that the recipient of a message is assumed to be an active information processor who modifies and alters the content of the communication. Although there is no one unified theory, the many researchers using this approach generally assume that the impact of persuasive communications such as advertising or other media messages can be best understood by understanding the thoughts that occur to people when they are exposed to a message. These cognitive responses are the results of the cognitive processes that occur during persuasion and thus it is assumed that they can be used to measure this processing.

The cognitive response approach has been used to examine a number of issues in the field of persuasive communication. Not surprisingly, research has consistently found that evaluative measures of cognitive responses are strongly related to other measures of the individual's attitude. This approach has been used to examine such issues as the enduring effects of communication, the effects of distraction on persuasive impact, and the role of the various source characteristics and individual differences in recipients (Petty, Ostrom, & Brock, 1981).

Recently, theorists from many domains have begun to argue that under many circumstances, shortcuts in information processing in the form of cognitive schema and heuristics can be used in place of the detailed processing suggested by these elaborate information-processing models of persuasion. This has led to the development of "dual process" theories that distinguish between two routes to persuasion (see Chaikin, 1980, 1987; Petty, this volume). A key implication of these dual process models is that the persuasive impact of a mass communication message will depend on which process is used by the audience to evaluate the message (the central or the peripheral processing route in Petty's work, for instance). Thus, researchers must understand the factors that determine which process is used by the audience as well as those that determine the persuasive impact of a message within each process, in order to develop successful persuasive communication.

In addition to models of how people process media messages, a third contemporary approach to persuasion argues that the process is not so rational, that affective, arousal, and motivational factors may influence people's behavior either directly or indirectly. A study by Gorn (1982) stimulated much of the work on the direct effects of affect in persuasion. Gorn developed an advertisement that paired a pen with liked and disliked music and found that students presented with the pen and liked music showed a significantly more positive preference for the pen than those presented with the same pen and disliked music. Because the music presumably contained no product information, Gorn argued that attitude and behavior change was accomplished via some process other than a belief-based, highly cognitive form of persuasion. He suggested that the positive affect toward the music was directly transferred to the product by way of classical conditioning. Thus, persuasion could occur without influencing cognition directly.

Although there has been much debate in the advertising and consumer behavior literature about whether classical conditioning was demonstrated in these and other studies (Allen & Madden, 1985; McSweeney & Bierley, 1984), many recent models of consumer communication have included some form of direct transfer of affect (e.g., MacKenzie, Lutz, & Belch, 1986; Moore & Hutchinson, 1985). Attitude toward the advertisement (or any message) represents this affective process. These researchers argue that, under some circumstances, the persuasive impact of a message will depend not on how well underlying beliefs are changed by the communication, but on how positively the ad is evaluated by the recipients.

Another approach to the role of affect examines its influence on the cognitive processing of advertising messages. Here, affect is thought to have an indirect effect on persuasion. An example of such theorizing is the work of Srull and Wyer (1986). They examined the role of mood in consumers' collection of ads and in their judgments about products. Srull wanted to incorporate affect into an information-processing perspective of persuasion. They argued that affect influences the judgment of an object by way of its impact on encoding and retrieval processes, and based these arguments on evidence that the effect of mood manipulations depends on processing manipulations that encourage some participants to make a judgment at the time of encoding and others at the time of retrieval. Presumably, when forming a judgment at the time of encoding, the mood at that time will influence the judgment, whereas if one forms a judgment later, upon retrieval, the mood at that time is the relevant one.

A second type of indirect effect of affect involves models in which affective and arousal processes influence which messages are attended to and processed. Primarily developed with respect to how individuals select what to attend to in general rather than just persuasive messages, this work is nonetheless useful in understanding persuasive communication. It represents a way to get at the neglected topic of selective exposure to the message. In developing a theory of entertainment, Zillmann, Weaver, Mundorf, and Aust (1986) argued that individuals consume media, in particular entertainment media, in order to manage their moods. This implies both that messages can influence moods and that individuals will choose to expose themselves to messages depending on their mood states. When the match is optimal, presumably persuasion may occur. The work of Donohew et al. (this volume) is predicated on a similar notion. They argue that individuals have an optimal level of arousal at which they feel most comfortable, and that they selectively expose themselves to communication that facilitates achieving this level. Individual differences in "sensation seeking" describe these differences in arousal. In these various models of the role of affect or arousal in persuasion, the goal is to develop better specification of the relationship between knowledge, affect, and behavior and to describe how persuasive communication can bring about changes in these domains.

This admittedly brief description of many research efforts in persuasive communication is illustrative of the variety and breadth of research in this area. The hallmark of these studies is the development of well-specified theoretical models of persuasion that are amenable to laboratory and field testing. The past 20 years or so of persuasion research has seen considerable elaboration of theories that attempt to predict audience behavior change as an outcome of the persuasion process.

SUMMARY

Our brief review of the historical development of research on mass media and public communication campaigns has glossed over many important lines of research not relevant to specific work in the development of persuasive communication campaigns (e.g., the considerable research on children and media has been ignored). The literature reviewed here would seem to be most important for current and future work on media-based interventions in specific areas of health behavior such as attempts at reducing drug abuse or AIDS-related high risk behaviors. With this goal in mind, three implications from the historical review offered here would seem to be most relevant.

First, the literature review suggests that examination of media's role in persuasion in any particular domain of social behavior (such as media's influence in changing social attitudes and behaviors related to drug abuse or AIDS) needs to look at media messages broadly for how mass media portray cultural and social meanings. Directed communication campaigns, such as those employing public service announcements against, for instance, drug abuse, are embedded within larger media portrayals and information about this social issue. There are subtle drug use messages often embedded within television programs and movies; there are news items about drug overdoses among movie stars and athletes; and there are news stories about public policy attempts to stop drug imports. All of these media messages may influence audience perceptions of the drug issue in addition to the focused PSA drug abuse media campaign. This implies that there should be some ongoing studies of media as social and cultural indicators of the information environment regarding specific health topics. Whether we are talking about social definitions of drugs or AIDS, the mass media, even outside directed public communication campaigns, are providing audiences with important social knowledge about these issues.

Second, for a specific, focused media campaign to be successful, media messages must be targeted to specific segments of the audience. In developing these campaigns, well-specified theoretical models of persuasion (and there are competing ones to choose from) need to be used to develop persuasive messages. The last 20 years or so of research on persuasion and behavior change suggest that well-formulated persuasive campaigns that are rooted in strong theoretical formulations of how to accomplish attitude and behavior change offer the greatest likelihood for success. Most of these models take into account how people process media messages.

Third, a cautionary note on expectations for media success in any sort of public communication campaign endeavor is necessary. The history of media research suggests that media power and influence is often balanced off by obstinate audiences who resist, reformulate, and selectively retain media messages. Media campaign designers need to hold realistic expectations about the goals of a media campaign. For instance, expecting a media campaign to increase awareness and knowledge about health risks is a very realistic goal. However, expecting a media campaign to bring about direct and massive behavior change is probably unrealistic.

In order to avoid the mistakes and failures in media programs intended to change people's behavior of 40 or 50 years ago, media-based campaigns should be integrated in larger community-based or institution-based interventions intended to bring about behavior change. Considering the formidable health policy issues confronting us, such as AIDS and drug abuse, considerable effort in the future is likely to be devoted to media-based public communication campaigns. It is important that such interventions have realistic expectations of media's influence. The history of media research is rich with lessons to be learned and heeded in the future.

REFERENCES

Ajzen, I., & Fishbein, M. (1980). *Understanding attitudes and predicting social behavior*. Englewood Cliffs, NJ: Prentice-Hall.

Allen, C. T., & Madden, T. J. (1985). A closer look at classical conditioning. *Journal of consumer Research, 12*, 301–315.

Bandura, A. (1986). *Social foundations of thought and action*. Englewood Cliffs, NJ: Prentice-Hall.

Bramson, L. (1961). *The political context of sociology*. Princeton, NJ: Princeton University Press.

Chaiken, S. (1980). Heuristic vs. systematic information processing and the use of source versus message cures in persuasion. *Journal of Personality and Social Psychology, 39*, 752–766.

Chaiken, S. (1987). The heuristic model of persuasion. In M. P. Zanna, J. M. Olson, & C. P. Herman (Eds.). *Social influence: The Ontario Symposium* (pp. 75–106). Hillsdale, NJ: Lawrence Erlbaum Associates.

De Fleur, M. L., & Ball-Rokeach, S. B. (1982). *Theories of mass communication* (4th ed.). New York: Longman.

De Tocqueville, A. (1900). *Democracy in America* (Vol. 2, H. Reeve, Trans.) New York: The Colonial Press. (Original work published 1835)

Fishbein, M., & Ajzen, I. (1975). *Belief, attitude, intention and behavior: an introduction to theory and research.* Reading, MA: Addison-Wesley.

Fishbein, M., & Middlestadt, S. E. (1987). Using the theory of reasoned action to develop educational interventions: Applications to illicit drug use. *Health Education Research: Theory and Practice, 2,* 361–371.

Fishbein, M., & Middlestadt, S. E. (1989). Using the theory of reasoned action as a framework for understanding and changing AIDS related behaviors. In V. M. Mays, G. Albee, J. M. Jones, & S. Schneider (eds.), *Primary prevention of AIDS: Psychological approaches* (pp. 93–110). Newbury Park, CA: Sage.

Gerbner, G., Gross, L. M., & Signorielli, N. (1986). Living with television: The dynamics of the cultivation process. In J. Bryant & D. Zillmann (Eds.) *Perspectives on media effects* (pp. 17–40). Hillsdale, NJ: Lawrence Erlbaum Associates.

Gorn, G. J. (1982). The effects of music in advertising on choice behavior: A Classical conditioning approach. *Journal of Marketing, 46,* 94–101.

Greenwald, A. G. (1968). Cognitive learning, cognitive response to persuasion and attitude change. In A. G. Greenwald, T. C. Brock, & T. M. Ostrom (Eds.), *Psychological foundations of attitudes* (pp. 147–170). New York: Academic Press.

Hovland, C., Lumsdaine, A., & Sheffield, S. (1950). Experiments in mass communication. In S. Stouffer, L. Gutman, E. Suchman, P. F. Lazarsfeld, & S. Star (Eds.). *Studies in social psychology in World War II* (Vol. 3). Princeton, NJ: Princeton University Press.

Hyman, H., & Sheatsley, P. (1947). Some reasons why information campaigns fail. *Public Opinion Quarterly, 11,* 412–423.

Katz, D. (1960). The functional approach to the study of attitudes. *Public Opinion Quarterly, 24,* 163–204. Katz, E., & Lazarsfeld, P. F. (1955). *Personal influence: The part played by people in the flow of communication.* Glencoe, IL: The Free Press.

Kelman, H. C. (1961). Processes of opinion change. *Public Opinion Quarterly, 25,* 57–78.

Klapper, J. T. (1960). *The effects of mass communication.* Glencoe, IL: The Free Press.

Lasswell, H. (1927). *Propaganda techniques in the world war.* London: K. Paul, Trench, Trubner.

Lazarsfeld, P. F., Berelson, B. R., & Gudet, H. (1948). *The people's choice.* New York: Columbia University Press.

Lippmann, W. (1922). *Public opinion.* New York: Harcourt Brace.

MacKenzie, S. B., Lutz, R. J., & Belch, G. E. (1986). The role of attitude toward the ad as a mediator of advertising effectiveness: A test of competing explanations. *Journal of Marketing Research, 23,* 130–143.

McCombs, M. E., & Shaw, D. (1972). The agenda setting function of mass media. *Public Opinion Quarterly, 36*(2), 176–187.

McGuire, W. (1985). Attitude and attitude change. In G. Lindzey & E. Aronson (Eds.), *Handbook of social psychology* (2nd ed., Vol. 2, pp. 233–346). Reading, MA: Addison-Wesley.

McSweeney, K., & Bierley, C. (1984). Recent developments in classical conditioning. *Journal of Consumer Research, 11,* 619–631.

Middlestadt, S. E. (1990). Developing a research-based campaign to increase financial contributions to a university library: An application of the theory of reasoned action. In R. W. Belk (Ed.), *Nonprofit marketing* (pp. 51–81). Greenwich, CT: JAI Press.

Moore, D. L., & Hutchinson, J. W. (1985). The influence of affective reactions to advertising: Direct and indirect mechanisms of attitude change. In L. F. Alwitt & A. A. Mitchell (Eds.), *Psychological processes and advertising effects.* Hillsdale, NJ: Lawrence Erlbaum Associates.

Paisley, W. J. (1981). Public communications campaigns: The American experience. In R. E. Rice & W. J. Paisley (Eds.) *Public communication campaigns (pp. 15-40). Beverly Hills: Sage.*

Peterson, R. E., & Thurston, E. L. (1933). *Motion pictures and the social attitudes of children.* New York: Macmillan.

Petty, T., Ostrom, T., & Brock, T. (1981). *Cognitive responses in persuasion.* Hillsdale, NJ: Lawrence Erlbaum Associates.

Rogers, E. M., & Storey, J. D. (1987). Communication campaigns. In C. R. Berger & S. H. Chafee (Eds.). *Handbook of communication science.* Newbury Park, CA: Sage.

Shiffrin, R. M., & Schneider, W. (1977) Controlled and automatic information processing: II. Perceptual learning, automatic attending, and a general theory. *Psychological Review, 84,* 127-190.

Siebert, F. S., Peterson, T., & Schramm, W. (1956). *Four theories of the press.* Urbana: University of Illinois.

Snyder, M., & DeBono, K. G. (1987). A functional approach to attitudes and persuasion. In M. P. Zanna, J. M. Olson & C. P. Herman (Eds.), *Social influence: The Ontario Symposium* (pp. 107-125). Hillsdale, NJ: Lawrence Erlbaum Associates.

Srull, T. K., & Wyer, S. Jr. (1986). The role of chronic and temporary goals in social information processing. In R. M. Sorrentino & E. T. Higgins (Eds.), *Handbook of motivation and cognition* (pp. 503-549). New York: Guilford.

Star, S., & Hughes, H. (1950). A report on an educational campaign: The Cincinnati plan for the United Nations. *American Journal of Sociology, 55,* 389-400.

Thrasher, I. M. (1933). *The gang: A study of 1,313 gangs in Chicago* (abridged). Chicago: University of Chicago Press.

Wartella, E., & Reeves, B. (1985). Historical trends in research on children and the media: 1900-1960. *Journal of Communication, 35(2),* 118-133.

Wicker, A. W. (1969). Attitudes vs. actions: The relationship of verbal and overt behavioral responses to attitude objects. *Journal of Social Issues, 25,* 41-78.

Zajonc, R. B., & Markus, H. (1982). Affective and cognitive factors in preferences. *Journal of Consumer Research, 9,* 123-131.

Zillmann, D., Weaver, J. B., Mundort, N., & Aust, C. I. (1986). Effects of an opposite-gender companions effect to horror on distress delight and attraction. *Journal of Personality and Social Psychology, 51,* 586-594.

Attitudes and Drug Abuse Prevention: Implications of the Elaboration Likelihood Model of Persuasion

Richard E. Petty
Sara M. Baker
Faith Gleicher
The Ohio State University

The first and most important truth about the war on drugs is that it is waged by and against individual people. The war will be won only if and when the people decide they will no longer accept drug abuse. The "war," then, is really about changing attitudes.
—Rinehart (Mayor, Columbus, Ohio; 1989, p. 1)

Popular opinion polls suggest that the nation's drug problem and the accompanying crime it engenders is the number one issue of concern to Americans today. In the simplest sense, two categories of solutions have been offered to solve the drug problem. One focuses on eliminating the *supply* of illicit drugs through various interdiction and law enforcement programs, whereas the other focuses on curtailing the *demand* for potentially harmful drugs. Importantly, the success of each approach depends in part on the *attitudes* of Americans toward specific drugs and specific drug programs. For example, efforts to curtail the supply of drugs will likely be more successful to the extent that public attitudes favor additional expenditures for law enforcement, and people think that this approach will be effective. Similarly, the demand for drugs is tied in part to peoples' attitudes about the desirability and/or danger of these substances as well as attitudes toward the effectiveness of drug treatment programs. The nature of public attitudes toward the drug problem and the various solutions to it can have important effects on funding for drug prevention programs.

For example, in November 1989, the voters in Kansas City, Missouri approved a $.025 sales tax for drug enforcement and rehabilitation efforts. The tax will raise over $100 million during its 7-year life span.

Given the relevance of attitudes to drug prevention efforts, it is not surprising that proponents of various solutions to the drug problem have attempted to influence the attitudes of individuals and the public at large. For example, in an attempt to garner public support for future efforts to reduce the supply of drugs, local law enforcement officials proudly display captured drugs before the media. The most frequent and systematic attempts to employ attitude change techniques to counter the drug problem, however, have been on the demand side. For example, the U.S. government has sponsored multimedia anti-drug campaigns (e.g., NIDA's "Cocaine, the Big Lie"; see Forman & Lachter, 1989), and local school and police organizations conduct influence programs in small group settings (e.g., project DARE; see DeJong, 1987). This chapter presents a brief overview of psychological approaches to social influence and outlines a general framework for understanding the processes responsible for attitude change. Because most of the empirical studies with respect to persuasion approaches to the drug problem have focused on modifying the demand for drugs rather than their availability (see Shoemaker, 1989; and other chapters in this volume), our focus is here as well.

BEHAVIORAL INFLUENCE
VIA PERSUASIVE COMMUNICATION

Many changes have taken place in Americans' knowledge, attitudes, and behaviors with respect to illicit drugs since the 1970s with some changes occurring in a desirable direction, and others in a less favorable direction. An understanding of the causal links among knowledge, attitudes, and behaviors, and some appreciation of the basic mechanisms by which change is achieved, should enhance the likelihood of selecting appropriate strategies to encourage optimal changes. Furthermore, a minimal understanding of basic research findings with respect to human influence may help guard against either overly optimistic or pessimistic assessments of the prospects for changing attitudes and behaviors with respect to illicit drugs. In the next section we outline some of the major theoretical perspectives on changing attitudes and behaviors with persuasive communications.

Overview of Approaches to Persuasion

Social psychologists concerned with the study of human influence have focused on the concept of "attitudes," or peoples' general predispositions to evaluate other people, objects, and issues favorably or unfavorably.

Among the attitudes relevant to the nation's demand for drugs are attitudes toward: (a) oneself (e.g., low self-esteem may contribute to drug use), (b) authority figures (e.g., parents, government officials, and teachers who eschew drug use), (c) peers (e.g., friends who may advocate drug use), (d) the drugs themselves (e.g., are they seen as harmful or exciting?), and (e) drug treatment programs (e.g., are they seen as worthwhile or wasteful?). The attitude construct has achieved its preeminent position in research on social influence because of the assumption that a person's attitude was an important mediating variable between the acquisition of new knowledge on the one hand, and behavioral change on the other. For example, initial drug abuse prevention efforts were based on the view that providing the "facts" about drugs would lead to dislike of drugs and behavioral avoidance (Moskowitz, Malvin, Schaeffer, & Schaps, 1984; Wallack & Corbett, 1987).

Since the 1940s, numerous theories of attitude change and models of knowledge–attitude–behavior relationships have developed (see reviews by Chaiken & Stangor, 1987; Cooper & Croyle, 1984; Petty, Unnava, & Strathman, 1991). One of the earliest assumptions of theories of attitude change was that effective influence required a sequence of steps (e.g., McGuire, 1985; Strong, 1925). For example, typical influence models contend that a person first needs to be *exposed* to some new information. The goal of any strategy of influence, of course, is to reach as many people in the target audience as possible. This will likely involve multiple channels of communication—face-to-face, mass media, and community programs in schools, work sites, churches, and so forth. Second, people must *attend* to the information presented. Because there are literally hundreds of messages competing for attention each day, it is not surprising that few are successful in arousing it (cf. Bogart, 1967). A third issue concerns *reception*, or what from the information presented enters long-term memory. Just because a person is consciously aware of an informational presentation, there is no guarantee that any aspect of what is seen and heard will create more than a fleeting impression. Interestingly, recent research has suggested that nonusers of drugs may be more attentive to and can recall more information from anti-drug mass media campaigns than current users of drugs (Bozinoff, Roth, & May, 1989).

Nevertheless, just because some new information is learned as a result of an educational campaign, this does not assure that this knowledge will lead to attitude or behavior change. Current research strongly indicates that attitude change depends on the manner in which a persuasive message is idiosyncratically elaborated, evaluated, and *interpreted* so that it makes some psychological sense to the person. Information that is received may trigger thoughts, images, and ideas, that are favorable, unfavorable, or neutral, or the information may not produce any cognitive or affective responses. The more favorable the cognitive or affective response to the information, the more likely that attitudes will change in a positive direction, but the more negative the cognitive or affective responses elicited, the more likely that attitudes will not change or will change in a direction opposite to that intended (cf. Greenwald, 1968; Petty, Ostrom, & Brock, 1981). Once the information received has elicited various thoughts and/or feelings, these must be *integrated* into an overall impression or evaluation which is then stored in memory (cf. Anderson, 1981). Only then is this overall evaluation or attitude capable of guiding subsequent *action*, the ultimate stage in the influence sequence (see Petty & Cacioppo, 1984).

Variants of this general information-processing model were often interpreted in theory and in practice as suggesting that a change early in the sequence would inevitably lead to a change later in the sequence. One problem with this reasoning is that the likelihood that a message will evoke each of the steps in the sequence may be viewed as a conditional probability. Thus, even if the likelihood of achieving each step in a campaign was 60%, the probability of achieving all six steps (exposure, attention, reception, interpretation, integration, and action), would be $.6^6$, or only 5% (see McGuire, 1989).

A second factor, however, is that some of the steps in the sequence may be independent of each other. For example, although a person's ability to learn and recall new information (e.g., facts about specific drugs) was often thought to be an important causal determinant of and prerequisite to attitude and behavior change, little empirical evidence has accumulated to support this view (McGuire, 1985; Petty & Cacioppo, 1981). Rather, the existing evidence shows that message learning can occur in the absence of attitude change, and that people's attitudes may change in the absence of learning the specific information in the communication.

For example, Figure 5.1 diagrams the reactions of six different people to an anti-drug public service announcement presented on television. The campaign sponsors want young people to learn the message that using marijuana is dangerous because it can lead to use of hard drugs. The spot features a popular celebrity who tells about two of his friends who were seriously harmed by drugs. As depicted in the figure, Person A gets nothing from the message (and will not be considered further). Persons B, C, D, & E all understand the gist of the message and would pass a typical recall or comprehension test on the specifics of the communication. Importantly, current models of persuasion suggest that it is unlikely that one can judge the effectiveness of the campaign solely by examining the *knowledge* acquired from the communication. Rather, an individual's idiosyncratic elaborations and interpretations of the message are critical. Person B actively counterargues the message, thinking that the people described in the message are atypical. Person C thinks that the people in the message may be typical, but that he is unique and invulnerable to the threat.

PERSON:

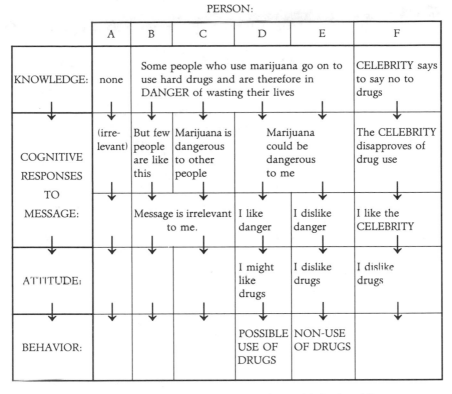

	A	B	C	D	E	F
KNOWLEDGE:	none	Some people who use marijuana go on to use hard drugs and are therefore in DANGER of wasting their lives				CELEBRITY says to say no to drugs
COGNITIVE RESPONSES TO MESSAGE:	(irre-levant)	But few people are like this	Marijuana is dangerous to other people	Marijuana could be dangerous to me		The CELEBRITY disapproves of drug use
		Message is irrelevant to me.		I like danger	I dislike danger	I like the CELEBRITY
ATTITUDE:				I might like drugs	I dislike drugs	I dislike drugs
BEHAVIOR:				POSSIBLE USE OF DRUGS	NON-USE OF DRUGS	

FIG. 5.1 Possible knowledge, beliefs, attitudes, and behavior of Persons A-F in response to a TV commercial featuring a celebrity who talks about two friends who used marijuana and went on to hard drugs and wasted their lives. Celebrity advocates "just say no."

Thus, both B and C dismiss the message as irrelevant to them, although for different reasons. Persons D and E have the initial response desired by the campaign sponsors. Both come to think that drug use could be dangerous to them. However, individual D likes danger and excitement (e.g., is a high sensation seeker; Zuckerman, 1983; see Donohew et al., this volume), and thinks that the drug might therefore be desirable. Person E, who shows the expected response of disliking danger, comes to dislike the drug (see Fishbein & Middlestadt, 1987, for further discussion of the role of idiosyncratic beliefs in influencing attitudes about drugs). The important point is that only one of the four people who processed the message and would pass a typical knowledge test showed attitude change in the desired direction. Finally, there is Person F who misses the point about the potential danger of drugs (and thus would fail the comprehension test), but does learn something—that the featured celebrity does not like drugs. Because Person F likes the celebrity, she also comes to dislike the drug men-

tioned in the ad. This result is expected by *balance theory* that states that
people feel more comfortable when they agree with people they like, and
disagree with people they dislike (Heider, 1958). Finally, note that Persons E and F have formed the same attitude, but as we explain later in
the chapter, some attitudes have greater implications for behavior than
others. That is, E's anti-drug attitude produces drug avoidance, but F's
does not. In short, Fig. 5.1 demonstrates that: (a) attitude change can occur in the absence of the presumably critical knowledge (Person F), (b)
the critical knowledge can be acquired without producing any attitude
change (Persons B and C), (c) the same knowledge can lead to opposite
attitudes (Persons D and E), and (d) attitudes that are ostensibly the same
can have different implications for behavior (Persons E and F).

This analysis may help to explain why previous research on drug education has often found that knowledge change was insufficient for attitude
and behavior change, or that attitude change was not followed by behavior
change. For example, Goodstadt, Sheppard, and Chan (1982) evaluated
an information-based program on alcohol. Students in the experimental
program were exposed to 10 lessons that covered myths about alcohol,
information about advertising, reasons for drinking, and the effects of alcohol on the family, driving, sports, fitness, and sexuality. When compared
with students in a control program who received no drug education, students in the experimental program showed greater knowledge about alcohol but failed to show any significant change in attitudes. After an extensive review of drug and alcohol education programs, Kinder, Pape, and
Walfish (1980) concluded that although programs were typically successful in increasing participants' knowledge about drugs, there was very little evidence that they were successful in changing attitudes and behavior
(see also Rundall & Bruvold, 1988).

Two Routes to Persuasion

Current psychological theories of influence focus on how and why various
features of a persuasion situation (i.e., aspects of the source, message, channel, context, and recipient) affect each of the steps in the communication
sequence (e.g., how does the credibility of the source affect attention to
the message?). The most work by far, however, focuses on how variables
affect the *interpretation* stage of information processing. This stage is sometimes viewed as the most critical because it is during this stage that the
message achieves some meaning, is evaluated favorably or unfavorably,
and is accepted or rejected.

According to the Elaboration Likelihood Model (ELM) of Persuasion,
the processes that occur during the interpretation stage can be thought

of as emphasizing one of two relatively distinct ''routes to persuasion'' (see Petty & Cacioppo, 1981, 1986). The first, or *central route*, involves effortful cognitive activity whereby the person draws on prior experience and knowledge to carefully scrutinize and evaluate the issue-relevant arguments presented in the communication (whether it appears in the mass media, comes from a friend, parent, or teacher). In order for this to occur, the person must possess sufficient motivation, ability, and opportunity to process the perceived merits of the information provided. The end result of this processing is an attitude that is well articulated and integrated into the person's belief structure. Attitudes changed by this route have been found to be relatively persistent, predictive of behavior, and resistant to change until they are challenged by cogent contrary information (see Petty & Cacioppo, 1986).

In addition, the more practice a person has in thinking about and defending a newly acquired anti-drug attitude, the more likely the person is to resist the challenges the new attitude surely will face. In his *inoculation theory*, McGuire (1964) used a biological analogy to suggest that just as people can be made more resistant to a disease by giving them a mild form of the germ, people can be made more resistant to attacks on their attitudes by inoculating their new opinions. The inoculation treatment consists of exposing people to a few pieces of attacking information and showing them how to refute it. Research clearly indicates that people whose attitudes are bolstered with inoculation treatments become less vulnerable to subsequent attacks on their attitudes than people whose attitudes are bolstered with supportive information alone (e.g., McGuire, 1964).

In stark contrast to the central route approach, some theories of persuasion do not place much credence on the arguments in a message or issue-relevant thinking. Instead, they postulate a *peripheral route* whereby simple cues in the persuasion context either elicit an affective state (e.g., happiness) that becomes associated with the advocated position (as in classical conditioning; Staats & Staats, 1958), or trigger a relatively simple inference or heuristic that a person can use to judge the validity of the message (e.g., Chaiken, 1987). Public service announcements (PSAs) attempt to employ this strategy when they rely on a well-liked celebrity or sports figure to induce attitude change rather than focusing on the merits of the arguments that are presented. We do not mean to suggest that peripheral approaches are necessarily ineffective. In fact they can be quite powerful in the short term. The problem is that over time, peoples' feelings about celebrities and sports figures change, the positive sources may become dissociated from the message, and normative sources of influence become less important as one grows older. Laboratory research has shown that attitude changes based on peripheral cues tend to be less persistent and resistant to subsequent pressures. Thus, people who hold anti-drug attitudes based solely on celebrity cues are less likely to resist arguments and pressure to use drugs than are people who have developed negative attitudes toward particular drugs after careful reflection on the personal dangers inherent in their use (see Persons E and F in Fig. 5.1).

In summary, attitudes changed via the central route tend to be based on active thought processes resulting in a well-integrated cognitive structure, but attitudes changed via the peripheral route are based more on passive acceptance (or rejection) of simple cues and have a less well-articulated structure. Figure 5.2 outlines two possible cognitive structures for the same information about drugs. The person represented in the top panel of the figure has an organized schema about drugs. When a drug is mentioned, the person easily is able to retrieve a negative attitude and the beliefs upon which this attitude is based. For the person represented in the bottom panel, however, thoughts and feelings about drugs are scattered throughout memory and are not likely to be highly accessible when a drug is mentioned. Rather, the information is organized around salient celebrity cues. This depiction makes it clear that although both the central and peripheral routes may produce similar amounts of attitude change initially, the structure of the attitudes may differ dramatically.

Our discussion of the central and peripheral routes to persuasion indicates that active participation in the persuasion process is critical to producing stable attitude changes that are influential in behavior and are resistant over time. Importantly, the trend in the 1980s in drug prevention programs was to incorporate a greater degree of active participation and "inoculation" by having participants discuss personal values with respect to drugs, actively question the information provided, and role play scenarios in which drugs are refused (Botvin, Baker, Renick, Filazzola, & Botvin, 1984; DeJong, 1987; Moskowitz et al., 1984). For example, Duryea (1983) exposed students to exercises in which they were confronted with several pro-drinking arguments and were shown how to refute them. When compared with a control group, the inoculation subjects were more likely to successfully refute pressure to participate in drinking and risky behavior when confronted with a hypothetical persuasion scenario in a classroom setting (see also, DuPont & Jason, 1984).

One program that is worthy of special note due to its commitment to creating an environment that fosters participants' active participation is the Alcohol and Substance Abuse Prevention Program developed at the University of New Mexico (Wallerstein & Bernstein, 1988). In this program, participants are provided with direct experience with the consequences of drugs by having them visit hospitals, jails, emergency rooms, and the like. The participants are responsible for seeking out information by developing their own questions, identifying problems that they see at various levels of societal and personal importance, relating the informa-

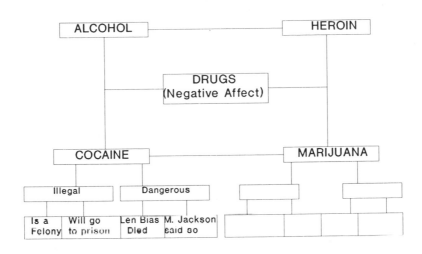

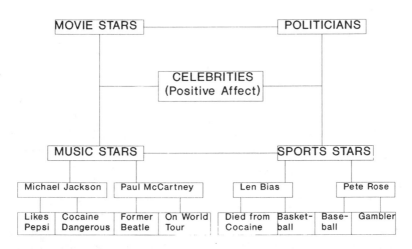

FIG. 5.2 Alternative cognitive schemas for information about drugs. Top panel presents a well-integrated drug schema. Bottom panel presents a poorly integrated one.

tion and experiences to their own lives, and thinking about what can be
done in order to deal with these problems in their own lives and in the
community.

The Role of Specific Variables
in the Elaboration Likelihood Model

Our discussion of the two routes to persuasion so far highlights two ways
in which variables can have an impact on persuasion. Variables may serve
as persuasive *arguments*, providing information as to the central merits of
an object or issue, or they may serve as simple *cues*, allowing favorable
or unfavorable attitude formation in the absence of a diligent consideration of the true merits of the object or issue. Two other ways in which a
variable can have an impact on persuasion are by affecting (a) the *extent
of argument elaboration* (i.e., the intensity with which the person thinks
about and evaluates the central merits of the issue-relevant information
presented), and (b) the direction of any *bias in elaboration* (i.e., are the
thoughts biased in a positive or negative direction; Petty & Cacioppo, 1990).
     The ELM holds that as the likelihood of elaboration is increased (whether
thinking about the arguments proceeds in a relatively objective or a more
biased fashion), the perceived *quality* of the issue-relevant arguments
presented becomes a more important determinant of persuasion. As the
likelihood of elaboration is decreased, however, peripheral cues become
more important. That is, when the elaboration likelihood is high, the central route to persuasion dominates, but when the elaboration likelihood
is low, the peripheral route takes precedence. The accumulated research
on persuasion has pointed to many variables that can be employed to either
increase or decrease the amount of thinking about a persuasive message.
Some variables, such as the perceived personal relevance of the communication (Petty & Cacioppo, 1979b) and an individual's level of "need for
cognition" (Cacioppo & Petty, 1982) determine one's overall *motivation*
to process issue-relevant arguments. Other variables, such as the extent
of message repetition (Cacioppo & Petty, 1989) or the nature of any distractions present (Petty, Wells, & Brock, 1976) determine a person's overall *ability* to process issue-relevant arguments. It is also important to note
that some variables affect information processing activity in a relatively
objective manner, whereas others may introduce a systematic bias to the
information-processing activity. For example, telling a highly involved audience that a message is specifically attempting to persuade them moti-
vates active resistance and counterarguing (Petty & Cacioppo, 1979a).
     One of the most important features of the ELM is that it holds that
any one variable can serve in each of the roles outlined here, although in

different situations. That is, a variable can serve as a persuasive argument in some contexts, act as a peripheral cue in others, and affect the intensity of thinking or the direction of processing bias in still other domains. For example, in separate studies, the attractiveness of a message source has (a) served as a simple peripheral cue when it was irrelevant to evaluating the merits of an attitude object and subjects were not motivated to process the issue-relevant arguments, (b) served as a message argument when it was relevant to evaluating the merits of the attitude object and the elaboration likelihood was high, and (c) affected the extent of thinking about the message arguments presented when the elaboration likelihood was moderate (see Petty & Cacioppo, 1986, for a review).

If any one variable can influence persuasion by several means, it becomes critical to identify the general conditions under which the variable acts in each of the different roles. The ELM holds that when the elaboration likelihood is high (such as when perceived personal relevance and knowledge are high, the message is easy to understand, no distractions are present, etc.), people typically know that they want and are able to evaluate the merits of the arguments presented and they do so. Variables such as source attractiveness have little direct impact on evaluations by serving as simple cues in these situations. Instead, they may serve as arguments if relevant to the merits of the issue, or may bias the nature of the ongoing cognitive activity. On the other hand, when the elaboration likelihood is low (e.g., low personal relevance or knowledge, complex message, many distractions, etc.), people know that they do not want and/or are not able to evaluate the merits of the arguments presented (or they do not even consider exerting effort to process the message). If any evaluation is formed under these conditions, it is likely to be the result of relatively simple associations or inferences. Finally, when the elaboration likelihood is moderate (e.g., uncertain personal relevance, moderate knowledge, moderate complexity, etc.), people may be uncertain as to whether or not the message warrants or needs scrutiny and whether or not they are capable of providing this analysis. In these situations they may examine the persuasion context for indications (e.g., is the source credible?) of whether or not they are interested in or should process the message.

An example might help to clarify the multiple roles that a variable can have in different situations. Consider the effect of a person's mood on persuasion. If the elaboration likelihood is very low, such as when a message is very low in perceived personal relevance, positive mood would be capable of serving as a simple cue, rendering people more positive toward whatever view is presented. On the other hand, if the elaboration likelihood is very high and people are clearly motivated and able to think about the arguments presented, positive mood should increase the likelihood that positive thoughts are accessed during processing. Finally, if the message is of uncertain relevance and people must decide whether or not to devote effort to thinking about the message, they may decide not to think about it if in a positive mood because of concern that thinking about the message will destroy their current good feeling (e.g., why think about a depressing drug message if you are in a good mood?; see Petty, Gleicher, & Baker, 1991, for further discussion).

Because any one variable can produce persuasion in multiple ways, it is important to understand *why* the variable has worked. For example, our discussion of the two routes to persuasion suggests that if a good mood has produced persuasion by serving as a simple cue under low elaboration conditions, the attitude induced will be less persistent, resistant, and predictive of behavior than if a good mood produced the same amount of persuasion, but worked by increasing positive thoughts to the message arguments under high elaboration conditions. In empirical research on drug abuse prevention, many source, message, recipient, and contextual variables have been examined, but little attention has been paid to the processes by which these variables work (cf. McCaul & Glasgow, 1985). For example, several studies have compared the effectiveness of peer-led prevention programs with those led by teachers (e.g., Botvin et al., 1984; Smart, Bennett, & Fejer, 1976). Unfortunately, in some of these studies the source was confounded with the nature of the message presented, and overall there has been little consistency in results indicating whether one type of source was more effective than another. The ELM holds that source, message, recipient, and contextual factors can work by different processes in different situations, and that the process is critical. Thus, even if previous research had shown that peers were more effective than teachers overall, it would be important to know if this was because a peer source was serving as a simple positive cue, or if peers enhanced attention to and processing of the substantive arguments presented.

Attitude–Behavior Links

Once a person's attitude has changed (e.g., has moved from pro- to anti-drug), it is important that the new attitude rather than old habits guide behavior. Considerable research has addressed the links between attitudes and behavior and a number of situational and dispositional factors have been shown to enhance the consistency between them. For example, attitudes have been found to have a greater impact on behavior when: (a) the attitudes in question are consistent with underlying beliefs, (b) the attitudes are based on high rather than low amounts of issue-relevant information and/or personal experience, (c) the attitudes were formed as a result of considerable issue-relevant thinking, and (d) cues in the situation indicate that the person's attitude is relevant to the behavior (see Ajzen, 1988, for a comprehensive review).

Two general models of the process by which attitudes guide behavior have achieved widespread acceptance. One type is exemplified by Ajzen and Fishbein's (1980) "theory of reasoned action," which assumes that "people consider the implications of their actions before they decide to engage or not engage in a given behavior" (p. 5). In this model, people are hypothesized to form intentions to perform or not to perform behaviors, and these intentions are based on the person's attitude toward the behavior as well as perceptions of the opinions of significant others (norms). The model focuses on the relatively thoughtful processing involved in considering the personal costs and benefits of engaging in a behavior. In particular, the model focuses on the perceived likelihood that certain benefits will be obtained or costs avoided, and the desirability (aversiveness) of those benefits (costs). The specific beliefs that are relevant to health-related actions have been outlined in the Health Belief Model (Rosenstock, 1974) and include beliefs about: (a) one's personal susceptibility to some negative condition (e.g., Will I become addicted if I take drugs? Will I experience withdrawal if I stop?), (b) the perceived severity of the condition, (c) the subjective benefits of engaging in a recommended action, and (d) the costs (financial, psychological, etc.) of the action. That is, people are assumed to engage in health-related actions (e.g., stopping smoking, avoiding drugs) to the extent that they believe that some health concern is serious, relevant to them, and the likely effectiveness and other benefits of the recommended action outweigh its costs. Although a number of studies have raised challenges to some of the specifics of the reasoned action and health-belief models, these frameworks have proven remarkably successful in accounting for a wide variety of behavior (see Janz & Becker, 1984; Sheppard, Hartwick, & Warshaw, 1988). As noted earlier, of course, this reasoned action approach is only applicable when people are sufficiently motivated and able to engage in a cognitively demanding cost–benefit analysis of some action.

In contrast to these theories of *reasoned* action, Fazio (1990) has proposed that much behavior is rather spontaneous and that attitudes can guide behavior by a relatively automatic process. Specifically, Fazio argued that attitudes can guide behavior without any deliberate reflection or reasoning if (a) the attitude is accessed (comes to mind) spontaneously by the mere presence of the attitude object; and (b) the attitude colors perception of the object so that if the attitude is favorable (or unfavorable), the qualities of the object appear favorable (or unfavorable). For example, when a drug abuser is confronted with cocaine, positive feelings based on past experience may come to mind automatically and cause the person to take the drug. The various costs and benefits of use may not be considered at all, or may be weighed only long after the drug is taken.

Fazio (1990) noted that motivational and ability factors will be important in determining whether the reasoned action or the automatic activation process occurs. That is, for behavioral decisions that are high in perceived personal consequences, attitudes are likely to guide behavior by a deliberate reflection process, but when perceived consequences are low, spontaneous attitude activation should be more important. Similarly, as the time allowed for a decision is reduced, the importance of spontaneous attitude activation processes should be increased over more deliberative processes. A teenager at a party who is confronted with likable peers who advocate drug use in a noisy environment with limited time for decision making, is not likely to engage in much cogitation. Rather, simple salient positive cues are likely to guide choices unless anti-drug attitudes are well ingrained and highly accessible.

BEHAVIORAL INFLUENCE
VIA SOCIAL LEARNING

In some domains an accessible attitude is easily translated into behavior (e.g., I like Candidate X, I will vote for this candidate in the upcoming election). In other domains, however, translating new attitudes into new behaviors is rather complex even if the person has the desire to act on the attitude. In the area of drug abuse, attitude change, although an important first step, may be insufficient to produce the desired behavioral responses. People may also need to acquire new skills and self-perceptions that allow newly acquired attitudes and intentions to be translated into action. Furthermore, once an attitude has yielded new behavior, this new behavior may not persist in the absence of incentives. Bandura's (1977, 1986) social (cognitive) learning theory provides a framework to understand these processes.

Like the central route approaches to persuasion described earlier, the social learning perspective views voluntary behavior as determined in part by the personal consequences that a person anticipates for various courses of action (Rosenstock, Strecher, & Becker, 1988). These consequences (rewards and punishments) may be anticipated because of prior personal experience, the observed experiences of others, or they may be expected simply as a result of cognitive reasoning processes.

According to social learning theory, producing behavior change may require that a person learns new actions (skills) or new sequences of already acquired actions. For example, a person may have developed a negative attitude toward drugs, but does not have the verbal skills to say no when under pressure.[1] Learning of new skills may occur via direct experience or by observing the behavior patterns of others (modeling). The most effective models are those people who are most similar to the target of influence or are people with whom the target identifies or admires. An important aspect of Bandura's social (cognitive) learning framework is the idea that people do not always behave optimally, even though they know the ''correct'' behaviors and have positive attitudes toward them. That is, people are not always motivated to translate their acquired skills into action.

One particularly important cognitive determinant of whether people's skills are put into action concerns peoples' assessments of their own capabilities or their judgments of *self-efficacy* or competence (Bandura, 1982). Judgments of self-efficacy are important because considerable research indicates that the higher the level of perceived efficacy, the more likely people are to persist in a new behavior that has been learned. Of the various ways to influence self-efficacy, providing guided practice and specific skills training have proven to be particularly powerful techniques (cf. Myer & Henderson, 1974).

A drug education program that incorporates elements of social learning theory along with the principle of active participation described previously is Project DARE (Drug Abuse Resistance Education; see DeJong, 1987). This program, which began as a joint activity of the Los Angeles Police Department and the Los Angeles Unified School District, has police officers lead sixth-grade students through a 17-session prevention program designed to help them recognize and resist the peer pressure that often leads to drug experimentation. Some sessions focus on providing information about the hazards of drug use and others incorporate inoculation techniques. Importantly, participants spend time practicing various resistance techniques through role-playing scenarios and engage in exercises aimed at building self-efficacy, assertiveness, and mature decision-making processes.

IMPLICATIONS OF THEORETICAL PERSPECTIVES FOR CHANGING ATTITUDES ABOUT DRUGS

Although considerable work has shown that it is possible to change people's knowledge about drugs, we have seen that these knowledge differences do not invariably turn into attitude and behavior change. Our brief

---

[1]Much of the work conducted within the social learning framework has focused on people who already want to change their behavior (e.g., snake phobics; people who want to change their diet as a result of having high cholesterol), and thus the initial attitude change process in not emphasized, because it has presumably occurred already.

review of basic theory and research has emphasized that information will only be successful in changing attitudes and behavior if people are motivated and able to process the information presented, and this processing results in favorable cognitive and affective reactions. Furthermore, once attitudes have changed, implementation of change may require learning new behavioral skills and perceptions of self-efficacy. Thus, current work on attitude and behavior change may help to account for some unsuccessful translations of anti-drug knowledge and/or attitudes into anti-drug behaviors. First, the anti-drug knowledge acquired may have been seen as irrelevant by the recipients, or may have led to unfavorable rather than favorable reactions. Second, even if positive attitude changes were induced, the changes may have been based on simple peripheral cues rather than elaborative processing of the message. Third, even if attitude changes were produced by the central route, the people influenced may have lacked the necessary skills or self-confidence to translate their new attitudes into action.

Perhaps the most important issue raised in our review is that although some attitudes are based on a careful reasoning process in which externally provided information is related to oneself and integrated into a coherent knowledge structure, other attitudes are formed as a result of relatively simple cues in the persuasion environment. Although both types of processes can lead to attitudes similar in their valence (how favorable or unfavorable they are), there are important consequences of the manner of attitude change. Because the goal of persuasion-based programs on drugs is to produce long-lasting changes in attitudes with behavioral consequences, the central route to persuasion appears to be the preferred influence strategy. Unfortunately, this is not simple. The recipient of the new information must have the motivation, ability, and opportunity to process the new information. As noted previously, one of the most important determinants of motivation to think about a message is the perceived personal relevance of that message. When personal relevance is high, people are motivated to scrutinize the information presented and integrate it with their existing beliefs, but when perceived relevance is low, messages may be ignored or processed for peripheral cues. Many people in the population may feel that anti-drug messages are not relevant to them or have few consequences for them. An important goal of any drug education strategy will be to increase people's motivation to think about anti-drug messages by increasing the perceived personal relevance of these messages.

Even if people were motivated to attend to and think about anti-drug messages, it is critical that people respond to these messages with favorable cognitive and affective reactions. It is likely that different types of information will be responded to favorably by different segments of the population. Considerable research is needed on the level of complexity to present to different audiences, and the type of information that when presented will elicit favorable thoughts and implications.

Finally, even if the appropriate attitudes are changed, a new attitude cannot influence behavior if it does not come to mind prior to the opportunity for behavior, or if people lack the necessary skills or confidence to implement their new attitudes. For example, if a person has recently come to the conclusion that crack cocaine should be avoided and has formed an appropriate negative attitude, this does no good if the negative attitude is not accessible when confronted with the drug. The new negative attitude might be retrievable, but only if cues in the environment provoke reflection. People will need to be encouraged to think before they act so that their *new* attitudes rather than old habits or salient situational cues are accessed. As noted previously, people will also need to acquire the behavioral skills to implement their new attitudes.

Alternatively, a person may have formed a tentative negative attitude toward some drug, but if the person's exploratory drug experience is positive, two contrary attitudes are formed—"this drug is supposed to be bad" and "this drug makes me feel good." Because beliefs and attitudes based on direct experience come to mind more readily than attitudes that are based solely on externally provided information, the effectiveness of the anti-drug attitude is at a competitive disadvantage (Fazio & Zanna, 1981). To the extent that these effects are anticipated, prevention programs can incorporate role-playing and other direct experiences in which students receive practice in dealing with these contrary feelings, should they arise.

In summary, we note that research on social influence has come a long way from the early notion that providing anti-drug information alone was sufficient to influence behavior. Social influence is a complex, although explicable process. We now know that the extent and nature of a person's cognitive responses to external information may be more important than the information itself. We know that attitudes can be changed in different ways (central vs. peripheral routes), and that some attitude changes are more stable, resistant, and predictive of behavior than others. We also know that even apparently simple variables (such as how likable a source is or what mood a person is in) can produce persuasion by very different processes in different situations. We hope our brief review of current thinking about attitude change processes may have some utility for developing and evaluating anti-drug communications.

REFERENCES

Ajzen, I. (1988). *Attitudes, personality, and behavior.* Chicago: Dorsey Press.

Ajzen, I., & Fishbein, M. (1980). *Understanding attitudes and predicting social behavior.* Englewood Cliffs, NJ: Prentice-Hall.

Anderson, N. H. (1981). Integration theory applied to cognitive responses and attitudes. In
    R. E. Petty, T.M. Ostrom, & T.C. Brock (Eds.), *Cognitive responses in persuasion* (pp.
    361–397). Hillsdale, NJ: Lawrence Erlbaum Associates.
Bandura, A. (1977). *Social learning theory.* Englewood Cliffs, NJ: Prentice-Hall.
Bandura, A. (1982). Self-efficacy mechanism in human agency. *American Psychologist, 37,*
    122–147.
Bandura, A. (1986). *Social foundations of thought and action.* Englewood Cliffs, NJ: Prentice-
    Hall.
Bogart, L. (1967). *Strategy in advertising.* New York: Harcourt.
Botvin, G. J., Baker, E., Renick, N. L., Filazzola, A. D., & Botvin, E. M. (1984). A cognitive-
    behavioral approach to substance abuse prevention. *Addictive Behaviors, 9,* 137–147.
Bozinoff, L., Roth, V., & May, C. (1989). Stages of involvement with drugs and alcohol:
    Analysis of effects of drug and alcohol abuse advertising. *Advances in Consumer Research,*
    16, 215–220.
Cacioppo, J. T., & Petty, R. E. (1982). The need for cognition. *Journal of Personality and So-*
    cial Psychology, 42, 116–131.
Cacioppo, J. T., & Petty, R. E. (1989). Effects of message repetition on argument processing,
    recall, and persuasion. *Basic and Applied Social Psychology, 10,* 3–12.
Chaiken, S. (1987). The heuristic model of persuasion. In M. P. Zanna, J. Olson, & C. Her-
    man (Eds.), *Social influence: The Ontario symposium* (pp. 3–39). Hillsdale, NJ: Lawrence
    Erlbaum Associates.
Chaiken, S., & Stangor, C. (1987). Attitude and attitude change. *Annual Review of Psycholo-*
    gy, 38, 575–630.
Cooper, J., & Croyle, R. (1984). Attitude and attitude change. *Annual Review of Psychology,*
    35, 395–426.
DeJong, W. (1987). A short term evaluation of project DARE (drug abuse resistance educa-
    tion): Preliminary indications of effectiveness. *Journal of Drug Education, 17*(4), 279–293.
DuPont, P. J., & Jason, L. A. (1984). Assertiveness training in a preventive drug education
    program. *Journal of Drug Education, 14*(4), 369–379.
Duryea, E. J. (1983). Utilizing tenets of inoculation theory to develop and evaluate a preven-
    tive alcohol education intervention. *Journal of School Health, 53*(4), 250–255.
Fazio, R. H. (1990). Multiple processes by which attitudes guide behavior: The MODE model
    as an integrative framework. In M. Zanna (Ed.), *Advances in experimental social psycholo-*
    gy (Vol. 23, pp. 75–109). New York: Academic Press.
Fazio, R. H., & Zanna, M. P. (1981). Direct experience and attitude-behavior consistency.
    In L. Berkowitz (Ed.), *Advances in experimental social psychology* (Vol. 14, pp. 161–202).
    New York: Academic Press.
Fishbein, M., & Middlestadt, S. E. (1987). Using the theory of reasoned action to develop
    educational interventions: Applications to illicit drug use. *Health Education Research, 2,*
    361–371.
Forman, A., & Lachter, S. (1989). The National Institute on Drug Abuse Cocaine Preven-
    tion Campaign. In P. Shoemaker (Ed.), *Communication campaigns about drugs: Govern-*
    ment, media, and the public (pp. 13–20). Hillsdale, NJ: Lawrence Erlbaum Associates.
Goodstadt, M. S., Sheppard, M. A., & Chan, G. C. (1982). An evaluation of two school-
    based alcohol education programs. *Journal of Studies on Alcohol, 43*(3), 352–369.
Greenwald, A. G. (1968). Cognitive learning, cognitive response to persuasion, and attitude
    change. In A. Greenwald, T. Brock, & T. Ostrom (Eds.), *Psychological foundations of atti-*
    tudes (pp. 147–170). New York: Academic Press.
Heider, F. (1958). *The psychology of interpersonal relations.* New York: Wiley.
Janz, N. K., & Becker, M. H. (1984). The health belief model: A decade later. *Health Educa-*
    tion Quarterly, 11, 1–47.

Kinder, B. N., Pape, N. E., & Walfish, S. (1980). Drug and alcohol education programs: A review of outcome studies. *The International Journal of the Addictions, 15*(7), 1035–1054.

McCaul, K. D., & Glasgow, R. E. (1985). Preventing adolescent smoking: What have we learned about treatment construct validity? *Health Psychology, 4,* 361–387.

McGuire, W. J. (1964). Inducing resistance to persuasion: Some contemporary approaches. In L. Berkowitz (Ed). *Advances in experimental social psychology* (Vol. 1, pp. 191–229). New York: Academic.

McGuire, W. J. (1989). Theoretical foundations of campaigns. In R. Rice & C. Atkin (Eds.), *Public communication campaigns* (pp. 43–65). Beverly Hills, CA: Sage.

McGuire, W. J. (1985). Attitudes and attitude change. In G. Lindzey & E. Aronson (Eds.), *Handbook of social psychology* (Vol. 2, 3rd ed., pp. 233–346). New York: Random House.

Moskowitz, J. M., Malvin, J. H., Schaeffer, G. A., & Schaps, E. (1984). An experimental evaluation of a drug education course. *Journal of Drug Education, 14,* 9–22.

Myer, A. J., & Henderson, J. B. (1974). Multiple risk factor reduction in the prevention of cardiovascular disease. *Preventive Medicine, 3,* 225–236.

Petty, R. E., & Cacioppo, J. T. (1979a). Effects of forewarning of persuasive intent on cognitive responses and persuasion. *Personality and Social Psychology Bulletin, 5,* 173–176.

Petty, R. E., & Cacioppo, J. T. (1979b). Issue-involvement can increase or decrease persuasion by enhancing message-relevant cognitive responses. *Journal of Personality and Social Psychology, 37,* 1915–1926.

Petty, R. E., & Cacioppo, J. T. (1981). *Attitudes and persuasion: Classic and contemporary approaches.* Dubuque, IA: Wm. C. Brown.

Petty, R. E., & Cacioppo, J. T. (1984). Motivational factors in consumer response to advertisements. In W. Beatty, R. Geen, & R. Arkin (Eds.), *Human motivation* (pp. 418–454). New York: Allyn & Bacon.

Petty, R. E., & Cacioppo, J. T. (1986). *Communication and persuasion: Central and peripheral routes to attitude change.* New York: Springer/Verlag.

Petty, R. E., & Cacioppo, J. T. (1990). Involvement and persuasion: Tradition versus integration. *Psychological Bulletin, 107,* 367–374.

Petty, R. E., Gleicher, F., & Baker, S. M. (1991). Multiple roles for affect in persuasion. In J. Forgas (Ed.), *Affect and judgment* (pp. 181–200). London: Pergamon.

Petty, R. E., Ostrom, T. M., & Brock, T. C. (Eds.) (1981). *Cognitive responses in persuasion.* Hillsdale, NJ: Lawrence Erlbaum Associates.

Petty, R. E., Unnava, R., & Strathman, A. (1991). Theories of attitude change. In H. Kassarjian & T. Robertson (Eds.). *Handbook of consumer behavior* (pp. 241–280). Englewood Cliffs, NJ: Prentice-Hall.

Petty, R. E., Wells, G. L., & Brock, T. C. (1976). Distraction can enhance or reduce yielding to propaganda. *Journal of Personality and Social Psychology, 34,* 874–884.

Rinehart, D. G. (1989). *Changing attitudes: The Columbus consensus on drug policy.* Columbus, OH: City of Columbus.

Rosenstock, I. M. (1974). Historical origins of the health belief model. *Health Education Monographs, 2,* 328–335.

Rosenstock, I. M., Strecher, V. J., & Becker, M. H. (1988). Social learning theory and the health belief model. *Health Education Quarterly, 15,* 175–183.

Rundall, T. G., & Bruvold, W. H. (1988). A meta-analysis of school-based smoking and alcohol use prevention programs. *Health Education Quarterly, 15*(3) pp. 317–334.

Sheppard, B. H., Hartwick, J., & Warshaw, P. (1988). The theory of reasoned action: A meta-analysis of past research with recommendations for modifications and future research. *Journal of Consumer Research, 15,* 325–343.

Shoemaker, P. J. (Ed.). (1989). *Communication campaigns about drugs: Government, media, and the public.* Hillsdale, NJ: Lawrence Erlbaum Associates.

Smart, R. G., Bennett, C., & Fejer, D. (1976). A controlled study of the peer group approach to drug education. *Journal of Drug Education, 6*(4), 305–311.

Staats, A. W., & Staats, C. (1958). Attitudes established by classical conditioning. *Journal of Abnormal and Social Psychology, 67*, 159–167.

Strong, E. K. (1925). *The psychology of selling and advertising.* New York: McGraw Hill.

Wallack, L., & Corbett, K. (1987). Alcohol, tobacco and marijuana use among youth: An overview of epidemiological, program and policy trends. *Health Education Quarterly, 14*, 223–249.

Wallerstein, N. & Bernstein, E. (1988). Empowerment education: Freire's ideas adapted to health education. *Health Education Quarterly, 15*(4), 379–394.

Zuckerman, M. (1983). *Biological bases of sensation-seeking, impulsivity, and anxiety.* Hillsdale, NJ: Lawrence Erlbaum Associates.

III

MASS COMMUNICATION, SOCIAL SYSTEMS, AND DRUG ABUSE PREVENTION

6

Toward a Theory
of Drug Epidemics

Lloyd D. Johnston
The University of Michigan

From the late 1960s to the early 1990s America has experienced a truly dramatic epidemic of illicit drug use, among its adolescents and young adults in particular. It has been an epidemic that to some degree has diffused to practically all other corners of the globe, although what piecemeal epidemiological data are available suggest that in no other region did the epidemic penetrate the youthful population as much as it did in North America (Johnston & Harrison, 1984; Smart & Murray, 1981; United Nations, 1987). During this time, I and my colleagues, Jerald Bachman and Patrick O'Malley, have spent much of our professional lives mapping and trying to understand the many tributaries, eddies, and streams that have comprised this great epidemic. It has been, after all, not exactly a single epidemic, but rather a constellation of epidemics involving the use of a broad array of psychoactive substances outside the medically or morally prescribed boundaries set down by society.

The overall drug epidemic has been comprised of the use of substances as diverse as drugs that are totally illegal to produce or possess (these include derivatives of natural substances like cannabis, coca, and opium, as well as synthetics like PCP and LSD); drugs that are legally manufactured for medical purposes and the use of which is controlled by law (like stimulants, sedatives, tranquilizers, and analgesics); and synthetic substances not legally controlled, but that still are used for their psychoactive effects (including the various inhalant drugs like glues, industrial solvents, the nitrites, etc.).

Perhaps we tend to think of this epidemic in more monolithic terms than we should, given this great diversity of substances that it encompasses, but on the other hand it may make sense, not only in facilitating discourse about this complex, multidimensional social problem, but also because the many different drug-using behaviors do in fact tend to clump together and do seem to have some orderly temporal connections among themselves. Many investigators, for instance, have demonstrated that these many different forms of illicit substance use correlate fairly strongly with each other, and further, that there tends to be some orderliness in the way individuals progress through these experiences (e.g., Johnston, 1973; Kandel, 1975; O'Donnell, Voss, Clayton, Slatin, & Room, 1976). In fact, not only is the use of these many illicit substances intercorrelated, their use also correlates with the use of quite an array of licit substances, including cigarettes, alcohol, "look-alike" stimulants, over-the-counter diet pills, sleeping pills, and so forth (Jessor & Jessor, 1977; Johnston, 1973; Johnston, O'Malley, & Bachman, 1987b; Kandel, 1975; Miller et al., 1983).

Because most social science research is comprised of single cross-sectional surveys, short-term experimental designs, or panel studies of single cohorts, it is fair to say that the great majority of social science studies on the use of these various substances have been somewhat time-bound. That is, they have tended to focus mostly on social and psychological differences among individuals at a given point in time (i.e., risk factors that might help to explain higher or lower use). Such emphases are valuable, of course—they provide many insights of both theoretical and practical significance. But, one wonders whether this examination of individual differences allows us to establish how the aggregate phenomenon of an epidemic came into being in the first place. I think it may tell us more about who is more vulnerable to the overall epidemic, or its component epidemics, than about the social forces that brought the epidemic itself about, or that may cause it to recede.

In this chapter, I address the issue of how this broad epidemic of illicit drug use came to be, and why different classes of drugs have held sway in it at different points in time.[1] In other words, I propose to specify and elaborate the forces that I believe explain much of the drug epidemic since the 1960s, and to generalize from that experience to the beginnings of a more general theory of secular (i.e., long-range) trends in drug use. To the

---

[1]For the purposes of this chapter I have not tried to integrate all of the hypotheses and concepts used in this theoretical formulation, which is specific to the drug use domain of behavior, with a number of other, more general theories of clear relevance from the sociological and psychological literatures—theories dealing with anomie and normlessness, social control, or social movements. Nor have I integrated it with the relevant literatures of certain social historians of this field, such as David Musto. I plan to make these integrations in later, expanded statements of the theory.

degree that this theoretical statement is accurate, it may prove useful in the near future in guiding social action aimed at trying to contain epidemics in the use of particular drugs, and in the longer term perhaps, in containing even more general epidemics of illicit drug use.

I take into account the constellation character of the overall epidemic—that is, to account for the changing proportions of young people willing to illicitly use drugs of whatever type. I also offer some theoretical explanation for three separate stages of the overall epidemic—onset, maintenance, and decline—as well as an explanation for changes in the use of individual drugs. To do this I rely heavily on our own data from the Monitoring the Future project, in particular on the portion that is comprised of repeated cross-sectional surveys of American high school seniors (Johnston, O'Malley, & Bachman, 1989).

Figures 6.1 through 6.7 help to illustrate more specifically the phenomena I explain here. They are all based on data from the Monitoring the Future project's annual surveys of American high school seniors beginning in 1975—some 7 or so years into the illicit drug use epidemic. It may be seen in the first five of these figures that the different drugs used illicitly by this population have changed considerably since 1975. Heroin, LSD, and barbiturates all began long-term declines from their peak levels at least as far back as 1975. On the other hand, tranquilizer use did not reach its peak until 1978, PCP and marijuana not until 1979, stimulants and methaqualone not until 1982, and cocaine not until 1985 or 1986. In other words,

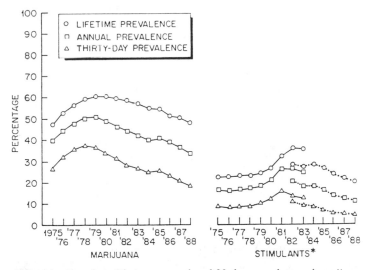

FIG. 6.1. Trends in lifetime, annual and 30-day prevalence of marijuana and stimulants (all seniors). *The dotted lines connect percentages which result if nonprescription stimulants are excluded.

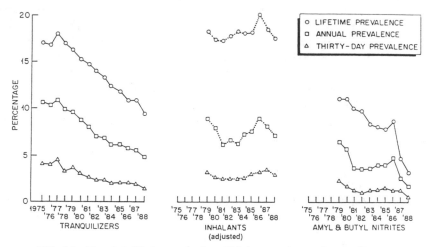

FIG. 6.2. Trends in lifetime, annual, and 30-day prevalence of tranquilizers, inhalants, and amyl and butyl nitrites (all seniors).

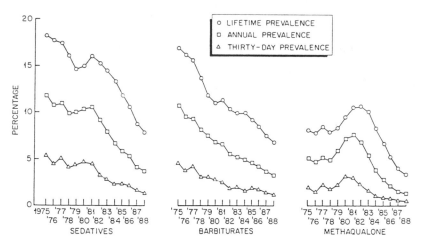

FIG. 6.3. Trends in lifetime, annual, and 30-day prevalence of sedatives, barbiturates, and methaqualone (all seniors).

some of these drugs were rising in popularity, whereas others were falling—and sometimes rising or falling quite sharply. Yet, as Figs. 6.6 and 6.7 show, the curves showing trends in the *overall* proportions of young people using any illicit drug, or any illicit drug other than marijuana or amphetamines, are quite smooth and orderly.

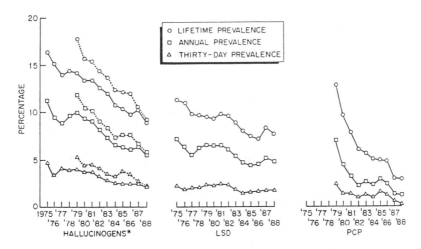

FIG. 6.4.   Trends in lifetime, annual, and 30-day prevalence of hallucinogens, LSD, and PCP (all seniors). *The dotted lines connect percentages that
are adjusted for underreporting of PCP.

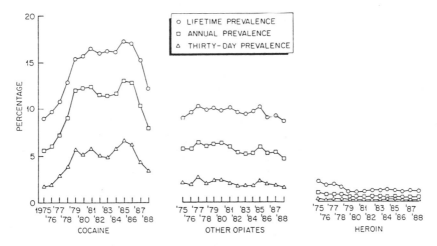

FIG. 6.5.   Trends in lifetime, annual, and 30-day prevalence of cocaine, other
opiates, and heroin (all seniors).

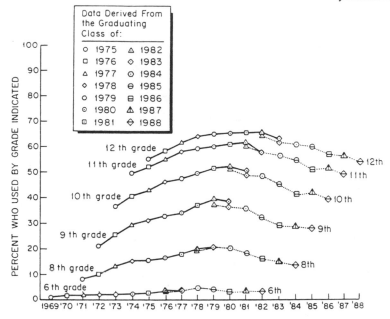

FIG. 6.6. Use of any illicit drug: Trends in lifetime prevalence for earlier grade levels (based on retrospective reports from seniors). *Note:* The dotted lines connect percentages that result if nonprescription stimulants are excluded.

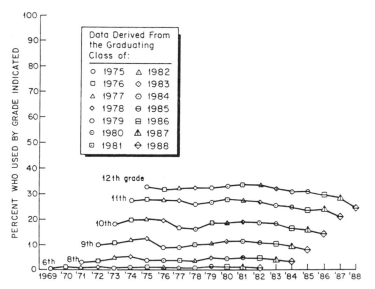

FIG. 6.7. Use of any illicit drug other than marijuana or amphetamines: Trends in lifetime prevalence for earlier grade levels (based on retrospective reports from seniors).

NECESSARY CONDITIONS FOR
THE EXPANSION OF AN EPIDEMIC

I believe there are five conditions that must pertain for a large spread in the popularity of a given drug or set of drugs to take place—conditions that I here label as *awareness, access, motivation, reassurance,* and *willingness to violate social norms.* I also argue that all of these conditions are necessary for a broad expansion in popular use to occur, as well as for a broad epidemic, once established, to continue.

Awareness

A population has to become aware of the existence of a drug and its psychoactive potential before it can entertain the idea of using it. Most young people in the silent 1950s were simply unaware of the behavioral alternatives of using marijuana, LSD, and the like—they were not active alternatives in their repertoire of behaviors. And most young people were not aware of drugs like methaqualone, cocaine, and PCP until the mid-1970s. Widespread awareness of other drugs such as ''ecstasy'' (MDMA) did not come until still later, and there are surely still others yet to arrive on the American scene. This is not to say, necessarily, that these drugs had not been discovered previously, but rather that there was no widespread awareness in the population of their potential use as psychoactive agents. The media undoubtedly play a significant role at some stage in spreading the awareness of a drug throughout the population, but prior to that there is likely to be a diffusion through networks of friendships and acquaintances, and perhaps through underground newspapers and magazines.

Things have changed for the practically indefinite future in terms of the smorgasbord of psychoactive alternatives of which American young people are aware. This constitutes a major change in the situation—one that not only helped give rise to the overall epidemic, but that also clearly helps to maintain its forward momentum.

Access

The second necessary condition I posit, which is not unrelated to awareness, is access. Obviously awareness without access cannot result in use, although rising access may well help to stimulate awareness. Because access is largely achieved through friendship networks, the advent of an epidemic is likely to have a snowball effect in that the more people are using, still more know people who are using and through whom they can have access. They, in turn, can become users, and can then provide access to still others in their friendship network, and so on (deAlarcon, 1969). This is probably most true for the *illegal* drugs, for which a new production and distribution system needs to evolve to feed the epidemic, and somewhat less true for the controlled psychotherapeutic drugs, which may already be widely dispersed in the population and thus be accessible through diversion, borrowing, and theft. (In fact, in many countries there is very little real control of the psychotherapeutic substances and easy accessibility is indeed widespread.) However, when the demand for psychotherapeutic drugs outstrips the amount that can be supplied by diversion from the legitimate domestic distribution system, then illegal importation or manufacture will evolve to supplement the supply.

We were recently able to document the rapid spread in access to crack cocaine. In 1985, crack was widely assumed to be confined to very few large cities, but we determined that by 1986, 52% of the high schools in our national sample had some prevalence of crack use and in a single year that proportion jumped to 77% (Johnston et al., 1989). Indeed, in 1988 some 42% of all seniors in the country said they could get crack fairly easily, if they wanted some. Quite obviously, commercial distribution networks made the drug quickly available to a large proportion of the communities in the country, and friendship networks undoubtedly took it from there.

The most accessible drugs, of course, are the legal uncontrolled substances that are widely available commercially for completely different purposes than the ones to which drug users put them—in particular, the inhalants. Such easy accessibility undoubtedly explains their popularity among younger children in this country; and that, in combination with their low price, helps to explain why inhalants have become a real problem among street children in developing countries, such as Mexico, as well. Clearly, access without awareness of the psychoactive potential of the drug is not enough to lead to use. As we have seen repeatedly, youngsters keep discovering new substances to use from among those that have been on store shelves for years—such things as Robitussin™, to take a very recent example.

As with awareness of the alternatives, widespread access to many drugs not really accessible to previous generations has developed as a result of the current American epidemic. The majority of American young people in the 1980s reported having some experience with illicit drug use, with the result that nearly all have friendship contacts; and although the extent of access still varies considerably by drug (see Fig. 6.8 and Table 6.1) a large segment of the youth population say that it would be "fairly easy" or "very easy" for them to acquire a number of the drugs if they wanted them. Obviously many more could achieve access if they made a concerted effort.

Now that an elaborated production and distribution system exists— having evolved to meet the massive demand of the epidemic to date—it is yet another important facilitating feature of our social landscape that will take a long time to decline. As a result it will help maintain the forward momentum of the epidemic.

Motivation

Awareness and access are not sufficient conditions to move individuals to actual use, of course. There must be some motivation to use, and here the story becomes more complex. Curiosity plays an important role in the initial use of most drugs (Johnston & O'Malley, 1986), and so do promises of "wonderful" experiences to be attained. And the things that might be promised—as every good tobacco company advertising executive knows—can be myriad. They may include not only the promised psychological effects, but status and image and sexual identity. In the illicit drug area the benefits promised have also included intrapersonal insight and creativity (in the cases of LSD and, more recently, MDMA or "ecstasy"), enhancement of sexual performance and the sexual experience (in the cases of marijuana, cocaine, and methaqualone), and enhanced work capacity (in the cases of cocaine and amphetamines).

Because these drug-using behaviors are illicit, they may also carry the benefits of symbolic defiance of parents and other authorities, and the expression of solidarity with a deviant group. And age-graded norms make

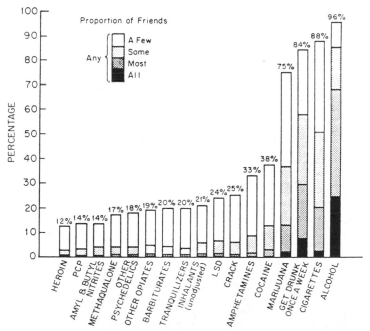

FIG. 6.8. Proportion of friends using each drug as estimated by seniors, class of 1988.

TABLE 6.1

Trends in Perceived Availability of Drugs, All Seniors

Q. How difficult do you think it would be for you to get each of the following types of drugs, if you wanted some?	Percentage saying drug would be "Fairly easy" or "Very easy" for them to get[a]														
	Class of 1975	Class of 1976	Class of 1977	Class of 1978	Class of 1979	Class of 1980	Class of 1981	Class of 1982	Class of 1983	Class of 1984	Class of 1985	Class of 1986	Class of 1987	Class of 1988	'87-'88 Change
Marijuana	87.8	87.4	87.9	87.8	90.1	89.0	89.2	88.5	86.2	84.6	85.5	85.2	84.8	85.0	+0.2
Amyl & Butyl Nitrites	NA	NA	NA	NA	NA	NA	NA	NA	NA	NA	NA	NA	23.9	25.9	+2.0
LSD	46.2	37.4	34.5	32.2	34.2	35.3	35.0	34.2	30.9	30.6	30.5	28.5	31.4	33.3	+1.9
PCP	NA	NA	NA	NA	NA	NA	NA	NA	NA	NA	NA	NA	22.8	24.9	+2.1
Some other psychedelic	47.8	35.7	33.8	33.8	34.6	35.0	32.7	30.6	26.6	26.6	26.1	24.9	25.0	26.2	+1.2
Cocaine	37.0	34.0	33.0	37.8	45.5	47.9	47.5	47.4	43.1	45.0	48.9	51.5	54.2	55.0	+0.8
"Crack"	NA	NA	NA	NA	NA	NA	NA	NA	NA	NA	NA	NA	41.1	42.1	+1.0
Cocaine powder	NA	NA	NA	NA	NA	NA	NA	NA	NA	NA	NA	NA	52.9	50.3	-2.6
Heroin	24.2	18.4	17.9	16.4	18.9	21.2	19.2	20.8	19.3	19.9	21.0	22.0	23.7	28.0	+4.3ss
Some other narcotic (including methadone)	34.5	26.9	27.8	26.1	28.7	29.4	29.6	30.4	30.0	32.1	33.1	32.2	33.0	35.8	+2.8
Amphetamines	67.8	61.8	58.1	58.5	59.9	61.3	69.5	70.8	68.5	68.2	66.4	64.3	64.5	63.9	-0.6
Barbiturates	60.0	54.4	52.4	50.6	49.8	49.1	54.9	55.2	52.5	51.9	51.3	48.3	48.2	47.8	-0.4
Tranquilizers	71.8	65.5	64.9	64.3	61.4	59.1	60.8	58.9	55.3	54.5	54.7	51.2	48.6	49.1	+0.5
Approx. N =	(2,627)	(2,865)	(3,065)	(3,598)	(3,172)	(3,240)	(3,578)	(3,602)	(3,385)	(3,269)	(3,274)	(3,077)	(3,271)	(3,231)	

Note: Level of significance of difference between the two most recent classes: s = .05, ss = .01, sss = .001. NA indicates data not available.

[a]Answer alternatives were: (1) Probably impossible, (2) Very difficult, (3) Fairly difficult, (4) Fairly easy, and (5) Very easy.

even generally licit behaviors, like smoking and drinking, illicit for younger age groups. These facts no doubt do much to explain the strong tendency of the drug epidemic to show up particularly among the more deviant segments of the population (Jessor & Jessor, 1977; Johnston 1973; Osgood, Johnston, O'Malley, & Bachman, 1988).

Once use is popular within certain groups, use by a newcomer can be a way of fitting in socially and partaking of a communal experience. In our analyses of the reasons young people offer for their drug and alcohol use, we have found that the one most commonly mentioned was ''to have a good time with my friends'' (Johnston & O'Malley, 1986). We also found that among youngsters more involved with drugs, reasons having to do with psychological coping were more frequently mentioned.

Motivation to use can be aroused and maintained by many means—a subject to which we return later—but certainly social modeling is likely to be one of the most powerful mechanisms through which interest, or motivation to use, can be brought about. The strong association found in the smoking area between smoking by one's parents and older siblings and the individual's own likelihood of becoming a smoker provides powerful evidence of this fact. It also serves to remind us that the modeling comes not just from friends, but also from others in one's immediate role set, from role models in the media, and even from complete strangers in the media (such as the models used in cigarette and alcohol ads).

Reassurance

Because nearly all people are aware of the possibility that ingesting a relatively unfamiliar chemical substance will be harmful (and, in many cases, the dangers have already been publicly stated), I believe that the fourth condition necessary for an epidemic is reassurance. The adverse effects, or costs, must not be seen to outweigh the benefits. Reassurance can be obtained in a number of ways: through assertion by others in one's immediate interpersonal sphere, through assertion by experts or self-proclaimed experts in the public sphere, and by direct observation of other people using and not suffering any obvious adverse consequences (i.e., by vicarious learning). The mere fact that many others use may be the most compelling form of reassurance and undoubtedly contributes to the snowball effect in the beginning of an epidemic, in that the increasing number of users provides reassurance to an ever-widening sphere of the population.

Willingness to Violate the Law and the Predominant Social Norms

The last condition that must be met for the rapid expansion of the use of a particular drug to occur is a willingness on the part of a large number of people to violate the law and the predominant social norms. The various classes of psychoactive substances we have been discussing vary considerably, not only in the degree to which their possession is legal, but in the extent to which their use is considered illicit (i.e., contrary to predominant social norms). Although not widely condoned, the use of many inhalant drugs is not considered very illicit either, whether by adolescents or adults. Of the illegal and the controlled psychotherapeutic substances, marijuana is clearly the least disapproved (Johnston et al., 1989). Table 6.2 illustrates the point. It also shows that for any given drug, experimental use receives less negative reaction than does occasional use, and occasional use less than regular use. The drugs can be rank-ordered on the extent to which their use is disapproved of; and that rank ordering matches very closely the extent to which they are seen as dangerous. This in part has led me to the hypothesis (first put forward in Johnston, 1985) that among the illicit drugs, perceived risk is a major determinant of personal disapproval, and derivatively, of peer disapproval. This point is discussed later.

The use of any of the illicit drugs at any level of involvement has been widely disapproved by the older adult segment of the population (e.g. Johnston et al., 1989), which reflects the long-term predominant norms of society. Thus, to use any of the illicit drugs without medical instruction is to violate predominant norms and usually the law as well. And for a widespread epidemic of the sort we have had since the 1960s to occur, a large proportion of the population—or at least of certain age groups in the population— must be willing to violate those norms and laws. This is a fairly unusual circumstance, and one that must be understood if we are to explain an epidemic that extends well beyond the most deviant sector of the population.

IMPORTANT HISTORICAL FORCES
IN THE MOST RECENT EPIDEMIC

All of the five factors discussed so far—awareness, access, motivation, reassurance, and willingness to violate laws and predominant norms—can be used to explain individual behavior, as well as people's behavior in the aggregate. But to explain the advent of the general epidemic of illicit drug use in the United States since the 1960s we need to look further at the historical forces that helped to bring about these conditions for a large number of illicit drugs.

In my opinion, the evolution of the American drug epidemic of the late 20th century is inextricably tied to two social changes that happened to coincide in the 1960s. One was the movement away from the outerdirectedness of the silent 1950s toward innerdirectedness—the movement toward the celebration of feelings, spontaneity, and intuitiveness. Drugs—in particular marijuana and LSD—came to be seen as appropriate vehicles for taking that journey to the "true" inner self. This shift toward innerdirected-

TABLE 6.2
Trends in Proportions of Seniors Disapproving of Drug Use

Percentage "disapproving"[a]

Q. Do you disapprove of people (who are 18 or older) doing each of the following?[b]	Class of 1975	Class of 1976	Class of 1977	Class of 1978	Class of 1979	Class of 1980	Class of 1981	Class of 1982	Class of 1983	Class of 1984	Class of 1985	Class of 1986	Class of 1987	Class of 1988	'87-'88 Change
Try marijuana once or twice	47.0	38.4	33.4	33.4	34.2	39.0	40.0	45.5	46.3	49.3	51.4	54.6	56.6	60.8	+4.2ss
Smoke marijuana occasionally	54.8	47.8	44.3	43.5	45.3	49.7	52.6	59.1	60.7	63.5	65.8	69.0	71.6	74.0	+2.4
Smoke marijuana regularly	71.9	69.5	65.5	67.5	69.2	74.6	77.4	80.6	82.5	84.7	85.5	86.6	89.2	89.3	+0.1
Try LSD once or twice	82.8	84.6	83.9	85.4	86.6	87.3	86.4	88.8	89.1	88.9	89.5	89.2	91.6	89.8	-1.8s
Take LSD regularly	94.1	95.3	95.8	96.4	96.9	96.7	96.8	96.7	97.0	96.8	97.0	96.6	97.8	96.4	-1.4ss
Try cocaine once or twice	81.3	82.4	79.1	77.0	74.7	76.3	74.6	76.6	77.0	79.7	79.3	80.2	87.3	89.1	+1.8
Take cocaine regularly	93.3	93.9	92.1	91.9	90.8	91.1	90.7	91.5	93.2	94.5	93.8	94.3	96.7	96.2	-0.5
Try heroin once or twice	91.5	92.6	92.5	92.0	93.4	93.5	93.5	94.6	94.3	94.0	94.0	93.3	96.2	95.0	-1.2
Take heroin occasionally	94.8	96.0	96.0	96.4	96.8	96.7	97.2	96.9	96.9	97.1	96.8	96.6	97.9	96.9	-1.0s
Take heroin regularly	96.7	97.5	97.2	97.8	97.9	97.6	97.8	97.5	97.7	98.0	97.6	97.6	98.1	97.2	-0.9s
Try amphetamines once or twice	74.8	75.1	74.2	74.8	75.1	75.4	71.1	72.6	72.3	72.8	74.9	76.5	80.7	82.5	+1.8
Take amphetamines regularly	92.1	92.8	92.5	93.5	94.4	93.0	91.7	92.0	92.6	93.6	93.3	93.5	95.4	94.2	-1.2
Try barbiturates once or twice	77.7	81.3	81.1	82.4	84.0	83.9	82.4	84.4	83.1	84.1	84.9	86.8	89.6	89.4	-0.2
Take barbiturates regularly	93.3	93.6	93.0	94.3	95.2	95.4	94.2	94.4	95.1	95.1	95.5	94.9	96.4	95.3	-1.1
Try one or two drinks of an alcoholic beverage (beer, wine, liquor)	21.6	18.2	15.6	15.6	15.8	16.0	17.2	18.2	18.4	17.4	20.3	20.9	21.4	22.6	+1.2
Take one or two drinks nearly every day	67.6	68.9	66.8	67.7	68.3	69.0	69.1	69.9	68.9	72.9	70.9	72.8	74.2	75.0	+0.8
Take four or five drinks nearly every day	88.7	90.7	88.4	90.2	91.7	90.8	91.8	90.9	90.0	91.0	92.0	91.4	92.2	92.8	+0.6
Have five or more drinks once or twice each weekend	60.3	58.6	57.4	56.2	56.7	55.6	55.5	58.8	56.6	59.6	60.4	62.4	62.0	65.3	+3.3s
Smoke one or more packs of cigarettes per day	67.5	65.9	66.4	67.0	70.3	70.8	69.9	59.4	70.8	73.0	72.3	75.4	74.3	73.1	-1.2
Approx. N =	(2,677)	(2,957)	(3,085)	(3,686)	(3,221)	(3,261)	(3,610)	(2,651)	(3,341)	(3,254)	(3,265)	(3,113)	(3,302)	(3,311)	

Note: Level of significance of difference between the two most recent classes: s = .05, ss = .01, sss = .001.
[a] Answer alternatives were: (1) Don't disapprove, (2) Disapprove, and (3) Strongly disapprove. Percentages are shown for categories (2) and (3) combined.
[b] The 1975 question asked about people who are "20 or older."

105

ness was evolving independently of the Vietnam War—which was the second and even more important historical change I want to discuss—but was greatly intensified by the consequences of that war.

Vietnam, of course, was the most prominent and determining feature in that period of American history. The alienation that it (and other historical events of the period, like Watergate) engendered among the young, gave rise to a generational rift of enormous importance. And drug use, largely *because* it was illicit, was adopted as an important symbol by the young—particularly by those most socially and politically alienated. In fact, it was an overdetermined form of symbolic expression, for drug use could be used not only to express open and very irritating defiance of the older generation and the establishment. It could be used (Particularly in the "passing of the joint") for the ritualistic expression of group solidarity and identity within a social movement, the counter-culture movement. And finally it could be used to call attention to the hypocrisy of the older generation in their acceptance of dangerous licit drugs and disapproval of supposedly "safe" illicit ones.

The Vietnam War, in my opinion, was the great catalyst that made the drug epidemic of the 1960s and 1970s a mass epidemic, rather than a relatively limited one. Not only did the symbolic expression add greatly to the "benefits" column in the decision-making ledger about whether to use, but the dramatic erosion of the legitimacy of the system in the eyes of so many young people greatly reduced the "costs" column, by permitting traditionally illicit and illegal behaviors to become licit within a certain age group—the young. In other words, widespread alienation among the young resulted in a breakdown of traditional norms, a motivation for rebellion, and spawning of a counter-culture movement, and certain drugs served the need created by those forces.

The empirical evidence that the use of illicit drugs—in particular marijuana and hallucinogens—were associated with anti-Vietnam and anti-government sentiment during that period is substantial (e.g., Clark & Levine, 1971; Johnston, 1973; Suchman, 1968), and this association was independent of being deviant in the more traditional sense of the term. Delinquency was virtually uncorrelated with anti-Vietnam sentiment even though both were strongly correlated with drug use (Johnston, 1973). With the end of the Vietnam War in 1973, however, this important catalyst to the drug epidemic was withdrawn, the counter-culture movement largely dissipated, and the symbolic expressive value of drug use, in those domains at least, largely eroded. This, I believe, sowed the seeds for a subsequent decline in the epidemic: The powerful catalyst was removed.

But that gets us ahead of the story. How do these historical events tie in with the five conditions stated as necessary for a large-scale epidemic of illicit drug use? First, they increased motivation to use. Second, the growing social movement of the counter-culture increased awareness and access. Gurus of the movement provided reassurance about the safety of marijuana and LSD, and there was also plenty of role modeling. Finally, I have already noted that the great extent of youth alienation from the system and from the older generation created the conditions in which young people could violate the older generations' laws and norms because they defined their authority as illegitimate. A large social movement defined drug use—and primarily marijuana and hallucinogen use in the early stages—as legitimate within that movement, and this legitimation spread to an entire age group in the general population. As a result, the social consequences of these illegal behaviors—including possible peer ostracism and certainly including the likelihood of being reported to authorities—changed substantially. There was safety in numbers, because so many young people were using marijuana that they knew that the legal system was incapable of apprehending, let alone processing, a significant proportion of the users.

And marijuana, I contend, was the drug that brought many young people across that psychological boundary of doing something that was illegal and illicit, based on predominant norms. It was the pathbreaking drug that tore a great hole through the fabric of traditional, normative social constraints and made it far easier for young people to consider using other drugs. Why did they never use the other drugs in such numbers as they used marijuana? I believe that it was because they never saw them as being as safe (see Table 6.3) and as a result of that never found them as acceptable (see Table 6.2).

But to help explain further how the five necessary conditions for an epidemic are brought about, I want to turn to the next part of the theory, which is that there are important public roles that are played out in the expansion phase of an epidemic.

PUBLIC ROLES IN THE EXPANSION PHASE OF AN EPIDEMIC

There are four critical public roles that are likely to be played out on the public stage during the expansion phase in the use of any illicit drug. I have chosen to label them the *proponents*, the *reassurers*, the *public role models*, and the *antagonists*.

The Proponents

Both awareness and motivation are likely to be brought to the population by the proponents of the use of a drug. The quintessential public proponent, of course, was Timothy Leary, who integrated LSD and marijuana use into a personal social philosophy that he codified in the phrase "tune in, turn on, and drop out." A proponent who integrates drug use into a

TABLE 6.3

Trends in Harmfulness of Drugs as Perceived by Seniors

Percentage saying "great risk"[a]

Q. How much do you think people risk harming themselves (physically or in other ways), if they...	Class of 1975	Class of 1976	Class of 1977	Class of 1978	Class of 1979	Class of 1980	Class of 1981	Class of 1982	Class of 1983	Class of 1984	Class of 1985	Class of 1986	Class of 1987	Class of 1988	'87-'88 Change
Try marijuana once or twice	15.1	11.4	9.5	8.1	9.4	10.0	13.0	11.5	12.7	14.7	14.8	15.1	18.4	19.0	+0.6
Smoke marijuana occasionally	18.1	15.0	13.4	12.4	13.5	14.7	19.1	18.3	20.6	22.6	24.5	25.0	30.4	31.7	+1.3
Smoke marijuana regularly	43.3	38.6	36.4	34.9	42.0	50.4	57.6	60.4	62.8	66.9	70.4	71.3	73.5	77.0	+3.5sss
Try LSD once or twice	49.4	45.7	43.2	42.7	41.6	43.9	45.5	44.9	44.7	45.4	43.5	42.0	44.9	45.7	+0.8
Take LSD regularly	81.4	80.8	79.1	81.1	82.4	83.0	83.5	83.5	83.2	83.8	82.9	82.6	83.8	84.2	+0.4
Try PCP once or twice	NA	NA	NA	NA	NA	NA	NA	NA	NA	NA	NA	NA	55.6	58.8	+3.2s
Try cocaine once or twice	42.6	39.1	35.6	33.2	31.5	31.3	32.1	32.8	33.0	35.7	34.0	33.5	47.9	51.2	+3.3s
Take cocaine occasionally	NA	NA	NA	NA	NA	NA	NA	NA	NA	NA	NA	54.2	66.8	69.2	+2.4
Take cocaine regularly	73.1	72.3	68.2	68.2	69.5	69.2	71.2	73.0	74.3	78.8	79.0	82.2	88.5	89.2	+0.7
Try "crack" once or twice	NA	NA	NA	NA	NA	NA	NA	NA	NA	NA	NA	NA	57.0	62.1	+5.1ss
Take "crack" occasionally	NA	NA	NA	NA	NA	NA	NA	NA	NA	NA	NA	NA	70.4	73.2	+2.8
Take "crack" regularly	NA	NA	NA	NA	NA	NA	NA	NA	NA	NA	NA	NA	84.6	84.8	+0.2
Try cocaine powder once or twice	NA	NA	NA	NA	NA	NA	NA	NA	NA	NA	NA	NA	45.3	51.7	+6.4sss
Take cocaine powder occasionally	NA	NA	NA	NA	NA	NA	NA	NA	NA	NA	NA	NA	56.8	61.9	+5.1ss
Take cocaine powder regularly	NA	NA	NA	NA	NA	NA	NA	NA	NA	NA	NA	NA	81.4	82.9	+1.5
Try heroin once or twice	60.1	58.9	55.8	52.9	50.4	52.1	52.9	51.1	50.8	49.8	47.3	45.8	53.6	54.0	+0.4
Take heroin occasionally	75.6	75.6	71.9	71.4	70.9	70.9	72.2	69.8	71.8	70.7	69.8	68.2	74.6	73.8	-0.8
Take heroin regularly	87.2	88.6	86.1	86.6	87.5	86.2	87.5	86.0	86.1	87.2	86.0	87.1	88.7	88.8	+0.1
Try amphetamines once or twice	35.4	33.4	30.8	29.9	29.7	29.7	26.4	25.3	24.7	25.4	25.2	25.1	29.1	29.6	+0.5
Take amphetamines regularly	69.0	67.3	66.6	67.1	69.9	69.1	66.1	64.7	64.8	67.1	67.2	67.3	69.4	69.8	+0.4
Try barbiturates once or twice	34.8	32.5	31.2	31.3	30.7	30.9	28.4	27.5	27.0	27.4	26.1	25.4	30.9	29.7	-1.2
Take barbiturates regularly	69.1	67.7	68.6	68.4	71.6	72.2	69.9	67.6	67.7	68.5	68.3	67.2	69.4	69.6	+0.2
Try one or two drinks of an alcoholic beverage (beer, wine, liquor)	5.3	4.8	4.1	3.4	4.1	3.8	4.6	3.5	4.2	4.6	5.0	4.6	6.2	6.0	-0.2
Take one or two drinks nearly every day	21.5	21.2	18.5	19.6	22.6	20.3	21.6	21.6	21.6	23.0	24.4	25.1	26.2	27.3	+1.1
Take four or five drinks nearly every day	63.5	61.0	62.9	63.1	66.2	65.7	64.5	65.5	66.8	68.4	69.8	66.5	69.7	68.5	-1.2
Have five or more drinks once or twice each weekend	37.8	37.0	34.7	34.5	34.9	35.9	36.3	36.0	38.6	41.7	43.0	39.1	41.9	42.6	+0.7
Smoke one or more packs of cigarettes per day	51.3	56.4	58.4	59.0	63.0	63.7	63.3	60.5	61.2	63.8	66.5	66.0	68.6	68.0	-0.6
Approx. N =	(2,804)	(2,918)	(3,052)	(3,770)	(3,250)	(3,234)	(3,604)	(3,557)	(3,305)	(3,262)	(3,250)	(3,020)	(3,315)	(3,276)	

Note: Level of significance of difference between the two most recent classes: s = .05, ss = .01, sss = .001. NA indicates data not available.

[a] Answer alternatives were: (1) No risk, (2) Slight risk, (3) Moderate risk, (4) Great risk, and (5) Can't say, drug unfamiliar.

more general philosophy or social movement has the most chance of giving rise to a major epidemic, insofar as that larger philosophy or movement takes hold. Given the historical conditions I have mentioned—a turning away from outerdirectedness and massive political and social disaffection among young people—Leary and a number of other proponents of the counter-culture movement (like Allan Ginsburg, John Sinclair, or Abbie Hoffman) had a powerful message for a receptive audience. There will surely be other periods in our history when there is widespread disaffection among the young, and these also will be periods of high risk for future ideologically driven epidemics of illicit drugs led by ideologically driven proponents.

Not all proponents, however, need be such florid, public, or ideologically driven figures as Leary and the other leaders of the counter-culture movement. In an earlier time, Sigmund Freud was a strong proponent of cocaine use, and newspaper accounts in recent years suggest that some psychotherapists were proponents of the drug MDMA or "ecstasy." When therapists or other professionals become proponents, they are also likely to take on the second role, which is sometimes separate, that of the reassurers.[2]

The Reassurers

The function of this role is related to achieving one of the necessary conditions for an epidemic—that of providing adequate reassurance about possible adverse consequences of use. There were many professionals who were publicly reassuring about the safety of marijuana—particularly during the first decade of the epidemic—although few are heard today. Timothy Leary played this role, as well as that of proponent, for LSD, trading on his expert power as a Harvard professor and scientist. Sigmund Freud did it in the case of cocaine, and some psychotherapists did it for MDMA. And a number of other names come to mind as having played the role of reassurer: Lester Grinspoon (1971), Robert Ashley (1975), Andrew Weil (e.g., Weil & Rosen, 1983), and Norman Zinberg (e.g., Zinberg & Robertson, 1972).

For the psychotherapeutic drugs, there was probably less need for a public role of reassurer, because these were FDA-approved drugs already widely prescribed by physicians. When taken within certain bounds, they would appear to be safe. In a sense, the reassurers for these drugs were the entire medical community. Interestingly, in the years since the beginning of the epidemic, these reassurers appear to have become less reassured themselves, and have reduced considerably their prescription of these drugs to young people (Johnston, O'Malley, & Bachman, 1987c).

---

[2]It is also important to note the degree to which the role of proponents can become institutionalized as it did in the form of NORML and underground papers like *High Times*.

In the case of heroin, no one took the public role of reassurer, at least not for many decades, which undoubtedly helps to explain the very low levels of use and very high perceived risks associated with that drug. And in the current era of AIDS, it is doubtful that anyone could play that role very convincingly—at least not for intravenous use.

For cocaine, as recently as the late 1970s and early 1980s, a reassurance function was being played by scientific professionals in the media (''Cocaine behaviors,'' 1982; ''The cocaine scene,'' 1977). The clinical and scientific evidence about the addictive and overdose hazards of the drug was so slow to accumulate that even many well-meaning professionals were fooled into believing it was not addictive or dangerous. The parallel to Sigmund Freud's experience is noteworthy.[3]

When a class of drugs is legal, representatives of the industry can become the reassurers, as has been the case with the tobacco industry. Not only can the content of advertising carry a reassuring message, as tobacco ads did quite explicitly for many years, but the mere existence of publicly sanctioned advertising gives a message of reassurance to youngsters, I would contend, because most would reason that a caring, responsible adult society would protect them from advertisements for anything that is addictive or otherwise dangerous for them. Even the mere legality of a product carries such an implicit message. Put another way, the government itself can take the role of reassurer both by letting a product be sold legally and by allowing it to be legally advertised or promoted in other ways.

The Public Role Models

Aside from the proponents, who actively encourage use, and the reassurers who say or imply that use is safe, there are others in the public eye who simply use drugs and whose use becomes known to broad segments of the public. They thus serve as role models. And there are still others who at the very least condone use, and who let their opinions be known in various ways, thus exerting an opinion-leader function. Such *public role models*, as I call them, can play an important role in the rise and maintenance of an epidemic, and surely did in the most recent one. Indeed, they played an important role in helping to bring drug use ''out of the closet.''

Some even verge on being proponents, and then the proper classification becomes a harder one to make. Paul McCartney's marijuana use, for example, was widely recognized, and the Beatles eulogized LSD use in their immensely popular song ''Lucy in the Sky with Diamonds.'' A great many

---

[3]It might also be noted that one argument that resulted in false reassurance was that a number of drugs—marijuana, peyote, and cocaine in particular—are derived from natural plants and, therefore, were considered somehow safer than synthetics. The argument gained currency, no doubt, because of its concordance with the ''back to nature'' movement of the times.

rock musicians and groups of that period—such as Jefferson Airplane and Jimi Hendrix—kept their drug use, and support of drug use, rather thinly veiled. And whatever veil they had was repeatedly lifted for the public by an unending stream of drug-related arrests, overdose deaths, and lesser emergencies among their number.

During the same period there were also many movies and television entertainment programs that were fairly overt in their condoning of drug use, such as the "Laugh In" series on television and the Cheech and Chong movies. Even a number of apparently "straight" performers, such as Johnny Carson, made light of drug use. More recently—and particularly as a result of the cocaine epidemic—drug use by many professional athletes has become common knowledge.

Athletes, rock musicians, and other entertainers are major influential role models for young people. Their use, or their condoning of use, has an important influence on young people by making drug use seem more acceptable and more "with it." They play a role in increasing both awareness and motivation, providing some reassurance as well as legitimation. And what may be most important is what young people *perceive* to be the practical and moral norms in these groups, regardless of what they actually are. In a recent paper, we reported survey results showing that the majority of young people believe that drug use, and the acceptance of drug use, are still widespread among professional athletes, among actors and actresses, and among rock performers (Johnston, in press). My own belief is that their perceptions greatly exaggerate what exists in reality, and perhaps always have. I hypothesize that this occurs because the few cases that come to light are so magnified by media coverage that young people end up with an exaggerated picture. If I am correct that their perceptions of drug use among these important role model groups are badly distorted and that this distortion may affect their own behavior, this would suggest an area for possible constructive intervention in the future.

The Antagonists

The last public role that I contend can contribute importantly to the rise, as well as the maintenance, of an epidemic is that of the antagonist. This role may not be a necessary one, but it is common and contributory.

For many drugs there were publicly visible antagonists—Harry Anslinger in the case of marijuana during the 1930s and Gabriel Nahas and many others in the 1970s. The effect of the antagonists on the epidemic is not always what they intend it to be: It seems to me that in a number of cases they have had the paradoxical effect of helping to stimulate or sustain the epidemic. The most emotional of the antagonists usually go beyond the realm of knowledge or credibility and have the effect of both solidifying pro-drug forces and sentiment and closing down the channels of communication with the drug-prone part of the population.

The federal government took on the role of antagonist in the early 1970s with a series of anti-drug commercials that came to be seen as untruthful and propagandistic. I believe it had the effect of hardening young peoples' resistance to any messages from "the system" about drugs, including those containing warnings based on fact. Fortunately, the government did the right thing, which was to drop that propaganda effort.

Politicians, too, can take on this role and in the process become negative referent figures for users and potential users in the relevant age groups. Richard Nixon based much of his presidential campaign on the evils of drug use and surely became a negative referent for many young people. I think the jury is still out on whether Nancy Reagan, with her "Just say no" campaign, became a negative referent for some.

It was the opinion of many young people during the early 1970s that the attack on marijuana and other drugs by the antagonists was really an attack on a much broader array of philosophical and political positions they held, and to a considerable degree I believe they were right. This almost surely had the effect of helping to solidify the pro-drug movement.

To sum up this section on social roles in the advent of an epidemic, the proponents and public role models stimulate awareness and increase motivation to use the drug, the reassurers provide the necessary reassurance about its safety, and the antagonists help to consolidate the pro-drug forces and make young people more resistant to cautionary messages. The growing demand resulting from all of these forces undoubtedly leads to a growing profit-driven production and distribution network, which in turn provides access to an ever larger portion of the population.

This series of processes I have described is most clearly observable in the case of marijuana, partly because the proponents, reassurers, antagonists, and public role models are so clearly identifiable. It should be remembered that most of the other drugs to come along got to "draft" behind marijuana, which had made so many young people willing to violate established norms and laws about drug use. Further, by achieving access to marijuana many young people put themselves in ready proximity for access to other drugs and to the modeling of their use. I argue that marijuana played a unique role in this epidemic and that its decline in recent years will play an important role in the decline of the overall epidemic.

OTHER FACILITATING FACTORS
OF THE MOST RECENT EPIDEMIC

In addition to the two historical forces already mentioned—the shift toward innerdirectedness and the increasing youthful alienation—I think the epidemic since the 1960s had other structural and demographic factors that contributed to its size. I only list them here for the sake of brevity.

First, there was a severe erosion in some of the societal institutions that have traditionally socialized young people and provided them with some measure of adult supervision or control. Breakdown of the control exerted by the nuclear family was occurring because of the rising divorce rates and the increase in the proportion of working mothers. The extended family and the community were both somewhat eroded by increased mobility and urbanization. Active membership in formal religious denominations was at a fairly low point historically. And the school systems were stretched by having to deal with much larger numbers of students, as the baby boom passed through adolescence. Somewhat by default, the media, and particularly television, took over much of the critical role of socialization in the society, but unfortunately, it was not an institution very well structured or motivated to promote the goal of responsible and caring socialization.

American young people also had more freedom than ever before in the sense that they more often had cars and a considerable amount of discretionary funds—a condition my colleague, Jerald Bachman (1983), has labeled "premature affluence." Having fewer social constraints and more discretionary resources made it easier for many of them to take up a new type of illicit behavior in the form of drug use.

Finally, it is my belief that American youngsters were growing up in this period with an increased expectation of continual stimulation and instant gratification without the requirement of much effort on their part—fostered largely by television but also by fast food restaurants, video games, fewer responsibilities in the home, and so on. Drug use, of course, is the ultimate in instant gratification without the necessity of intervening effort. In summary, I think there were some important structural, technological, and demographic changes that created a fertile ground in which the drug epidemic could grow, and that still contribute to the maintenance of the epidemic today.

FORCES MAINTAINING AN EPIDEMIC

One could argue that there is a middle phase in the full cycle of an epidemic—one that occurs after the forces that had given rise to it have led a large segment of the population to use drugs, but before the forces that will eventually end it have come into play.

Continuing Awareness and Accessibility

Some of the forces that tend to sustain an epidemic have already been mentioned: the widespread awareness among upcoming birth cohorts of a wide range of behavioral alternatives for altering mood and consciousness, and the widespread accessibility provided by the supply and production system that was spawned by the epidemic in its expansion phase. Once established, organizations tend to seek survival and perpetuation (Katz & Kahn, 1966) and the major drug cartels are no exception to this principle.

Inter-Cohort Role Modeling

Forward momentum is also provided by the large numbers of slightly older youngsters who are users. Put more concretely, there is an ongoing process of extensive role modeling for younger children by older peers and siblings, which for the younger ones has the effect of raising their motivation to use, providing reassurance about consequences, and legitimating the violation of drug-related laws and norms in the larger society.

Institutional Support Mechanisms

Also contributing to the maintenance of the epidemic are the institutional support mechanisms that have evolved—like NORML and magazines such as *High Times*. All of these forces help to maintain the forward momentum of the epidemic. The drug epidemic continued to an impressive extent beyond the life of some of the key forces that had given rise to it—in particular, the counter-culture movement spawned by the Vietnam War. In an earlier paper (Johnston, O'Malley, & Bachman, 1987a), we presented evidence that illicit drug use among American young people is no longer a symbolic expressive behavior—certainly not within the political domain—and thus has become primarily a hedonistic phenomenon.

Continual Introduction of New Drugs

Still another factor that helps to maintain the epidemic is the continual introduction of new drugs onto the scene. These help to sustain interest and replace other drugs that have fallen from popularity. Because a significant number of youth and young adults have already crossed the psychological and social boundaries to using other illicit drugs, there is greater receptiveness to new ones that may be introduced subsequently. The existing distribution system is ready to add new drugs to its product line and thereby provide widespread access to them rather quickly.

Other Factors

Other forces that might also sustain the epidemic are possible. The symbolic expressive value of drugs could have remained longer had the Vietnam War not come to an end, or drug use could have become associated with, or expressive of, other political or philosophical positions. It is also possible that illicit drug using habits could be passed on from generation to generation through intergenerational modeling. Concern has been expressed about the last possibility—that the people who grew up in the drug generation will pass on their drug using habits to their children—but so far I have not seen good evidence to substantiate the case. My own hypothesis is that such effects will be fairly minimal because (a) many users quit themselves later in the life cycle; (b) concern about possible modeling effects leads parents to either quit or conceal their use from their children; and (c) few parents find it acceptable for their children to use drugs even if they did themselves, meaning that the attitudes they pass on are generally not supportive of use.

FORCES LEADING TO THE DECLINE OF AN EPIDEMIC

As we have seen, the use of the different illicit drugs, which has reached epidemic levels among American young people, began to decline at quite different historical points. That suggests that factors specific to those drugs, and not common across the whole illicit drug use epidemic, played important roles in their decline. Two such primary forces are discussed at some length here—one having to do with the loss of reassurance about the safety of using a drug, and one having to do with lowered motivation to attain the psychological experience that the drug, or class of drugs, offers. The loss of reassurance about safety has probably been the most important, and likely will be in future drug epidemics as well.

The Importance of Perceived Risk

During the expansion and maintenance phases of an epidemic of use of a particular drug, the public is reassured about its safety by those who take the public roles of reassurers and also by the substantial number of users who appear to use it without significant physical or psychological damage.[4]

---

[4]The consequences of use may be social as well as physical or psychological, of course. For example, the probability of being caught by various types of authorities (i.e., parents, school authorities, police) is undoubtedly taken into account, as well as the likely severity of the consequences should apprehension occur. But such factors have not been very effective deterrents of behavior so far in the United States because the probability of apprehension was very low and the consequences for possession for personal use relatively limited. (See, e.g., Johnston, O'Malley, & Bachman, 1981.) One reason that the probability of apprehension has been so low was that within the younger age band in the population there was relatively little sympathy with the law—particularly in relation to marijuana and particularly in the earlier years of the epidemic (Johnston et al., 1989).

Deducing from the American experience since the 1960s, we have con-cluded that the decline phase in the use of particular drugs has a great deal to do with the evolution of an awareness of the adverse consequences of use—particularly in relation to physical and psychological health.

This theoretical explanation for the decline of many of the specific drugs is one that we have been developing and empirically substantiating for some years. In a sense, we acted on this hypothesis at the beginning of the study in 1975 by devoting a considerable amount of instrumentation to measur-ing the degree of risk perceived to be associated with various levels of use of the various drugs (Johnston & Bachman, 1980). However, the first confirm-ing evidence did not really begin to accumulate until 1979, when a dramatic increase in the perceived risks of marijuana began to occur among American young people, and simultaneously marijuana use began to drop. It was early in this process that we described perceived risk as the likely deter-mining factor (Johnston, 1982; Johnston, Bachman, & O'Malley, 1981). The evidence was expanded with data on the reasons abstainers and quitters gave for their non-use of marijuana *and* in the trends in the frequency with which they gave those reasons (Johnston, 1982, 1985). Another hypothesis that was advanced in the latter article stated that changes in perceived risk may be driving changes in disapproval (and derivatively, peer norms), be-cause the magnitude of the changes in perceived risk were much greater than those in personal disapproval. Trends in marijuana use and in these attitudes continued to evolve throughout the 1980s in ways consistent with this theoretical position, and we have been able to eliminate one major alternative hypothesis—that changes in access or availability caused the downturn (Johnston et al., 1989). Another alternative hypothesis was ad-dressed in a recent article and found inadequate—namely that a shift among young people toward a more conservative lifestyle could have caused the downturn in use (Bachman, Johnston, O'Malley, & Humphrey, 1988). In that article it was also shown that if one holds constant across time the level of perceived risk, no downturn in use is to be found. In summary, the hypo-thesis about the importance of perceived risk in deterring use has now achieved extensive empirical support, particularly in the case of marijuana. A more detailed summary of that empirical evidence is provided in chap-ter 7, along with some new evidence on the importance of perceived risk.

Unfortunately, the Monitoring the Future study did not include ques-tions about the perceived risk of PCP during the period of its rapid fall, which I am quite sure would have substantiated the same hypothesis in the case of that drug. But the very high level of perceived risk which we found in the mid 1980s for PCP, *after* the period of great decline, is consis-tent with such an interpretation. (In fact, experimenting with PCP is now seen as carrying ''great risk'' by more seniors than any other drug, including heroin; see Table 6.3.)

The more recent epidemic of cocaine use proved stubbornly resistant to societal efforts to control it in the early 1980s. Based on the apparent importance of perceived risk in the downturn in marijuana use (and most likely in the earlier declines in the use of LSD, PCP, and methamphetamines), we predicted that a turnaround in perceived risk would have to occur for cocaine as well if the prevalence of use was to fall (Johnston, O'Malley, & Bachman 1984, 1985). We further expected that it would have to happen for experimental and occasional use, because regular use was already coming to be seen as more dangerous, yet prevalence had not declined (Fig. 6.10). Because very few cocaine users see themselves as regular users—particularly in high school—the attitude shift would have to get closer to the relevant behavior, we reasoned. Between 1986 and 1987, a sharp change occurred in the perceived risk of occasional and experimental use (Fig. 6.9) and, as predicted, the prevalence of use began to fall (Fig. 6.5). Both trends continued in 1988. This gives further support for the theory, and suggests an elaboration, namely, that it is the level of use most commonly adopted for which perceived risk is most relevant for changing behavior. A shift in perceived risk of regular use was relevant for marijuana because so many young people were regular users. (Current daily use stood at 11% among seniors in 1978; see Fig. 6.10.) On the other hand, the perceived risk of regular use for cocaine did not translate into changed use levels because very few were regular users. This derivative hypothesis is consistent with the findings of the more general attitude change literature, which shows that attitudes are more likely to affect behavior to the extent that they are specific to the behavior (e.g., Ajzen & Fishbein, 1977).

Another hypothesis that is derived from the marijuana and cocaine experiences is that it is perceived risk of regular use that is likely to move

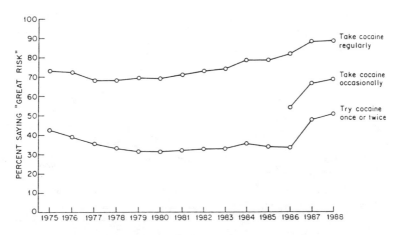

FIG. 6.9. Trends in perceived harmfulness: Cocaine (all seniors).

first, to be followed later by similar changes in the perceived risk of occasional use and experimental use. Because experimental and occasional use are necessary steps along the pathway to regular use, which in turn may carry risks of habituation or addiction, it seems logical that if regular use comes to be seen as more dangerous, so will the intervening steps associated with getting to that stage.

Still another hypothesis derived largely from this experience is that during the decline phase in the epidemic of a given drug, those subgroups—whether defined in terms of demographics or lifestyle variables—which have attained the highest levels of use will tend to show the greatest rate of decline (assuming that addiction has not widely occurred). We have reported such findings in relation to gender, region, and urbanicity (Johnston et al., 1989) and in relation to religiosity, grades, and time spent out of the home (Bachman et al., 1988).

Concordance With the Health Belief Model

Many of the findings presented here regarding the importance of perceived risk as a deterrent to the use of a drug, fit nicely into the more general theoretical framework of the Health Belief Model (Janz & Becker, 1984; Maiman & Becker, 1974; Rosenstock, 1974). The Health Belief Model was developed over the last 40 years to help explain and predict people's behavior in the domains of disease prevention, medical care utilization, delays in seeking medical care, and compliance with medical regimens. It was used for the most part to understand how best to get people to *under-*

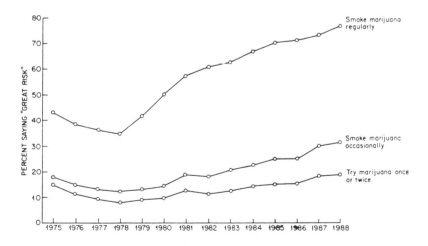

FIG. 6.10.   Trends in perceived harmfulness: Marijuana (all seniors).

take some behaviors that would be disease-preventing in their effect, so it is different in that regard from the domain of behavior under discussion here—illicit drug use—where the goal is to get people to *desist* or *abstain* from certain behaviors. Still, the major motivation of the behavior is the prevention of morbidity and mortality, and the major influences on behavior are posited to be perceived threat or danger, and perceived personal susceptibility.

Within the Health Belief Model, the principal determinants of an individual's readiness to take particular actions to avoid a disease are (a) the perceived seriousness or severity of the disease or condition, (b) the person's perceived susceptibility or vulnerability to that disease, or condition, and (c) the person's belief that the particular action is feasible and would be efficacious in reducing susceptibility or severity. Obstacles to, or costs of, the avoidance behavior are also taken into account. The theory also holds that cues to action, or triggers, are important to instigating the behavior, once the necessary beliefs about severity, susceptibility, and the benefits are in place. The cue or stimulus may be internal, such as a symptom or perception of a body state, or external—from the mass media, interpersonal communication, and so on (Maiman & Becker, 1974; Rosenstock, 1974).

In the cases of both marijuana and cocaine, it would appear that young people's assessment of the severity of the consequences that can follow from use have changed. Cocaine, for example, is now widely acknowledged to have the potential for addiction and for death from overdose—beliefs that were not widely held, even among professionals in the field, as recently as the late 1970s. Perceived susceptibility has also changed in that the perceived probability of such severe consequences has risen even for experimental and occasional use. Thus, dangers previously seen as relevant only to heavy users, which probably very few young people ever expected to become, are now seen as relevant to lighter users, which many more of them are. In this case, the efficacy of the preventive behavior in question—namely, quitting or abstaining from use—is fairly obvious, and really need not be demonstrated.

So, although abstaining from drug use does not fit the mold of positive behavior aimed at preventing disease which is typical of the Health Belief Model, nor are all of the positive goal states sought relevant to disease (e.g., goals such as compliance with the law, with parental wishes, or with changing peer norms), this model does have a considerable amount of applicability to the phenomenon under study here. Of particular relevance, perhaps, is the application of rational decision-making processes in the explanation of much adolescent drug-using behavior. (Maiman & Baker, 1974, present a comparison and integration of the Health Belief Model with six other psychological theories of decision making.)

A Possible Case of Reversed Effects of Perceived Risk

Before leaving the role of perceived risk in the decline phase of a number of drugs, I would like to mention that this model—and the Health Belief Model more generally—is based on the assumption that a considerable portion of the user and potential-user populations are motivated to protect their own health and will act rationally toward that end. In other words, an increase in the perceived dangers of a drug will motivate them to abstain from use or cease it. The data from the Drug Abuse Warning Network, however, show that even when the dangers of a drug become widely recognized—as in the case of PCP—there are still significant pockets of use in certain inner-city populations. It is my hypothesis that in some youth populations—particularly inner city males who spend a lot of time on the street—the risks associated with a drug have little or no deterrent value, either because their motivation to protect their health is lower generally, or more likely, because using such drugs is seen as an effective way to express one's fearless and "macho" nature.[5] (Put in terms of the Health Belief Model, it may amount to an unrealistic denial of personal susceptibility.) Such beliefs may actually make such drug use *more* likely, by defining use as a "macho" statement. If I am right in this regard, it would help to explain why some of the most dangerous forms of drug use—heroin, PCP, and crack, for example—appear to occur disproportionately in these populations. It might also suggest that prevention efforts in these areas need to be directed more at challenging the notion that using such drugs is macho than at solely emphasizing the dangers of the drugs.

PUBLIC ROLES IN THE DECLINE PHASE OF AN EPIDEMIC

The time it takes for the population to come to recognize the risk of a drug and begin to modify its behavior accordingly depends in large part on the functioning of people in three additional social roles of importance to a drug epidemic—the knowledge providers, the educators, and the unfortunate public role models.

The Knowledge Providers

The knowledge providers are the clinicians, social scientists, and biomedical scientists who give rise to a body of factual information about the consequences of using a drug. Probably most of that information is accurate,

---

[5]In Washington, DC PCP is known on the street as "Saint Elizabeth's," after the Federal mental hospital to which so many PCP users get taken. Obviously these youngsters know something about the extremely adverse consequences of this drug, but still a number of them continue to use it.

although I do not assume that it need be to have an impact. Although the effects of this knowledge are important, the occupants of these roles are usually not publicly visible figures. Nevertheless, they play an important function in reversing an epidemic by providing the knowledge base necessary for later persuasive communication.

Institutional mechanisms in turn play a key role in developing this knowledge base, because government agencies like the National Institute on Drug Abuse set funding levels and priorities for the work of the knowledge providers. Data-collection systems such as the Drug Abuse Warning Network and the cocaine hotlines also provide important clinical data about the rates at which various kinds of clinical consequences occur for the various drugs. These, too, add to the knowledge base of relevance.

The relative importance of the clinical data versus data coming from experimental or large epidemiological studies depends partly on the nature of the effects of the drug. To the extent that the effects are short-term or acute, that is, they occur during or immediately following ingestion (e.g., as in the case of PCP), clinicians dealing with emergency medicine are likely to be the ones to sound the alarm first. To the extent that the effects are long-term, and to the extent that they occur with relatively low probability (e.g., as in the case of cigarettes), it is more likely to be the epidemiologists or biomedical scientists who establish convincing evidence of the dangers involved.

The Educators

Within the present theoretical framework the educators are those individuals, groups, and organizations who disseminate to the public what the knowledge providers have found. In other words, they make the public aware of the hazards of drug use—particularly the addiction, and other physical and psychological hazards. (Often the antagonists attempt to play this role but, as I have said, they are usually unsuccessful because their objectivity, and therefore their credibility, becomes questioned.) The educators might be recognized public figures, but during this epidemic they have mostly been people not in the public eye.

One important group of educators is comprised of those in the media who package and present new knowledge to the public in a variety of ways, such as in news programs, dramatic programs, documentary specials, and so on. Such media coverage of drugs and their hazards—in particular, marijuana and cocaine—has been particularly ubiquitous since the late 1970s. In recent years the media have also played a more conscious and intentional role as educators through their public service advertising campaigns against drug use. The National Institute on Drug Abuse disseminated the ad campaign entitled "Cocaine: the Big Lie" with the help of the Advertising Council, and the National Media-Advertising Partnership was formed to develop an ongoing series of campaigns that have focused on marijuana and cocaine. They run the risk of acquiring the role of untrustworthy antagonists, rather than that of educators, but so far our evidence suggests that they have maintained a high level of credibility with their intended audience (Johnston, in press).

Scientific and governmental organizations may also play important intervening roles between the knowledge providers and the educators in compiling and giving credibility to a body of knowledge. Recent examples would include the summary reports by the Institute of Medicine (1982) and Canada's Addiction Research Foundation (1981) with regards to the health consequences of marijuana.

Of course, outside of the public media, important educator roles are played by schools and parents and youth organizations in teaching young people face-to-face about the hazards of various drugs. Their effectiveness no doubt depends in part on the knowledge base to which they have access and on their credibility, just as does the effectiveness of the more public educator figures. It may never be possible to separate out the relative importance of these different educator groups in bringing about the changed beliefs about the dangers of drug use that we observe among young people. Nevertheless, it seems to me likely that they have a synergistic effect to the extent that each tends to reinforce the cautionary messages youth receive from the other educator groups.[6]

Unfortunate Public Role Models

Finally, the education of the public may also be carried out in an unintentional way by those whose adverse consequences from drug use serve as object lessons for large segments of the population. These are the public role models who get into trouble with drugs and thus provide an opportunity for vicarious learning by the general public. Overdose deaths of public figures like rock stars and actors likely had some educational effects, although because many of these have involved heroin—and because heroin has long been seen as very dangerous—they may not have had a great impact. On the other hand, the cocaine-related deaths of athletes Len Bias and Don Rogers in 1986 were initially thought to be related to casual cocaine use, and because these levels of cocaine use were not widely assumed

---

[6]Note that I have emphasized here only one of the traditional functions of educators, broadly defined—that of communicating knowledge about the consequences of drug use. There are a number of important functions they play in relation to drug use, not the least of which is social skills training.

to be dangerous (Johnston et al., 1989), these deaths very likely had considerable impact. Certainly our evidence on trends is consistent with that interpretation (see Table 6.4). Put another way, vicarious learning about the hazards of drugs can occur both in the public arena, as well as in one's own role set as discussed earlier. Within the context of the Health Belief Model, these highly public events may have served as the "cues" or social stimuli needed to precipitate changes in behavior for many young people. The more day-to-day events, described as the work of the educators, through the mass media and elsewhere, may also provide these stimuli, although the importance of such a cuing function may be less in the arena of drug use than in other areas addressed by the Health Belief Model, because it is not the undertaking of a behavior that is to be brought about by the educators—as is usually true under the Health Belief Model—but rather the avoidance of a behavior.

Public Roles and the Lag Time in Knowledge Development and Dissemination

It is unfortunately the case that the time lag between the onset of the widespread use of a drug in the population and the accumulation of evidence about adverse consequences can be a long one. Most often the clinical and scientific data needed from the knowledge providers by the educators is not gathered until the epidemic is already occurring—partly because the clinical evidence may take some time to accrue if there is much of a time lag between the initiation of use and the occurrence of the adverse consequences, and partly because the planned scientific laboratory or epidemiological studies may not be initiated in great number until the drug is identified as having attained some appreciable level of use in the population. Those studies then have their own time lag to completion.

As was mentioned earlier, cigarettes probably illustrate the extreme case in the time required for the knowledge providers to gather the necessary evidence on the consequences to deter use, and this was because the effects come almost entirely from chronic use. Most of the illicit drugs took less time for their adverse consequences to be recognized. Still, in the case of cocaine, although the epidemic of use began about 1976, it was not until the early 1980s that enough clinical and other scientific evidence accumulated so that the educators could begin to drown out the reassurers in their calls for caution. This happened because there tends to be quite a long time lag, on the order of 6 or 7 years, between the initiation of use and the development of addiction and other severe consequences (Gold, 1984). Marijuana also had quite a long delay between the onset of an epidemic of use (in the late 1960s) and the accumulation of convincing evi-

TABLE 6.4

Trends in Annual Prevalence of 18 Types of Drugs

Percentage who used in last 12 months

	Class of 1975	Class of 1976	Class of 1977	Class of 1978	Class of 1979	Class of 1980	Class of 1981	Class of 1982	Class of 1983	Class of 1984	Class of 1985	Class of 1986	Class of 1987	Class of 1988	'87-'88 Change
Approx. N =	(9,400)	(15,400)	(17,100)	(17,800)	(15,500)	(15,900)	(17,500)	(17,700)	(16,300)	(15,900)	(16,000)	(15,200)	(16,300)	(16,300)	
Marijuana/Hashish[a]	40.0	44.5	47.6	50.2	50.8	48.8	46.1	44.3	42.3	40.0	40.6	38.8	36.3	33.1	-3.2sss
Inhalants[a]	NA	3.0	3.7	4.1	5.4	4.6	4.1	4.5	4.3	5.1	5.7	6.1	6.9	6.5	-0.4
Inhalants Adjusted[b]	NA	NA	NA	NA	8.9	7.9	6.1	6.6	6.2	7.2	7.5	8.9	8.1	7.1	-1.0
Amyl & Butyl Nitrites[c,h]	NA	NA	NA	NA	6.5	5.7	3.7	3.6	3.6	4.0	4.0	4.7	2.6	1.7	-0.9s
Hallucinogens	11.2	9.4	8.8	9.6	9.9	9.3	9.0	8.1	7.3	6.5	6.3	6.0	6.4	5.5	-0.9s
Hallucinogens Adjusted[d]	NA	NA	NA	NA	11.8	10.4	10.1	9.0	8.3	7.3	7.6	7.6	6.7	5.8	-0.9
LSD	7.2	6.4	5.5	6.3	6.6	6.5	6.5	6.1	5.4	4.7	4.4	4.5	5.2	4.8	-0.4
PCP[c,h]	NA	NA	NA	NA	7.0	4.4	3.2	2.2	2.6	2.3	2.9	2.4	1.3	1.2	-0.1
Cocaine	5.6	6.0	7.2	9.0	12.0	12.3	12.4	11.5	11.4	11.6	13.1	12.7	10.3	7.9	-2.4sss
"Crack"[g]	NA	NA	NA	NA	NA	NA	NA	NA	NA	N A	NA	4.1	4.0	3.1	-0.9s
Other cocaine[c]	NA	NA	NA	NA	NA	NA	NA	NA	NA	N A	NA	NA	9.8	7.4	-2.4ss
Heroin	1.0	0.8	0.8	0.8	0.5	0.5	0.5	0.6	0.6	0.5	0.6	0.5	0.5	0.5	0.0
Other opiates[e]	5.7	5.7	6.4	6.0	6.2	6.3	5.9	5.3	5.1	5.2	5.9	5.2	5.3	4.6	-0.7s
Stimulants[e]	16.2	15.8	16.3	17.1	18.3	20.8	26.0	26.1	24.6	NA	NA	NA	NA	NA	NA
Stimulants Adjusted[e,f]	NA	NA	NA	NA	NA	NA	NA	20.3	17.9	17.7	15.8	13.4	12.2	10.9	-1.3s
Sedatives[e]	11.7	10.7	10.8	9.9	9.9	10.3	10.5	9.1	7.9	6.6	5.8	5.2	4.1	3.7	-0.4
Barbiturates[e]	10.7	9.6	9.3	8.1	7.5	6.8	6.6	5.5	5.2	4.9	4.6	4.2	3.6	3.2	-0.4
Methaqualone[e]	5.1	4.7	5.2	4.9	5.9	7.2	7.6	6.8	5.4	3.8	2.8	2.1	1.5	1.3	-0.2
Tranquilizers[e]	10.6	10.3	10.8	9.9	9.6	8.7	8.0	7.0	6.9	6.1	6.1	5.8	5.5	4.8	-0.7
Alcohol	84.8	85.7	87.0	87.7	88.1	87.9	87.0	86.8	87.3	86.0	85.6	84.5	85.7	85.3	-0.4
Cigarettes	NA	NA	NA	NA	NA	NA	NA	NA	NA	NA	NA	NA	NA	NA	NA

Notes: Level of significance of difference between the two most recent classes: s = .05, ss = .01, sss = .001. NA indicates data not available.
[a]Data based on four questionnaire forms. N is four-fifths of N indicated.
[b]Adjusted for underreporting of amyl and butyl nitrites.
[c]Data based on a single questionnaire form. N is one-fifth of N indicated.
[d]Adjusted for underreporting of PCP.
[e]Only drug use which was not under a doctor's orders is included here.
[f]Based on the data from the revised question, which attempts to exclude the inappropriate reporting of nonprescription stimulants.
[g]Data based on a single questionnaire form in 1986 (N is one-fifth of N indicated), and on two questionnaire forms in 1987 (N is two-fifths of N indicated).
[h]Question text changed slightly in 1987.

dence about its potential hazards (by the late 1970s), and even now many questions about the effects of long-term use remain unanswered.

Not all drugs took so long for evidence to accumulate about their adverse effects. Methamphetamine got a bad name on the street early in the epidemic as word got out that "speed kills." LSD use began to fall in the early 1970s as concerns about the possible dangers of chromosomal and brain damage spread. It is quite possible that this new "knowledge" was, in fact, wrong, but it had the same effect nonetheless, because it was believed. Concern about "flashback" experiences with LSD also mounted. In the mid to late 1970s a new drug, PCP (phencyclidine), entered the scene and rose rapidly in popularity as its proponents spoke glowingly of its benefits. But its capacity to lead people to violent and sometimes self-destructive behavior became known within a few years, because these are acute effects, not long-term ones, and, as a result, its popularity plummeted as fast as it had risen (see Fig. 6.4). In the mid-1980s crack cocaine began to rise in popularity fairly suddenly, as awareness of the drug spread rapidly, as did widespread access to it (Johnston et al., 1989). In this case, the evidence of its addictive potential accumulated quite quickly, because the "honeymoon period" for crack is relatively short, and word of its dangers was carried in a great surge of media coverage in 1986 (Merriam, 1989). The Monitoring the Future data suggest that crack use leveled among seniors by 1987—and started to decline in 1988. The fact that this turnaround started only a couple of years after the epidemic of crack use took hold may make it one of this society's most successful experiences in controlling the epidemic of use of an illicit drug. The knowledge base on its hazards accumulated quickly—not because of the rapid application of planned research but because the drug's very short time to addiction quickly generated convincing clinical evidence. The media then virtually flew with the story and, judging by our data on the perceived risks of crack (see Table 6.3), the message was indeed convincing to young people.

OTHER FACTORS CONTRIBUTING TO THE RECENT DECLINES

I am not suggesting that perceived risk is the major corrective force for all drugs—just that it has the potential to be a powerful corrective force for many drugs for which the knowledge base about risks has yet to accumulate. Several other factors are suggested here.

Two psychotherapeutic drugs for which we have long-term information on both use and perceived risk—amphetamines and barbiturates—have both shown significant declines, but there is very little evidence that shifts in perceived risks have been the determining factors. The annual prevalence of barbiturate use fell by two thirds between 1978 and 1987, yet perceived risk actually fell a little during that interval, instead of rising. It did not begin to rise until 1987 (Table 6.3), which may have resulted from the health concerns about marijuana, cocaine, and crack beginning to generalize to all illicit drugs. It could also be argued that the decreasing number of users provided less collective reassurance for possible new recruits. Amphetamine use began its decline considerably later—after 1982—but the sharp drop in use between 1982 and 1986 was not accompanied by any change in perceived risk. Again, perceived risk did not begin to rise until 1987. Nor did the norms regarding the use of these two drugs shift much before 1986 (Table 6.2). As mentioned earlier, because these are established psychotherapeutic drugs, it would seem likely that their risks have been fairly accurately known for some time.

A Possible Substitution Across Drugs

It thus appears that other factors contributed to the decline in the use of these two drugs. According to the trend data on perceived availability, it does not appear that any significant change in access occurred either, and surely awareness of these drugs remained widespread. In the case of amphetamines it could be that those most interested in the effects obtained with stimulant drugs chose cocaine over amphetamines—particularly as the price of cocaine declined—although the cross-time trend curves for amphetamines and cocaine do not show reciprocal trends: both were rising in popularity in the late 1970s, and cocaine use remained relatively stable in the early to mid-1980s when amphetamine use was dropping. However, it might be argued that cocaine would have begun to decline earlier had there not been some shifting over from amphetamine to cocaine use. Although it is not entirely clear at this point whether substitution or other factors account for the considerable decline in amphetamine use in recent years, it is useful to be reminded that substitution of one drug for another can be the cause of such a decline.

Reduced Motivation to Attain the Drug's Effects

One set of factors not discussed up to this point are the reinforcing properties of the drugs themselves. These obviously differ dramatically across drugs in both quantitative and qualitative terms. Put another way, different drugs are used to attain quite different psychological states (e.g., Johnston & O'Malley, 1986), and it is quite conceivable that young peoples' desire or motivation to achieve those states will vary over time. This may well explain why barbiturates and tranquilizers have been declining steadily in popularity since the mid-1970s, because both are central nervous system (CNS) depressants. Heroin use also fell by half, to virtually trace levels among seniors, in the latter half of the 1970s. (Methaqualone, another CNS depressant, rose slightly in popularity in the late 1970s—quite likely because it was used in conjunction with cocaine, which was also rising then—but its use also has fallen quite dramatically, since 1980.[7]) I am inclined to conclude from these several facts that the demand for illicit CNS depressants in general declined because young people became less interested in attaining their effects. In other words, there was a decline in demand which was not driven by perceived risks, or by availability. Were we to enter another historical period like the Vietnam era, which was both very painful and very anxiety provoking for young people, I would predict that CNS depressants may well rise again in popularity.[8]

Factors Influencing the Overall Epidemic

There were some additional factors that have played a role in the decline in the proportion of young people using drugs, other than the increases in perceived risk for a number of drugs (and, in particular, the lead drug, marijuana) or a decrease in interest in particular drug effects. Perhaps most important was the passing of the Vietnam War and the alienated, youthful, counter-culture to which it gave rise. The Woodstock generation has grown up and the symbolic value of drug use among youth has dissipated. Also of importance in my opinion, but hard to demonstrate empirically, was the wearing off of the "fad" quality of drug use—it simply no longer was something new and outrageous; thus some of the other social and symbolic gains from use have also dissipated. For as long as the current cohorts of adolescents can remember, American adolescents have been using drugs.

The severe recession of the early 1980s brought about a shortage of entry level jobs for the baby-boom generation, which I believe caused greater concern with job attainment and, derivatively, school performance. Drug use tends to be seen as inimical to good performance in school. Finally, a healthy lifestyle movement was evolving in the country in the early 1980s, which may have made the health consequences of drug use all the more

---

[7]It is true that the legal manufacture of methaqualone ceased in the early 1980s, but had there been a strong demand, it seems likely that an illicit production or importation system would quickly have evolved to provide a ready supply.

[8]One might well ask why demand for alcohol did not decline steadily across the same period since it too is a CNS depressant. The major differences, it would seem, are that alcohol use has many social benefits associated with it and an industry constantly promoting it. It is also a traditionally accepted behavior, modeled and condoned by older age groups. Even in the case of alcohol, there has been some gradual decline in use in recent years.

salient. I believe all of these forces—issues of war and peace, economic prosperity and recession, and general shifts in lifestyle—influence levels of illicit drug use, and often in ways that we never really quantify very accurately. Nevertheless, they should be recognized as potentially important factors in the beginning of the decline phase of this epidemic, and as examples of potentially important classes of variables that may influence future ones.

Finally, there may be some evidence that the bad reputation being acquired by some of the most popular drugs—in particular, marijuana and cocaine—may be generalizing to the full range of illicit drugs. It also appears that the normative constraints against illicit drug use, which eroded so badly among young people in the 1960s and 1970s, are returning (as evidenced both by a hardening of peer norms across the board and by increased support for legal restraints on the use of drugs; Johnston et al., 1989). These should help to reduce the proportion of youth willing to try or use any of the illicit drugs, regardless of their perceived dangers.

SUMMARY

I have tried to offer a theory—derived largely from the American drug epidemic since the 1960s—which accounts for both an overall epidemic and for changes in the use of specific drugs. Forces contributing to three general phases—expansion, maintenance, and decline—have been described. A set of necessary conditions for expansion was postulated: awareness, access, motivation, reassurance, and willingness to violate certain laws and predominant social mores. Four public social roles which help to bring about these conditions for various drugs were also postulated: the proponents, the reassurers, the public role models, and the antagonists.

A number of forces were put forward to explain how the forward momentum of an epidemic continues, even beyond the point where some of the historical forces that gave rise to it (e.g., the Vietnam War) have ceased to exist. These included continued awareness of alternatives, continued access through a supply system that has become established and that seeks to perpetuate itself, and continual inter-cohort role modeling for younger adolescents by slightly older ones.

Finally, it is argued that the decline phase for many drugs occurs as a result of users and potential users becoming increasingly aware of the hazards of use. This interpretation can be construed as a specific application of the Health Belief Model, which has been used to explain health-motivated behavior in a number of other domains. Three public social roles were posited as being important to bringing about such an increase in perceived risk: the knowledge providers, the educators, and the unfortunate public role models. It is argued that as perceived risk increases, use declines, as well as tolerance for use.

It was pointed out that an increase in perceived risk cannot account for the decline in the use of all drugs, and also may not be enough to cause a decline in all subpopulations. In particular, a decline in motivation to achieve the effects obtained with CNS depressants is hypothesized as accounting for declines in the use of tranquilizers, barbiturates, methaqualone, and possibly heroin. Nevertheless, an increased concern about the dangers of use appears to have been a critical factor in the general decline of several very important drugs; in particular, marijuana, cocaine, crack cocaine specifically, LSD, and PCP.

REFERENCES

Addiction Research Foundation. (1981). *Report of an ARF/WHO scientific meeting on adverse health and behavioral consequences of cannabis use.* Toronto, Ontario, Canada: Author.

Ashley, R. (1975). *Cocaine: Its history, uses and effects.* New York: St. Martin's Press.

Ajzen, I., & Fishbein, M. (1977). Attitude-behavior relationships: A theoretical analysis and review of empirical research. *Psychological Bulletin, 84,* 888–918.

Bachman, J. G. (1983). Premature affluence: Do high school students earn too much? *Economic Outlook U.S.A., 10*(3), 64–67.

Bachman, J. G., Johnston, L. D., O'Malley, P. M., & Humphrey, R. H. (1988). Explaining the recent decline in marijuana use: Differentiating the effects of perceived risks, disapproval, and general lifestyle factors. *Journal of Health and Social Behavior, 29,* 92–112.

Clark, J. W., & Levine, E. L. (1971). Marijuana use, social discontent, and political alienation: A study of high school youth. *American Political Science Review, 65,* 120–130.

Cocaine behavior: "Recreational" sniffing found no riskier than alcohol or tobacco; heavy use "enslaving." (1982, February 25). *Washington Post,* pp. A1, A2.

The cocaine scene: What the doctors say. (1977, May 30). *Newsweek,* pp. 20–22, 25.

deAlarcon, R. (1969). The spread of heroin abuse in a community. *Bulletin of Narcotics, 21*(3), 17–22.

Gold, M. S. (1984). *800-COCAINE.* New York: Bantam.

Grinspoon, L. (1971). *Marijuana reconsidered.* Cambridge, MA: Harvard University Press.

Institute of Medicine. (1982). *Marijuana and health.* Washington, DC: National Academy Press.

Janz, N. K., & Becker, M. H. (1984). The health belief model: A decade later. *Health Education Quarterly, 11*(1), 1–47.

Jessor, R., & Jessor, S. L. (1977). *Problem behavior and psychological development: A longitudinal study of youth.* New York: Academic Press.

Johnston, L. D. (1973). *Drugs and American youth.* Ann Arbor, MI: Institute for Social Research.

Johnston, L. D. (1982). A review and analysis of recent changes in marijuana use by American young people. In *Marijuana: The national impact on education* (pp. 8–13). New York: American Council on Marijuana.

Johnston, L. D. (1985). The etiology and prevention of substance use: What can we learn from recent changes? In C. L. Jones & R. J. Battjes (Eds.), *Etiology of drug abuse: Implications for prevention* (NIDA Research Monograph No. 56, DHHS Publication No. (ADM) 85-1335, pp. 155–177). Washington, DC: U.S. Government Printing Office.

Johnston, L. D. (in press). The interface between epidemiology and prevention. In W. Bukoski (Ed.), *Drug abuse prevention research: Methodological issues* (NIDA Research Monograph). Washington, DC: National Institute on Drug Abuse.

Johnston, L. D., & Bachman, J. G. (1980). *Monitoring the future: Questionnaire responses from the nation's high school seniors, 1975.* Ann Arbor, MI: Institute for Social Research.

Johnston, L. D., Bachman, J. G., & O'Malley, P. M. (1981). *Highlights from student drug use in America, 1975–1981.* Rockville, MD: National Institute on Drug Abuse.

Johnston, L. D., & Harrison, L. D. (1984, September). *An international perspective on alcohol and drug use among youth.* Paper presented at the Swedish Academy of Medical Sciences' Third International Berzelius Symposium, Stockholm, Sweden.

Johnston, L. D., & O'Malley, P. M. (1986). Why do the nation's students use drugs and alcohol? Self-reported reasons from nine national surveys. *Journal of Drug Issues, 16,* 29–66.

Johnston, L. D., O'Malley, P. M., & Bachman, J. G. (1981). *Marijuana decriminalization: The impact on youth, 1975–1980* (Monitoring the Future Occasional Paper No. 13). Ann Arbor, MI: Institute for Social Research.

Johnston, L. D., O'Malley, P. M., & Bachman, J. G. (1984). *Highlights from drugs and American high school students: 1975–1983.* Rockville, MD: National Institute on Drug Abuse.

Johnston, L. D., O'Malley, P. M., & Bachman, J. G. (1985). *Use of licit and illicit drugs by America's high school students: 1975–1984.* Rockville, MD: National Institute on Drug Abuse.

Johnston, L. D., O'Malley, P. M., & Bachman, J. G. (1987a, October). *Lifestyle orientations in late adolescence and patterns of substance abuse.* Paper presented at the Sixth Annual Scientific Symposia of the American College of Epidemiology, New Orleans, LA.

Johnston, L. D., O'Malley, P. M., & Bachman, J. G. (1987b). *National trends in drug use and related factors among American high school students and young adults, 1975–1986.* Rockville, MD: National Institute on Drug Abuse.

Johnston, L. D., O'Malley, P. M., & Bachman, J. G. (1987c). Psychotherapeutic, licit, and illicit use of drugs among adolescents: An epidemiologic perspective. *Journal of Adolescent Health Care, 8,* 36–51.

Johnston, L. D., O'Malley, P. M., & Bachman, J. G. (1989). *Drug use, drinking, and smoking: National survey results from high school, college, and young adult populations, 1975–1988.* Rockville, MD: National Institute on Drug Abuse.

Kandel, D. B. (1975). Stages in adolescent involvement in drug use. *Science, 190,* 912–914.

Katz, D., & Kahn, R. L. (1966). *The social psychology of organizations.* New York: Wiley.

Maiman, L. A., & Becker, M. H. (1974). The health belief model: Origins and correlates in psychological theory. *Health Education Monographs, 2*(4), 336–353.

Merriam, J. E. (1989). National media coverage of drug issues, 1983–1987. In P. J. Shoemaker (Ed.), *Communication campaigns about drugs: Government, media, and the public* (pp. 21–28). Hillsdale, NJ: Lawrence Erlbaum Associates.

Miller, J. D., Cisin, I. H., Gardner-Keaton, H., Harrell, A. V., Wirtz, P. W., Abelson, H. I., & Fishburne, P. M. (1983). *National survey on drug abuse: Main findings, 1982.* Rockville, MD: National Institute on Drug Abuse.

O'Donnell, J. A., Voss, H. L., Clayton, R. R., Slatin, G., & Room, R. G. W. (1976). *Young men and drugs—A nationwide survey* (NIDA Research Monograph No. 5). Washington, DC: U.S. Government Printing Office.

Osgood, D. W., Johnston, L. D., O'Malley, P. M., & Bachman, J. G. (1988). The generality of deviance in late adolescence and early adulthood. *American Sociological Review, 53,* 81–93.

Rosenstock, I. M. (1974). Historical origins of the health belief model. *Health Education Monographs, 2*(4), 328–335.

Smart, R. G., & Murray, G. F. (1981). A review of trends in alcohol and cannabis use among young people. *Bulletin on Narcotics, 33,* 77–99.

Suchman, E. A. (1968). The "hang-loose" ethic and the spirit of drug use. *Journal of Health and Social Behavior, 9,* 146–155.

United Nations, Division of Narcotic Drugs. (1987). Review of drug abuse and measures to reduce the illicit demand for drugs by region. *Bulletin on Narcotics, 39*(1), 3–30.

Weil, A., & Rosen, W. (1983). *Chocolate to morphine: Understanding mind-active drugs.* Boston, MA: Houghton Mifflin.

Zinberg, N. E., & Robertson, J. A. (1972). *Drugs and the public.* New York: Simon & Schuster.

How Changes in Drug Use are Linked to Perceived Risks and Disapproval: Evidence From National Studies That Youth and Young Adults Respond to Information About the Consequences of Drug Use

Jerald G. Bachman
Lloyd D. Johnston
Patrick M. O'Malley
The University of Michigan

Some years ago the "conventional wisdom" in the drug abuse prevention field was that "information alone is not effective in influencing behavior, and that negative information or 'scare tactics' are especially ineffective" (Jessor, 1985, p. 258). Although we agree that obvious scare tactics may not be effective, recent findings suggest that in most other respects the conventional wisdom once again turns out to be unwise. In this chapter we summarize a growing body of evidence that supports our belief that large proportions of youth and young adults are, in fact, responsive to information about the risks and consequences of drug use.

The first line of evidence involves the downturn in the use of marijuana during the last decade. We reported some years ago that increased awareness of risk accompanied (or slightly preceded) the decline in marijuana use, and we offered the rather straightforward hypothesis that the more danger young people associate with a drug, the less likely they will be to use it (Johnston, 1982; Johnston, Bachman, & O'Malley, 1981). More recently we examined in considerable detail the ways in which perceived risk and disapproval are related to marijuana use (Bachman, Johnston, O'Malley, & Humphrey, 1988). Most recently we have applied the same type of analysis to cocaine use (Bachman, Johnston, & O'Malley, 1990). In our present summary of key findings we have borrowed extensively from the latter two reports.

Still another line of evidence comes from work currently underway, extending our earlier analyses of links between changes in drug use and post-high school experiences (Bachman, O'Malley, & Johnston, 1984). The earlier work found that a number of changes in drug use were linked primarily to living arrangements, and the current work continues to find such patterns. But additional findings that are particularly relevant to the present topic have emerged. We have uncovered declines in drug use that were directly linked to pregnancy, and that were generally much larger than the changes linked to other post-high school experiences.

EXPLAINING THE RECENT DECLINES
IN MARIJUANA AND COCAINE USE

The most widely used of the illicit drugs during recent decades has been marijuana. Rates of use rose during the 1960s and most of the 1970s, so that by 1979 fully two thirds of young adults (age 18–25), and nearly as many high school seniors, reported some consumption of the drug. However, 1979 marked something of a turning point, and during the 1980s marijuana use among young people declined steadily (Fishburne, Abelson, & Cisin, 1980; Johnston, O'Malley, & Bachman, 1988; National Institute on Drug Abuse, 1988; O'Malley, Bachman, & Johnston, 1988). The use of the more dangerous illicit drug cocaine followed a somewhat different trajectory: Prevalence rose during the late 1970s, remained relatively unchanged during the first half of the 1980s, and only very recently showed clear signs of a decline (Johnston et al., 1988).

Although the declines in usage rates of marijuana and cocaine began at clearly different points in time, they have two very important features in common: (a) each was accompanied, or slightly preceded, by increases in perceived risks and disapproval; and (b) neither was accompanied by any decline in perceived availability of the drug. This is evident in Figs. 7.1 and 7.2, which display trend data based on the high school senior classes of 1976 through 1988.

The findings in Figs. 7.1 and 7.2, and those presented in the rest of this chapter, are from the Monitoring the Future project, which annually administers questionnaires to nationally representative samples of high school seniors. Data on drug use are obtained from about 16,000 to 17,000 respondents each year, whereas data on perceptions and attitudes about drugs are obtained from subsamples of about 3,000 each year. The study design has been described extensively elsewhere (e.g., Bachman & Johnston, 1978; Johnston, O'Malley, & Bachman, 1988), and the methods underlying these particular analyses are detailed in other reports (Bachman et al., 1988; Bachman et al., 1990).

The trends for marijuana, shown in Fig. 7.1, show the strong reciprocal relationship between the steady rises in perceived risk (beginning in 1979)

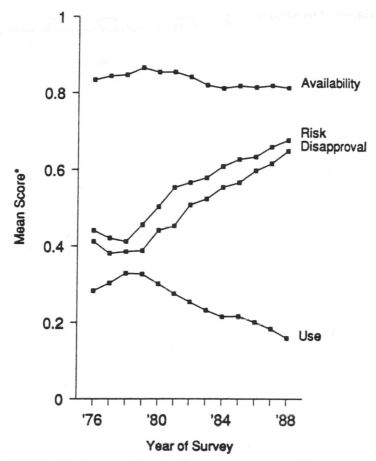

FIG. 7.1. Trends in annual marijuana use, perceived availability, perceived risk, and disapproval (high school seniors, 1976-1988). *All items were scaled with the minimum possible score set equal to zero and the maximum possible score set equal to 1.

and disapproval (beginning in 1980), and the decline in use of the drug (beginning in 1980). Also evident in Fig. 7.1 is the fact that perceived availability changed very little. Throughout the whole period the great majority of seniors thought it would be fairly easy or very easy to get marijuana, thus suggesting that availability did not play any important role in the recent decline in marijuana use.

The data for cocaine, shown in Fig. 7.2, are in many respects different from the marijuana data shown in Fig. 7.1. (The questionnaire items about marijuana and cocaine use identical sets of answer categories, and Figs. 7.1 and 7.2 display mean scores for all items on the same scale so as to highlight contrasts between the two drugs.) Throughout the study, levels of

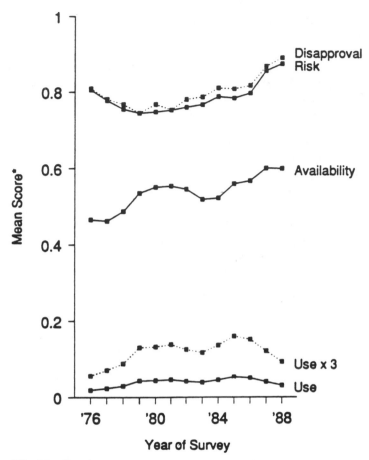

FIG. 7.2. Trends in annual cocaine use, perceived availability, perceived risk, and disapproval (high school seniors, 1976-1988). *All items were scaled with the minimum possible score set equal to zero and the maximum possible score set equal to 1.

perceived risk and disapproval have been much higher for cocaine, perceived availability somewhat lower, and self-reported use a great deal lower. Indeed, mean usage rates for cocaine are so low that we found it necessary to include in Fig. 7.2 a second trend line that magnifies the usage data in order to make the changes clearer. But in spite of these very large differences between the marijuana and cocaine data, it is also evident that for cocaine, like marijuana, the recent decline in use corresponded to sharp rises in perceived risk and disapproval. These increases in negative views about cocaine are all the more striking when we note that in 1986 they were already fairly close to the "ceiling." It is also clear in Fig. 7.2 that when cocaine use began its decline, there was no decrease in perceived availability—on the contrary, availability reached new peaks in 1987 and 1988.

Competing Explanations for the Declines in Drug Use

We called early attention to the link between trends in marijuana use and trends in perceived risks of marijuana (Johnston et al., 1981), and noted the additional evidence that (a) concerns about marijuana's effects on physical and psychological health were among the leading reasons seniors gave for not using marijuana, (b) such mentions were increasing, and (c) there was no change in the widespread perception that marijuana was easily available (Johnston, 1982, 1985). Johnston (1985) thus argued that changes in beliefs and attitudes, rather than any decline in supply, led to changes in demand for marijuana.

Jessor (1985) found such arguments plausible but "not yet compelling." He pointed out that aggregate trend data do not clearly establish causal order, and "it remains quite possible that regular use of marijuana declined and beliefs about its harmfulness subsequently increased rather than the other way around." Jessor also noted that "it is possible to entertain an equally plausible alternative hypothesis to account for both the increased perception of harm from regular use and the actual decline in regular use, namely, that there has been an increase in the general conventionality of adolescents during this same historical period. Such an increase in conventionality would also imply greater receptivity to messages from authorities about the harmfulness of drug use" (p. 259). In other words, while the A causes B (i.e., attitudes cause behavior) interpretation of the trends is plausible, Jessor saw two other plausible interpretations: B causes A (i.e., behavior causes attitudes), or C causes both A and B (i.e., conventionality causes both attitudes and behaviors). These alternative explanations have been addressed in our more recent analyses, and we summarize the relevant findings here.

General Versus Specific Predictors of Drug Use

We found it useful to divide predictors (i.e., correlates) of marijuana use into two categories: (a) individual "lifestyle variables" that relate not only to marijuana use but also to the use of other drugs, to delinquent behavior, and to a variety of other "problem" behaviors; and (b) drug-specific factors that relate directly to marijuana use. This distinction, although too sharp and simple to correspond fully to the real world, was nonetheless useful in organizing data and analyses related first to marijuana use, and then to cocaine use.

With respect to general lifestyle factors, we and others have consistently found that certain kinds of individuals are more likely than others to use drugs, and that such individuals are also more likely to get involved in other kinds of "problem" behavior (Bachman et al., 1988; Bachman, Johnston, & O'Malley, 1981; Jessor, Chase, & Donovan, 1980; Jessor & Jessor, 1977; Johnston, 1973; Johnston, O'Malley, & Eveland, 1978; Smith & Fogg, 1978; and for further reviews and summaries see also Glynn, Leukefeld, & Ludford, 1983; Jessor, 1979; Jones & Battjes, 1985; Kandel, 1978, 1980, 1982; Lettieri & Ludford, 1981; Murray & Perry, 1985). But, as we noted in an earlier analysis, the particular forms of deviant or "problem" behavior can vary from one historical period to another:

> In the 1960s and 1970s illicit drug use emerged as an increasingly "popular" form of deviance; so instead of simply smoking cigarettes and using alcohol, many of today's teenagers also use marijuana, and some use other illicit drugs. The emerging pattern of relationships with the use of cocaine may illustrate our point particularly well. In 1975, cocaine use was low and was not very strongly correlated with the background and lifestyle factors treated in this report. By 1979, usage levels were higher and the correlations were much stronger; however, the *patterns* of correlation were the familiar ones consistently in evidence for alcohol, marijuana, and other illicit drugs taken as a group. In other words, the kinds of young people most "at risk" tend to remain much the same, while the kinds and amounts of substances used shift somewhat from year to year. (Bachman et al. 1981, p. 67)

These observations, based on analyses of high school seniors in the classes of 1975 through 1979, continue to hold true. Drug use continues to be greater than average among those less successful in adapting to the educational environment (as indicated by truancy and low grades), those who spend many evenings out for recreation, those with heavy time commitments to a job, and those with relatively high incomes. Additionally, drug use continues to be below average among those with strong religious commitments and among those with conservative political views.

Given that individual differences in drug use are clearly correlated with the lifestyle factors listed earlier, it is not surprising that the gradual decline in marijuana use during the 1980s might suggest that young people were finally getting "better" or less "trouble-prone" or more "conventional." Of course in one respect, namely marijuana use, that is exactly what was happening. But that is not the same as saying that more *general* changes in lifestyle were the *underlying cause* of the decline in marijuana use.

An alternative approach to explaining changing levels in the use of particular drugs is to focus on drug-specific factors, those things that relate primarily to the use of a particular drug rather than to drug use in general (or problem behavior in general). Such factors include potential effects of using the drug, availability, friends' acceptance or disapproval of use, as well as individuals' *perceptions* of each of these dimensions. In contrast to the more general correlates of drug use and other deviant behaviors, these drug-specific factors are more subject to change over fairly short periods of time. Moreover, changes in factors related to one drug may be quite different from changes (or non-changes) in factors related to another drug, as illustrated in Figs. 7.1 and 7.2 (see Johnston et al., 1988, for other examples).

In our efforts to understand the decline in marijuana use, we examined both general lifestyle factors and drug-specific factors, in each case asking whether such factors might account for the secular (i.e., consistent, long-range) trend downward in use during the 1980s. We asked similar questions most recently in our examination of the decline in cocaine use since 1986. The next sections summarize the answers we found.

Lifestyle Factors Predicting Marijuana Use. We examine first the possibility that the decline in marijuana use during the 1980s was the result of one or more lifestyle changes among young people during that period. To take a specific example, let us suppose that young people became more committed to religion (i.e., that rates of attendance increased, and increased proportions reported religion to be very important in their lives). As noted earlier, religious commitment is negatively correlated with marijuana use, so any shift toward greater religious involvement should produce a shift toward fewer marijuana users. For the sake of illustration, let us make the further assumption that the recent decline in marijuana use is due *solely* to an increase in religious commitment (i.e., no other direct causal factors need be considered). Suppose now that we were to plot mean levels of marijuana use for each of four levels of religious commitment, showing the trends among seniors from the classes of 1976 through 1986. Under the scenario just described, we would expect to see four essentially flat trend lines: seniors with high religious commitment would report practically no marijuana use, and that would not change from year to year (although the proportion of seniors in that category would be a good deal larger in 1986 than in 1980); similarly, seniors with little or no religious commitment would report relatively high levels of marijuana use, and the mean amounts of use would not change from year to year (although the numbers of such "low commitment" seniors would decline). In other words, if shifting religious commitment fully accounted for the changes in marijuana use, then controlling for that factor (by separating seniors into four categories) would completely "remove" the trend—the lines would be essentially flat.

Figure 7.3 displays the actual trend lines, and it is clear that the facts of the matter are not at all consistent with the scenario just outlined. Statistically controlling religious commitment does not "explain" the trend in marijuana use; the pattern remains clearly evident both for the strongly religious and for those with little involvement in religion. At each level of religious commitment, marijuana use was higher for those in the class of 1978 than for those in the class of 1976, but from 1979 onward marijuana use declined steadily with each succeeding class. There is, however, an important difference in the strength of the trends shown in Fig. 7.3. The upward and then downward trend in marijuana use appears only weakly among seniors with strong religious ties, whereas it is more pronounced among those who reported little religious commitment. It thus appears that those most "protected" by their high religious commitment were least influenced by shifts in the popularity of marijuana.

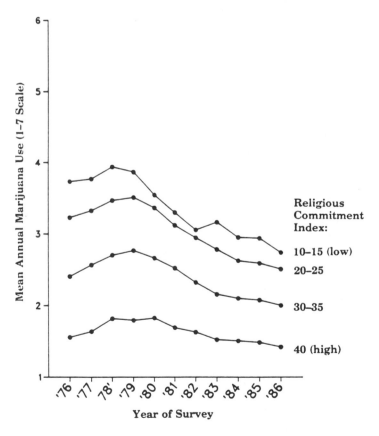

FIG. 7.3. Trends in annual marijuana use shown separately for four levels of religious commitment (high school seniors, 1976-1986).

We repeated analyses of the sort illustrated in Fig. 7.3, examining bivar iate relationships between marijuana use and seven other lifestyle factors (grades, truancy, hours of part-time work during the school year, weekly income, liberal versus conservative political beliefs, and frequency of evenings out for recreation). Each of these factors showed some correlation with marijuana use in each of the graduating classes of 1976 through 1986. However, none of them could "explain" the decline in marijuana use. The trend remained evident for every subgroup defined along each of the other lifestyle variables—the trend lines for marijuana use always increased from 1976 through 1978 or 1979, and thereafter declined. But here again the strength of the trend differed from one category to another. We found it always stronger in the "higher-risk" categories (e.g., those high in truancy, those with poor grades, those who frequently spent their evenings away from home).

Our analysis also examined whether any of the lifestyle factors showed substantial changes either in level (e.g., whether there were increases in religious commitment from 1979 to 1986), or in pattern of correlation with marijuana use. We found few such changes, none were large enough to begin to explain the trend in marijuana use, and some were not even in the right direction to do so. (Indeed, religious commitment actually *declined* slightly during the 1980s, quite the opposite of what we outlined in our illustrative scenario.) Reviewing all of this evidence, we found little reason to conclude that shifts in these lifestyle factors were the cause of the recent decline in marijuana use. If anything, we felt that a reverse causal explanation might be more consistent with some of the data: It may be that the decline in marijuana use during the 1980s made some contribution to small reductions in truancy and frequency of evenings out which we observed during that period.

One limitation of these findings is that they do not extend beyond the bivariate level: each lifestyle predictor was examined separately. Thus, our next step was to combine these predictors multivariately, and see whether they could jointly account for the general trend in marijuana use. It is beyond the scope of this chapter to spell out the analysis procedure (see Bachman et al., 1988, for a full reporting of methods and findings), but the key findings can be summarized briefly. Pooling data from 11 senior classes (1976–1986), we found that the lifestyle variables (plus gender) treated as joint predictors could account for about 25% of the variance in marijuana use. A measure of the secular trend from 1976 through 1986 could account for a much smaller amount of the variance in individual marijuana use—about 1.5%. We noted that "this finding serves as a useful reminder that although year-to-year variations in marijuana use over the past decade are important and interesting, such variations remain small in comparison to the wide range of variability among seniors within each year of the study" (Bachman et al., 1988, p. 105). The key finding for present purposes, however, was that the two sets of explained variance did not overlap very much: at least two thirds of the secular trend was found to be independent of the full set of lifestyle factors.

The multivariate analyses also examined drug-specific predictors, with a very different set of outcomes. Before reporting those findings, however, we examine how lifestyle factors are related to the very recent changes in cocaine use.

Lifestyle Factors Predicting Cocaine Use. Although the overall levels of cocaine use among high school seniors have been far lower than the levels of marijuana use, and although the trend patterns are distinctly different for the two drugs, the basic conclusions relating to lifestyle factors are much the same. We extended our analysis to include the senior classes of 1976 through 1988, and examined the same set of lifestyle variables that we used in our analysis of marijuana use. We found the overall trend in cocaine use evident in every subgroup of every variable: cocaine use rose from 1976 through 1980, and later declined from 1986 through 1988. The pattern is illustrated in Fig. 7.4.

Figure 7.4 also illustrates another general finding that emerged for cocaine use just as it did for marijuana use: The trend is more pronounced for those in "higher risk" categories. Thus, the rise in cocaine use from 1976 through 1980 shows up more sharply among those with low religious commitment ("high risk" individuals), and so does the later decline in use; but among strongly religious seniors there was little cocaine use during any of the years studied, and thus the trend is very weak.

We also examined cocaine use at the multivariate level, following the same strategy that we used in examining marijuana. We focused on the 4-year interval from 1985 through 1988, which encompassed the recent decline in cocaine use (see Bachman et al., 1990, for an explanation of the choice of this interval, and for further details on procedures and findings). The multivariate analyses revealed no overlap at all between the variance in individual cocaine use explained by the lifestyle factors and the variance linked to the temporal trend in cocaine use. Although lifestyle factors are very important correlates of cocaine use, taking full account of their predictive value in no way diminishes or "explains" the temporal trend in using this drug. In order to account for the trends in both marijuana and cocaine use, we must turn to a different set of measures.

Drug-Specific Factors Predicting Marijuana Use. Between 1978 and 1986, the proportion of high school seniors perceiving no risk in regular marijuana use dropped from 12% to near zero (1.2%), whereas the proportion of those perceiving great risk doubled from 37% to 75%. During that

same period, the proportion of seniors not disapproving of regular marijuana use dropped by nearly two thirds, from 31% to 11%, whereas the
proportion of those strongly disapproving rose from 41% to 67%. Were
these sharp changes in attitudes sufficient to account for the decline in
actual use of marijuana among high school seniors? The findings in Fig.
7.5 suggest that they were.

Figure 7.5 displays mean rates of marijuana use for seniors who saw
little or no risk in regular marijuana use, for those who saw moderate risk,
and for those who saw great risk. The figure clearly shows the very strong
relationship between perceived risk and use. It also shows that there was
little overall change in usage rates among those who saw little or no risk.
They consistently averaged near "5" on the scale, which corresponds to
10–20 uses of marijuana during the prior 12 months. At the other end of

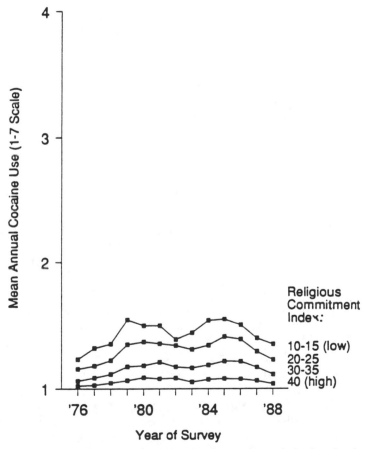

FIG. 7.4. Trends in annual cocaine use shown separately for four levels
of religious commitment (high school seniors, 1976-1988).

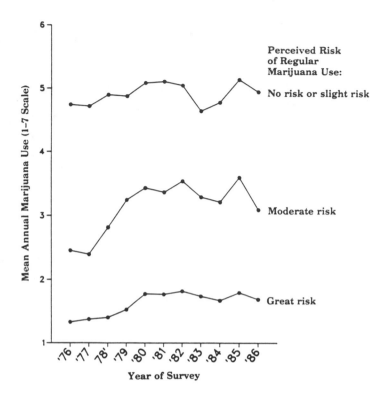

FIG. 7.5. Trends in annual marijuana use shown separately for three levels of perceived risk of regular marijuana use (high school seniors, 1976-1986).

the scale, those who perceived great risk showed very little use ("1" on that scale refers to no use, whereas "2" denotes use only once or twice during the year), and those rates did not change very much either—especially after 1980.

So what is it that *has* been changing? As we noted earlier, the big change occurred in the *proportions* of seniors in these groups. In other words, the relationship between perceived risk and use did not seem to change very much. What did change is that a great many more seniors began to take the risks more seriously. That finding is fully consistent with the "A causes B" interpretation—that increased perceptions of risk led to the decline in use.

The data concerning disapproval of marijuana use tell much the same story. Those who disapproved strongly of regular marijuana use also reported low levels of actual use (means averaged 1.4 on the scale of 1 to 7), those who "merely" disapproved showed consistently higher mean levels of use (about 2.8), and those who did not disapprove showed much higher mean levels of use (about 5.2). In other words, although each year following 1979 there were increased numbers of seniors who disapproved of regular marijuana use, the amounts of use associated with each level of disapproval remained essentially the same. Thus "nondisapprovers" still report high mean levels of actual marijuana use, but nowadays there are very few seniors who do not disapprove of regular marijuana use.

These findings suggested to us that if there had not been substantial secular trends in *attitudes* about marijuana, starting in the late 1970s, then the (smaller) secular trend in *actual use* would not have occurred. We thus concluded that controlling for the recent rise in perceived risks and disapproval is one way of accounting for the corresponding downturn in marijuana use.

But Jessor's (1985) question naturally arises here: is a reverse explanation—the "B causes A" interpretation—equally plausible? Could one just as well explain the shifts in *attitudes* by controlling trends in *behaviors?* Analyses that were essentially the mirror image of those described previously (and shown in Fig. 7.5) produced a negative answer to that question. We found that "controlling for the behavior of marijuana use does nothing to reduce or 'explain away' the upward trend from 1978 through 1985 in negative attitudes about marijuana. Subgroups consisting of frequent users, infrequent users, and non-users, all show substantial increases in the proportions who disapprove of marijuana use and perceive that such use is risky" (Bachman, Johnston, O'Malley, & Humphrey, 1986, p. 14). In addition, these findings held true not only for views about regular use, but also for views about occasional and experimental use of marijuana.

The multivariate analyses of predictors of marijuana use described earlier were extended to include the drug-specific attitudes. We found that perceived risks of regular marijuana use accounted for 33% of the variance in use, whereas disapproval accounted for 46%. (We could not include these two measures in the same regression analysis because they appeared on separate questionnaire forms. Nevertheless, the findings for the two measures are sufficiently similar that we do not think that their inclusion as joint predictors, were that possible, would lead us to any different conclusions. We note in passing that a new questionnaire form, first administered in 1989, includes both the perceived risk and the disapproval items.) The more important finding from this phase of the analysis was that inclusion of the secular trend term generated no increase in explained variance. Put differently, in the presence of either of the attitude measures, the secular trend effect is reduced to zero, and this is exactly what the findings in Fig. 7.5 would lead us to expect. Incidentally, the conclusions drawn here hold equally well whether or not the lifestyle measures are included in the equation.

In summary, our multivariate analyses indicated that the secular trend in marijuana use could not be explained in terms of the lifestyle factors, but the trend *could* be explained by either of the drug-specific measures.

Drug-Specific Factors Predicting Cocaine Use. Throughout the course of the Monitoring the Future project at least three quarters of the seniors in each graduating class perceived the regular use of cocaine as posing great risks, and similar proportions expressed strong disapproval of such use. These proportions have increased substantially in recent years, so that 88% in the class of 1986 saw great risks in regular use, and fully 95% in the class of 1988 expressed that view. The proportions of seniors expressing strong disapproval were nearly as large: 83% in the class of 1986, rising to 90% in the class of 1988. Again we are interested in whether the sharp changes in attitudes were sufficient to account for the recent decline in actual drug use—in this case the drop in cocaine use between 1986 and 1988.

Figure 7.6 parallels Fig. 7.5, but now of course the focal drug is cocaine. Again we see a strong relationship between perceived risk and use, although we also note that mean usage levels are distinctly lower than the corresponding levels for marijuana shown in Fig. 7.5. The upper two trend lines in Fig. 7.6, like those in Fig. 7.5, do not show a recent decline in drug use. On the contrary, whereas the percentage of seniors in the "moderate risk" category dropped from 9% in 1986 to only 4.2% in 1988, the mean level of cocaine use among such individuals actually may have *increased*. (The small numbers of cases, and the corresponding "raggedness" of the trend line, leads us to be very cautious about any single point in the "moderate risk" category; however, the overall trend is upward, and that may well be true also for 1986–1988.) The top trend line in Fig. 7.6 is based on even fewer cases, dropping from 2.7% of seniors in 1986 to only 1.2% in 1988. Among these most atypical individuals there is no evidence of a recent decline in cocaine use—here again any overall trend is in an upward direction.

The bottom trend line in Fig. 7.6, representing seniors who perceived "great risk" in regular cocaine use, does show a decline in cocaine use from 1986 through 1988. But because such large majorities of seniors are in the "great risk" category, trends in perceptions of risk are not adequately controlled. When perceived risks of *trying cocaine once or twice* are similarly displayed, there are no clear declines in mean use trends from 1986 through 1988 (see Bachman et al., 1990).

The multivariate analyses linking cocaine use to drug-specific factors tell the same story. Just as we found for marijuana use, in the presence of either of the attitude measures the recent trend in cocaine use is reduced to zero.

These findings suggest a conclusion similar to the one for marijuana: if there had not been a substantial trend in *attitudes* about cocaine, then

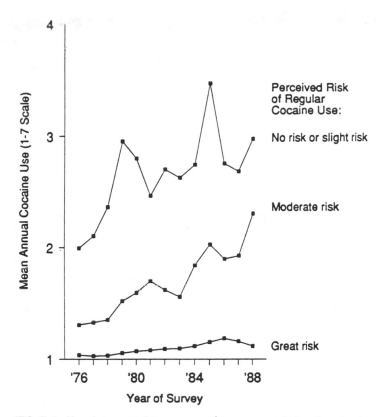

FIG. 7.6. Trends in annual cocaine use shown separately for three levels of perceived risk of regular cocaine use (high school seniors, 1976-1988).

the (smaller) trend downward in cocaine *use* very likely would not have occurred.

Conclusions About the Declines in Marijuana and Cocaine Use

Our findings have highlighted a number of large and important differences between these two illicit drugs. Young people have been far more likely to view cocaine use as risky, and something to be disapproved, than has been the case for marijuana use. Consistent with these differences in attitudes, actual use of cocaine among high school seniors has been a great deal lower than marijuana use. But in spite of these large differences in attitudes and usage rates, the findings for both drugs show close linkages between attitude changes and declines in rates of use.

Another important difference between the two drugs involves the shape and timing of the secular trends. Although use of both drugs was increasing up to 1978, the secular trends were distinctly different after that. Marijuana use declined fairly steadily from 1979 onward, so that by 1988 the amount of use had been cut about in half. For cocaine, on the other hand, the first large drop did not occur until after the 1986 survey, but then it was so steep that only two years later amount of use was cut by about 40%.

It is hard to see how these two different secular trends could have been caused by some general trend toward young people becoming more "conservative" or less "trouble-prone" in recent years. Moreover, such an argument would be further strained to accommodate still other trend patterns for other drugs. Changes in *drug-specific* factors, on the other hand, clearly correspond to the declines in both marijuana and cocaine use. Moreover, the several bivariate and multivariate analyses summarized here all strongly suggest that if these changes in attitudes toward each drug had not occurred, then we would not have observed the recent declines in use.

One important question that remains is: Why have these changes in attitudes occurred? Here we move somewhat beyond our data, but not beyond our willingness to speculate. We think that changes in the social environment, particularly changes in information, have led to the secular trends in perceptions of risk, which in turn have led to secular trends in disapproval and in actual drug use.

In the case of marijuana, early efforts to discourage its use often made exaggerated claims about harmful effects. Meanwhile, students could see friends and acquaintances whose use of the drug did not lead to such disastrous consequences. More recently, however, reports about the health consequences have been more balanced, have received better and more extensive media coverage, and have been based on more extensive research. Additionally, reports about psychological consequences such as poor school performance, reduced interest in extracurricular activities, and impaired interpersonal relationships all acquired the ring of truth: Regular use of marijuana became widespread for a long enough time to give most students at least some contact with classmates who exhibited some of these negative outcomes. In other words, direct observation of the effects of marijuana use became consonant with messages from "the system."

In the case of cocaine the recent shifts in attitudes and behaviors have been more abrupt, and we think that is because the new information about cocaine arrived in such a dramatic fashion. In May 1986 college basketball star Len Bias died as a result of cocaine use. The extensive press coverage of this tragedy included reports that Bias had never used cocaine prior to the occasion that resulted in his death. Although that later proved to be incorrect, the early publicity left a strong impression that even trying cocaine could be very dangerous. Within several weeks another star athlete, professional football player Don Rogers, also died as a result of cocaine use. These young men in prime physical condition, already successful and famous, were the kind of individuals with whom many high school students could identify. Their deaths, so widely reported and discussed, may have had at least some of the same impact that would have resulted from a classmate's death due to cocaine. In any case, the two tragedies provided a focal point for extensive media coverage of cocaine use and its risks (including death rate statistics, other physical effects, addictive potential, and the like), and that surely contributed to higher levels of public concern about the drug. Certainly the findings reported here are consistent with that interpretation.

CHANGES IN DRUG USE DURING PREGNANCY

The Monitoring the Future project includes a follow-up component: Each year we mail questionnaires to subsamples of those whom we first surveyed as high school seniors. One of our purposes in carrying out the follow-up surveys has been to ascertain how the new roles and responsibilities of young adulthood affect drug use. Several years ago we reported on changes in drug use during the first 3 years after high school. We found that post-high school drug use is highly predictable from senior year drug use; but in addition, usage rates for alcohol, marijuana, and other illicit drugs (but not cigarettes) seem to be influenced by post-high school living arrangements. In particular, those who married showed declines in drug use, those who continued to live with their parents (unmarried) showed little change on average, and those in other living arrangements showed increases in drug use (Bachman, O'Malley, & Johnston, 1984). Further analyses of follow-up data, extending to 8 years beyond high school, have replicated the findings on living arrangements. They have also uncovered some other patterns of change, one of which is particularly relevant to the focus of this chapter.

Beginning with the follow-up survey in 1984, we asked respondents whether they or their spouses were pregnant. The findings reported here are based on data from about 20,000 females, 1 to 8 years beyond high school (i.e., ages ranging from about 19 to 26), surveyed in 1984, 1985, 1986, 1987, or 1988.

The basic finding of interest can be summarized briefly: Pregnant women are very likely to stop or reduce their use of various drugs, and their rates of "quitting" far exceed those of any other subgroup we have examined. This holds true for the illicit drugs marijuana and cocaine, and shows up even more dramatically for alcohol and cigarettes.

These findings originally emerged in the context of large-scale multivariate analyses, which controlled a variety of background factors including high school academic experiences and lifestyle, along with current factors such as marital and parental status, living arrangements, current employment, and recent unemployment experiences. The findings for pregnancy are not greatly affected by controls for these other factors, particularly once we control for marital status. Accordingly, in this chapter we present the data in a much simplified format. Specifically, we focus on proportions of females, both pregnant and nonpregnant, whose follow-up responses indicate that they no longer engage in a form of drug use that they *did* report as seniors. We refer to this as *quitting*, although we recognize that it is quite a simplification given that we use only two reference points—the senior year of high school and a follow-up 1 to 8 years later. In spite of that, the findings are sufficiently strong and clear that this approach works quite well.

We begin with the findings for alcohol, which are displayed in Fig. 7.7. The left-hand side of the figure presents "quitting rates" for drinking behavior that includes having five or more drinks in a row at least once in the past 2 weeks. About 30% of female high school seniors report such behavior, and those individuals are the basis for the percentages shown. As the figure indicates, among those who were pregnant at the time of the follow-up, fully 95% had "quit." Put differently, among the roughly 30% of pregnant women who had reported such drinking as seniors, only

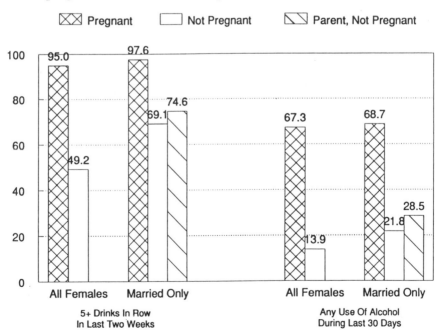

FIG. 7.7. Alcohol "quitting rates" linked to pregnancy (females age 19–26 surveyed in 1984–1988).

5%—or 1.5% of *all* pregnant women—also reported such use in the follow-up survey. (We note in passing that among pregnant women who had not reported such drinking as seniors, virtually none reported such use at the time of the follow-up.)

Among all *nonpregnant* females who had reported such drinking as seniors, only about half (49%) had "quit." There is, however, an important confounding factor when we compare all pregnant females with all nonpregnant ones: The pregnant women are much more likely to be married, and marriage has its own clear and substantial relationship with "quitting." In order to deal with this problem, we also display in Fig. 7.7 the quitting rates for married women only. For these individuals the pregnancy effect is still quite large, but the marriage effect is also evident. (Also displayed separately in Fig. 7.7 is the subset of married and nonpregnant women who already have children, and it can be seen that "quitting" rates for this subgroup are somewhat higher than for the total group of nonpregnant married women.)

Given widespread publicity connected with fetal alcohol syndrome, it may not be surprising that very few pregnant women report having as many as five or more drinks in a row during the past 2 weeks. A much more impressive kind of "quitting" involves no use of alcohol at all, and the right-hand portion of Fig. 7.7 displays those findings—specifically, it shows the proportions of females who as seniors did report some use of alcohol during the past month (somewhat more than 60% of all female seniors did so) but who at the time of the follow-up reported no use of alcohol during the past month. Among all nonpregnant females very few (about 14%) had "quit" monthly use, and although marriage and parenthood raised the rate of "quitting," it is still true that large majorities of nonpregnant females continued some consumption of alcohol. Among pregnant women, however, fully two thirds had "quit" any current consumption of alcohol. (Moreover, among those pregnant women who had not reported current alcohol use as seniors, the rates of use at follow-up were even lower.)

We now turn briefly to the relationships between pregnancy and "quitting" other drugs, as displayed in Table 7.1. We note first that pregnant women are much more likely to quit (or at least reduce their rates of) smoking than nonpregnant women. Indeed, our panel analyses of cigarette use have consistently shown rather high rates of stability and little responsiveness to post-high school experiences (except for an initial rise in amount of cigarettes consumed in the first year or 2 after leaving high school). Presumably because of the addictive properties of tobacco, we have not observed substantial declines in smoking as the result of marriage—although rates of other drug use do decline. We were thus particularly impressed to find that fully half of all pregnant women who had been daily smokers as seniors had managed to "quit," in contrast to only about one quarter

TABLE 7.1
"Quitting Rates" Linked to Pregnancy
(Females Age 19-26, Surveyed in 1984-1988).

	5+ Drinks in Past 2 Weeks	30-Day Alcohol	Daily Cigarette Use	½ Pack or more per Day	30-Day Marijuana	30-Day Cocaine
All Females						
Pregnant	95.0	67.3	52.3	49.5	83.2	91.9
Not pregnant	49.2	13.9	24.6	25.1	55.4	67.6
Married Females						
Pregnant	97.6	68.7	58.8	55.5	86.2	93.5
Not pregnant	69.1	21.8	28.9	27.7	63.8	79.0
Parent, not pregnant	74.6	28.5	29.0	27.3	65.9	84.1

of the nonpregnant women. Looking at a higher rate of smoking—half a pack or more a day—we again found that half of the pregnant women, but only one quarter of the others, had been able to "quit" at that level of use. (Some had only reduced use to less than half a pack daily, but many had stopped smoking altogether.) Limiting the analysis to married women increases the "quit" rates by only a few percentage points, and parenthood makes no additional difference.

Among all female seniors who reported some use of marijuana during the past 30 days, the majority had "quit" such monthly use at the time of the follow-up. However, among all nonpregnant women about 45% continued use, whereas only 17% of all pregnant women did so. These continuation rates are lower when we restrict the analysis to married women— 36% among the nonpregnant, and only 14% among those pregnant.

We computed similar "quitting" and "continuation" statistics for monthly cocaine use, although the numbers of cases grow small when we focus on females who as seniors reported some use of cocaine during the past 30 days. But among such individuals, only about 8% of those pregnant continued use, compared with 32% of the nonpregnant. Limiting the analysis to married women reduces those proportions further, to 6.5% and 21%.

There are many ways of presenting the relationships between pregnancy and drug use, in addition to the "quit" or "continuation" rates shown here. But no matter which way we look at it, the findings clearly show that being pregnant has a distinct impact on drug use, above and beyond the effects of marital status, living arrangements, employment, and a variety of other factors. It is obvious that large proportions of young women today reduce or eliminate their use of psychoactive drugs during pregnancy, and presumably they do so primarily out of concern for the health of their unborn children.

We assume also that these concerns arise because of the transmission of information, both by health professionals and by the media. Furthermore, we suspect that at least some of this information has been changing in recent years. In the very limited period from 1984 through 1988—the years in which we asked about pregnancy—it was not clear whether we would uncover any shifts in the effects of pregnancy on drug use, but we thought it was worth exploring. In general, we did not find much change. One important exception, shown in Fig. 7.8, involves "quitting" rates for alcohol. Although the data are a bit uneven from year to year, we can see especially for the measure of monthly use that quitting rates rose even during as short a period as the last 4 years. This suggests that messages about negative effects of alcohol on fetuses are coming through more clearly with each succeeding year.

CONCLUSIONS

What can we conclude from all the findings summarized here? What do they imply about the "conventional wisdom" that information alone is not effective in dissuading young people from drug use? We are reminded

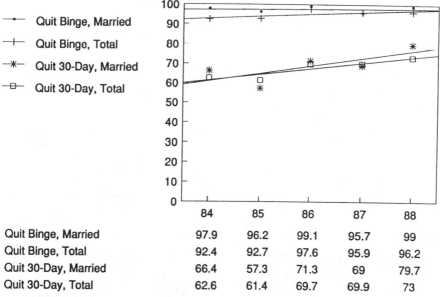

	84	85	86	87	88
Quit Binge, Married	97.9	96.2	99.1	95.7	99
Quit Binge, Total	92.4	92.7	97.6	95.9	96.2
Quit 30-Day, Married	66.4	57.3	71.3	69	79.7
Quit 30-Day, Total	62.6	61.4	69.7	69.9	73

FIG. 7.8.   Trends in quitting alcohol, 1984-1988, among pregnant women, ages 19–26.

of Lee Cronbach's (1975) comments on the short half-life of findings in the social sciences: "Generalizations decay. At one time a conclusion describes the existing situation well, at a later time it accounts for rather little variance, and ultimately it is valid only as history" (pp. 122–23).

Perhaps we should start treating the old conventional wisdom about information and drug use as "history." We are not sure that it ever was valid, but certainly there is reason to doubt it today. Recent evidence suggests that large proportions of youth and young adults *do* pay attention to new information about drugs, especially about the risks involved, and they moderate their behavior accordingly. We find that very encouraging.

REFERENCES

Bachman, J. G., & Johnston, L. D. (1978). *The monitoring the future project: Design and procedures* (Monitoring the Future Occasional Paper 1). Ann Arbor, MI: Institute for Social Research.

Bachman, J. G., Johnston, L. D., & O'Malley, P. M. (1981). Smoking, drinking and drug use among American high school students: Correlates and trends, 1975–1979. *American Journal of Public Health, 71,* 59–69.

Bachman, J. G., Johnston, L. D., & O'Malley, P. M. (1990). Explaining the recent decline in cocaine use among young adults: Further evidence that perceived risks and disapproval lead to reduced drug use. *Journal of Health and Social Behavior, 31*(2), 173–184.

Bachman, J. G., Johnston, L. D., O'Malley, P. M., & Humphrey, R. H. (1986). *Changes in marijuana use linked to changes in perceived risks and disapproval* (Monitoring the Future Occasional Paper 19). Ann Arbor, MI: Institute for Social Research.

Bachman, J. G., Johnston, L. D., O'Malley, P. M., & Humphrey, R. H. (1988). Explaining the recent decline in marijuana use: Differentiating the effects of perceived risks, disapproval, and general lifestyle factors. *Journal of Health and Social Behavior, 29,* 92–112.

Bachman, J. G., O'Malley, P. M., & Johnston, L. D. (1984). Drug use among young adults: The impacts of role status and social environments. *Journal of Personality and Social Psychology, 47,* 629–645.

Cronbach, L. J. (1975). Beyond the two disciplines of scientific psychology. *American Psychologist, 30,* 116–127.

Fishburne, P. M., Abelson, H. I., & Cisin, I. (1980). *National survey on drug abuse: Main findings, 1979* (DHHS Publication No. (ADM) 80-976). Washington, DC: U.S. Government Printing Office.

Glynn, T. J., Leukefeld, C. G., & Ludford, J. (Eds.). (1983). *Preventing adolescent drug abuse: Intervention strategies* (NIDA Research Monograph No. 47, DHHS Publication No. (ADM) 83-1280). Washington, DC: U.S. Government Printing Office.

Jessor, R. (1979). Marijuana: A review of recent psychological research. In R. Dupont, A. Goldstein, & J. O'Donnell (Eds.), *Handbook on drug abuse* (pp. 337–355). Washington, DC: U.S. Government Printing Office.

Jessor, R. (1985). Bridging etiology and prevention in drug abuse research. In C. L. Jones & R. J. Battjes (Eds.), *Etiology of drug abuse: Implications for prevention* (NIDA Research Monograph No. 56, DHHS Publication No. (ADM) 85-1335, pp. 257–268). Washington, DC: U.S. Government Printing Office.

Jessor, R., Chase, J. A., & Donovan, J. E. (1980). Psychosocial correlates of marijuana use and problem drinking in a national sample of adolescents. *American Journal of Public Health, 70,* 604–613.

Jessor, R., & Jessor, S. L. (1977). *Problem behavior and psychological development: A longitudinal study of youth.* New York: Academic Press.

Johnston, L. D. (1973). *Drugs and American youth.* Ann Arbor, MI: Institute for Social Research.

Johnston, L. D. (1982). A review and analysis of recent changes in marijuana use by American young people. In *Marijuana: The national impact on education* (pp. 8-13). New York: The American Council on Marijuana.

Johnston, L. D. (1985). The etiology and prevention of substance use: What can we learn from recent changes? In C. L. Jones & R. J. Battjes (Eds.), *Etiology of drug abuse: Implications for prevention* (NIDA Research Monograph No. 56, DHHS Publication No. (ADM) 85-1335, pp. 155-177). Washington, DC: U.S. Government Printing Office.

Johnston, L. D., Bachman, J. G., & O'Malley, P. M. (1981). *Highlights from student drug use in America, 1975-1980* (DHHS Publication No. (ADM) 81-1066). Washington, DC: U.S. Government Printing Office.

Johnston, L. D., O'Malley, P. M., & Bachman, J. G. (1988). *Illicit drug use, smoking, and drinking by America's high school students, college students, and young adults, 1975-1987* (DHHS Publication No. (ADM) 89-1602). Washington, DC: U.S. Government Printing Office.

Johnston, L. D., O'Malley, P. M., & Eveland, L. K. (1978). Drugs and delinquency: A search for causal connections. In D. B. Kandel (Ed.), *Longitudinal research on drug use: Empirical findings and methodological issues* (pp. 137-156). Washington, DC: Hemisphere.

Jones, C. L., & Battjes, R. J. (Eds.). (1985). *Etiology of drug abuse: Implications for prevention* (NIDA Research Monograph No. 56, DHHS Publication No. (ADM) 85-1335). Washington, DC: U.S. Government Printing Office.

Kandel, D. B. (1978). Convergences in prospective longitudinal surveys of drug use in normal populations. In D. B. Kandel (Ed.), *Longitudinal research on drug use: Empirical findings and methodological issues* (pp. 3-38). Washington, DC: Hemisphere.

Kandel, D. B. (1980). Drug and drinking behavior among youth. *Annual Review of Sociology, 6,* 235-285.

Kandel, D. B. (1982). Epidemiological and psychosocial perspectives on adolescent drug use. *Journal of the American Academy of Child Psychiatry, 21,* 328-347.

Lettieri, D. J., & Ludford, J. P. (1981). *Drug abuse and the American adolescent* (NIDA Research Monograph No. 38, DHHS Publication No. (ADM) 81-1166). Washington, DC: U.S. Government Printing Office.

Murray, D. M., & Perry, C. L. (1985). The prevention of adolescent drug abuse: Implications of etiological, developmental, behavioral, and environmental models. In C. L. Jones & R. J. Battjes (Eds.), *Etiology of drug abuse: Implications for prevention* (NIDA Research Monograph No. 56, DHHS Publication No. (ADM) 85-1335, pp. 236-256. Washington, DC: U.S. Government Printing Office.

National Institute on Drug Abuse. (1988). *National household survey on drug abuse: Main findings, 1985* (DHHS Publication No. (ADM) pp. 88-1586). Washington, DC: U.S. Government Printing Office.

O'Malley, P. M., Bachman, J. G., & Johnston, L. D. (1988). Period, age, and cohort effects on substance use among young Americans: A decade of change, 1976-86. *American Journal of Public Health, 78*(10), 1315-1321.

Smith, G. M., & Fogg, C. P. (1978). Psychological predictors of early use, late use, and nonuse of marijuana among teenage students. In D. B. Kandel (Ed.), *Longitudinal research on drug use: Empirical findings and methodological issues* (pp. 101-113). Washington, DC: Hemisphere.

8

Changing Attitudes Toward Drug Use: The Effects of Advertising

Gordon S. Black
The Gordon S. Black Corporation

THE ATTITUDINAL BASIS OF DRUG USE

Unselling Drugs

The Partnership for a Drug Free America has an ambitious mission: *unselling illegal drugs* in the United States. The Partnership is directed at discouraging the purchase and consumption of its three target products—marijuana, cocaine, and crack. The Partnership's task is to marshall the resources of the advertising and media industries to produce advertising that encourages nonusers not to start and users to decrease or terminate their use.

This research project was commissioned by the Partnership for two purposes: (a) to provide information that might be useful in the design of advertising aimed at discouraging drug use, and (b) to track the effectiveness of the advertising effort itself, over time.

The first wave of the research, which was conducted in February 1987, involved interviews with 7,325 respondents across the United States. These anonymous respondents were recruited at shopping malls and other central locations. They were asked to fill out a questionnaire concerning their attitudes toward illegal drugs, and their use of them.

The Partnership for a Drug Free America

The Partnership for a Drug Free America is a volunteer, private sector coalition of the advertising communities—all of those who work together in the fields of advertising, media, and public communication. The coalition brings together a number of national associations, including The American Association of Advertising Agencies, The Association of National Advertisers, The National Association of Broadcasters, The American Advertising Federation, The Outdoor Advertising Association of America, The Station Representatives Association, The Magazine Publishers Association, The Advertising Council, The Association of Independent Television Stations, The Television Bureau of Advertising, The Radio Advertising Bureau, and The Newspaper Advertising Bureau.

Although this is an impressive list of national associations, the Partnership is in reality the thousands of individuals in media who are providing free air time and space, and thousands more who are creating, producing, directing, acting in, and editing the advertising without charge. They are creating the television, radio, newspaper, and magazine advertisements that have appeared across the United States. The supporting cast includes the people in agencies all across the country who have solicited stations, magazines, and newspapers on behalf of the Partnership, and the thousands of people who feel this effort is so important that they have intervened to make it possible for the ads to be placed in the media without cost.

To understand the breadth of the Partnership, the effort constitutes the largest single advertising effort ever undertaken in the United States, and it is entirely a volunteer enterprise.[1]

The objectives of the Partnership are: (a) decreased acceptance of drug use; (b) increased social disapproval of use; (c) increased awareness of risks; (d) increased communication by parents; and (e) decreased demand over time. The Partnership's task is to create a multifaceted, multidimensional, multitargeted, multimedia campaign aimed at supporting the objectives just stated.

The Research Objectives

The research is a three- to four-wave tracking study. The first wave is essentially a baseline measurement of the attitudinal basis of drug abuse. The objectives of this research are to: (a) provide information useful to

---

[1]Those of us who have conducted the research are indebted to three people for their support: Richard T. O'Reilly, the very gifted national director who guided our efforts until his untimely death in August 1987; Thomas Hedrick, the Partnership's marketing director who very ably stepped in to keep the momentum going; and Fred Posner, of NW Ayer, who managed to understand that research companies also have to work for paying clients when they do volunteer work.

the design of advertising; (b) obtain specific recall measures of the advertising; and, (c) track attitudinal changes over the course of at least the first 3 years of this advertising effort.

THE BASE LINE WAVE

The first wave analysis was completed in November 1987. The research design was prepared by the Research and Strategy Committee, under the direction of Fred Posner. The first draft of the questionnaire was prepared by Dr. Gordon S. Black, who also supervised two large pretests. The final draft of the adult questionnaire involved the support and participation of the people on the committee and the experts.[2] Jackie Silver was primarily responsible for the children's 9- to 12-year-old) questionnaire.

Sampling Methodology and Site Selection

The study was conducted during the first months of 1987 by screening prospective respondents at malls and colleges across the United States. Interviews were conducted by 98 field services at 150 malls and other central locations. These locations were chosen to approximate a correct regional distribution, and a correct central city/suburban/rural distribution. Participating were 122 colleges and universities throughout the United States. They were selected according to the following criteria: correct regional distribution, type of school (2-year/4-year; public/private, religious/secular), and size of school. Although the study was *not a full national probability study*, every effort was made to obtain the closest possible approximation to a fully representative national sample.

Samples and Weighting

There were four discrete samples: children between the ages of 9 and 12, teenagers between the ages of 13 and 17, college students, and adults. The

---

[2]The Research and Strategy Task Force consisted of Fred Posner, NW Ayer; Jim Donius, NW Ayer; Jackie Silver, Backer Spielvogel Bates; Jim Crimmons, DDb Needham; Leonard Bayer, Gordon S. Black Corporation; David Clemm, Gordon S. Black Corporation; Laurie Robertson, NW Ayer; Stuart Agres, Lowe Marschalk; Lew Pringle, BBDO; Gordon S. Black, Gordon S. Black Corporation; Tony Adams, Campbell Soup Company; Joy Jones, NW Ayer; and John Brodsky, NW Ayer.

The panel of experts were Charles Schuster, Director, NIDA; Dr. Edgar Adams, Research Director, NIDA; Dr. Beatrice Rouse, NIDA; Dan Langdon, Director of Public Information, Phoenix House; Lloyd Johnston, Program Director, Institute of Social Research, University of Michigan; and Douglas Lipton, Deputy Director, Substance Abuse, State of New York.

sample sizes were as follows: 884 children ages 9–12; 798 teenagers ages 13–17; 942 college students; and 4,737 adults.

Where necessary, the data were weighted to project the counts to the total population. These adjustments included the following variables: region, race within region, age, gender (teenagers), and type of school (college). On the whole, the largest weights were to compensate for sample imbalances by age. Because of the importance of age, each year was corrected to represent its true proportion.

The Multivariate Design

The fundamental *dependent* variables in this analysis are variables that measure *reported drug use*, present and future. These are the variables the analysis attempts to explain, and they include marijuana and cocaine use during the past 12 months as well as *likely* use of both drugs during the next 12 months. The analysis centers around these four variables.

The *independent* or *predictor* variables include over 100 factors, organized into logical groups. These include 37 items concerning attitudes and beliefs about the use of drugs; 8 items on the first use of drugs and substances; 12 items about risk of using substances under different conditions; 5 items concerning friends using substances; 5 items about difficulty of obtaining substances; 17 items on appeals of use; and 26 items pertaining to reasons for not using drugs.

On the whole, these items are measured using a consistent scale for every item within a group. The purposes of the multivariate analysis are several:

1. To greatly reduce a list of 113 factors to those that have the best predictive power with regard to the four dependent variables that measure drug use, past and future.
2. To develop a series of models that show the relationships between these variables and drug use, identifying those variables that have the greatest predictive value.
3. To evaluate the relative importance of variables drawn from each of the different sets just cited, for the purpose of determining which variable category is the most powerful and predictive.
4. To eliminate variables that have little predictive merit, even to the point of eliminating them from subsequent waves of the research.

The method for conducting this analysis is through *regression analysis*. Although this method has some limitations for this type of data, it is by far the fastest and most efficient way to proceed. There is a *vast* amount of information contained in these four separate studies, and efficiency is a central criterion for getting the job accomplished.

The problems of the analysis are compounded by the high degree of multicolinearity within particular variable sets. For example, nearly all of the attitudes and beliefs are correlated (i.e., people who agree with one item are likely to agree with a second, and so forth).

Moreover, most of the variables in the questionnaire are related to one degree or another with drug use and the differences are in the degree of the association.

In this analysis, our *primary objective* is to reduce and simplify a complex set of associations into several relatively simple and straightforward models—models that provide guidance for those directing the creation of advertising.

A COMPARISON WITH NIDA HOUSEHOLD/ HIGH SCHOOL SENIORS STUDIES

The primary purpose of this study was to establish the base line for tracking attitudes as they changed during the Partnership's program. The research measured drug use as an important variable that was related to the respondent's basic attitudes, but our sampling methodology could only approximate a national sample. Therefore, the findings in this research regarding the use of drugs are less reliable than those obtained through the work of the National Institute of Drug Abuse (NIDA).

NIDA funds two major national tracking studies: the national household study and the national study of high school seniors and young adults, both conducted by Dr. Lloyd Johnston of the Survey Research Center (SRC) at the University of Michigan.

One major task was to analyze the basic similarities and differences between these two invaluable data sources and the current one. Underlying demographic factors in these studies were compared. Data from the current study were weighted to match them to the two NIDA studies. This effort was undertaken with the considerable cooperation of Dr. Beatrice Rouse of NIDA and Dr. Lloyd Johnston of the Survey Research Center of the University of Michigan.

A comparison of our data with those of the two Federal studies reveal both similarities and differences. On the whole, differences with the high school data for 1986 are small, with the exception of cocaine use in the past 30 days, where the SRC has 6.2% and this study has 13.7%. The attitudes toward the "risk" of marijuana and cocaine use are very similar in the SRC and Gordon S. Black Corporation (GSBC) studies. The data on college students from the SRC sample are also quite similar to those found in the GSBC study, and the data on young adults (18–27) in the two studies are virtually identical. The GSBC study consistently shows higher levels of marijuana and cocaine consumption than the data on use from the NIDA national household sample of teenagers. The discrepancy is greatest for cocaine use, particularly cocaine use in the past 30 days and in the past year. Marijuana use is also lower in the NIDA data, but the difference is not as great as with cocaine. The NIDA data on young adults show lower consumption figures than those of the GSBC data, but the differences are much smaller than those of teenagers.

Although these differences are of no particular importance for the purposes of the GSBC study, the pattern of discrepancy is interesting. For the most part, the SRC *drug use data* on high school seniors, college students, and young adults are very similar to the GSBC data. Given the radically different sampling techniques and locations, the degree of similarity is surprising and striking, particularly on the comparable attitude measures.

Both of these studies used written questionnaires that are filled out under conditions that guarantee considerable confidentiality. In both instances, there was no practical way an interview could have been associated with a specific individual in the study.

The other NIDA study was conducted within the household. There is a question of whether this environment constitutes a "threatening environment," particularly for the younger respondents. Every effort was made in the household study to reassure the respondents that the information they imparted to the interviewer was confidential. One might question, however, whether the users will entrust such information to a stranger when the interview is conducted directly in the home, usually with the parents or spouses at home, if not present within the room.

The pattern of findings *suggests* the possibility that the interviewing circumstances were threatening, particularly to younger respondents. The discrepancy in the reported use was greater among the teenagers than among the young adults, was greater for cocaine (the more opposed drug by parents) than for marijuana, and was greater for recent behavior than for past behavior with both drugs.

The data in the GSBC study were obtained through a different and less representative method of sampling respondents, and the differences reported here may be solely a product of the samples. However, the pattern is somewhat surprising and suggests the possibility of a different interpretation (i.e., that interviews in a household lead to under-reporting by vulnerable respondents).

PRINCIPAL FINDINGS

The Pattern of Drug Use

The pattern of drug abuse as disclosed in this research is very similar to the findings reported in other national studies.

Both Marijuana and Cocaine Use are Already Established by Age 13.
Of children aged 9 through 12, 16% have already been approached to buy
or use drugs. Of the 9- to 12-year-olds, 15% agree it is easy to get marijuana.
By age 13, 12% report having tried marijuana and 8% have tried cocaine.

The incidence of all forms of use increases steadily into the late 20s,
when it starts to decline. Lifetime cocaine use peaks at 38% among those
26 to 30, and lifetime marijuana use peaks at over 70%. College students
report lower use patterns than their noncollege counterparts. *Lifetime use*
reflects the pattern of exposure through experimentation over time, and
the growth in lifetime use as one moves down on the age scale demonstrates the increasing penetration of drugs during the 1960s, 1970s, and
early 1980s.

Although one might be optimistic about the future use of drugs based
on the data that show that respondents *intend* to use less drugs during the
next 12 months, this finding has been present in other studies during years
in which no decline in drug use was apparent.

9- to 12-Year-Olds

A special questionnaire was administered to children 9 through 12 years
old. In this questionnaire, the children were asked some of the questions
posed to adults, but the questionnaire was specifically written for this age
group. In particular, the children were not asked directly about drug use.
They were, however, asked about a number of issues known to be related
to a vulnerability to drug use.

Key Findings

Exposure Has Already Taken Place for Many in This Group. Of
these children 16% have been approached to buy or use drugs, 15% agree
it is easy to get marijuana, 7% agree cocaine is easy to get, and 13% have
friends who already use marijuana.

Social Pressures and Factors Support Drug Abuse. The study shows
that 39% believe it is hard to say "no" to friends about drugs, 37% say
drug users are "popular." Thirty-one percent believe drug users have many
friends, and 26% believe people can easily stop if they want.

Vulnerability Factors

The purpose of the multivariate statistical analysis was to isolate and
identify the key factors producing *higher levels of vulnerability* to drug abuse.
Among the 9- to 12-year-olds, the key factors increasing vulnerability included the following, in order of their importance:

1. Talking to *older siblings* was the strongest predictor of early vulnerability to drug abuse (i.e., those whose older siblings talk to them about drugs are more vulnerable).
2. Peer-group influences were the second most influential factor predicting vulnerability to drug abuse. These include just talking with their friends about drugs, doing what their friends do, finding it hard to say no to their friends, positive images of drug users, and the belief that drug users are not different.
3. Fear is the major deterrent to drug use in this age group. The fear is a fear of getting hooked, particularly to cocaine, but 10% of the respondents would like to try crack just once, and this attitude increases vulnerability.

By far the most important finding is the extraordinarily important role that older siblings play in increasing the vulnerability of their younger brothers and sisters. This is not a role that the older siblings wish to play, but they play it none the less. Of teenagers, 60% greatly fear influencing their brothers and sisters with their use of pot and 66% greatly fear influencing them with their cocaine use.

Teenagers

Although the pattern of drug abuse vulnerability emerges quite clearly during pre-teenage years, the level of abuse rises sharply throughout the teenage years. That pattern is supported by a set of factors that shape the degree of teenagers' vulnerability.

Key Findings

1. The *age of first use* is the single most powerful predictor of the current frequency of abuse (i.e., the earlier one begins the pattern of abuse, the greater the frequency of abuse today and the less likely the reduction in the future). The average age of first use for marijuana and cocaine appears relatively constant for teenagers. Of the teenage age cohort groups, 15%–20% report trying marijuana by age 13. Of these teenagers, 4%–5% report trying cocaine by age 13.
2. Among teenagers, all drug use—present and future—is related to having friends who use drugs. The relationship is so strong among teenagers that if your child has friends who smoke marijuana and do coke, then your child probably does the same.
3. Teenagers' *fear* of marijuana overall is not a good predictor of their use of the drug. To the extent that teenage users fear anything, 48%

of regular teenage users fear getting caught by the law, 38% fear influencing siblings with their behavior, 36% fear impure marijuana, and 29% fear the impact on school performance.

4. The approval of the use of drugs at parties drives drug use among teenagers. Of teenagers, 22% agree that it is fun to have drugs at parties. Only 53% agree that they do not like to hang around drug users.

5. Other attitudes that are strongly pro-drug use among teenagers are: 29% see drug users as popular; 28% believe drugs are just part of growing up; 25% believe pot increases creativity; 24% believe coke is not risky, or don't know; 22% report they like being high on drugs; 11% say it is OK to sell coke to a friend; and 10% would like to try crack just once.

6. The reported ease of obtaining cocaine and crack increases dramatically during teenage years and is related to cocaine use. Of the 13-year-olds, 13% report that it is easy or fairly easy to obtain cocaine and crack. Of the 14- and 15-year-olds, 25% report that it is easy or fairly easy to obtain cocaine and crack. Of the 16- and 17-year-olds, 38% report that it is easy or fairly easy to obtain cocaine and 30% report that it is easy or fairly easy to obtain crack.

7. Teenage cocaine users report significant fears about drug use. Sixty-five percent fear getting caught by parents, 59% fear impure cocaine or crack, 58% fear physical damage, 58% fear psychological damage, 51% fear reaction of school authorities, and 51% fear becoming dependent on the drug.

Vulnerability Factors

The following is the order of importance of the various factors in producing a higher degree of vulnerability for drug abuse among teenagers.

1. The age of the first use of marijuana and cocaine, and the age of *first regular* use strongly predicts future marijuana and cocaine use.

2. The number of friends who use marijuana predicts marijuana use, and the number of friends who use cocaine predicts cocaine use.

3. Fear of dying predicts lower cocaine use; fear of getting hooked predicts lower marijuana use. People who fear getting caught with cocaine are less likely to be users.

4. Those who think its fun to have cocaine at a party are more likely to be users.

College Students

College students show a distinctly lower level of use of drugs than high school students in our data, and they are even more markedly lower than people their age not attending college. Also, the college students display different patterns of fears and concerns about drugs and drug abuse.

Key Findings

1. Among regular marijuana users in college, 58% fear getting caught by the law, 49% fear impure marijuana, 47% fear reaction of parents, and 38% fear impact on school performance.
2. Regular cocaine users in college show markedly more concerns. Seventy-five percent fear reaction of parents, 73% fear dying from crack use, 67% fear getting caught by the law, 65% fear impure cocaine or crack, 61% fear dying from cocaine, and 60% fear reaction of school authorities.
3. Many college students have attitudes that are supportive of continued drug use. Thirty-two percent see drug users as no different from others, 27% believe that using cocaine is a status symbol, 22% report that cocaine makes the user feel powerful, 22% feel that drugs help you forget your troubles, and 21% say parties are more fun with drugs.

Vulnerability Factors

1. Having friends who get stoned on pot is the best predictor of marijuana use, and age of first using marijuana is a good predictor of current use.
2. Age of first using cocaine is the best predictor of cocaine use.
3. Attitudes shape both marijuana and cocaine use, particularly the attraction of use at parties, attitudes toward drugs as stepping stones to use harder drugs, the perceived riskiness of cocaine, and the basic acceptance of drug use as part of growing up.
4. Cocaine use is lower among those who think it is hard to get. This relationship is not true of marijuana use.
5. The more college students perceive cocaine as risky, the less they use it. That is not true for high school students and teenagers, nor is it true for marijuana.
6. College students who fear feeling guilty are less likely to be users of marijuana and cocaine, and this is not true for teenagers or adults.

Adults

When we speak of adults, we are really speaking about distinctly different groups. First, there are the young adults, mostly between 18 and 35 years old, who are the worst abusers of drugs. Second, there are those between

35 and 50 years old, who came of age during the generational excesses of the 1960s and 1970s. This group still has abusers, but a much lower use pattern. Finally, above the age of 50, drug abuse is relatively uncommon.

Key Findings

1. Among regular adult users of marijuana, 52% fear getting caught by the law, 36% fear impure marijuana, 34% fear negative influence on children or younger siblings, and 28% fear the reaction of parents.
2. Regular adult users of cocaine are much more fearful than those who use marijuana. It was found that 68% fear dying from crack use, 65% fear getting caught by the law, 65% fear reaction of employers, 62% fear impure cocaine or crack, and 61% fear physical damage.
3. Some attitudes also support the use of drugs by adults. Twenty-nine percent think cigarettes are worse than pot, 26% think it is OK to smoke pot in private, 20% feel that cocaine is a status symbol, and 11% feel that occasional cocaine use is not risky.

Vulnerability Factors

1. Age of first use of cocaine and age of first use of marijuana.
2. Fear of reaction of loved one or spouse.
3. Fear of psychological effects.
4. Friends who are using cocaine (not seen for marijuana).

Parents

The data suggest that there is substantial uncertainty and perhaps misconception among parents about their children. Fully 25% to 35% consistently respond that "they are not sure" about their children's behavior concerning drugs. Moreover, substantial groups believe that their children are not at risk, even though drug use reports suggest that the majority of children are likely to use marijuana and nearly 4 in 10 will use cocaine. According to the data, 51% of the parents believe their kids will not take drugs. Only 34% believe their kids will actually try drugs, with 30% who are not sure. Fifty percent believe their kids have never tried drugs, but 61% report that drugs have affected children they know.

The parents do report efforts to engage in behavior aimed at dealing with the possibility of drug use by their children. Seventy percent have discussed the dangers of drug use with their children and 71% have expressed strong disapproval of drug use to them. Thirty-six percent have discussed their concern with the parents of children who use drugs. Only

11% have complained to school officials about the use of drugs by other children at school, and only 8% have reported suspected drug use to the police. Only 6% have removed drugs from their children's possession.

The Demographics of Drug Use

The demographics of drug use are important because they suggest the kinds of models and settings that are appropriate for targeting advertising. Drug use is now so pervasive, however, that abuse is relatively common among every social group and in every part of the country. Therefore, although the differences described in the following summary are differences of degree, not of kind, they do provide some guidance.

Key Demographic Findings

1. Women today are nearly identical to men in their use of marijuana and cocaine.
2. Blacks and Hispanics are more likely to be drug abusers than the general population.
3. Drug abuse is more common among the very affluent and the very poor, and is significantly less common among middle income groups.
4. Regular church attendance is strongly related to much lower levels of drug abuse among all populations.

Hispanics

The Hispanic sample is not large enough to produce interpretable results for children, teenagers, or college students. Normally, we do not interpret a sample of less than 100, and these three have samples of between 50 and 60.

However, a review of these few cases showed a pattern where Hispanics were in most instances similar in their responses to non-Hispanic Whites. The similarity between the Hispanics and non-Hispanic Whites suggests that a separate campaign *in terms of content* is unnecessary, although it is obviously important to develop ads that use Hispanic settings and individuals.

In the adult sample, there are nearly 300 Hispanics, which provides a confidence interval of plus or minus 5.7%. It is thus possible to make comparisons between Blacks, Whites, and Hispanics on the full range of variables.

Key Findings

1. Hispanics are much *less inclined* than Blacks or Whites *to fear the effects of drugs.* Among Hispanics, 19% agree that they are not scared of drugs compared with 12% among others. They are twice as likely

to see *slight or no risk* in cocaine use. But Hispanics are more likely to report *becoming hooked on cocaine*—6% for Hispanics compared with 3% for Blacks and 2% for Whites.

2. Hispanics appear to engage in more *pro-active* behavior aimed at discouraging drug use. They are *much more likely* to report having attempted to discourage use among their friends or their children. Of this group, 19% report removing drugs from their kids, compared with 10% for Blacks and 5% for Whites. But Hispanics are *much more likely* to believe that their children will not use drugs, contrary to the evidence that their children use drugs as much as White children.

Blacks

In every sample but the adults, Blacks show a pattern of greater vulnerability to drug use than Whites. Among children 9 to 12 years old, Black children are twice as likely to have been approached to buy or use drugs than White children—27% for Blacks and 13% for Whites. Among the teenagers, 18% of the Blacks have used cocaine in the past year and 35% have used marijuana, and that is contrasted with 11% for cocaine and 30% for marijuana in the rest of the population. Even among adults, marijuana use is slightly higher for Blacks than for the rest of the sample, but the difference is small.

By any standard, Blacks are at greater risk for the use of marijuana and cocaine than Whites. Moreover, that use reportedly begins at a slightly earlier age for Blacks. Among Blacks, 23% of the teenagers *tried* marijuana by age 13 and 12% tried cocaine by that age, whereas for Whites the numbers are 16% for marijuana and 5% for cocaine.

The question, of course, is why and what role, if any, attitudinal differences play in these differences in use.

Before summarizing some of these differences between Whites and Blacks, it is important to know that the similarities between White and Black attitudes and behavior far exceed the differences. On the whole, there are many relatively small differences where Blacks are *slightly* more favorable toward drugs than Whites. Generally, the two demographic groups are quite alike in their views on most issues. The differences are of relatively *small degree*.

Key Findings

1. The most profound differences between Blacks and Whites are found in the youngest group—the 9- to 12-year-olds. Of these, 27% of the Black children have been approached to buy or use drugs, compared with 13% for Whites. Of the Black children, 39% say it is easy to obtain marijuana,

and 16% say it is easy to obtain cocaine, with 11% and 6% respectively for Whites. Black children see drug users as "popular": 46% for Blacks and 29% for Whites, and as "having lots of friends": 33% for Blacks and 16% for Whites. Of the Black children, 28% think drug users are "no different", with 13% for Whites. Many Black children think drug users are good at sports (27%), or are good students (20%), and these attitudes are not shared by as many Whites (16% and 7% respectively).

2. Although Black teenagers tend to be exposed earlier and show a greater frequency of drug use, Black teenagers' *attitudes* are generally quite similar to those of Whites. By far the greatest and most important difference is in the variables that measured the *perceived harmfulness* of using both marijuana and cocaine. Of the Black teenagers, 25%–29% perceive *no risk* in using cocaine or marijuana. Only 6% to 12% of the White teenagers see *no risk* in using these drugs. Black teenagers rate drugs of nearly every type as "more attractive" than Whites.

3. The attitudes of Black college students are very similar to those of White college students, with some attitudes slightly more positive and others slightly more negative.

4. The largest difference between Black and White adults is that Blacks are more likely to find it easy to obtain marijuana, cocaine, and crack. The percentages of Black adults saying it is very easy to obtain marijuana, cocaine, and crack are 44%, 34%, and 31% respectively, as contrasted with 27%, 17%, and 14% for Whites. Adult Blacks are less likely to see drug users as boring, stupid, or foolish, and they are more likely to believe that occasional cocaine use is not risky, and that cigarettes are worse than marijuana. Black and White parents have similar expectations of their children's behavior with regard to drugs, but Black adults show consistently less pro-active behavior than Whites, although the differences are small. Black and White adults have very similar fears as to the possible consequences of drug use.

RECOMMENDATIONS FOR DRUG ABUSE PREVENTION

Children 9 to 12

1. All efforts at educating children—by schools, parents, and the advertising of the Partnership and others—must push into these lower age groups!
2. The idea of the drug user as "popular," the local "hero," must be dispelled, using negative images of drug users as models.

3. The role of the older sibling provides an avenue for attacking the defenses of teenagers, who do not want the responsibility for negatively influencing their younger brothers and sisters.
4. The pro-active aspect of friendship in discouraging drug use among friends needs to be emphasized.

Teenagers

1. Emphasize the need to delay the onset of the first use of drugs. Aim educational programs at the early teenage years.
2. Evaluate ways to make friendship an asset against drug use, as opposed to a liability. Emphasize through responsibility inducing themes what a real friend is. Emphasize the importance of expressing social disapproval of drug use.
3. Point out the impact of older siblings on younger ones.
4. Attack the notion that it is fun to have drugs at parties by pointing out how stupid the behavior of the drug users is, a point that teenagers agree with.
5. Avoid too many death and dying themes, but use the fears of getting caught, impure drugs, physical and psychological damage, and so on.

College Students

Many of the recommendations made concerning teenagers apply to college students. We obviously cannot push the age of first use up, but the data for college students support the need to do that with the younger children. Also, all of the themes about responsible friendship hold for college students. Finally, the use of drugs at parties is as significant with college students as it is with teenagers.

College students have more fears than teenagers about drug use. These fears constitute themes that can be emphasized without concern about the credibility of the advertising. They also have more realistic fears about death from cocaine and crack, and they are afraid of impure cocaine and marijuana.

These elements provide thematic material which may prove useful in the development of advertising and other materials.

Adults

The findings pertaining to adults, listed earlier, provide many of the themes that can be developed as part of a campaign. Obviously, parental responsibility themes are already a part of the overall campaign, and these are valuable. In addition, many of these adults are amenable to "social responsibility" themes concerning the consequences of their behavior. Do they really want to support the violence, the terror abroad, and the corruption at home that are the necessary products of their "right to use" drugs?

Moreover, we have yet to develop themes that help adults understand what they can do when they confront drug abuse at parties, on the job, or elsewhere. What is their responsibility for their friends and families? And how can parents, as influencers, deal more effectively with instilling a strong anti-drug ethic in their children?

Parents

1. Continue the emphasis of "pro-active" behavior among the parents.
2. Encourage additional forms of "pro-active" behavior such as working with school officials, neighborhood groups, local police, and so forth, to control the distribution of drugs.
3. Equip parents with information about the probability of their children using drugs and how to detect it, particularly by noting their actual behavior. Emphasize the risks for very young children.

Catering to Demographic Groups

1. Use more female, Black, and Hispanic actors and actresses, with appropriate themes and in appropriate settings.
2. Consider developing "social responsibility" themes directed to appeal to people who think of themselves as "liberal."
3. Focus greater emphasis on young adults not in college, particularly the ages of 18 to 30 where abuse is the most severe.

Hispanics

1. On the whole, the *message content* designed for Whites is also appropriate for Hispanics.
2. Ads should be designed to appeal to Hispanics using Hispanic settings and characters, with the obvious caution that the Hispanic community is itself ethnically very diverse.
3. Attitudinally, Hispanics appear to fear the effects of drugs less than Whites, and fear may be a less effective tactic in this community.
4. Hispanic parents are more pro-active concerning drugs, but they underestimate significantly the vulnerability of their children.

Blacks

1. We must have a more frequent use of Black characters and situations involving Blacks in our commercials, because of the consistently greater incidence of drug use among Black young people. This is particularly true for pre-teenage children, where Blacks are *twice* as vulnerable as Whites. For Black teenagers, early exposure and "teen pressure" for exposure are factors that require attention. If the ads could do anything for these children, it would be to dispel the view of drug users and sellers as popular and as having many friends.

2. Blacks report a greater "ease of access" to drugs, suggesting that drug sellers can operate more in the open within the Black community than within the White one. Parents of Black children should be told how easily their children can obtain drugs. This greater ease of access is also a statement of how community standards and institutional constraints serve to restrict the freedom of the drug dealers. Ads should be aimed at these institutional audiences (e.g., police, schools, neighborhood groups, churches, etc.).

3. Media and education must be specifically developed for dealing with the greater vulnerability of Black children.

4. The percentage of Black teenagers who perceive *no risk* in drug use is extremely high, and it is a point of ignorance that needs to be attacked with Black characters and situations.

5. Among college students, the ads can be very similar for Blacks and Whites.

THE FOLLOW-UP WAVE

Since the beginning of April 1987, the advertising initiated and created by the Partnership for a Drug Free America has been appearing in media all over the United States.

This section has two main functions. First, to summarize the changes in attitudes that have occurred during the first year. Second, to analyze the relationship between those changes and the advertising effort of the Partnership.

The objective of this analysis is to compare *matched samples* of Americans obtained through two waves of research conducted a year apart. The benchmark, or base line wave was completed during February 1987, before any Partnership advertising had begun, and the second, follow-up wave was completed during February and early March of 1988. The sample sizes of the two waves are listed in Table 8.1.

TABLE 8.1
Sample Sizes of Two Waves

		Wave 1	Wave 2
Children 9–12	$N =$	881	1,190
Teenagers 13–17	$N =$	798	1,031
College students	$N =$	947	1,491
Adults	$N =$ 4,749		4,665

Note: The adult sample, which is of people 18 and over, includes the college students. In the analysis, the college component is weighted downward to correct for the oversampling.

All of the respondents other than college students were recruited in 89 malls and other central locations across the United States. The college students were recruited in central locations on 130 college campuses. All respondents filled out the questionnaire in private, and procedures were employed to provide full confidentiality.

The samples were weighted to approximate a representative national sample. The largest weights compensate for sample imbalances by age because of the importance of age in drug use.

Each component sample was compared on every available demographic and geographic variable in order to search for any source of bias in the two samples. We found no instance in which the two waves differed by a statistically significant amount! The two waves appear closely matched, and that makes it easier to evaluate any changes that occur in the drug-related variables.

What We Are Looking For

The earlier analysis (1987) identified a structure of relationships that predicted past, present, and future cocaine and marijuana use. That study singled out the importance of several factors, including the age of first using drugs, the role of friendship networks and social factors in promoting drug use (or retarding it), and the special role of siblings in affecting younger children.

This phase of the research attempts to specify the attitudinal and other changes that have occurred since the Partnership started its advertising campaign. All variables were compared for statistically significant differences between the two waves. In reporting the findings, we are only reporting statistically significant results. We are ignoring all other data in this report.

The research also attempts to identify attitudinal changes that are attributable to relative exposure of respondents to the advertising effort. The Partnership identified 10 media areas around the United States in which the public would have received at least a 50% heavier weight than in other areas. The respondents in each of these areas were grouped so as to produce a division into "higher" media exposure and "lower" media exposure.

An analysis of variance was performed on each of these groups, comparing the 1987 results with the 1988 results in both segments. The results of this analysis are summarized in this report.

MAJOR FINDINGS

Many attitudes and orientations have become distinctly more antagonistic toward drug use in all of the samples over the past year. The changes are most pronounced in the college sample, followed by children (9–12), with somewhat less, but important, change among the adults and teenagers. There is virtually no significant movement in the opposite direction (i.e., toward views more sympathetic to drug use). Factors that could not be expected to change (e.g., lifetime drug use or age of first use) are virtually identical in the two samples.

In areas with high media exposure, the changes were substantially greater on most variables than in the rest of the United States. This is true for all the samples, but the college sample is too small in this part of the analysis. Exposure was extensive for many of the television ads, and they were generally very positively received. The observable differences between the "high" and the "rest of U.S." areas are very consistent and in some instances very large.

Among the college students, where attitudinal changes appear to be the greatest, there are statistically significant declines in cocaine consumption, primarily among the "occasional users." Statistically significant declines in consumption were not present in other segments. Among 9- to 12-year-olds, the percentage of those approached to buy or use drugs increased slightly, from 16% to 18%.

College Students

From Ragtime to Woodstock, college students often have paved the way for changes in society. During the 1960s and 1970s, college students were among the first groups to increase their consumption of illegal drugs. In the past year, however, their attitudes and fears have become clearly more anti-drug. Even more impressive is the first evidence of a decline in occasional cocaine use. The statistically significant changes range from 4% to 14% shifts across the entire data set. These changes are even more profound among the Black college students.

1. Out of 32 basic attitudes, 15 became more anti-drug; only 1 became more pro-drug, with shifts ranging from 3% to 12%.
2. Out of 18 positive images of nondrug users, 16 increased in frequency of mention, whereas none declined.
3. Out of 11 negative images of marijuana users, 8 increased in frequency of mention.
4. Out of 11 negative images of cocaine users, 9 increased in frequency.
5. Out of 26 fears of the consequences of drug use, 20 increased, whereas none declined, with shifts ranging from 5% to 10%.
6. Black students' fear of the consequences of drug use increased dramatically on six items, shifting 17%–31%.
7. Black students show greater changes than Whites throughout the data. Now their attitudes are more in line with those of Whites.
8. Occasional cocaine use has decreased 5 percentage points among college students, from 11% to 6%.
9. Occasional cocaine use by friends has decreased 5 percentage points, from 36% to 31%.

Many variables that were found in the first report to be important deterrents changed positively. If these important attitudes continue to shift, then the first major behavioral changes should have occurred (and did occur) in this segment. Hopefully, the changes evident in the college segment are indicative of the changes to come in the rest of society.

Children 9 to 12

The childrens' attitudes changed somewhat less than those of the college students, but the changes that are present have important long-term implications. If attitudes against drug use in this population harden, then the age of first use is likely to rise and consumption will diminish. The results indicate that this "hardening" has begun. There is evidence of a reported decline in usage by friends, and strong indications of increased fear of drugs among these respondents. Both factors were found to be vital in deterring drug use. The changes are not as large or as widespread as those that occurred among college students, but they are consistently in the right direction and on many of the most important items.

Finally, there was a slight increase in the number of children approached to buy or use drugs, which is an important indication of the persistence of the attempts to increase supply to the youngest people.

1. Out of 19 basic attitudes, 7 became more anti-drug; only 1 became more favorable toward drugs, with shifts ranging from 3% to 5%.

2. Out of 7 positive images of drug users, 3 decreased in frequency, and no positive images increased. Users are less likely to be seen as "popular": down 4 percentage points. Users are less likely to be seen as "having many friends": down 5 percentage points.

3. Out of 4 variables indicating usage by friends, 2 decreased; none increased. 3% fewer children have friends who use marijuana, from 12% to 9%.

4. Black children became more anti-drug on 6 out of 19 basic attitudes, with shifts of up to 15%.

5. At the same time, the percentage of these children approached to buy or to use drugs increased slightly from 16% to 18%.

The objective of the Partnership with regard to children has been to shift attitudes toward a more antagonistic stance toward drugs prior to the point when significant exposure occurs. That hardening is taking place. If it continues, it should delay early trials. At the same time, current exposure is unchanged, indicating the persistence of those seeking to induce these children into drugs.

Adults 18 and Over (Including College Students)

The adult segment has shown some, although fewer, positive changes. There are some major attitudinal shifts, but they are less dramatic and far-reaching than those observed in the college and children segments. However, this is to be expected because in the first wave, the adults were found to be the most anti-drug to begin with, especially in the population above the age of 35. Thus, the population as a whole cannot be expected to change as much in such a short time period. The fact that there are important and significant changes is very encouraging.

1. Out of 32 basic attitudes, 6 became more anti-drug; none has changed toward a more pro-drug posture, with shifts ranging from 3% to 8%.

2. Out of 26 fears of the consequences of use, 10 have changed and none went in the wrong direction, with shifts ranging from 3% to 4%.

3. Out of 11 negative images of marijuana users, 6 increased.

4. Out of 11 negative images of cocaine users, 7 increased.

5. Out of 18 positive images of nonusers, 8 increased.

6. Black adults show positive attitudinal shifts of 6% to 14%. However, Black parents underestimate the risks of drugs to their children. Only 20% of Black parents feel their children are likely to use drugs, but 33% of Black teenagers already use marijuana.

The most negative finding in this section is that parents today are less likely to think their children are susceptible to drug use. Several of these items moved toward a less realistic view of the children's behavior—"less realistic" in the face of the data demonstrating the high levels of use and exposure. Of parents, 32% say their children have never been exposed to drugs. The truth is that 18% of children (9–12) have been approached to buy or use drugs, 40% of 16- and 17-year-olds have friends who use cocaine occasionally, and 76% of 16- and 17-year-olds have friends who use marijuana occasionally.

Teenagers (13–17)

Teenagers have experienced the fewest attitudinal shifts of the four segments. There have been some significant and positive changes, but they are not as large or as widespread as with other segments. Changing teenagers' attitudes is vital because the growth of drug use is so pronounced during these years.

All of the changes, however, are in the direction of less favorability toward drug use and drug users, and the consistency is important even if the number of changes is smaller. The teenage population is going to require a greater communication effort.

1. Out of 32 basic attitudes, 7 became more anti-drug, none became more pro-drug.
2. Out of 12 variables measuring the perceived risk of using drugs and alcohol, 7 increased. Five percent more feel it is "risky" to smoke marijuana regularly, from 80% to 85%; 5% more feel it is "risky" to do cocaine regularly, from 86% to 91%.
3. Five more teenagers fear the psychological and physical effects of marijuana.
4. Black teenagers show both increased fear of drugs and more anti-drug attitudes, with shifts ranging from 6% to 14%.
5. Nonusers are more likely to be seen as "a leader" and "attractive."

In particular, teenagers today perceive greater risk associated with drug use, especially regular drug use. Moreover, the attitudinal movement among Black teenagers is particularly encouraging.

The Advertising

The second purpose of the research is to track the effectiveness of the advertising and to investigate the correlation between exposure to the advertisements and attitudinal change.

The data collected on advertisement recall indicate two positive and clear trends: First, many of the advertisements have received excellent exposure. Second, they were rated very positively by the viewers. For example, 95% of the college students report seeing the "Man frying egg" advertisement, and 75% give it a "very positive rating." In general, the advertisements that have been seen the most are also perceived most positively by the viewers. The popularity of these advertisements is consistent throughout all age and racial groups.

Most importantly, there is strong evidence that the advertising is a powerful contributing factor in the improvement in attitudes toward drugs. The degree of "media weight" (i.e., the number of separate "exposures") in different markets varied considerably due to the cooperation of local media organizations. Because of this variation, it is possible to construct a "natural experiment," where the markets with the greatest media weight are isolated for analysis and comparison with the remainder of the United States. The top 10 markets, which comprise just over 10% of the total population, received an average of four times more Partnership advertising than the rest of the U.S.

Children 9–12

Although very little of the advertising in this campaign was aimed at this age group, children in high exposure areas show several important changes (see Table 8.2). Disagreement with three pro-drug statements in-

TABLE 8.2
Children in High Media Areas Become More Anti-Drug

	Percent Who Disagree	
	High Media Area	Balance U.S.A.
Using drugs makes you feel grown-up		
1987	60%	70%
1988	73%	75%
Variance	+13	+5
It is hard to get hooked on drugs		
1987	69%	73%
1988	80%	76%
Variance	+11	+3
I would try drugs if my friends did		
1987	84%	86%
1988	92%	91%
Variance	+8	+5
1987 n =	135	748
1988 n =	174	1016

creased by 8% to 13% in high media areas, compared with 3% to 5% in the balance of the United States. Conversations about drugs with parents, teachers, and siblings increased 9% to 15%, against *no increase* in the rest of the United States (see Table 8.3).

Teenagers

The teenage segment was, from the outset, considered to be the hardest segment to reach with the advertising. Overall, they show the fewest changes during the past year in the entire sample. When the respondents in the high exposure areas are separated, this group shows some very dramatic results.

1. On eight basic attitudes, the teenagers show changes of 8% to 20%, whereas the respondents in the rest of the U.S. changed by a negative 4% to plus 6% (see Table 8.4).
2. They see nonusers more positively, with shifts ranging from 13% to 18%; changes in the rest of the country ranged from negative 2% to positive 5% (see Table 8.5).
3. The teens in the high exposure areas show equally encouraging changes in their views of marijuana and cocaine users, with little or no changes in these items in the rest of the United States (see Tables 8.6–8.8).

Adults

The adults in the study demonstrate an equally significant number of items in which there is sharp improvement in attitudes in the high exposure areas, but little or no change in the rest of the United States.

1. On 10 basic attitudes, adults changed from 5 to 15 points in high exposure areas, with much less or no change in the rest of the United States (see Tables 8.9 and 8.10).
2. Adults in the high exposure areas show significant increases in their willingness to discourage others from using drugs, with no change in the rest of the country (see Table 8.11).
3. Parents in these areas are more willing both to complain to school officials and to discuss the dangers of drug use with their children (see Table 8.12).
4. In high exposure areas, fears of drug use increase significantly on 19 separate items, with increases from 5% to 10% (see Table 8.13).
5. Like teenagers, adults in the high exposure areas view both the non-users more positively and the users more negatively, again, with much smaller changes in the rest of the United States (see Tables 8.14–8.16).

TABLE 8.3
Children in High Media Areas Talking About Drugs More

	High Media Area	Balance U.S.A.
To siblings		
1987	31%	40%
1988	46%	40%
Variance	+15	0
To parents		
1987	64%	69%
1988	74%	70%
Variance	+10	+1
To teachers		
1987	50%	55%
1988	59%	55%
Variance	+9	0
1987 n =	135	748
1988 n =	174	1016

TABLE 8.4
Teens in High Media Areas Become More Anti-Drug

	Percent Who Agree	
	High Media Area	Balance U.S.A.
Marijuana is a stepping stone to harder drugs		
1987	70%	67%
1988	82%	73%
Variance	+20	+6
Taking drugs scares me		
1987	65%	66%
1988	76%	70%
Variance	+11	+4
Drugs make you do worse		
1987	72%	73%
1988	80%	75%
Variance	+8	+2
1987 n =	114	684
1988 n =	154	877

TABLE 8.5
Teens in High Media Areas See Nonusers More Positively

| | Percent Who Agree | |
	High Media Areas	Balance U.S.A.
Secure		
1987	39%	42%
1988	57%	43%
Variance	+18	+1
Intelligent		
1987	63%	68%
1988	78%	66%
Variance	+15	−2
Well-adjusted		
1987	45%	45%
1988	60%	48%
Variance	+15	+3
Reliable		
1987	47%	47%
1988	60%	48%
Variance	+13	+1
Adventurous		
1987	23%	24%
1988	36%	29%
Variance	+13	+5
1987 n =	114	684
1988 n =	154	877

TABLE 8.6
More Teens in High Media Areas Disagree With Pro-Drug Statements

| | Percent Who Disagree | |
	High Media Areas	Balance U.S.A.
It's OK for adults to sell a gram of cocaine to friends		
1987	73%	79%
1988	90%	79%
Variance	+17	0
It's OK for adults to sell an ounce of marijuana to friends		
1987	66%	72%
1988	82%	72%
Variance	+16	0

(Continued)

TABLE 8.6
(Continued)

	Percent Who Disagree	
	High Media Area	*Balance U.S.A.*
The more popular people smoke marijuana		
1987	46%	53%
1988	57%	49%
Variance	+11	−4
It's OK for adults to use cocaine in private		
1987	74%	76%
1988	85%	77%
Variance	+11	+1
People who use drugs are no different than anyone else		
1987	54%	61%
1988	64%	55%
Variance	+11	−1
1987 n =	114	684
1988 n =	154	877

TABLE 8.7
Teens in High Media Areas See Marijuana Users More Negatively

	Percent Who Agree	
	High Media Areas	*Balance U.S.A.*
A loner		
1987	30%	42%
1988	52%	42%
Variance	+22	0
Has no future		
1987	50%	57%
1988	67%	56%
Variance	+17	−1
Lazy		
1987	55%	62%
1988	72%	58%
Variance	+17	−4
Depressed		
1987	39%	44%
1988	53%	46%
Variance	+14	+2
A loser		
1987	47%	52%
1988	60%	52%
Variance	+13	0
1987 n =	114	684
1988 n =	154	877

TABLE 8.8
Teens in High Media Areas See Cocaine Users More Negatively

	Percent Who Agree	
	High Media Areas	Balance U.S.A.
Nervous		
1987	48%	52%
1988	72%	52%
Variance	+24	0
A loner		
1987	34%	47%
1988	56%	47%
Variance	+22	0
Lazy		
1987	45%	55%
1988	62%	54%
Variance	+17	−1
Has no future		
1987	62%	63%
1988	75%	63%
Variance	+13	0
1987 n =	114	684
1988 n =	154	877

TABLE 8.9
Adults in High Media Areas Become Less Pro-Drug

	Percent Who Disagree	
	High Media Areas	Balance U.S.A.
People who try drugs are adventurous		
1987	63%	61%
1988	75%	66%
Variance	+12	+5
Smoking cigarettes is more harmful than smoking marijuana		
1987	53%	50%
1988	61%	55%
Variance	+8	+5
It's fun to have drugs at a party		
1987	74%	74%
1988	81%	74%
Variance	+7	0

(Continued)

TABLE 8.9
Continued

	Percent Who Disagree	
	High Media Areas	Balance U.S.A.
Marijuana isn't harmful if used only occasionally		
1987	61%	58%
1988	67%	60%
Variance	+6	+2
Using cocaine is a status symbol		
1987	68%	67%
1988	74%	66%
Variance	+6	−1
Marijuana increases your creativity		
1987	68%	65%
1988	73%	63%
Variance	+5	−2
1987 n =	725	3,972
1988 n =	715	3,917

TABLE 8.10
Adults in High Media Areas Become More Anti-Drug

	Percent Who Agree	
	High Media Areas	Balance U.S.A.
I don't want to hang around with people who use drugs		
1987	70%	74%
1988	85%	80%
Variance	+15	+6
People on drugs act stupid/foolish		
1987	74%	75%
1988	82%	74%
Variance	+8	−1
Taking drugs scares me		
1987	83%	85%
1988	90%	84%
Variance	+7	−1
It's easy to become hooked on marijuana		
1987	71%	72%
1988	78%	71%
Variance	+7	−1
1987 n =	725	3,972
1988 n =	715	3,912

TABLE 8.11
Adults in High Media Areas Take More Action Against Drug Use

	Percent Who Took Action in the Last Year	
	High Media Areas	Balance U.S.A.
Discouraged a friend from using marijuana		
1987	21%	27%
1988	31%	27%
Variance	+10	0
Discouraged a friend from using crack		
1987	18%	20%
1988	23%	17%
Variance	+5	−3
Discouraged a friend from using cocaine		
1987	22%	26%
1988	27%	24%
Variance	+5	−2
1987 n =	688	3,797
1988 n =	685	3,821

TABLE 8.12
Parents in High Media Areas Take More Action Against Drugs

	Percent Who Took Action in the Last Year	
	High Media Areas	Balance U.S.A.
Complained to school officials about the use of drugs by children at the school		
1987	8%	11%
1988	18%	11%
Variance	+10	0
Discuss the dangers of drug use with your children		
1987	73%	69%
1988	78%	66%
Variance	+5	−3
1987 n =	412	2,176
1988 n =	491	2,139

TABLE 8.13

Fear Increases Sharply Among Adults

	Percent Who Greatly Fear	
	High Media Area	Balance U.S.A.
Reaction of parents if they discovered you were using marijuana		
1987	59%	62%
1988	69%	66%
Variance	+10%	+4%
Reaction of parents if they discovered you were using cocaine or crack		
1987	72%	74%
1988	82%	78%
Variance	+10%	+4%
Reaction of husband/wife or boyfriend/ girlfriend if they discovered you were using cocaine or crack		
1987	71%	72%
1988	80%	75%
Variance	+9%	+3%
Reaction of employer, school for marijuana		
1987	69%	68%
1988	78%	71%
Variance	+9%	+3%
Getting caught with enough marijuana to get in trouble with the law		
1987	68%	68%
1988	76%	72%
Variance	+8%	+4%
Getting caught with enough cocaine or crack to get in trouble with the law		
1987	76%	80%
1988	84%	81%
Variance	+8%	+1%
The influence your use of cocaine or crack might have on your brothers, sisters, or children		
1987	76%	77%
1988	84%	80%
Variance	+8%	+3%
Dying from crack use		
1987	84%	85%
1988	91%	85%
Variance	+7%	0
Dying from cocaine use		
1987	79%	80%
1988	86%	81%
Variance	+7%	+1%

(Continued)

TABLE 8.13
(Continued)

	Percent Who Greatly Fear	
	High Media Area	Balance U.S.A.
Becoming addicted to or dependent on cocaine or crack		
1987	81%	82%
1988	88%	83%
Variance	+7%	+1%
Reaction of your husband/wife or boyfriend/ girlfriend if they discovered you were using marijuana		
1987	58%	60%
1988	65%	61%
Variance	+7%	+1%
Reaction of employer, school for cocaine		
1987	80%	80%
1988	87%	82%
Variance	+7%	+2%
Having your motivation or your ability to perform at work, school, or sports suffer from marijuana		
1987	63%	62%
1988	70%	64%
Variance	+7%	+2%
Having your motivation or your ability to perform at work, school, or sports suffer from cocaine or crack		
1987	80%	79%
1988	87%	81%
Variance	+7%	+2%
Damage your reputation might suffer if your use of cocaine or crack became known by others		
1987	75%	75%
1988	82%	77%
Variance	+7%	+2%
The danger that marijuana might contain other harmful substances you could not know about		
1987	66%	67%
1988	73%	69%
Variance	+7%	+2%
Psychological damage from marijuana		
1987	54%	54%
1988	61%	58%
Variance	+7%	+4%

(Continued)

TABLE 8.13
(Continued)

	Percent Who Greatly Fear	
	High Media Area	Balance U.S.A.
The danger that cocaine or crack might contain other harmful substances you could not know about		
1987	81%	84%
1988	86%	84%
Variance	+5%	0
Physical damage from cocaine or crack		
1987	83%	83%
1988	88%	85%
Variance	+5%	+2%
1987 n =	662	3,635
1988 n =	655	3,685

TABLE 8.14
Adults in High Media Areas See Nonusers More Positively

	High Media Area	Balance U.S.A.
Intelligent		
1987	62%	66%
1988	71%	71%
Variance	+9%	+5%
In control		
1987	56%	59%
1988	64%	62%
Variance	+8%	+3%
Someone I would probably like		
1987	62%	64%
1988	69%	68%
Variance	+7%	+4%
A leader		
1987	36%	41%
1988	42%	44%
Variance	+6%	+3%
Easy going		
1987	24%	23%
1988	29%	24%
Variance	+5%	+1%
1987 n =	727	4,022
1988 n =	720	3,945

TABLE 8.15
Adults in High Media Areas Describe Marijuana Users More Negatively

	High Media Area	Balance U.S.A.
A loner		
1987	45%	40%
1988	54%	47%
Variance	+9%	+7%
Adventurous		
1987	18%	19%
1988	27%	21%
Variance	+9%	+2%
Shy		
1987	19%	20%
1988	27%	21%
Variance	+8%	+1%
Depressed		
1987	45%	46%
1988	52%	50%
Variance	+7%	+4%
1987 n =	727	4,022
1988 n =	720	3,945

TABLE 8.16
Adults in High Media Areas Describe Cocaine Users More Negatively

	High Media Area	Balance U.S.A.
A loser		
1987	51%	50%
1988	63%	58%
Variance	+12%	+8%
Has no future		
1987	56%	56%
1988	66%	63%
Variance	+10%	+7%
Depressed		
1987	43%	43%
1988	49%	48%
Variance	+6%	+5%
1987 n =	727	4,022
1988 n =	720	3,945

DISCUSSION AND CONCLUSIONS

The data are remarkable for the consistency of the effect of respondents in the high exposure areas. With many of these changes, virtually all of the shifts in attitudes over the past year appear in those areas. The effect is so strong and so widespread in the data set that it suggests the possibility that such advertising has to reach a threshold before it begins to have much effect in the rest of the country.

Drug abuse attitudes and beliefs are not the same as views on consumer products. In most instances, these attitudes are held strongly by individuals, with few people who are indifferent or undecided. Moreover, these attitudes are strengthened by reinforcing effects from friends, family, and other influencing agents. The data have already shown the powerful impacts, both favorable and unfavorable, of friendship networks on drug abuse.

Even with the strength of the orientations, however, the data strongly support the conclusion that advertising can affect the attitudes of Americans toward drug abuse.

IV

MASS COMMUNICATION AND THE INDIVIDUAL: TARGETING MESSAGES AND PROGRAMS AT SENSATION SEEKERS

9

Sensation Seeking and Drug Abuse Prevention From a Biological Perspective

Michael T. Bardo
University of Kentucky

Charles W. Mueller
*University of Hawaii
and
Kapiolani Medical Center*

A number of theories of drug abuse have been postulated, each emphasizing the importance of different legal, social, psychological, and biological factors. Although there has been much debate about the impact of these various factors, most researchers would now agree that certain individual differences predispose some people toward abuse more than others (e.g., Khantzian, 1985). This view has led some investigators to search for the critical factors that may predict an individual's risk for abuse.

Identification of the social, psychological, and biological factors that predict drug abuse risk may have important implications for structuring programs aimed at preventing the onset of abuse in adolescents and young adults. In this chapter, we review briefly the literature that suggests that at least one psychological trait, sensation seeking (SS), is related to drug abuse. Following this, we review the evidence that suggests that sensation-seeking and drug-seeking traits may be related because they involve a similar biological mechanism. We conclude with some speculation about the relevance of biological factors in drug abuse prevention programs.

RELATIONSHIP BETWEEN SENSATION SEEKING AND DRUG ABUSE

There has long been an interest in identifying personality characteristics related to drug abuse. The ''addiction-prone'' personality has been studied using a wide variety of theoretical models and empirical methods (for a

review see Barnes, 1979). Although general support for this notion is rather
limited, there is some evidence suggesting that impulsive personality factors are related to drug abuse.

Zuckerman's concept of sensation seeking has proven to be one of the
most promising of these approaches, because of its theoretical coherence,
its relationship to other models of individual differences (e.g., Eysenck,
1967) and to other bodies of literature (e.g., schizophrenia vulnerability;
McCann, Mueller, Hays, Scheuer, & Marsella, in press), as well as its extensive research base (Zuckerman, 1979). Zuckerman defined sensation
seeking along the lines of needs, specifically the need for complex experiences and the willingness to take risks for these experiences. Sensation seeking consists of four related subcategories: thrill and adventure seeking, experience seeking, disinhibition, and boredom susceptibility.
Although SS was originally proposed as an optimal arousal model, more
recently it has been reformulated as a brain reward model. This change
is important, in that the newer formulation places less emphasis on the
differences between substances of abuse (e.g., stimulants and depressants)
and focuses instead on their common reward value.

A number of studies have shown that SS correlates moderately with drug
abuse (see Zuckerman, 1987). For example, Jaffe and Archer (1987) examined drug use and personality characteristics of college men and women.
Participants completed an assessment battery that included an alcohol and
drug survey and selected personality scales and subscales. Results indicated that the overall SS score was the most powerful predictor of substance
abuse. Discriminant analyses indicated that the SS score was the single
most important variable in identifying drug taking patterns and in distin-
guishing between single and multiple drug users. Other studies have replicated these findings using different sample populations, including blue-
collar workers, sailors, soldiers, and clients in residential substance abuse
programs. In general, the relationship between SS and drug abuse is not
limited to any particular drug. However, the relationship appears to be
more robust among males than among females.

The most significant criticism of these studies is their reliance on correlational methods. Longitudinal studies are needed and there has been
some work in this area using measures related to SS. For instance, Jones
(1981) found themes of undercontrol and impulsivity in adolescent boys
who later became alcoholics. It is important to note, however, that these
correlations are moderate in degree. Clearly other processes and factors
affect drug abuse.

Recent evidence suggests that SS and drug abuse may be related only
within a subgroup of abusers. Different typologies of alcoholism and drug
abuse have been proposed. One such typology distinguishes a type of abuse
that is early in onset, impulsive and inheritable, from a second type that

is more common but less debilitating (Cloninger, 1987). Both theoretical and empirical work seem to indicate that SS is most closely related to abuse risk that is inheritable. Many of these chronic abusers manifest traits associated with antisocial personality disorder or ''psychopathy.'' These traits remain even after a period of abstinence. Men with an antisocial personality disorder score high on SS, especially on the disinhibition scale, again pointing to the relationship between this type of abuse and SS. Of course, although many psychopaths and chronic drug abusers are high sensation seekers, most high sensation seekers are neither.

What then are the mechanisms that affect this relationship? In the next section, we review some of the potential biological underpinnings of the relationship between SS and drug abuse.

BIOLOGICAL FACTORS IN SENSATION SEEKING AND DRUG ABUSE

Genetics

A number of individual differences appear to be influenced by genetics, including intellectual, psychopathological, and personality factors. SS is one such personality trait believed to be under some genetic influence. To test this influence, Fulker, Eysenck, and Zuckerman (1980) administered the SS scale to 422 pairs of adult twins. These included monozygotic (MZ) and dizygotic (DZ) same-sex twins and DZ different-sex twins. The authors used complex biometric-genetical statistics through which they attempted to identify specific sources of variation on given scores. Their results indicated that SS scores were primarily a function of genetic and within-family environmental factors. Genetic factors accounted for 58% of the variance in SS scores. This percentage of inheritability is comparable to that seen with intelligence measures when corrected for measurement error. Further, these investigators found that little variance was explained by between-family factors. However, there was some evidence that the pattern of inheritance might be different for men and for women, especially on the thrill- and adventure-seeking scale and on the disinhibition scale.

Although compelling, these results must be viewed with caution. First, they need to be replicated, particularly using adoption studies. Second, studies such as these, which compare MZ and DZ twins reared together, partially confound genetic and environmental influences. Identical twins, because of their similar physical attributes, may well elicit more similar environmental interactions than fraternal twins. This may be particularly true for interactions outside the immediate family (peers and other adults).

Just as SS may be inheritable, evidence also indicates that genetic factors may play a role in alcoholism (Searles, 1988). Although the overall evidence is equivocal and contradictory at times, it is generally agreed that alcoholism runs in families. Children of alcoholics are more likely to become alcoholics than are children of nonalcoholics. Males with greater genetic commonality show higher concordance rates for alcoholism than do those with less biological relatedness (e.g., siblings vs. first-degree cousins). Some twin studies have found higher concordance among MZ than among DZ twins. Some of the confusion and the conflicting results in the literature may be due to difficulties determining zygosity and to differing definitions of alcoholism and alcohol abuse. Also, as just mentioned, MZ twins may share a more common environment than do DZ twins, further hampering interpretations. Nevertheless, twin studies seem to support two tentative conclusions: Alcoholism may be more influenced by genetics than is alcohol use, and male alcoholism may be more influenced genetically than female alcoholism.

The strongest evidence for the inheritability of risk for alcoholism may come from adoption studies. Such studies conducted in Denmark, Sweden, and the United States provide some evidence for a genetic influence on alcoholism. Cloninger, Bohman, and Sigvardsson (1981) studied 862 adopted men in Sweden. Using Swedish national public records from social and medical agencies, they examined the influence of biological and environmental factors on alcohol abuse. The authors found that alcohol abuse was meaningfully described on a continuum from no abuse, to mild, moderate and severe abuse. Discriminant analyses then identified factors that predicted inclusion into each group. Their results indicated that mild and severe alcohol abusers were best identified by biological and environmental factors combined. These two groups were thought to have a similar genetic predisposition, but to differ in the extent to which environmental factors contributed to their alcohol abuse. The moderate abuse group was discriminated predominantly by biological factors. Specifically, the biological fathers' own alcohol abuse and general criminal history predicted inclusion into this group. These results support the notion that biological and environmental factors interact to predict risk for alcoholism, and that there are two types of alcohol abuse, distinguished by their degree of inheritability.

Other studies have yielded similar results. For instance, Carodet and Gath (1978) found that adoptees who were alcoholics were more likely to have alcoholic biological fathers than were nonalcoholic adoptees. This difference was not influenced by other factors they examined (e.g., age at adoption, or socioeconomic status of adoptive family). Interestingly, many of these alcoholic adoptees were found to have manifested a socialized conduct disorder as children.

These and other genetic studies have not gone without some criticism. For example, it has been pointed out that the inheritability of alcoholism among women is less clear than among men. Definitions of alcoholism and alcohol abuse also vary widely across studies. This is especially troublesome when a given study finds a genetic effect at one level of abuse or dysfunction but not at another. Such varying definitions can also lead to artifactual findings. Adoption studies are not free from alternative explanations, including the obvious potential effects of prenatal and perinatal environmental influences. Moreover, every adoption study published to date can be criticized on specific methodological grounds (cf. Searles, 1988).

Little is known about the genetic influences on the abuse of drugs other than alcohol by humans. However, some recent studies using animal models have suggested that abuse of a variety of psychoactive drugs is inheritable. For example, Crabbe, McSwigan, and Belknap (1985) have reviewed the literature that suggests that different inbred strains of mice exhibit a marked difference in reactivity to the analgesic effect of morphine. This difference in behavior may reflect a variety of inherited biological factors, including differences in drug disposition, density of opiate receptors in the brain, and levels of endogenous opioids. Further work is needed in order to determine whether or not such factors differ genetically in humans.

Platelet Monoamine Oxidase (MAO)

MAO is an enzyme involved in the metabolism of various biogenic amines, including dopamine, norepinephrine, serotonin, and tyramine. At least two different forms of the enzyme, which have differential affinities for various amines, have been identified: MAO-A and MAO-B. MAO has a ubiquitous distribution in the body, being found in the brain, liver, and gastrointestinal tract. In the brain, MAO is located both inside and outside of neurons, although the enzyme which is bound to intraneuronal mitochondria is thought to be most important in the metabolism of neurotransmitters such as dopamine, norepinephrine and serotonin. In human and nonhuman primates, MAO is also associated with blood platelets, although its role in the blood is not known for certain. What is clear, however, is that measuring platelet MAO is not a reliable index of MAO activity within the brain, as these biochemical parameters are not significantly correlated (Young, Laws, Sharbrough, & Weinshilboum, 1986).

Despite our lack of knowledge regarding the functional significance of platelet MAO, several studies have indicated that this enzyme may be correlated with the inheritance of SS (for review see Zuckerman, 1987). For example, Schooler, Zahn, Murphy, and Buchsbaum (1978) examined male and female young adult volunteers for blood platelet MAO activity and for scores on the SS scale. With both males and females, there was a significant negative correlation between MAO activity and SS scores. This negative correlation was found to be strongest when MAO activity was correlated with either the general SS scale or the experience-seeking subscale. Further, males had significantly lower MAO activity than females, which may be related to the fact that males tend to score higher on SS than females. Interestingly, a questionnaire filled out by these same subjects also provided data indicating that those with low MAO activity attended more high sensation events such as rock concerts and museums, whereas those with high MAO activity reported sleeping more and watching more television.

One problem with some of the studies reporting that MAO and SS are negatively correlated is that age was not partialled out as a confounding variable in the statistical analysis. Some evidence indicates that MAO activity may increase and SS may decrease as a function of age (Bridge et al., 1985; Klinteberg, Schalling, Edman, Oreland, & Asberg, 1987). Thus, using a subject population with a wide range of ages may lead to an artifactual negative correlation between MAO activity and SS. Fortunately, this possibility has been controlled for in several other studies. For example, Arque, Unzeta, and Torrubia (1988) used a normal subject population of male and female volunteers with an age range of 18 to 56 years and found that MAO activity and SS were negatively correlated even after age was partialled out in the statistical analysis. Moreover, significant negative correlations have also been obtained when the subject population was all of the same age (von Knorring & Oreland, 1985).

Perhaps a more serious problem in examining the relationship between MAO activity and SS is the potential confounding effect of drug abuse in altering MAO activity. As discussed previously, high SS individuals are more prone to use drugs than low SS ones. This opens the possibility that high SS individuals have lower MAO activity as a result of greater drug use. To assess this possibility, Ward, Catts, Norman, Burrows, and McConaghy (1987) examined the effect of cigarette smoking on the relationship between MAO activity and SS in male and female college students. They found that cigarette smokers had lower MAO activity than nonsmokers. When both smokers and nonsmokers were combined in an overall statistical analysis, a significant negative correlation between MAO activity and SS was obtained with males. However, when the statistical analyses were performed separately for smokers and nonsmokers, no significant correlations were obtained. In a related study, von Knorring and Oreland (1985) found that cigarette smokers used more alcohol, marijuana, amphetamines, and other drugs than did nonsmokers. The smokers also had lower MAO activity and higher SS scores than nonsmokers. In this study, a significant negative correlation between MAO activity and

SS was obtained with smokers, but not with nonsmokers. These studies indicate that drug use within the sample population may be an important factor to consider in examining the relationship between MAO activity and SS.

Although differences in drug intake may contribute to the negative correlation between MAO activity and SS, this confounding factor may be ruled out by using one of several research approaches. First, correlation coefficients may be analyzed after partialling out the influence of drug-taking differences within the subject population. Second, subject populations that are not actively engaged in recent drug-taking behavior may be used, perhaps including pre-adolescents who have never experienced drugs, or adults who are in a prolonged period of total abstinence. Third, controlled animal studies may be conducted if a satisfactory model of SS can be devised. For example, Redmond, Murphy and Baulu (1979) found that platelet MAO activity in male rhesus monkeys was negatively correlated with high-stimulation behaviors such as playing, social contact, and dominance displays, but positively correlated with low-stimulation behaviors such as self-grooming and being alone. Such approaches may strengthen the evidence indicating that MAO activity and SS are functionally linked.

Following the observed relationship between MAO and SS, evidence is now also accumulating to indicate that platelet MAO activity may be related to risk for drug abuse. A study by von Knorring, Oreland, and von Knorring (1987) showed that 18-year-old males who abused a variety of drugs such as alcohol, marijuana, amphetamines, and opiates had significantly lower MAO activity than males who reported no drug abuse history. Similarly, a number of studies have reported that patients hospitalized for alcoholism have lower MAO activity than normal control subjects (for review see Cloninger, 1987). Alexopoulos, Lieberman, and Frances (1983) showed further than the nonalcoholic first-degree relatives of hospitalized alcoholics also had significantly lower MAO activity than normal control subjects. This latter finding is important because it suggests that the decrease in MAO activity in alcoholics is not induced by alcohol.

More recent work in this area suggests that platelet MAO activity may be a biological marker only for the subtype of alcoholism that shows the greatest inheritability. A study by von Knorring, Bohman, von Knorring, and Oreland (1985) examined MAO levels in male and female outpatient alcoholics who had been abstinent for at least 4 weeks. The male alcoholics had lower MAO activity than normal control subjects, but this finding was only evident within a subgroup of patients that showed the highest inheritability of alcoholism. Interestingly, these alcoholics also reported significantly more abuse of drugs other than alcohol and scored significantly higher on the SS scale when compared with the subgroup of patients that showed low inheritability of alcoholism. This suggests the possibility that MAO activity may eventually offer a biological marker for SS and drug abuse risk, at least with some individuals.

Brain Neurotransmitters

Despite the extensive literature that has examined platelet MAO, there is presently little direct evidence to indicate whether there are any biochemical differences within the brain between high and low SS individuals. This lack of information is due largely to the technical problems involved in quantifying brain biochemical activity in humans. Although drug receptors can be measured using positron emission tomography (PET) and levels of neurotransmitters can be quantified postmortem, these approaches may yield only a limited view of the functional activity of brain neurotransmitter systems.

In one study, Zuckerman, Ballenger, and Post (1984) took samples of cerebrospinal fluid (CSF) from a spinal lumbar puncture of male and female volunteers who were also administered the SS scale. The CSF was analyzed for metabolites of the biogenic amines, dopamine, norepinephrine, and serotonin. Bivariate correlations between each metabolite and SS were performed after partialling out the effects of age, height, and weight. The results revealed a significant negative correlation between levels of the norepinephrine metabolite methoxy-hydroxyphenylglycol (MHPG) and scores on the SS scale for both males and females, perhaps indicating that high SS individuals have a lower level of norepinephrine activity in the brain than low SS individuals. If both norepinephrine metabolite and MAO levels are decreased in high SS individuals, then this suggests that there may be a deficit in both the release and metabolism of the neurotransmitter in the brain. However, these results must be interpreted cautiously because CSF metabolite levels may not directly reflect neurotransmitter release in discrete brain regions.

An alternative approach to studying the neurochemical mechanisms involved in SS is to use animal models. Although SS as defined by Zuckerman's scale clearly cannot be measured in laboratory animals, some components of the SS trait may be represented with an animal analogue. In particular, it has been shown that complex novel visual stimuli are preferred by high SS humans more than by low SS humans (Lambert & Levy, 1972). Similarly, various strains of mice display inheritable differences in the exploration of novel stimuli (Peeler & Nowakowski, 1987). Reactivity to novelty may therefore offer a useful rodent analogue to study the neurochemical basis of one component of the SS trait.

Using animal models, a number of investigations have implicated a critical role for dopamine (DA) in the exploration of novel stimuli. For example, in an investigation in our laboratory (Bardo, Neisewander, & Pierce, 1989), we assessed the effect of various drugs on novelty-seeking behavior in rats. The animals were first exposed to one of two different stimulus environments. Following this, they were given free-choice access to both the familiar and novel environments simultaneously. The novel environment was preferred over the familiar one, and all animals spent more time in the novel environment. This novelty preference behavior was blocked completely when the animals were tested under the influence of the DA antagonist haloperidol. The blockade of novelty preference was not due to the locomotor depressant action of haloperidol, as other drugs that alter locomotor activity did not affect novelty preference. Instead, haloperidol may have blocked the DA receptors that mediate the rewarding value of novel stimulation.

Other studies have shown that lesions of the mesolimbic DA system in rats disrupt the normal exploratory behaviors directed toward novel stimuli (Fink & Smith, 1980). The mesolimbic DA system is a neuronal fiber path that runs from the ventral tegmental area of the midbrain to the nucleus accumbens of the limbic system. Strong evidence now indicates that the mesolimbic DA pathway mediates the rewarding effects of various stimuli, including food, water, intracranial self-stimulation, and psychoactive drugs (for review see Wise, 1983). Indeed, novelty-seeking and drug-seeking behaviors are, perhaps, both reinforced because they both activate a common mesolimbic DA system within the brain.

Much of the evidence implicating the mesolimbic DA system in drug reward comes from studies conducted with laboratory animals in which they were conditioned to administer drugs to themselves. Like humans, most animals will perform an operant response that is reinforced by intravenous self-administration of a psychoactive drug (see Weeks & Collins, 1987). The operant response rate is determined by the magnitude of reinforcement derived from the drug dose used. In general, it is found that higher self-administration response rates are evident with low drug doses than with high drug doses. Using this technique, it has been shown that rats responding for intravenous amphetamine reward will increase their response rate when challenged with a low dose of a DA antagonist (Yokel & Wise, 1975). This suggests that the DA antagonist essentially decreased the amphetamine reward derived from each injection. Further, high doses of DA antagonist were found to terminate amphetamine self-administration behavior altogether, which is indicative of extinguishing the rewarding value completely. Similarly, a lesion within the mesolimbic nucleus accumbens has also been shown to disrupt amphetamine self-administration in rats (Lyness, Friedle, & Moore, 1979).

In another, recent study, Di Chiara and Imperato (1988) examined the extracellular levels of DA within the nucleus accumbens of rats to which various drugs were administered. In general, drugs that are abused by humans (e.g., amphetamine, cocaine, morphine, ethanol, and nicotine) were found to increase DA levels, whereas drugs not abused by humans (e.g., imipramine, atropine, and diphenhydramine) did not affect DA levels. These results support the idea that the ability of a drug to act as a rewarding stimulus is dependent on its ability to increase synaptic DA concentrations within the nucleus accumbens.

Perhaps individual differences in the sensitivity of the mesolimbic DA system to drug reward may underly, at least in part, the individual differences seen in drug abuse liability. In humans, the magnitude of reward derived from the first drug experience can predict the subsequent degree of risk for drug addiction (Haertzen, Kocher, & Miyasato, 1983). Although there is no direct evidence to indicate whether this difference in drug reward reflects a difference in the sensitivity of the mesolimbic DA system, some evidence derived from animal experiments indicates that this may be the case. For example, Kiianmaa and Tabakoff (1983) found that strains of mice that differed in their behavioral sensitivity to a low dose of ethanol showed a differential activation of the DA system within the brain.

These results suggest that high SS individuals may have a mesolimbic DA system that is more sensitive to the rewarding effects of drugs than that of low SS individuals. In a study conducted by Carrol, Zuckerman, and Vogel (1982), high and low SS male volunteers were administered amphetamine, diazepam (Valium) or placebo drug treatments in a double-blind design in which various physiological, affective, and psychomotor tests were administered. In addition, the subjects were asked to identify the drug they had received and to rate it for enjoyment on a 7-point scale. Interestingly, although the effects of diazepam and amphetamine on the physiological and psychomotor variables did not differ significantly between high and low SS subjects, the enjoyment of both drugs was significantly greater in the high SS subjects than in the low SS subjects. Perhaps high SS individuals enjoy the stimulation provided by drugs and novelty because they both activate a similar mesolimbic DA reward system.

IMPLICATIONS FOR
DRUG ABUSE PREVENTION PROGRAMS

Alcoholism, and likely other types of drug addiction, runs in families. This suggests that some prevention programs should be targeted at children raised by substance abusing parents. Many such programs are already in place at the community level. A more controversial issue concerns the case of adoption. Should adoptive parents be informed about the substance abuse history of the biological parents and relatives? If so, can the adoptive parents be counseled to reduce the risk of substance abuse in the child?

Numerous programs have been implemented in an attempt to prevent or delay drug abuse in adolescents. These programs have relied on a variety of techniques, including peer-oriented support groups, law enforcement education programs (e.g., DARE) and mass media public service announcements. Although the effectiveness of each of these programs requires further investigation, it seems clear that one prerequisite for the success of any program is that it captures the attention of those individuals at highest risk for drug abuse. Perhaps the psychobiological factors that predispose an individual to abuse drugs may also predispose that individual to attend preferentially to different prevention messages.

Indeed, some evidence indicates that high and low SS individuals may differ in their physiological reactivity to sensory information. For example, Neary and Zuckerman (1976) measured the skin conductance changes in high and low SS college students exposed to complex colored visual stimuli. It was found that high SS individuals were more aroused than low SS individuals by the initial stimulus presentation, although there was no difference between the groups in the rate of habituation to repeated stimulus presentations. In another study, Herning, Hickey, Pickworth, and Jaffe (1989) found that delinquent adolescents at risk for drug abuse showed a deficit in the processing of repeated simple auditory stimuli as measured by two different electrophysiological measures. These studies provide some initial evidence that adolescents at risk for drug abuse may be biologically prepared to attend more to novel complex stimuli than to simple repetitive stimuli.

Drug abuse prevention programs may also benefit by research that seeks to identify the specific biological factors that predispose an individual to drug abuse. As described previously, recent evidence suggests that sensation-seeking and drug-seeking behaviors may be mediated by similar mechanisms within the brain. Perhaps high sensation seekers find both drugs and novelty to be especially rewarding because they have a hypersensitive mesolimbic DA reward system. These individuals may have a "biological drive" to seek those stimuli that activate the DA reward system. If this is the case, then these individuals could be targeted for prevention programs that provide novel and arousing sensory events that may "satisfy" this brain reward system, thus decreasing the relative rewarding value of drugs. Such sensory stimulation may come from various events, including travel, amusement park rides, physical exercise, and high-energy sports activities. Whether such sensory events may substitute for the rewarding value provided by drugs remains to be determined.

REFERENCES

Alexopoulos, G. S., Lieberman, K. W., & Frances, R. J. (1983). Platelet MAO activity in alcoholic patients and their first-degree relatives. *American Journal of Psychiatry, 140*, 1501–1504.

Arque, J. M., Unzeta, M., & Torrubia, R. (1988). Neurotransmitter systems and personality measurements: A study in psychosomatic patients and healthy subjects. *Neuropsychobiology*, 19, 149–157.

Bardo, M. T., Neisewander, J. L., & Pierce, R. C. (1989). Novelty-induced place preference behavior in rats: Effects of opiate and dopaminergic drugs. *Pharmacology, Biochemistry & Behavior*, 32, 683–689.

Barnes, G. E. (1979). The alcoholic personality: A reanalysis of the literature. *Journal of Studies of Alcohol*, 40, 571–634.

Bridge, T. P., Soldo, B. J., Phelps, B. H., Wise, C. D., Francak, M. J., & Wyatt, R. J. (1985). Platelet monoamine oxidase activity: Demographic characteristics contribute to enzyme activity variability. *Journal of Gerontology*, 40, 23–28.

Carodet, R. J., & Gath, A. (1978). Inheritance of alcoholism in adoptees. *British Journal of Psychiatry*, 132, 252–258.

Carrol, E. N., Zuckerman, M., & Vogel, W. H. (1982). A test of the optimal level of arousal theory of sensation seeking. *Journal of Personality and Social Psychology*, 42, 572–575.

Cloninger, C. R. (1987). Neurogenic adaptive mechanisms in alcoholism. *Science*, 236, 410–416.

Cloninger, C. R., Bohman, M., & Sigvardsson, S. (1981). Inheritance of alcohol abuse: Cross fostering analysis of adopted men. *Archives of General Psychiatry*, 38, 861–868.

Crabbe, J. C., McSwigan, J. D., & Belknap, J. K. (1985). The role of genetics in substance abuse. In M. Galizio & S. A. Maisto (Eds.), *Determinants of substance abuse: Biological, psychological and environmental factors* (pp. 13–64). New York: Plenum Press.

Di Chiara, G., & Imperato, A. (1988). Drugs abused by humans preferentially increase synaptic dopamine concentrations in the mesolimbic system of freely moving rats. *Proceedings of the National Academy of Science USA*, 85, 5274–5278.

Eysenck, H. J. (1967). *The biological basis of personality*. Springfield, IL.: Charles C. Thomas.

Fink, J. S., & Smith, G. P. (1980). Mesolimbic and mesocortical dopaminergic neurons are necessary for normal exploratory behavior in rats. *Neuroscience Letters*, 17, 61–65.

Fulker, D. W., Eysenck, S. B. G., & Zuckerman, M. (1980). A genetic and environmental analysis of sensation seeking. *Journal of Research in Personality*, 14, 261–281.

Haertzen, C. A., Kocher, T. R., & Miyasato, K. (1983). Reinforcements from the first drug experience can predict later drug habits and/or addiction: Results with coffee, cigarettes, alcohol, barbiturates, minor and major tranquilizers, stimulants, marijuana, hallucinogens, heroin, opiates and cocaine. *Drug and Alcohol Dependence*, 11, 147–165.

Herning, R. I., Hickey, J. E., Pickworth, W. B., & Jaffe, J. H. (1989). Auditory event-related potentials in adolescents at risk for drug abuse. *Biological Psychiatry*, 25, 598–609.

Jaffe, L. T., & Archer, R. P. (1987). The prediction of drug use among college students from MMPI, MCMI, and sensation seeking scales. *Journal of Personality Assessment*, 51, 243–253.

Jones, M. C. (1981). Midlife drinking patterns: Correlates and antecedents. In D. Eichorn, J. Clausen, N. Haan, M. Honzik, & P. Mussen (Eds.), *Present and past in middle life* (pp. 223–242). New York: Academic Press.

Khantzian, E. J. (1985). The self-medication hypothesis of addictive disorders: Focus on heroin and cocaine dependence. *American Journal of Psychiatry*, 142, 1259–1264.

Kiianmaa, K., & Tabakoff, B. (1983). Neurochemical correlates of tolerance and strain differences in the neurochemical effects of ethanol. *Pharmacology, Biochemistry & Behavior*, 18 (Suppl 1), 383–388.

Klinteberg, B., Schalling, D., Edman, G., Oreland, L., & Asberg, M. (1987). Personality correlates of platelet monoamine oxidase (MAO) activity in female and male subjects. *Neuropsychobiology*, 18, 89–96.

Lambert, W., & Levy, L. H. (1972). Sensation seeking and short term sensory isolation. *Journal of Personality and Social Psychology*, 24, 46–52.

Lyness, W. H., Friedle, N. M., & Moore, K. E. (1979). Destruction of dopaminergic nerve terminals in nucleus accumbens: Effect on d-amphetamine self-administration. *Pharmacology, Biochemistry & Behavior*, 11, 553–556.

McCann, S., Mueller, C., Hays, P., Scheuer, A. & Marsella, A. (in press). The relationship between anhedonia and sensation seeking. *Journal of Personality and Individual Differences.*

Neary, R. S., Zuckerman, M. (1976). Sensation seeking, trait and state anxiety, and the electrodermal orienting response. *Psychophysiology, 13,* 205–211.

Peeler, D. F., & Nowakowski, R. S. (1987). Genetic factors and the measurement of exploratory activity. *Behavioral and Neural Biology, 48,* 90–103.

Redmond, D. E., Murphy, D. L., & Baulu, J. (1979). Platelet monoamine oxidase activity correlates with social affiliative and agonistic behaviors in normal rhesus monkeys. *Psychosomatic Medicine, 41,* 87–100.

Schooler, C., Zahn, T. P., Murphy, D. L., & Buchsbaum, M. S. (1978). Psychological correlates of monoamine oxidase activity in normals. *The Journal of Nervous and Mental Disease, 166,* 177–186.

Searles, J. S. (1988). The role of genetics in the pathogenesis of alcoholism. *Journal of Abnormal Psychology, 97,* 153–167.

von Knorring, A. L., Bohman, M., von Knorring, L., & Oreland, L. (1985). Platelet MAO activity as a biological marker in subgroups of alcoholism. *Acta Psychiatrica Scandinavica, 72,* 51–58.

von Knorring, L., & Oreland, L. (1985). Personality traits and platelet monoamine oxidase in tobacco smokers. *Psychological Medicine, 15,* 327–334.

von Knorring, L., Oreland, L., & von Knorring, A. L. (1987). Personality traits and platelet MAO activity in alcohol and drug abusing teenage boys. *Acta Psychiatrica Scandinavica, 75,* 307–314.

Ward, P. B., Catts, S. V., Norman, T. R., Burrows, G. D., & McConaghy, N. (1987). Low platelet monoamine oxidase and sensation seeking in males: An established relationship? *Acta Psychiatrica Scandinavica, 75,* 86–90.

Weeks, J. R., & Collins, R. J. (1987). Screening for drug reinforcement using intravenous self-administration in the rat. In M. A. Bozarth (Ed.), *Methods of assessing the reinforcing properties of abused drugs* (pp. 35–43). New York: Springer-Verlag.

Wise, R. A. (1983). Brain neuronal systems mediating reward processes. In J. E. Smith & J. D. Lane (Eds.), *The neurobiology of opiate reward processes* (pp. 405–437). Amsterdam: Elsevier.

Yokel, R. A., & Wise, R. A. (1975). Increased lever pressing for amphetamine after pimozide in rats: Implications for a dopamine theory of reward. *Science, 187,* 547–549.

Young, W., Laws, E., Sharbrough, F., & Weinshilboum, R. M. (1986). Human monoamine oxidase: Lack of brain and platelet correlation. *Archives of General Psychiatry, 43,* 604–609.

Zuckerman, M. (1979). *Sensation seeking: Beyond the optimal level of arousal.* Hillsdale, NJ: Lawrence Erlbaum Associates.

Zuckerman, M. (1987). Biological connection between sensation seeking and drug abuse. In J. Engel & L. Oreland (Eds.), *Brain reward systems and abuse* (pp. 165–176). New York: Raven Press.

Zuckerman, M., Ballenger, J. C., & Post, R. M. (1984). The neurobiology of some dimensions of personality. In: J. R. Smythiies & R. J. Bradley (Eds.) *International review of neurobiology* (Vol. 25, pp. 391–436). New York: Academic Press.

Sensation Seeking and Targeting of Televised Anti-Drug PSAs

Lewis Donohew
Elizabeth Lorch
Philip Palmgreen
University of Kentucky

This chapter addresses a limited but vitally important objective—how to reach out in an effective manner via televised public service announcements (PSAs) to particular "at-risk" audiences to motivate participation in other phases of drug abuse prevention programs. Anti-drug PSAs have become an increasingly popular tool in prevention campaigns, but media-*only* campaigns have been largely unsuccessful in bringing about changes in behavior (Flay, 1981, 1983). Media have been more successful in the context of comprehensive public health campaigns involving both media and nonmedia efforts to reach target populations, as in the Stanford Three-Community Study (Flay & Sobel, 1983). There is a need, however, to strengthen the mass media component of campaigns against drug abuse. Studies of the use of the mass media for drug abuse prevention that included anti-drug or alcohol PSAs show that many PSA campaigns failed to bring about meaningful change because they failed to reach their target audience (Capalaces & Starr, 1973; Delaney, 1978, 1981; Field, Deitrick, Hersey, Probst, & Theologus, 1983; Hanneman, 1973; Hanneman & McEwen, 1973; Harris & Associates, 1974; Hu & Mitchell, 1981; Morrison, Kline, & Miller, 1976; Plant, Pirie, & Kreitman, 1979; Rappaport, Labow, & Williams, 1975).

There are several reasons for this, according to Flay and Sobel (1983):

1. *lack of dissemination*—in several campaigns studied the PSAs were aired outside of prime time and/or on noncommercial stations, and then only infrequently, thus greatly reducing reach and frequency of exposure;

209

2. *lack of targeting*—many anti-drug PSAs have been directed at unidentifiable audience segments; and

3. *selectivity*—individual attitudes, values, and norms affect exposure to drug-related messages—drug users and those at high risk for becoming users are likely to avoid anti-drug PSAs.

The lack of dissemination problem, although difficult, can be addressed by well-planned and carefully executed approaches to convincing media gatekeepers of the need to air more PSAs more frequently in prime time (Flay & Sobel, 1983). A recent example of a successful collaboration between message designers and the media is the "Partnership for a Drug Free America" campaign (Black, 1988). Solving the targeting and selectivity problems, however, will require much additional research. According to Flay and Sobel (1983), and, more recently, Atkin and Freimuth (1989), much more emphasis should be placed on formative message research in the laboratory before proceeding to more expensive field evaluations, and certainly prior to program dissemination: "Only after it has been established than an efficacious communication product has been developed, is it worth disseminating it" (Flay & Sobel, 1983, p. 26).

A series of studies funded by the National Institute on Drug Abuse, one of which is reported on here, is focused directly on the problem of developing and testing methods of enhancing the effectiveness of televised anti-drug PSAs. These PSAs often are submerged in an overwhelming clutter of programming and product advertisements and must be capable of: (a) immediately attracting the attention of target audience members; and (b) motivating these viewers to attend to the remainder of the message. In addition, such messages require relatively high levels of information-processing intensity and/or involvement to achieve informational and persuasive goals. Further, motives for watching television ordinarily do not include exposure to advertising and PSAs.

Designing effective televised anti-drug PSAs for use in comprehensive prevention campaigns is thus a difficult task. Ways must be found to motivate both attention to the entire message and high-level processing of its content. A promising way of accomplishing these goals according to previous research by Donohew and associates is to target messages according to sensation-seeking level, a biologically based characteristic (Zuckerman, 1978, 1983, 1988) found to be associated with both communication (Donohew, Palmgreen, & Duncan, 1980) and drug use (Donohew, 1990; Zuckerman, 1978).

Sensation Seeking

Need for sensation—a need related to preferences for novel, complex, and ambiguous stimuli (e.g., Zuckerman, 1988)—has been measured both as a personality trait (Pearson, 1970, 1971; Zuckerman, 1978, 1983, 1987; Zuckerman, Kolin, Price, & Zoob, 1964) and as part of a more general activation theory of information exposure (Donohew, Finn, & Christ, 1988; Donohew et al., 1980).

Zuckerman incorporated Berlyne's arousal potential qualities of stimulation and factors that reduce arousal potential, including repetition, constancy, and over familiarity as ends of a sensation-seeking continuum united in an optimal level of arousal theory of the sensation-seeking motive. A Sensation Seeking Scale (SSS) was constructed to measure the characteristic (Zuckerman, Eysenck, & Eysenck, 1978). As described by Zuckerman (1978, 1988) the four subscales of the SSS are:

1. Thrill and Adventure Seeking: A desire to seek sensation through physically risky activities that provide unusual situations and novel experiences (e.g., parachuting and scuba diving).
2. Experience Seeking: A desire to seek sensation through a nonconforming lifestyle, travel, music, art, drugs, and unconventional friends.
3. Disinhibition: A desire to seek sensation through social stimulation, parties, social drinking, and a variety of sex partners.
4. Boredom Susceptibility: An aversion to boredom produced by unchanging conditions or persons and a great restlessness when things are the same for any period of time.

Describing differences between high and low sensation seekers, Zuckerman (1988) has observed that:

> The high sensation seeker is receptive to novel stimuli; the low tends to reject them, preferring the more familiar and less complex. The high sensation seeker's optimal level of stimulation may depend on the levels set by the characteristic level of arousal produced by novel stimuli. Anything producing lower arousal levels may be considered "boring." . . . Apart from the voluntary avoidance of high intensities of stimulation, the low sensation seeker may have a type of nervous system that rejects such stimulation or inhibits cortical reactivity to high intensity stimuli. (pp. 181–182)

Findings from both current and previous research by Donohew (1988, 1990; Donohew et al., 1990) strongly indicate that sensation seeking offers an avenue for targeting prime at-risk groups and designing messages and programs to reach them. The studies consistently indicate highly significant differences in marijuana use between high- and low-sensation seekers at both the junior and senior high school age levels. Among junior high school students, high-sensation seekers (HSS) were clearly the first to use marijuana. The disparity between high- and low-sensation seekers (LSS) in drug use among members of this age group was so great that it was difficult to find enough subjects for the experimental condition calling for low-sensation seeking users. Results are essentially the same when the measure of drug use is marijuana, alcohol, tobacco, cocaine, and other substances (see Table 10.1).

Zuckerman and associates (1978) found that 74% of college undergraduates scoring high on his sensation-seeking scale had used one or more drugs, as opposed to 23% of those scoring low on the scale. Association of sensation seeking with drug use has been supported in a number of other studies. Using a variety of personality measures, Segal and Singer (1976) found that the SSS provided the most discrimination between nonusers and various user groups. Use of specific drugs, such as amphetamines, marijuana, hashish, and LSD correlates strongly with sensation seeking. Studies of sensation seeking and alcohol use tended to employ the disinhibition subscale of the SSS. Positive relationships were found between alcohol use and the disinhibition subscale in adolescents (Bates, Labouvie, & White, n.d.) and college student populations (Schwarz, Burkhart, & Green, 1978) but not among alcoholic populations (Kish & Leahy, 1970; Pare, 1973). Studies conducted with drug abusers found that medium and high-sensation seekers had experimented with drugs at an earlier age than low-sensation seeking abusers, and had more varied drug experience (Zuckerman, 1978).

In the area of communication, persons with high need for sensation also tend to tolerate or even require stronger messages for attracting and holding their attention (Donohew et al., 1988; Donohew et al., 1980). Findings from communication studies thus far indicate that individual differences in need for sensation and, to a lesser extent, in prior drug use play a major role in exposure to and comprehension of drug abuse prevention messages, and in arousal (skin conductance), attitudinal, and behavioral intention responses to the messages.

TABLE 10.1
Sensation Seeking and Drug Use Among
Junior and Senior High School Students[*]

	Junior High LSS n = 658	Junior High HSS n = 565	Senior High LSS n = 450	Senior High HSS n = 420
Marijuana	6.2	24.7	13.0	38.3
Cocaine	.6	3.4	1.8	6.6
Liquor	20.7	58.3	28.5	67.1
Beer	24.9	58.3	38.0	70.5
Uppers	1.4	14.9	2.0	14.8
Downers	.5	11.2	1.6	6.6

[*] These figures represent percentage of students at the 7th- through 12th-grade levels who indicated using particular drugs at least once during the last 30 days.

The messages used in the experimental studies by Donohew and associates were most effective with two prime target groups:

1. those likely to be at greater risk of becoming drug users—high-sensation seekers (HSS) who had not used marijuana but were ambivalent in their attitudes toward its use, making them likely to be at greater risk for becoming users; and
2. low-sensation seeking (LSS) moderate users of marijuana, whose drug use behaviors were somewhat beyond the risk-taking norm for their personality type and who were found to have mixed attitudes toward marijuana use.

These two groups indicated the most interest in further exposure to prevention messages. Two other groups in the study showed less interest in the message:

1. high-sensation seeking drug users, who indicated favorable attitudes toward marijuana use; and
2. low-sensation seeking nonusers who were highly unfavorable to marijuana use.

These results take on more meaning when considered in the context of a drug abuse prevention campaign employing the mass media. They are particularly pertinent when the objective of the mass media portion of the campaign is to generate awareness and attitude change and to stimulate responses that bring audiences into situations where interpersonal contact can be initiated.

Optimal Levels of Arousal

Arousal theories hold that behavioral efficiency increases as arousal increases to some optimal level, then falls off as arousal level continues to increase (Berlyne, 1971; Cacioppo & Petty, 1983; Cacioppo, Petty, & Tassinary, 1988; Hebb, 1955). These theories also have implications for exposure to particular stimuli. As noted by Martindale (1981):

> . . . the more arousal potential a stimulus has, the more attention an organism will devote to it. Up to a certain point, this increasing attention will be accompanied by increasing pleasure. Presumably, this will lead the organism to approach the stimulus in question. Beyond this point, the increasing attention will be accompanied by increasing displeasure. (p. 257)

Information Exposure. As described earlier, need for arousal is fundamental to human behavior and serves an important function in the mechanisms guiding exposure to the mass media. The activation theory of information exposure referred to earlier (Donohew et al., 1980) is grounded in assumptions that individuals operate most effectively at an optimal level of arousal that varies across individuals (see Fig. 10.1). The theory assumes that motivation for exposure to a message involves both cognitive need for information and physiological need for stimulation (Donohew et al., 1988; Finn, 1983, 1984). It proposes that individuals enter information exposure situations with the expectation of achieving or maintaining this optimal state of activation. It should be noted, however, that the monitoring of this "expectation" may be carried out at a low level of awareness. If the level of activation falls below or exceeds the desired level, individuals will tend to turn away from the source of information and seek more or less exciting stimuli, as appropriate to their needs. If the activation level reaches or remains within some range perceived to be acceptable, individuals will continue to expose themselves to the information. Under conditions of very high arousal, even high-sensation seekers would be likely to avoid a message. One shortcoming of this theory, however, is that it is difficult to specify just what is high arousal because there does not yet exist a parsimonious procedure for establishing individual arousal baselines. It is assumed, however, that for HSS individuals the most likely state at any given point in time is *stimulus hunger*, and for LSS it is *stimulus satiation*. Thus, individuals with a high need for activation would most of the time be in an *arousal-seeking* mode and those with lower needs would be in an *arousal-avoidance* mode.

The optimal level of arousal theory does not imply, however, that individuals read, watch, or listen to only those items that maintain arousal levels within desired boundaries. As Donohew et al. (1988) noted:

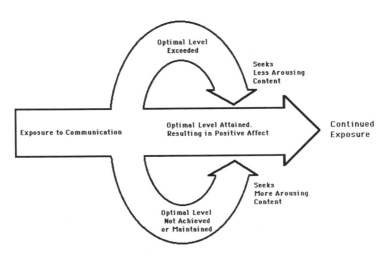

FIG. 10.1. Activation model of information exposure.

Although arousal needs do appear to guide (people) in their selections, they may choose to override these affective tugs for any of a number of reasons, such as desire to learn more about a topic of importance to them in which they perceive themselves to be deficient. (p. 195)

NEED FOR FORMATIVE RESEARCH

The previous discussion strongly implies that messages designed to appeal to the needs of high-sensation seekers will be more effective in reaching and influencing this high-risk group.

We are testing this proposition in a series of laboratory experiments in which both HSS and LSS subjects are exposed to anti-drug PSAs either high in sensation value or low in sensation value. We define sensation value as the degree to which formal and content audiovisual features of a televised message elicit sensory, affective, and arousal responses.

Thus, a major goal preparatory to conducting these studies was to develop two PSAs for a target audience of 18- to 22-year-olds, one aimed at HSS and the other at LSS individuals. The 18–22 age group displays the highest, or nearly the highest, usage levels for a number of different drugs, according to the 1985 National Household Survey on Drug Abuse. For example, 39.1% of this group had used marijuana in the past 12 months, and 23.5% in the past 30 days (highest among the age groups). The group also ranked first in cocaine use, with 17.5% using cocaine in the past 12 months and 8.7% in the past 30 days, compared to figures of 8.2% and 3.9% respectively for the 16–17 age group.

Message Design and Pretesting

The process of attaining this goal included several steps. First, characteristics of televised messages that have differential appeal for HSS and LSS individuals were determined. Second, this information was used to develop several concepts for PSAs, three of which were developed into high sensation value (HSV) and low sensation value (LSV) storyboards and pretested with 18- to 22-year-olds. Third, based on pretest responses and production considerations, one concept was chosen and its storyboards modified for final production. The PSAs were produced by an award-winning producer who participated in all aspects of their development.

The strategy for accomplishing the first step was based on the notion that HSS individuals seek stimuli producing higher levels of arousal than LSS individuals (Zuckerman, 1988). Therefore, it was thought that various production characteristics or "formal features" of televised messages might produce different responses in the two groups of people. For example, a more unusual format, a greater frequency of editing techniques, faster and more frequent movement, and more intense music might be characteristics that would increase the "sensation value" of a televised message, thus increasing its appeal to HSS viewers. With this in mind, a large number of commercials and PSAs were reviewed, from which nine commercials and three PSAs were selected for testing. This material included a variety of content and production techniques and was thought to represent wide variations in sensation value: from a peaceful, slow-paced ad for Classico spaghetti sauce to an intense, music video format Pontiac ad.

Focus group interviews were conducted and quantitative data were collected in order to determine responses to each of the spots. Participants were drawn from a randomly generated list of 500 registered voters, ages 18–22, in Fayette County, Kentucky, and from University of Kentucky communication classes. Those who agreed to participate were asked to complete the Zuckerman Sensation Seeking Scale and to return it by mail. The median for the sample was 20. Those with scores between 19 and 21 were excluded. Those scoring 18 or below were classified as low-sensation seekers and those scoring 22 or above as high-sensation seekers. From these pools, four six-person focus groups of HSS subjects and four six-person focus groups of LSS subjects were created.

The members of each group participated in a session of approximately 2 hours. The first part of the session was a general discussion about advertising, during which subjects were asked about various techniques used in commercials and to pick their most and least favorite commercials. After the general discussion, the group was shown 6 of the 12 selected commercials. Two different orders of presentation were employed. After viewing each spot, the group members gave their opinions and discussed what they particularly liked or disliked about it. After all six spots had been shown, subjects were asked to choose the spots they liked most, and those they liked least. Focus group discussions were audiotaped and transcribed. Transcripts were coded for mention of positive and negative ad/PSA attributes. Each member of the project team also read all transcripts as part of a more qualitative assessment of the preferences of HSS and LSS respondents.

The remainder of each session consisted of the collection of quantitative measures from individual members of each group. Five of the focus group participants were brought into a communications laboratory to view the remaining six spots they had not discussed. (Because of the capacity of the laboratory, the participant with the sensation-seeking score closest to the median was excused.) Physiological arousal was measured while the subjects viewed the spots, and ratings of how much they liked the spots and measures of recall of the spots were obtained after viewing.

Overall, consistent conclusions emerged from the focus group data and the quantitative measures. The value of the formative research process was emphasized when it was discovered that characteristics producing differential appeal were not so straightforward as a consideration of formal features and their relation to sensation value might have implied. First, HSS and LSS viewers responded similarly to a number of characteristics. For example, rock music and the fast-paced music video format, humor, and a good story line with believable characters that the audience could relate to were liked by both groups, and neither HSS nor LSS viewers wanted to be "preached to" in a PSA. Second, differences between the two groups were more subtle than expected. Although rock music was favored in general, HSS subjects preferred more intense, hard-edged music than LSS subjects. HSS subjects also reacted more positively to novel formats and unusual uses of formal features (e.g., extreme close-ups and heavy use of sound effects in the absence of music). Higher levels of suspense, tension, drama, and emotional impact also were more strongly favored by HSS viewers. LSS participants preferred more closure at the end of a story (e.g., they responded positively to a tag line summing up the message of one PSA), whereas HSS subjects expressed a preference for drawing their own conclusions (e.g., they were more likely to see the same tag line as an example of "preaching" and as insulting to their intelligence).

Based on the data from the focus groups, a number of possible message concepts were developed for high sensation value (HSV) and low sensation value (LSV) versions of an anti-drug PSA. The goal was to target the versions specifically at HSS or LSS viewers, respectively, while controlling as many message variables (e.g., general format and theme, actors, length, narrator) as possible across the HSV and LSV versions. Nevertheless, one content difference was intentionally introduced. Past research (Donohew, 1988) suggests that LSS individuals are relatively unlikely to become users unless society, probably as represented by peers, intervenes. Thus, it was decided that the LSV message should aim at the development of peer-resistance skills. In contrast, research findings (Donohew, 1988) suggest that HSS individuals are at greater risk to become drug users, and may be influenced best by encouraging the substitution of alternative stimulating but prosocial activities. Three message concepts were eventually selected and developed into HSV and LSV storyboards.

To assess the effectiveness of the concepts and the differentiation of the HSV and LSV versions, two focus groups and two individual reaction groups were conducted. These groups were drawn from 18- to 22-year-olds in University of Kentucky classes. Sensation-seeking scores were obtained for all participants; cutpoints of 18 and 22 were used to define LSS and HSS subjects. The three sets of storyboards were presented as color slides with accompanying audio and visual instructions read by the moderator. Participants saw all six storyboards, with presentation order of the three main concepts and the two versions of each varying across groups. In the two focus groups (containing approximately 10 participants each), an open-ended discussion was held after the viewing of each storyboard. In the two reaction groups, participants completed individual questionnaires after each storyboard. Subjects were asked about the message's ability to gain attention and to provoke thinking about drug abuse, and about their likes and dislikes for the message. They also were asked to choose between the two versions of each message and to provide reasons for the choice.

The concept chosen for production represented a pinball game. A hand was shown pulling back the plunger to start the ball through the machine. As the ball bounced off bumpers, scenes of social activities (LSV) or exciting alternatives to drug use (HSV) were shown. When the possibility of drug use was introduced, the game "tilted" and the ball entered the game's "Dead End Alley" depicting drug abuse and negative consequences of using drugs, as highlighted by a shot of an ambulance exiting the alley. The PSAs ended by presenting 1-800-hotline numbers to call for information about peer-resistance skills (LSV) or alternatives to drug use (HSV). In a "motivational introduction" version of each PSA, the hand pulling back the plunger in the initial scene was accompanied by a dramatic voiceover saying, "The game is life."

The pinball concept was selected for a number of reasons. Subjects in the focus and reaction groups generally perceived it as novel, creative, and attention-getting, and many of its specific features drew positive comments. It also had production advantages. The concept called for a combination of animation and live action. This combination permitted costs to be kept reasonable, and also allowed a greater degree of manipulation of specific features to distinguish the HSV and LSV versions.

In addition to the positive features of the pinball concept, the pretesting also revealed that a number of modifications were necessary before final production. The alternatives to drug use and the social situations presented were perceived as insufficiently realistic, and so were modified in accord with participants' responses. The data also revealed that the LSV version needed to be made more appealing to LSS viewers. Several changes were made to accomplish this, including the attenuation of the emotional impact and the strengthening of tag lines at the end of the spot.

INITIAL EVALUATION STUDY: RATIONALE

The purpose of the initial evaluation study was to determine the effectiveness of each version of the pinball PSA with high- and low-sensation seekers. In this study, the PSA was presented in the context of other media messages under controlled laboratory conditions designed to promote high attention. Although several dependent variables were included (e.g., mood, attitude toward drug use, free and cued recall of content), the only measure reported here is behavioral intention to call a drug hotline as advocated in the PSA. (The results for other variables are reported elsewhere.) It was expected that the high sensation value anti-drug PSAs would induce a stronger behavioral intention with high-sensation seekers, whereas the low-sensation value PSAs would be more effective with low-sensation seekers. In addition, it was expected that a PSA that included the verbal audio motivational introduction would be more effective than an otherwise identical PSA without such an introduction. A final question for this investigation was: Does level of drug use mediate the effects of the above message variables?

METHOD

Independent variables were (a) sensation seeking—high or low; (b) message sensation value—high or low; (c) motivational introduction to the PSA—presence or absence of a brief verbal audio message (as described earlier) to attract and motivate continued attention; and (d) drug use— a quantitative measure of frequency of use of various illicit drugs in the past 30 days. These were employed in a 2x2x2x2 randomized groups design.

Selection of Subjects

The 18- to 22-year-old subjects were recruited from a variety of sources, including drivers license listings, recruitment ads in a local newspaper and a shoppers weekly, a local public university, and a local 2-year community college. Included in the final analyses of the experiment were 207 subjects.

Sensation Seeking

Subjects completed the Zuckerman (1979) sensation-seeking scale, Form V. A median split on the sum of the 37 nondrug-related items was used to define low- and high-sensation seekers, who then were randomly assigned to one of the experimental conditions ($n = 165$) or the control group ($n = 42$).[1]

---

[1]Because time constraints did not allow subjects to be run individually, they were run in groups of two to five persons (usually four or five persons). These groups (rather than individuals) were randomly assigned to the experimental conditions or control group.

Laboratory Procedure

Subjects were seated facing a color television monitor, and told they would be shown several televised ads/messages. The videotape began with 4 minutes of a story from "CBS Sunday Morning," and continued with two 30-second commercials, one of the test PSAs, then three more 30-second ads, and a repeat of the PSA. Subjects then completed behavioral intention, attitude, and drug use scales, and indicated their age, gender, and educational level. Control group subjects participated in all procedures except the anti-drug PSAs were not included in the video content.

RESULTS

The most important result from a targeting perspective is the interaction (in factorial ANOVA) between message sensation value and sensation seeking ($p = .059$) with an index of intent to call a drug hotline as the dependent variable. Values greater than 1.00 on the index indicate a stronger intention of the experimental group to call the appropriate hotline than that of the appropriate control group.[2] As hypothesized, the behavioral intention to call the hotline of low-sensation seekers was more affected by the low-sensation message than by the high-sensation PSA (see Fig. 10.2). High-sensation seekers, on the other hand, were somewhat more persuaded by the high-sensation message.

A strong main effect emerged on behavioral intention for motivational introduction ($p = .011$). The PSA versions with the motivational intro generally were more effective ($\bar{X} = 1.33$) in inducing subjects to call the appropriate hotline, relative to the appropriate control group, than those exposed to the non-intro messages ($\bar{X} = 1.01$). The results indicate that careful attention should be paid to the verbal audio characteristics of the introductory portion of televised anti-drug PSAs.

Another significant two-way interaction, between sensation seeking and use/non-use of illicit drugs in the past 30 days ($p = .023$), revealed a somewhat surprising pattern (see Fig. 10.3). It was expected that high-sensation seeking users of illicit drugs would, for both behavioral and biological reasons, be the most resistant to anti-drug messages. Instead, in this comparison this group displayed the strongest behavioral intention to call the hotline advocated in the PSA relative to the appropriate control group ($\bar{X} = 1.40$). Low-sensation seeking users of drugs, on the other hand, displayed

---

[2]Variables employed to determine the appropriate control group were sensation seeking (high or low) and drug use (user vs. nonuser). Thus HSS users in the experimental group were compared to HSS users in the control group, and so on.

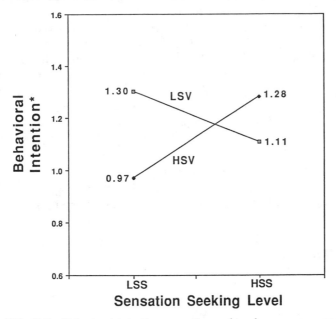

FIG. 10.2. Behavioral intention: sensation seeking by message sensation value.

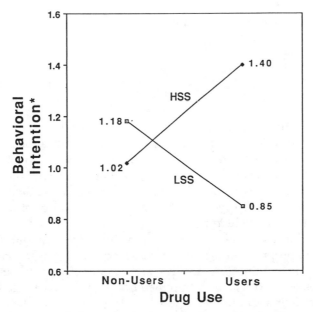

FIG. 10.3. Behavioral intention: sensation seeking by drug use.

negative effects on behavioral intention ($\bar{X}$ = .85). Low-sensation seeking non-users of drugs showed some positive impact of the message ($\bar{X}$ = 1.18). Finally, high-sensation seeking non-users, a group particularly at risk to become drug users, on the surface appeared to be unaffected by the appeal to call the hotline ($\bar{X}$ = 1.02). This finding, however, ignores the effects of message sensation value and motivational introduction. Further analysis revealed that the HSV intro version of the PSA was highly effective with HSS non-users ($\bar{X}$ = 1.58). In other words, this important at-risk group was reached effectively with the message hypothesized to do so (i.e., a message high in sensation value that included a motivational introduction).

HSS users, on the other hand, were positively affected by both HSV messages (with and without intro) and by the LSV message with intro as well. The subgroup of HSS users exposed to the LSV intro message was very small (n = 7), however, and any inferences based on it must be highly tentative.

DISCUSSION

This study has important implications for the development and targeting of effective televised anti-drug PSAs. First, it underscores the importance of formative research in the production of anti-drug messages. As noted in a recent review:

> health educators have not typically used systematic approaches at the pre-production stage, as mass media campaign efforts often proceed in the absence of a research foundation. Instead, messages tend to be produced in a haphazard fashion based on creative inspiration of copywriters and artists, patterned after the normative standards of the health campaign genre. (Atkin & Freimuth, 1989, p. 132)

Although this study began with the theory-based goal of creating messages that would have differential appeal for high- and low-sensation seekers, our initial conceptualizations of the defining characteristics of high- and low-sensation value messages were modified in several ways by the results of the pre-production formative research. We learned of characteristics that seemed to have general appeal for this age group, and discovered relatively subtle features that held differential appeal for HSS and LSS viewers. Without the formative research, much time and money might have been spent on inappropriate strategies for reaching the target groups.

Two elements of the formative research approach should be stressed: (a) In our opinion, the focus group methodology was particularly useful. As argued by Wimmer and Dominick (1987), focus group responses often are more complete than those from individual interviews, because one respondents' remarks tend to stimulate others to pursue different lines of thinking. Although focus group and quantitative reaction data were generally consistent in our formative research, the focus group responses tended to be more revealing of some of the subtle differences between high- and low-sensation seekers. (b) The formative research included multiple stages: After developing message concepts based on principles and characteristics identified in the first stage, each message concept was tested in a second stage. The concept finally selected was then modified for production in a third stage. Each stage was crucial to the development of effective messages.

A second implication is that the results of the initial evaluation study provide rather convincing evidence that sensation-seeking and message sensation value can be employed in concert to target televised anti-drug PSAs at young adults who are users of illicit drugs or at risk of becoming users. They also indicate the importance of developing effective verbal message introductions that motivate and/or facilitate further message processing.

The specific nature of the most effective messages within different audience subgroups may depend on the goal of the media campaign. If the goal of the media campaign is modest behavioral change, such as inducing young adults to call a hotline for drug-related information or to put them in touch with face-to-face intervention programs, then this study offers clear guidelines for designing messages to reach non-drug users with different needs for sensation. For high-sensation seeking non-users, a group whose members are particularly at risk to become users, a message that stresses exciting alternatives to drug use and is high in sensation value clearly is more likely to be effective than one that stresses peer-resistance skills and is lower in sensation value. Motivated by a biologically based need for sensation, these individuals are attracted to information about activities that fulfill this need. They may indeed already be involved in many such activities. Low-sensation seeking non-users, on the other hand, appear to be much more influenced by a message that stresses peer-resistance skills and is low in sensation value than by a message that features exciting alternatives to drug use and is high in sensation value. A question worth investigating is whether members of this group actually are frequently subjected to peer-group pressure to use drugs, or whether they simply fear such pressure. In any case, their lower need for sensation makes information about exciting alternatives to drug use much less salient than it is to high-sensation seekers.

The finding that high-sensation seeking *users* are vulnerable to appeals based on exciting alternatives and may also be open to those featuring peer resistance information is somewhat surprising, and indicates the need for further research (being carried out by the first author) into the development of peer group networks among high- and low-sensation seekers. It may be that high-sensation seekers at some point in their psychosocial development begin to choose others as friends who share their propensity for thrilling and exciting activities, including drug use. If indeed the relevant peer groups of HSS drug users contain disproportionate numbers of other HSS users, then information about peer-resistance skills would be sorely needed by those who desire to stop or decrease their use of drugs. In any event, it is encouraging to note that high HSS users, who might be expected to be the most impervious to media influence, nonetheless were vulnerable on the behavioral intention index to both kinds of message appeals employed here. Although many of those classified as "users" in this study were only low to moderate in their use of illicit drugs, our findings caution against assuming that HSS users are "unreachable" in a media PSA campaign. The messages, however, must be carefully designed and targeted.

Finally, it should be recognized that the differences between HSV and LSV messages were intentionally restricted for experimental purposes. Therefore, the HSV PSAs employed in the present study do not represent an extreme in message sensation value. The focus group findings implied, however, that it might be difficult to make a message "too strong" for HSS—that highly sensation fear appeals may work for those with particularly strong sensation needs (something not considered in research on fear appeals). In the HSV messages used here, any serious drug-related health consequences were only *implied* by the PSA ambulance scene and by the written message: "Drugs can take you out of the game."

More direct, dramatic depictions of serious consequences might be too much for LSS to accommodate, but may prove effective with HSS. If so, then messages that represent the upper ranges of the message sensation value dimension might be expected to show even stronger differential or "targeting" effects on HSS and LSS than those in the present study. Given that televised anti-drug PSAs are turning to more explicit depictions of drug use consequences, this is a question worth investigating.

ACKNOWLEDGMENT

This research described here was funded under Grant No. DA 05312 from the National Institute on Drug Abuse.

REFERENCES

Atkin, C. K., & Freimuth, V. (1989). Formative evaluation research in campaign design. In R. E. Rice & C. K. Atkin (Eds.), *Public communication campaigns (pp. 131–150). Newbury Park, CA: Sage.*

Bates, M. E., Labouvie, E. W., & White, H. R. (n.d.). *The effect of sensation seeking needs on alcohol and marijuana use in adolescence.* Unpublished manuscript, Rutgers University, Center of Alcohol Studies, New Brunswick, NJ.

Berlyne, D. (1971). *Aesthetic and psychophysiology.* New York: Appleton-Century-Crofts.

Black, G. S. (1988). *Changing attitudes toward drug use-1988.* Rochester, NY: Gordon S. Black Corp.

Cacioppo, J., & Petty, R. (1983). Foundations of social psychophysiology. In J. Cacioppo & R. Petty (Eds.). *Social psychophysiology: A sourcebook* (pp. 3–36). New York: Guilford.

Cacioppo, J., Petty, R., & Tassinary, L. (1988). Communication, social cognition and affect: A psychophysiological approach. In L. Donohew, H. Sypher, & T. Higgins (Eds.), *Communication, social cognition, and affect* (pp. 219–245). Hillsdale, NJ: Lawrence Erlbaum Associates.

Capalaces, R., & Starr, J. (1973). The negative message of anti-drug spots: Does it get across? *Public Telecommunications Review, 1,* 64–66.

Delaney, R. W. (1978). *Comparison impact of two approaches to primary alcoholism prevention in Florida—1978.* Sarasota, FL: Department of Health and Rehabilitative Services, Alcohol Abuse Prevention Project.

Delaney, R. (1981). *NIAAA information and feature service.* The National Clearinghouse for Alcohol Information of the National Institute on Alcohol Abuse and Alcoholism, Rockeville, MD.

Donohew, L. (1988). *Effects of drug abuse message styles: Final report.* A report of a study conducted under a grant from the National Institute on Drug Abuse.

Donohew, L. (1990). Public health campaigns: Targeting strategies and a model. In E. B. Ray & L. Donohew (Eds.), *Communication and health: Systems, processes, and applications* (pp.). Hillsdale, NJ: Lawrence Erlbaum Associates.

Donohew, L., Finn, S., & Christ, W. (1988). The nature of news revisited: the role of affect, schemas, and cognition. In L. Donohew, H. Sypher, & T. Higgins (Eds.), *Communication, social cognition, and affect* (pp. 195–218). Hillsdale, NJ: Lawrence Erlbaum Associates.

Donohew, L., Helm, D., Lawrence, P., & Shatzer, M. (1990). Sensation seeking, marijuana use, and responses to drug abuse prevention messages. In R. Watson (Ed.). *Prevention and treatment of drug and alcohol abuse.* Clifton, NJ: Humana.

Donohew, L. Palmgreen, P., & Duncan, J. (1980). An activation model of information exposure. *Communication Monographs, 47,* 295–303.

Field, T., Deitrick, S., Hersey, J. C., Probst, J. C., & Theologus, G. C. (1983). *Implementing public education campaigns: Lessons from alcohol abuse prevention* (Summary report to NIAAA). Washington, DC: Kappa Systems.

Finn, H. S. (1983). An information theory approach to reader enjoyment of print journalism (Doctoral dissertation, Stanford University, 1982). *Dissertation Abstracts International, 43,* 2481A–2482A.

Finn, S. (1984). Information-theoretic measures of reader enjoyment. *Written Communication, 2,* 358–376.

Flay, B. R. (1981). On increasing the chances of mass media health promotion programs causing meaningful changes in behavior. In M. Meyer (Ed.), *Health education by television and radio* (pp.). Munich: Saur.

Flay, B. R. (1983). *State-of-the-art in mass media and smoking behavior.* Paper presented at NCI Workshop on the role of mass media in smoking prevention and cessation, Washington, DC.

Flay, B. R., & Sobel, J. L. (1983). The role of mass media in preventing adolescent substance abuse. In T. J. Glynn, C. G. Leukefeld, & J. P. Lundford (Eds.), *Preventing adolescent drug abuse: Intervention strategies.* NIDA Research Monograph Series (47).

Hanneman, G. J. (1973). Communicating drug abuse information among college students. *Public opinion quarterly, 37*(2), 171–191.

Hanneman, G. J., & McEwen, W. J. (1973). Televised drug abuse appeals: A content analysis. *Journalism quarterly, 50*(2), 329–333.

Harris, L., & Associates. *Public awareness of the NIAAA advertising campaign and public attitudes toward drinking and alcohol abuse.* Rockville, MD: The National Institute on Alcohol Abuse and Alcoholism: Report #2352.

Hebb, D. C. (1955). Drives and the CNS (conceptual nervous system). *Psychological Review,* *62,* 243–254.

Hu, T., & Mitchell, M. E. (1981). *Cost effectiveness evaluation of the 1978 media drug abuse prevention television campaign.* A final report submitted to the Prevention Branch, National Institute on Drug Abuse, Rockville, MD.

Kish, G. B., & Leahy, L. (1970). Stimulus-seeking, age, interests and aptitudes: An amplification. *Perceptual and Motor Skills, 30,* 670.

Martindale, C. (1981). *Cognition and consciousness.* Homewood, IL: Dorsey.

Morrison, A. F., Kline, F. G., & Miller, P. (1976). Aspects of adolescent information acquisition about drugs and alcohol topics. In R. Ostman (Ed.), *Communication research and drug education* (pp.). London: Sage.

Pare, W. P. (1973). *Sensation seeking and extraversion in hospitalized alcoholics.* Unpublished manuscript.

Pearson, P. H. (1970) Relationships between global and specified measures of novelty-seeking. *Journal of Consulting and Clinical Psychology, 34,* 199–204.

Pearson, P. H. (1971). Differential relationships of four forms of novelty experiencing. *Journal of Consulting and Clinical Psychology, 37,* 23–30.

Plant, M. A., Pirie, F., & Kreitman, N. (1979). Evaluation of the Scottish Health Education Unit's 1976 campaign on alcoholism. *Social Psychology, 14,* 11–24.

Rappaport, M., Labow, P., & Williams, J. (1975). *The public evaluates the NIAAA public education campaign: A study for the U.S. department of health, education, and welfare, public health service, alcohol, drug abuse, and mental health administration* (2 vols.). Princeton, NJ: Opinion Research Corp.

Schwarz, R. M., Burkhart, B. R., & Green, B. (1978). Turning on or turning off: Sensation seeking or tension reduction as motivation determinants of alcohol use. *Journal of Consulting and Clinical Psychology, 46,* 1144–1145.

Segal, B., & Singer, J. L. (1976). Daydreaming, drug and alcohol use in college students: A factor analytic study. *Addictive Behaviors,* 227–235.

Wimmer, R. D., & Dominick, J. R. (1987). *Mass media research: An introduction.* Belmont, CA: Wadsworth.

Zuckerman, M. (1979). *Sensation seeking: Beyond the optimal level of arousal.* Hillsdale, NJ: Lawrence Erlbaum Associates.

Zuckerman, M. (1983). *Biological bases of sensation seeking, impulsivity, and anxiety.* Hillsdale, NJ: Lawrence Erlbaum Associates.

Zuckerman, M. (1988). Behavior and biology: Research on sensation seeking and reactions to the media. In L. Donohew, H. Sypher, & T. Higgins (Eds.), *Communication, social cognition, and affect* (pp. 173–194). Hillsdale, NJ: Lawrence Erlbaum Associates.

Zuckerman, M., Eysenck, S. B., & Eysenck, H. J. (1978). Sensation seeking in England and America: Cross-cultural, age, and sex comparisons. *Journal of Consulting and Clinical Psychology, 46,* 139–149.

Zuckerman, M., Kolin, E. A., Price, L., & Zoob, I. (1964). Development of a sensation-seeking scale. *Journal of Consulting Psychology, 28,* 477–482.

Zuckerman, M., Neary, R. S., & Brustman, B. A. (1970). *Sensation seeking scale correlates in experience (smoking, drugs, alcohol, "hallucinations," and sex) and preference for complexity (designs.)* Proceedings of the 78th Annual Convention of the American Psychological Association.

V

INTERPERSONAL, SCHOOL, AND COMMUNITY APPROACHES

personality factor to explain drug abuse are not discussed here because they do not readily lend themselves to interpersonal interventions.

Findings derived from social learning theory (Akers, 1985; Bandura, 1977) and its spinoff, socialization theory (Jessor & Jessor, 1977; Kandel & Andrews, 1987) indicate the importance of the behavior of peers in the initiation of smoking, drinking, and illegal drug use. Adolescents learn to drink, smoke, and use drugs by observing this behavior in their parents, older siblings, or friends. Programs derived from this theoretical perspective focus preventive education and activities on peer groups and also aim to reduce drug, alcohol, and tobacco use in groups such as parents who might serve as role models for adolescents. Learning theory can be useful in designing intervention programs by helping to ensure that youths receive information and intervention on a schedule that maximizes their acquisition, recall, and application of prevention materials (Schinke, Moncher, Palleja, Zayas, & Schilling, 1988).

Persuasive communication theories (Kiesler, Collins, & Miller, 1969; Leventhal, 1968, 1971; McGuire, 1973) indicate that latent cues from others, such as parents' implicit attitudes or ambivalence, influence a child's attitudes toward drug use. Appeals aimed at preventive behaviors are more effective if they stress the risks from neglecting such behaviors, the value of taking preventive action, and ways to overcome any barriers to preventive behavior.

Both mass media and interpersonal approaches are based on findings from persuasive communication theories. Persuasive messages that are uncomplicated ("Say no to drugs"), material that is easy to learn, and behaviors that are consistent with a person's lifestyle are more often followed than complicated procedures that require major changes in daily routine (Sackett & Haynes, 1976). Construction of persuasive messages and the use of fear appeals are important in developing prevention strategies, but these message characteristics are beyond the scope of this chapter. However, I discuss one model derived from persuasive communication theories, the health belief model (Becker, 1974; Becker et al., 1977; Becker & Maiman, 1983).

Advocates of the health belief model contend that whether or not people take actions regarding health problems or preventive behaviors is determined by their perceived susceptibility of getting an illness, the perceived seriousness of that illness, the perceived benefits and barriers to taking action and triggers that cause people to take action. Impaired professionals (i.e., affected by drugs or alcohol) such as nurses or physicians, persons who are well-educated regarding the negative effects of addiction, repeatedly stress that although they understood the seriousness of the disease, they thought they were too strong and knowledgeable to ever become addicted. In short, they did not perceive themselves as susceptible to addiction. Work with impaired medical professionals (AMA Council on Mental Health, 1973; Sullivan, 1987a, 1987b) shows that many academically and professionally successful professionals become addicted to drugs or alcohol. These findings argue against education alone as an effective deterrent to substance abuse. The triggers to action as described in the health belief model may be mass media announcements suggesting to call a hot line, an accident, arrest or other embarrassing event, or an expression of concern from another person regarding one's drinking, smoking, or drug use.

Utilizing the health belief model in designing prevention programs suggests that one should provide information regarding the serious consequences of drug use, the susceptibility of targeted persons to becoming addicted or other negative consequences of use, the value of participation in prevention programs or in alternative activities designed to reduce the likelihood of substance use, and how to combat or reduce any barriers to taking action. Strategies to provide triggers such as public service announcements would follow from the model, also.

Group dynamics and subculture theories (Lewin, 1951, 1953; Sherif & Sherif, 1964; Zigler & Child, 1969) indicate that groups pressure individuals into conformity with their norms. If an adolescent wishes to be a part of a group, and the group engages in smoking, drinking, or drug use, the individual will conform to the group norms and engage in these behaviors also. Social pressure may also be harnessed in prevention activities to keep groups of adolescents drug-free.

Self-derogation theory (Kaplan, 1975, 1976, 1980) indicates that attitudes of self-rejection come from group experiences that the individual is unable to cope with, adapt to, or defend oneself against. These situations lead to loss of self-esteem and to an increase in self-derogation. Development of attitudes of self-rejection results in a decreased desire to conform to the expectation of the group that rejected one. Consequently, the rejected individual is motivated to seek out alternative groups who may have deviant patterns such as drug use, but will accept the individual and thereby increase that individual's self-esteem. For example, the male student who is rejected by the fraternity of his choice or does not make the football team may disavow interest in any organized fraternity or sports activity, and may join a group with deviant behaviors such as drug use to gain acceptance.

The theory of motivated actors (Dembo, Blount, Schmeidler, & Burgos, 1986) stems from the finding of an inverse effect in inner-cities between friends' use of hard drugs and personal drug use. The greater use of hard drugs by friends, the less likely youth would be to use alcohol and marijuana. Rather than assuming that the individual was pushed to drug use by the social group, Dembo et al. posited a boomerang effect whereby the individual resists using hard drugs after observing their effects on his ur her friends. Youngsters using soft drugs such as alcohol and marijuana in high-risk environments rejected hard drug-using peers. Although most interpersonal theories see the individual as responding to social and environmental pressures, Dembo et al. perceive persons as guiding their own behavior in an attempt to actualize self-defined values.

Some theorists believe that drug use develops as an attempt to cope with personal stress. Strained social relationships and a heightened sense of powerlessness or helplessness may induce adolescents to rely more heavily on substance abuse as a means of emotional self-regulation. Drug use requires little effort or ability, promises instant effect, and provides a sense of personal control (Labouvie, 1986). Stressors may be cognitive such as perceived helplessness, fatalism, or low self-esteem; they may stem from the social milieu such as poverty, unemployment, or racial discrimination; or they may stem from the environment such as noise, substandard and crowded housing, and environmental safety hazards (Schinke et al., 1988). Programs teaching relaxation techniques and other strategies to cope with stress stem from the stress and coping theoretical perspective.

Another perspective assumes that certain environments such as inner-cities are risk factors for drug abuse (Dembo et al., 1986). Therefore, programs in inner cities should provide extrinsic rewards for nonuse of drugs. Dembo et al. feel that recognition programs for nonusers should be public policy and should be linked to community organizations, religious organizations, and respected neighborhood role models. Efforts should also be made to reduce the environmental pressures that encourage drug use.

SETTINGS FOR DRUG ABUSE PREVENTION

Drug abuse prevention programs may take place in a variety of settings: in the home through self-help programs and consumer education; in the community, through the mass media, through laws passed at all levels of government; in schools; in workplaces; and in medical care settings.

GENERAL RESEARCH FINDINGS

Research and experience have determined that information alone is not sufficient to deter drug abuse. Findings from research on impaired physicians and nurses reinforce that statement. Some drug education programs assume that information about commonly abused substances and their effects will change attitudes and behaviors. Such an assumption ignores the peer-contexts of drinking, smoking, and drug use.

Adolescent drug use is rarely initiated or sustained outside of the context of the social group. Peer influences on drug use are much stronger than parental influences (Kandel & Andrews, 1987). The influence of parents has been found to be strongest at the early stage of drug involvement, preceding initiation of substance use. A strong parent–child bond restrains youths from using drugs. Once youths have experimented with drugs, however, parental control is exerted only indirectly through choice of friends by the adolescent. Once drug use has begun, imitation of peers is the dominant form of social influence, especially regarding immediate lifestyle, although parental influence remains important for issues dealing with future life goals (Kandel & Andrews, 1987).

Older siblings are important influences on initial drug use, frequently obtaining tobacco, alcohol, or drugs for their younger brothers and sisters (Needle et al., 1986). Slightly older peers serve as role models, encouraging drug use. The employment of older peers as role models may be helpful, also, in programs aimed at preventing substance abuse. Using slightly older peers to deliver program materials has proved effective in smoking education programs (Fisher, 1977; Foon, 1986).

Peer influences may result from *perceptions* of peer attitudes and behaviors rather than from actual peer behavior. Studies with college students indicate that they misperceive their peers as more liberal regarding drinking behavior than they actually are. Perkins and Berkowitz (1986) indicated that preventive responsible attitudes already exist in most users. Therefore, prevention and treatment programs may not need to change attitudes, but should correct the exaggerated images of peer drinking and drug use to make it easier for students to act on their own attitudes of moderation. Moskowitz (1983) contended that drug-specific prevention strategies should elicit and reinforce existing attitudes among youth that oppose alcohol and drug use. By exposing an entire cohort, within a school for example, to the strategy, one could invest those anti-drug sentiments with normative properties.

It should be noted that we have emphasized adolescent drug use and prevention programs targeting youth. There is evidence of a progression of drug use whereby the use of legal substances precedes the use of illegal substances. Youths tend to use beer and wine first, then proceed to tobacco and hard liquor. Marijuana is seldom used without first using tobacco, hard liquor, or both. The use of marijuana generally precedes the use of other illicit drugs (Kandel, 1975). Because many youths start using beer and other addictive substances before the teen years, prevention programs aimed at adolescents and younger children prior to initiation of drug use might be more effective than programs aimed at older age groups.

 DRUG ABUSE PREVENTION PROGRAMS

Research and theory combine to provide direction for designing drug abuse prevention programs targeting youth. Such programs should include four components: information, education or skills training, alternatives to drug use, and interventions utilizing role models such as peer counselors (LoSciuto & Ausetts, 1988).

Adolescents use drugs to enhance positive affective states, for excitement, at parties, to be with friends, and to handle negative affective states including worries, nervousness, and boredom (Binion, Miller, Beauvais, & Oetting, 1988). Drug abuse interventions should address the same needs that lead to drug use.

Preventive interventions utilizing interpersonal communication approaches include the teaching of interpersonal and intrapersonal competencies, creation of an environment that can respond to emotional and social needs as well as to needs for information, and provision of alternative activities in a social setting.

Interpersonal and intrapersonal competencies include strategies to build or enhance self-esteem, assertiveness skills, and skills to combat peer pressures. Adolescents need to be taught how to say "no" to drugs. Decision-making techniques, problem-solving techniques, and techniques to cope with anxiety, nervousness, and anger are also beneficial educational skills that might be provided by abuse prevention programs. Some of these skills have been successfully taught through role-playing activities.

Environments may be created to respond to adolescents' emotional and social needs. Teachers may be trained to provide socially rewarding learning environments through techniques of positive reinforcement. However, teacher-training alone has not been a successful method of drug abuse prevention because teachers vary in their enthusiasm and in the amount of prevention material and activity they actually carry back to the classroom (Schaps, Moskowitz, Malvin, & Schaeffer, 1986).

Parents have also been encouraged to provide supportive home environments by setting aside time each day to talk privately with each of their children, reducing verbal criticism and increasing positive interpersonal communication by encouraging compliments and thanking their children. Parents are asked to encourage their children to learn how to solve their own problems, to give their children privileges and responsibilities appropriate to their abilities, and to use consistent, positive but firm, discipline. Programs may be designed that involve existing peer groups such as scout troops. Interpersonal support systems may also be created for youth to help them deal with stressful feelings.

Another preventive strategy is to provide alternative activities in a social setting. Just as individuals attempting to give up smoking or alcohol find relief in exercise and alternative activities, the availability of these activities in a drug-free environment may serve as a preventive strategy.

Although many prevention programs have proved successful, one that teaches adolescents skills to withstand drug pressures is the SODAs model developed by Gilchrist (Gilchrist, Schinke, Trimble, & Cvetkovich, 1987).

This program teaches people to stop, weigh the options rationally, choose among available options (hopefully with alternative drug-free activities readily available), act using learned communications skills and give themselves praise for remaining drug-free.

We have emphasized the social nature of drug use and the importance of peers in the initiation and continued use of drugs. It must be noted that, in doing so, we have omitted a large group of drug abusers who have become addicted to legally obtained prescription drugs. These users often drink and use pills outside of the peer context. They include many women who have been treated by physicians for symptoms of stress as well as elderly patients who have been overmedicated or have experienced drug interactions due to treatment for multiple chronic conditions. Although discussion of programs for these at-risk groups is outside the scope of this chapter, it should be emphasized that they, too, need prevention programs targeted toward them, and programs targeting adolescents are unlikely to work with many adults and elderly abusers.

Further research is needed to evaluate drug prevention programs and to tie successful programs to theory in an effort to understand the reasons underlying their success. Combinations of theoretical positions may be necessary to explain drug abuse and to devise successful programs for prevention and treatment. Drug abuse is a complex issue and programs targeting one at-risk group may not be applicable for others equally at risk. However, like information, an interpersonal communication element is likely to be a necessary, but not sufficient, component in a successful drug abuse prevention program.

REFERENCES

Akers, R. L. (1985). *Deviant behavior: A social learning approach* (3rd ed.). Belmont, CA: Wadsworth.

AMA Council on Mental Health. (1973). The sick physician. *Journal of the American Medical Association, 223,* 684–687.

Bandura, A. (1977). *A social learning theory.* Englewood Cliffs, NJ: Prentice Hall.

Becker, M. (1974). *The health belief model and personal health behavior.* San Francisco: Society for Public Health Education.

Becker, M., Haefner, D., Kasl, S., Kirscht, J., Maiman, L., & Rosenstock, I. (1977). Selected psychosocial models and correlates of individual health-related behaviors. *Medical Care, 15* (May Supplement), 27–46.

Becker, M., & Maiman, L. (1983). Models of health-related behavior. In D. Mechanic (Ed.), *Handbook of health, healthcare, and the health professions* (pp. 539–568). New York: The Free Press.

Binion, A., Miller, C. D., Beauvais, F., & Oetting, E. R. (1988). Rationales for the use of alcohol, marijuana, and other drugs by eighth-grade Native American and Anglo youth. *International Journal of the Addictions, 23,* 47–64.

Dembo, R., Blount, W. R., Schmeidler, J., & Burgos, W. (1986). Perceived environmental drug use risk and the correlates of early drug use or nonuse among inner-city youths: The motivated actor. *International Journal of the Addictions, 21,* 977–1000.

Fisher, L. (1977). These students helped design their own smoking education programs. *American Lung Association Bulletin, 63*(5), 2–9.

Foon, A. E. (1986). Smoking prevention programs for adolescents: The value of social psychological approaches. *International Journal of the Addictions, 21,* 1017–1029.

Gilchrist, L. D., Schinke, S. P., Trimble, J. E., & Cvetkovich, G. T. (1987). Skills enhancement to prevent substance abuse among American Indian adolescents. *International Journal of the Addictions, 22,* 869–879.

Jessor, R., & Jessor, S. L. (1977). *Problem behavior and psychosocial development: A longitudinal study of youth.* New York: Academic Press.

Kandel, D. (1975). Stages in adolescent involvement in drug use. *Science, 190,* 912–914.

Kandel, D. B., & Andrews, K. (1987). Process of adolescent socialization by parents and peers. *International Journal of the Addictions, 22,* 319–342.

Kaplan, H. B. (1975). *Self-attitudes and deviant behavior.* Pacific Palisades, CA: Goodyear.

Kaplan, H. B. (1976). Self-attitudes and deviant response. *Social Forces, 54,* 788–801.

Kaplan, H. B. (1980). *Deviant behavior in defense of self.* New York: Academic Press.

Kiesler, C. S., Collins, B. A. & Miller, N. (1969). *Attitude change: A critical analysis of theoretical approaches.* New York: Wiley.

Labouvie, E. W. (1986). Alcohol and marijuana use in relation to adolescent stress. *International Journal of the Addictions, 21,* 333–345.

Leventhal, H. (1968). Experimental studies of anti-smoking communications. In E. F. Borgatta & R. R. Evans (Eds.), *Smoking, health and behavior* (pp. 95–121). Chicago: Aldine.

Leventhal, H. (1971). Fear appeals and persuasion: The differentiation of a motivational construct. *American Journal of Public Health, 61,* 1208–1224.

Lewin, K. (1951). *Field theory in social science.* New York: Harper & Row.

Lewin, K. (1953). The field theory approach to adolescence. In J. M. Seidman (Ed.), *The adolescent: A book of readings* (pp. 32–42). New York: Holt, Rinehart & Winston.

LoSciuto, L., & Ausetts, M. A. (1988). Evaluation of a drug abuse prevention program: A field experiment. *Addictive Behaviors, 13,* 337–351.

Mayo, E. (1933). *The human problems of an industrial civilization.* New York: Macmillan.

McGuire, W. J. (1973). Persuasion, resistance, and attitude change. In I. de Sola Pool, F. W. Frey, W. Schramm, N. Maccoby, & E. B. Parker (Eds.), *Handbook of Communication* (pp. 216–252). Chicago: Rand McNally.

Moskowitz, J. (1983). Preventing adolescent substance abuse through drug education. In T. Glynn, C. Leukefeld, & J. Ludford (Eds.), *Preventing adolescent drug abuse: Intervention strategies* (National Institute on Drug Abuse Research Monograph 47, DHEW Publ. No. (ADM) 83-1280, pp. 233–249). Washington, DC: US Government Printing Office.

Needle, R., McCubbin, H., Wilson, M., Reineck, R., Lazar, A., & Mederer, H. (1986). Interpersonal influences in adolescent drug use: The role of older siblings, parents and peers. *International Journal of the Addictions, 21,* 739–766.

Perkins, H. W., & Berkowitz, A. D. (1986). Perceiving the community norms of alcohol use among students: Some research implications for campus alcohol education programming. *International Journal of the Addictions, 21,* 961–976.

Sackett, D. L., & Haynes, R. B. (1976). *Compliance with therapeutic regimens.* Baltimore: The Johns Hopkins University Press.

Schaps, E., Moskowitz, J. M., Malvin, J. H., & Schaeffer, G. A. (1986). Evaluation of seven school-based prevention programs: A final report on the Napa project. *International Journal of the Addictions, 21,* 1081–1112.

Schinke, S. P., Moncher, M. S., Palleja, J., Zayas, L. H., & Schilling, R. F. (1988). Hispanic youth, substance abuse, and stress: Implications for prevention research. *International Journal of the Addictions, 23*, 809–826.

Sherif, M., & Sherif, C. W. (1964). *Reference groups: Exploration into conformity and deviation of adolescents.* New York: Harper & Row.

Sullivan, E. J. (1987a). A descriptive study of nurses recovering from chemical dependency. *Archives of Psychiatric Nursing, 1*, 194–200.

Sullivan, E. J. (1987b). Comparison of chemically dependent and nondependent nurses on familial, personal and professional characteristics. *Journal of Studies on Alcohol, 48*, 563–568.

Zigler, E. A., & Child, I. L. (1969). Socialization. In G. Lindsey & E. Aronson (Eds.), *The handbook of social psychology* (Vol. 3, 2nd ed., pp. 450–589). Reading, MA: Addison Wesley.

12

Prevention, Peer Clusters, and the Paths to Drug Abuse

E. R. Oetting
Colorado State University

Susan Spooner
University of Northern Colorado

Fred Beauvais
James Banning
Colorado State University

The purpose of this chapter is to stimulate creative thinking about prevention alternatives; it is not aimed at providing answers or solutions, but rather, at suggesting methods that can organize prevention planning and possibly identify new approaches to prevention. Four dimensions are involved in prevention planning: (a) prevention goals, (b) general purpose of the intervention, (c) the target of the intervention, and (d) the type of method used. The first dimension, prevention goals, is derived from peer-cluster theory. The other three dimensions are dealt with through a general intervention model, the "cube."

Goals for prevention of adolescent drug use are, in part, prescribed by peer-cluster theory (Oetting & Beauvais, 1986a, 1986b, 1987a) a psychosocial model that points out the critical mediating role in drug use played by the youth's close friends. Although the theory points out the central role played by the peer cluster and suggests that a major goal of prevention should be to influence the structure and function of peer clusters, it also indicates that membership in a drug-using peer cluster is related to other social and psychological factors, and those factors suggest other prevention goals. We, therefore, present a path diagram that shows how personal, social, and cultural characteristics are linked together in relation to drug use, and how those links indicate goals for prevention.

The other three dimensions involved in prevention planning are the orthogonal sides of the "cube," a conceptual model of intervention strategies (Morrill, Hurst, & Oetting, 1980; Morrill, Oetting, & Hurst, 1974).

The cube is an engineering tool; it provides a method for classifying interventions, for exploring ideas, and for creating alternatives. The cube points out that (a) an intervention can be aimed at either the individual or a relevant group, (b) either direct or indirect methods can be used, and (c) the purpose can be remedial, preventive, or developmental. The final section of this chapter provides examples to illustrate these four dimensions of prevention planning, taking goals from peer-cluster theory and relating them to prevention programs suggested by the cube.

PEER-CLUSTER THEORY

Although underlying psychosocial factors create the potential for drug use, that potential is almost always realized through the peer cluster: other youth, siblings, and close friends who are similar in age and who have close associations with the youth. A peer cluster is a small tight group of close friends. It may be several youth who "hang out" together. It may be a pair of best friends, or a couple. In younger children a peer cluster is almost always a same-sex group; in older adolescents it may be a mixed-gender group. It is the attitudes, beliefs, and behaviors of the peer cluster that determine adolescent drug use.

When adolescents use drugs, it is almost always in a peer context. Even when they use drugs alone, it usually reflects the conviction of a group of peers that using drugs alone is "the way to go." Peers provide drugs. Peers initiate each other into drug use. Peers discuss drugs and model drug use, shaping both drug attitudes and drug behaviors. The peer cluster decides where and when drugs should be used, how much to use, how specific drugs will affect you, and how you should behave when taking specific drugs. A peer cluster can also decide that drugs are anathema and develop the attitudes and ideals that reject drug involvement.

Peer-cluster theory is a theory about *adolescent* drug use, about those years when drug use is initiated and when it evolves. It is not a theory about adult addicts or alcoholics, although they almost always got their start in substance abuse as adolescents who were involved in peer clusters. It is not a theory about drug effects or the addictive power of drugs, although drugs would not continue to be used unless they were potent psychoactive agents. Peer-cluster theory is not irrelevant for addicts, however, because those who become addicted had to start somewhere, and that start was almost always in an adolescent peer cluster.

Peer-cluster theory alters the concept of peer pressure. The vision of the "evil stranger" forcing drugs on the "innocent youth" is one that appeals to the Norman Rockwell in us, but it does not match reality. In the real world, it is not the anonymous pusher who introduces drugs, it is the child's best friends who suggest and initiate everything: shoplifting, pickup basketball games, vandalism, skateboarding, anonymous phone calls, "dungeons and dragons," mutual masturbation—and drug use. And every child is as much a "pusher" as a "pushee." When adolescents insist, "I am NOT subject to peer pressure!", they are not lying, despite the absolute *necessity* of owning one, and only one, brand of coat, or of having pink hair just like their friends. They know that the peer cluster is a true mutual society. No one applies pressure, everyone simply agrees on how they are all going to be "different."

THE PATHS TO DRUG USE

Recognizing that the peer cluster plays a dominant role in adolescent drug use, however, only leads to the next question: What makes one youth join a peer cluster that moves toward drug use and another make friends who decide that drugs are not for them? There are a considerable number of psychosocial factors that increase the potential for drug use. The figures in this chapter show results from some of our path analyses (Oetting & Beauvais, 1987b; Oetting, Swaim, Edwards, & Beauvais, 1989; Swaim, Oetting, Edwards, & Beauvais, 1989, with some theoretical additions, to bring in important variables we have not yet fully tested. They provide an organized way to list factors and to show how they relate to drug use and to each other.

These path models are not temporal; they do not predict from the past to the future. They only show how correlations partial out. We want to use them here, however, to produce prevention ideas, so we drop scientific caution and talk about these relationships as though they are real, causal, and have a time dimension. In doing so, we engage to a certain extent in science fiction. If, however, a prevention idea grows out of these models, one of the best experimental tests of causation would be to engage in a rigorously controlled test, manipulating change in a certain characteristic and assessing subsequent impact on peer cluster formation and on later drug use.

We present three path models that suggest prevention goals. The first considers emotional distress variables, negative feelings that might relate to drug use. The second examines socialization links: the influence of family, religion, school, and peers. The third model considers cultural identification.

Emotional Distress and Adolescent Drug Use. The idea that drugs and alcohol are used because they assuage depression and anxiety is an axiom in some quarters. Despite theory and popular belief, the search for the emotional distress roots that "cause" drug use has not been very successful. A frequent response when we tell our "recovering alcoholic" friends that we have failed to confirm this popular idea is, "But I used alcohol when I was depressed." Unfortunately, they also used alcohol when they were not depressed and most research studies show that, although people do use alcohol and drugs when they are emotionally distressed, people who are chronically emotionally distressed do not use alcohol or drugs much more than anyone else (Green, Blake, & Zehaysern, 1973; Jones, 1973; Miranne, 1981; Oetting, Swaim, Edwards, & Beauvais, 1989; O'Malley, 1975; Schooler, White, & Cohen, 1972; Simon, Primavera, Simon, & Orndoff, 1974; Spevack & Pihl, 1976; Correlations usually account for only about 1% of the variance in drug use).

Our path model shows that although there are some small relationships between chronic emotional distress and having drug-involved friends, depression and anxiety are not the major culprits (Swaim et al., 1989). The emotion that is important is one that is rarely considered in research studies, anger. Figure 12.1 shows the paths from emotional distress to adolescent drug use. Anger is not only linked to peer drug associations, it mediates whatever influence other emotional distress characteristics might have on drug use.

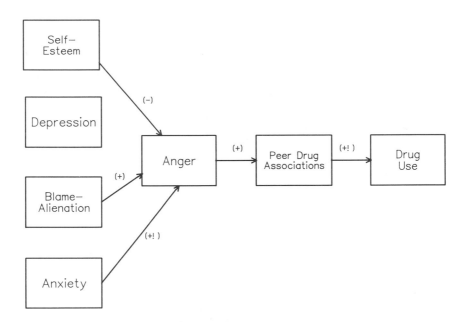

FIG. 12.1. Simplified path model linking emotional distress and peer drug associations to adolescent drug use. (Nonrecursive paths linking exogenous variables are left out.)

The fact that anger seems to play a role in drug-using peer groups is not a new idea to those who work with youth. It is not uncommon to hear a group of youth described as angry and rebellious. On the other hand, peer clusters are rarely described as depressed or anxious.

Even self-esteem (the trait most likely to appear in drug research proposals) seems to have little direct influence on drug use. There is a slight negative correlation with anger, suggesting that what influence self-esteem does have may be because low self-esteem is slightly linked to increased anger, although even this relationship is confusing. When the variance associated with blame/alienation and anxiety is partialled out, the residual correlation between anger and self-esteem is slightly positive.

In general, however, chronic emotional distress of almost any kind seems likely to increase chances of anger. What does this suggest about prevention?

1. The major influence on drug use is still the peer cluster. Is there a way to change the peer cluster?
2. The emotion we should focus on first is not depression or anxiety, but anger. What can be done about anger or what can be done to keep anger from increasing involvement in a drug using peer cluster?
3. We should not totally ignore depression, anxiety, and low self-esteem. If we could reduce these problems, it might help reduce anger, and that, in turn, might lower the chances that youth will develop drug-involved peer clusters. But programs aimed at increasing self-esteem or at reducing depression and anxiety are starting several steps away from any direct influence on drugs, so perhaps prevention programs with the goal of affecting these traits would have to start very early.
4. Whatever we do about depression, anxiety, or self-esteem must not just affect that trait. If it is going to influence drug use, it has to reduce the anger that grows out of those problems and, in turn, the effect anger has on involvement in a drug using peer cluster.

If we followed through on every link of this chain, then our efforts would have at least a chance to prevent formation or involvement in drug-using peer clusters and could lead to a consequent reduction in drug use.

Even though emotional distress is not a very potent predictor of drug use, efforts to deal with emotional distress problems for *some* people may still be worthwhile. There is always something that is not covered by a simple model, and this path model is no exception. We have become convinced that there is a small group of children who suffer from early, multiple, and serious problems, including emotional problems. These youth do not have much influence on general models like our path diagrams because there are only a few of them, and they may not be in school where we get most of our subjects. They have emotional problems, they have drug problems, *and* they have high levels of delinquency. They progress to more serious difficulties in all areas: school, crime, drugs, and life. We believe that a high proportion of these deviant children end up committing serious crimes or becoming heavy, chronic drug abusers. If we can reach these children, we have to reach them early and we have to impact them heavily—in both of these areas: providing early treatment of emotional and self-esteem problems and altering the pernicious influence of peer clusters consisting of youth with high potential for both delinquency and drug use.

There are other personal traits that are tied to drug use that we did not include in this model because they are not related to emotional distress. They might, however, produce ideas for prevention. Peer clusters who share a high need for excitement are more likely to experiment with drugs (see chapter 10 by Donohew et al., this volume).

Socialization Links and Adolescent Drug Use. Socialization links are the connections between a youth and the major elements of the social environment: the community, the family, schools, religion, and peers. Although emotional distress is not highly related to drug use, the strength of an adolescent's relationship with every one of these major socialization forces correlates substantially with drug use. A review of numerous studies confirming this conclusion appears in the paper on socialization characteristics by Oetting and Beauvais (1987b). This statement, in itself, may have implications for prevention—you might have more effect on drug use if you ignored emotional distress and aimed prevention efforts at these socialization links.

The path model in Fig. 12.2 shows how socialization characteristics are related to drug use (Oetting & Beauvais, 1987b). The image created by this model is a vivid one. At the base of the model is the family. It all starts there. The family radiates its influence out in a number of different directions. Each of these, in turn, focuses down again and influences the formation of peer clusters. The conclusion is that family problems can lead to multiple other problems that, in turn, can lead to drug-using clusters. But the central and early role played by the family should not make us insensitive to the importance of school and religion. Both can directly influence the formation of drug using or non-drug-using peer clusters, whether or not there are family problems.

What are the implications for prevention? Once again in this model, the peer cluster is the dominant force in predicting actual drug use, suggesting that changing the peer cluster is likely to have the most influence on drug involvement. There are other possible targets as well, but the path model shows that the peer cluster mediates the influence of the other socialization links and suggests that, if prevention is going to work, the changes that do occur in other socialization links will probably have to somehow alter or influence the peer cluster.

The centrality of the family suggests that disruption of the family is a major underlying factor, influencing many aspects of life, and that prevention aimed at the family might be highly valuable. The model also shows, however, that the influence of the family is not direct. Even if the family is changed, there has to be time for the improvement to influence school, religion, and peer-cluster formation, so family-oriented prevention might have to start early.

Efforts to improve school adjustment might also have to start early because increasing liking for school and performance in school is going to be difficult and take time. There may be other school-based prevention efforts, however, that would have immediate effects. When you put youth together, you increase the chances that they will form peer clusters and the school may, unintentionally, be encouraging growth of deviant peer clusters in this way. Subtle prejudices, for example, may put youth with school problems in trade-oriented classes, whereas successful youth are placed together in classes like debate or Latin. Remedial classes may force together youth who share school problems. Even school punishments can lead to formation of peer clusters; for instance, a detention group may bring together youth with high potential for deviance. An "alternative school" that provides an opportunity for dropouts to finish high school may be very valuable in reducing dropout, but may, at the same time, bring together youth who have high potential for drug use. We have found very

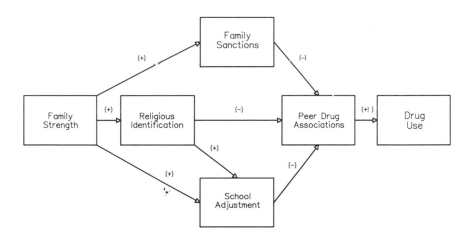

FIG. 12.2. Simplified path model of socialization characteristics and adolescent drug use.

high rates of drug involvement in some of these schools (Beauvais & Oetting, 1986; Swaim et al., 1989). Reconstructing the school system so it does not encourage formation of deviant peer clusters might be worth trying.

Cultural Identification and Drug Use.   Figure 12.3 is almost entirely theoretical because we have not actually constructed and tested path models for cultural identification. It is, however, based on our research with Native-American and Mexican-American youth, and is probably reasonably accurate.

The youth's cultural identification is based firmly on the family's cultural identification (Oetting & Beauvais, 1989; Oetting, Edwards, & Beauvais, 1989). In this country, most minority families have some identification with both the minority culture and the majority White-American culture. That identification, in turn, influences and is influenced by the extent to which the youth has minority or majority friends, is involved in minority or majority cultural activities, and develops goals, values, and behaviors that are closely related to cultural content. Some of those behaviors and beliefs may be linked to drug use (such as the idea that adult males in that culture drink heavily or the concept that young women of that culture should be "innocent" and not drink or use drugs).

Probably more important is the fact that a high level of cultural identification, whether with the majority or the minority culture, is a source of general strength and potency. It is related to improved school adjust-

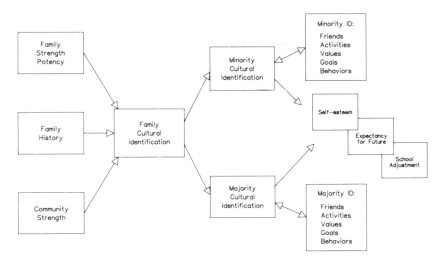

FIG. 12.3.   Theoretical path model showing the roots and the effects of an adolescent's cultural identifcation.

ment, to increased self-confidence and pride, and to higher self-esteem, and all of those may, in the long run, improve the youth's ability to avoid drugs (Oetting & Beauvais, 1989). At the other extreme are adolescents from families that are "outcasts" in the community, youth whose parents are not successful in either the minority or the majority culture and who, themselves, have learned to expect failure. These anomic youth have no strong cultural ties, and often have multiple problems that are likely to eventually involve them with drug using peer clusters.

Culture-based prevention might be aimed at breaking up cultural stereotypes that encourage alcohol or drug use, or could be aimed at generally increasing cultural pride and identification. The path model suggests that improving cultural identification may be valuable for the youth, that it may enhance self-esteem and even influence school adjustment. There are, however, a number of steps between cultural identification and drug use. The effect of improved cultural identification on drug use is likely to be very indirect and may, therefore, take a long time and be relatively small.

That does not mean that culture can be ignored. It is important to make sure that prevention programs are culturally congruent. If they are not, they are likely to be denigrated or sabotaged by adults who value that culture. In addition, the small group of severely culturally alienated and anomic youth is probably headed for serious problems, and increasing its cultural identification could be a valuable element in an overall prevention plan.

Path Models and Prevention Goals. The path models suggest a series of links and influences and indicate that prevention programs need to consider ultimate goals, immediate goals, and intermediate goals. The *ultimate goals* of drug abuse prevention are reduction of drug use and reduction of the damage done by drugs. But the path models suggest that there are other *immediate goals* that may also eventually lead to reduction in use, notably reducing pro-drug influence of the peer cluster, improving family relationships, increasing adaptive anger management skills, and improving school adjustment. These immediate goals provide ideas for useful prevention programs, but their influence on drug use can be indirect and partial, and that must be remembered in program planning, implementation, and assessment.

The more steps between drug use and an immediate goal, the longer it may take for an effect on the actual use of drugs to take place. For example, changing the peer cluster may lead to a very rapid change in drug use, whereas altering anger may take some time to first affect the formation of peer clusters and then for that to reduce drug use.

When the links are indirect and involve several steps, it may also be necessary to provide longer term follow-up, with *intermediate goals* to make sure the changes stay in place long enough to influence the next step in the change. It may be possible to include program elements aimed at increasing effect on the next step in the chain. The models, for example, suggest at least a possibility that increasing cultural identification of anomic youth may eventually have an effect on drug use, but there may be many steps in between these goals. Long-term follow-up might be planned to first link improved cultural identification to better school adjustment, and then to encourage formation of peer clusters of youth who share better school adjustment and increased cultural pride.

A CONCEPTUAL MODEL
FOR INTERVENTION STRATEGIES

Caplan's (1964) early conceptual model for classifying preventive intervention strategies is applicable to the path model and peer-cluster theory of drug abuse. In Caplan's nomenclature, primary prevention interventions (prevention) would affect the paths (emotional distress, socialization links, and cultural identification) leading to peer clusters marked by drug abuse. Secondary prevention strategies (treatment) would focus on reducing the duration of the damage associated with drug abuse. Finally, tertiary prevention (rehabilitation) would aim at the reduction of the impairment resulting from drug abuse. Although the Caplan model is useful, the complexity of peer-cluster theory and the path models with the links of ultimate, immediate, and intermediate goals calls for a more heuristic model that can assist in the development of a wide range of intervention strategies. The "cube" provides a tool that organizes this task (Morrill et al., 1974).

In the early 1970s lip service to prevention or "outreach programming" was paid, but not much was going on and few models were available. Treatment professionals were too busy pulling bodies out of the river to go upstream and find out who was throwing the bodies in. So the cube was constructed to stimulate thinking about new approaches and strategies of intervention. The multidimensional nature of the cube is helpful in stimulating ideas for intervention, given the richness of the path model and peer cluster theory of drug abuse. The cube (really a parallelepiped) appears in Fig. 12.4.

The cube indicates that any intervention has three dimensions: the *purpose* of the intervention, the *target* of the intervention, and the *method*, how the intervention is implemented.

The Purpose of the Intervention. The first thing that the cube points out is that intervention can be reactive or proactive. The first column, remediation, is reactive, it occurs after the damage is done. Proactive intervention can take two forms, prevention or development. Both of them "prevent," but prevention is aimed at stopping a specific identified problem from occurring; in our case that problem would be drug abuse. A prevention program (in the classification system of the cube) is focused on a specific problem, is aimed at factors that lead directly to that problem, and is designed for people who are at risk for that problem.

Developmental programs might come under the general category of prevention, but they have a different philosophy. Rather than being problem oriented, they are asset oriented. A developmental program is one that is aimed at enhancing people's potential and improving their functioning. That kind of enhancement could prevent the emergence of problems, but its major aim is to promote positive growth. Developmental purposes are usually longer term and broader than prevention purposes and are not aimed only at populations that are at risk.

The Target of the Intervention. The ultimate target is probably always individual drug abuse, but the attack does not always focus on the individual. The model points out that there are other targets that should also be considered: (a) primary groups, (b) associational groups, and (c) the ecology, the environmental factors surrounding the person. Primary

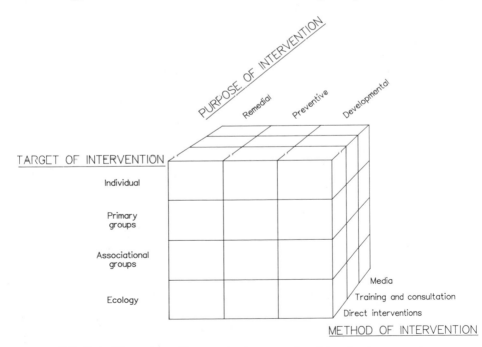

FIG. 12.4. Dimensions of intervention for prevention of drug involvement. (Copyright © 1974 by Morrill, Oetting, and Hurst. Reprinted by permission.)

groups are those that are closest to the individual, that have the most impact and influence on the individual's behavior. The family and the extended family (if it is close knit) are obvious and important primary groups, but for drug-using adolescents the peer cluster is probably the dominant primary group.

Associational groups are one step removed from primary groups. They do not have the intimacy or immediacy of primary groups, but are important for the person. They could be organizations like the Boy Scouts or groups like the football team, the community theater, or the marching band. Members of an associational group are aware that they share similar interests or goals and are together to pursue those goals.

Ecology is a "catchword," but we use it as a shorthand to cover the wide range of environmental influences that affect the individual. Moos (1974) captured the full range of these influences in his classification of human environments: (a) geographical and meteorological variables, (b) architectural and physical design variables, (c) behavioral settings, (d) dimensions of organizational structure, (e) personal and behavioral characteristics and organizational climate, and (g) functional or reinforcement analyses of the environment. The concept of mesosystem as used by Bronfenbrenner (1979) also captures our use of the concept of ecology. A mesosystem comprises the interrelations among two or more settings in which a person actively participates. In reference to the developing young person, these mesosystems would include the relations among home, school, neighborhood, and a variety of settings relating to work and recreation. It is not only the social aspects of these settings that are important, the physical environment also affects the person. People exist and survive by interacting within their "ecology" and this ecology can serve as an important target for preventive interventions.

People are aware that they are members of "ecologies" and identify with their institutions, organizations, and neighborhoods. Examples would include: Roosevelt Junior High, the eighth-grade class, Cherry Creek neighborhood, or Middletown, U.S.A. A very small charismatic church might be an important associational group, with a strong shared common purpose, whereas a typical large church might be classified as part of the ecology, because it is a looser aggregation of people who may have many different purposes and goals. In summary, the cube suggests that interventions designed to reach the individual drug abuser can be targeted through the use of primary groups, associational groups, and through a number of different ecological interventions.

The Method of Intervention. Direct intervention involves contact with the target, aimed at altering or changing it, whether it is an individual or a group. Drug treatment, family therapy, or a "Just say 'No' " program would be direct interventions.

Indirect interventions are aimed at the target, but work through influencing or changing another source of influence. An example would be training or consultation to help teachers identify drug use in the classroom and deal with it appropriately. The target is the youth, but the method is indirect.

Both direct intervention and consultation and training are personal; they involve interaction with the professional. Media interventions differ in that there is no personal contact. The person or group must be reached through nonpersonal communication. The obvious media are radio, television, newspapers, and magazines, but media can include any nonpersonal communication method that can reach the target. Examples would include direct mail, billboards, computer games, books and novels, music, and self-help tapes.

USING THE CUBE

At this point we have a four-dimensional model: the path models, that suggest goals; and the cube, that classifies targets, purposes, and methods of intervention. This should allow us to classify and organize prevention ideas systematically. For example, one use would be examining policy: If all of the prevention programs sponsored by the Office of Substance Abuse Prevention (OSAP) were listed, where would they fall? Would there be open spaces, suggesting alternatives that are not being tried or supported?

Figure 12.5 shows the results of classifying a random sample of prevention programs funded by OSAP in 1988. Because the purpose is to see what kind of programs are being tried, a single program may be classified in more than one location if it has significant elements related to more than one cell of the cube.

These results suggest that OSAP programs are focusing on direct services: treatment and prevention for targeted individuals, but that there is a surprising variety of programs. Quite a few programs, for example, have components that are developmental (i.e., not aimed directly either at a high risk group or at behaviors that are closely linked to drug use). Most of these are programs for minority youth and use cultural values, language, and cultural norms to enhance an individual's sense of self-worth, or to develop cognitive and behavioral skills.

A few programs provide remedial services through the primary group (usually the family of the drug-using youth). There are some instances of developmental interventions through groups, and of direct interventions based on the community ecosystem. Some programs, for example, target

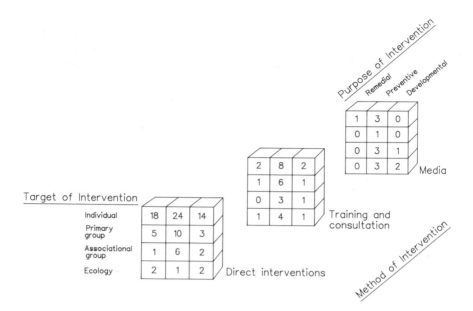

FIG. 12.5. Classification of a one third sample of Office of Substance Abuse Prevention funded programs for 1988. (The 43 programs may be classified in more than one cell.)

the ecosystem by teaching people techniques for improving the community or by helping them learn how to enhance the developmental impact of the community. This last one is so difficult to get at—and even harder to measure in terms of results—that few programs attempt it except as an "adjunct" part of their efforts.

There are several indirect programs, aimed at improving the skills of those who deal with problem youth. Most of them cater to individual service providers, typically teaching them prevention strategies. Some offer similar training to primary and associational group members (families, fellow students).

A surprisingly large number of programs, 13, include media interventions aimed at individuals, primary or associational groups, as well as the community's ecosystem. Such strategies take the form of producing print materials, videos, publicity campaigns, or training packages. Most of these items focus on prevention, although 3 of them have developmental aspects.

Overall, as might be expected, most interventions are remedial and preventive, focusing directly on high-risk target populations of individuals. But there are also interesting and innovative ideas that broaden the scope of programmatic strategies. They include training, consultation, and media interventions that are developmental and a number of programs involving both primary and associational groups, and even the ecological system at the community level. The OSAP-funded programs show more variety than we might have expected. The exercise demonstrates that the cube can be useful for classifying programs.

The cube may also be useful for assessment. For example, the National Academy of Science will soon be providing NIDA with a scientific review of drug abuse prevention research (Review of Prevention Research, 1989). A meta-analysis classifying the prevention effect size according to the cells of the cube might show blocks within the cube where prevention has been effective and other blocks, or even rows or columns, where prevention has had little effect.

The cube, however, should be most useful for program planning. It does not provide answers, but it can suggest prevention ideas that should be considered. At one level, we could take a particular problem or goal, and start through the cube, looking at *every* cell and trying to find an effective and economical way of providing a prevention program. The result would be a multifaceted attack on the problem, hitting it from every angle. At another level, we might use the cube for brainstorming, a source for finding a new prevention idea that might be particularly effective for a specific goal.

Some brief examples may improve understanding of this four-dimensional model, the goals derived from peer-cluster theory and the programs defined by the cube, and how it can be used. The first step is to select an immediate goal from the path models. The obvious one to start with is the the *peer cluster*, with the goal of reducing the impact of peer drug associations.

What can be done to prevent the peer cluster from leading to drug abuse? To mount a total attack on the pernicious influence of drug-using peer clusters, we might explore how *every* cell of the cube would relate to that goal, from individual/remedial/direct to ecology/developmental/media. The following samples show how that process might work:

Goal: Change the Negative Effects of the Peer Culture

Approach: Individual/Direct/Remedial. This is the first cell in the cube, the traditional treatment approach. In this cell the professional has direct communication with the person who is already drug involved and needs to get away from drugs. The program in this cell involves remediation. Because we are, in this book, concerned only with prevention, we could have simply left out the remediation column of the cube. But if we did so, we might miss some good ideas. So we shift our approach slightly so it still deals with remediation, but has a prevention flavor (i.e., tertiary prevention, preventing return to drug use, or preventing further progression into drug use of a treatment client).

The goal, taken from the path model, focuses on changing the effect of the peer cluster. If the treatment client leaves the program and returns to the street, what will he or she do? Probably go out with old friends. What will they do? Probably push the client right back into using drugs. This cell of the cube suggests that we ask how counseling, therapy, or other direct professional treatment can prevent this from happening. There are many possible ideas, but two are enough to illustrate their nature: (a) we might simply make sure that treatment includes discussion of peer clusters and their influence, or (b) we might include vocational/educational counseling as part of treatment based on the idea that new peer clusters may grow out of training, school, or work, and those new peer clusters might not be drug-oriented.

Approach: Primary Group/Direct/Remedial. If we considered these same clients but moved down one cell of the cube, the target would be a primary group, which could be the peer cluster itself. We might bring the whole peer cluster into treatment, doing something analogous to structured family therapy. Another alternative would be to develop social activities as part of post-treatment follow-up activities that encourage formation and maintenance of non-drug-using peer clusters.

Approach: Associational Group/Prevention/Training and Consultation. For further illustration, let us move to a cell right in the middle of the cube. The goal is still to influence peer clusters so they have less potential for encouraging drug use. Because youth belong to many different associational groups, we might start by listing all of them, and considering how we could develop a multifaceted program to reach all of these potential groups. More realistically, we pick one associational group as a target, say the Youth Recreation Center. This cell of the cube then suggests that the professional work *indirectly*, through training or consultation, with those who actually work with (or within) the Youth Center.

One possible approach consistent with this cell of the cube could involve teaching Youth Center staff and recreation directors the essentials of peer-cluster theory. Consultation could help them examine their programs to see how those programs might be throwing together youth who have a high tendency for either seeking excitement or for deviance. The consultant could help them redesign programs so that youth with high sanctions against using drugs are involved in small group activities, making sure their influence was spread out. The focus is on the peer cluster, so preventing youth from sneaking away and individually taking drugs is not a goal related to this cell of the cube, but programs and monitoring might be designed to make sure that youth could not get away *together* to use drugs.

A complete analysis would continue to explore the other cells of the cube, but these three examples should illustrate how that process would work. The cube does not actually suggest the content of programs, it only indicates the form or structure that a program might take. Creative ideas for content must still derive from intelligence guided by experience. For further illustration of how the cube works, we should change to a different goal.

Goal: Increase Cultural Identification

We chose this example because it illustrates a situation where the type of program suggests looking only at certain dimensions of the cube. We have already commented on the "distance" between cultural identification and drug use. The emphasis on indirect and long-term effects of cultural identification and a sense that a cultural identification program is aimed more at personal and social growth than at eliminating drug use per se, suggest that such programs should be located in the developmental column of the cube. Any of the cells in that block of the cube might then suggest possible programs.

Improving cultural identification may ultimately lead to a reduction in adolescent drug use, but the path model in Fig. 12.3 suggests that there may be many steps in between. Whatever effect there is on drug use is likely to be through the influence of cultural identification on other factors, which, in turn, influence drug use. Being indirect, the effect may also be small. If we were only considering efficiency in reducing drug use, this effort could have a poor cost/benefit ratio. It is possible, however, through creative efforts, to close the gap between cultural identification and drug use. One good example occurred on a western Indian reservation. On this reservation there is a tradition of wearing shirts decorated with multicolored ribbons. These ribbons have spiritual significance. One of the youth counselors developed a custom that whenever students wore their ribbon shirts to school they pledged to not use drugs on that particular day. After a while this became a mark of honor among the students.

There may be other valid reasons for wanting to improve cultural identification. It could lead to significant social, psychological, and cultural benefits for the youth other than reduction in drug use. It might have secondary benefits for the overall prevention program: It might, for instance, improve working relationships with elders and show that there is sensitivity to the minority culture and respect for it, and this attitude could enhance ability to provide more direct prevention programs for youth.

The path model in Fig. 12.3 shows that increasing identification with *either* the minority culture or the majority one can serve as a source of strength and potency. Traditional approaches would be either to emphasize acculturation to the majority culture, based on the feeling that minority identification only holds people back from taking their place in society, or to emphasize involvement with the minority culture, based on the idea that this strengthens traditional values and beliefs. Both approaches are based on the idea that cultures are mutually exclusive, that an increase in identification with one is at the cost of another. In contrast, our cultural identification theory states that identification with one culture does not have to be at the cost of loss of identification with another (Oetting & Beauvais, 1989). When we talk about increasing identification with the majority culture, therefore, we are not in any way denigrating identification with the minority culture nor are we suggesting a loss of that identification. The first goal we consider, therefore, is programs that might enhance identification with the *majority* culture.

Approach: Developmental/Individual/Training. Cultural identification includes a large component of cultural skill and success, success that marks the existence of a meaningful stake in that culture. Language, for example, is an important element of identification, and where majority language skills are weak, special training programs in English might be useful mechanisms for improving cultural stake. Education and job success are also often markers of majority success. The individual might be provided with counseling, training in job acquisition skills, and training to increase employability, any of which may lead to increases in stake in the majority culture. Note that, because our theory indicates that identification with different cultures does not have to be in conflict, programs that enhance minority cultural identification should be developed at the same time that we try to improve stake in the majority culture.

Approach: Developmental/Ecology/Consultation. When the youth's neighborhood is a ghetto, a barrio, or a reservation, it greatly increases the chances of drug use. The causes may be manifold: prejudice, lack of opportunity, dilapidated housing, lack of community facilities, lack of recreational alternatives, poor transportation systems, educational and economic disadvantagement, more alcohol and drug using role models, and so on. All of these send messages that work against cultural pride.

Consultation to change these environments could be aimed at altering any or all of these factors, programs such as creating a youth Outward Bound program, a volunteer housing repair system, or getting the drug sellers off the streets. Consultation could also involve working with the members of the community or neighborhood to help them develop and create local programs that encourage community activities that are rooted in the minority culture and increase pride in it.

Another role of the consultant might be to examine the messages about culture that are presented by the physical environment. As an example, Fig. 12.6 shows the murals in the entrance to the library of a major western

FIG. 12.6. Murals in the library of a major western university showing ethnic stereotyping of White-Americans, Mexican-Americans, and Native-Americans.

university. What message is communicated when the scientists and doctors are White, the blue-collar workers are Hispanic, and the traditional artists are Indian?

Figure 12.7 shows another kind of message. The gang graffiti communicate danger and also communicate that society is unable to control deviant behavior. They include drug "messages." Graffiti also suggest substituting a stake in gang culture for identification with either the minority or majority culture.

Although the eventual goal of these developmental ideas may be to reduce drug use, they are being implemented at a level far removed from adolescent drug involvement. To assess program effectiveness, therefore, it is necessary to look at immediate outcomes, short-term intermediate outcomes, and long-term ultimate outcomes. The immediate goal is to change cultural identification, so accurate measures of that characteristic will be needed. The short-term intermediate outcomes need to focus on those changes that we believe, from the path models, may eventually have some effect on drug use: self-esteem, school adjustment, and expectancy for the future.

Because this is a developmental program, we also need to consider secondary or ancillary outcomes that may have positive value even though they do not eventually lead to prevention of drug abuse. These can be very im-

FIG. 12.7.   Gang graffiti in a barrio area of a western city.

portant in estimating the cost effectiveness of a program. The Job Corps, for example, had less effect than expected on minority employment, but had a considerable effect in reducing venereal disease and nonmarital pregnancy. Similarly, in this program improving self-esteem may have little effect on drug use, but may have other important benefits.

Developmental programs may have more overall impact on people than remedial or preventive programs. If we taught people to swim, we would not have to worry about someone throwing them in the river. But that effect is likely to be diffuse and therefore difficult to quantify, particularly if we look at only one outcome such as drug use. To determine whether there is an eventual effect of the developmental programs described here on drug use might require very long-term follow-up, and may not be practical. The small size of such an effect and the variability introduced by historical events may make it almost impossible to detect. This makes the shorter term intermediate goals of developmental programs even more important. They may provide enough benefits to warrant continuation of a program despite the difficulty of proving that it has an ultimate effect on the specific outcome of drug abuse.

SUMMARY

This book is about persuasive communication, but that would cover nearly every possible intervention, because almost any intervention is eventually going to involve persuading people to alter their actions or attitudes. Within that definition psychotherapy or counseling are certainly persuasive, training and consultation must be convincing to be effective, and unless an advertisement or music video is persuasive enough to alter beliefs or behaviors it would be useless. Where and how should persuasive communication be applied to prevention?

We have presented a complex four-dimensional model for organizing, categorizing, and planning prevention programs. The model uses path models based on peer-cluster theory to identify specific prevention goals. The goals are examined in relation to the three dimensions of the cube, the target of the intervention, the purpose of the intervention, and the method of intervention. The opportunities are multiple, so where do we start?

The path models suggest that there are some goals that should have high priority because there is evidence that changing these characteristics might have an immediate and strong impact on drug abuse. This chapter suggests trying to modify the effects of the peer cluster, the family, school, and anger. There are other goals that might not have as much immediate effect, but may be more important in the long run, such as improving economic conditions and increasing legitimate opportunities for those who live in impoverished and crime-ridden neighborhoods. At the same time we should consider programs that might have smaller effects on any one individual, but that reach so many people that the accumulated effect is meaningful. Examples include the public service messages described by Black (chapter 8, this volume), and programs to mobilize community action (Beauvais & Oetting, 1989).

Each cell of the cube suggests a different approach that might be taken to prevention, and within that cell, the number of possibilities is only limited by the imagination and creativity of the planner. Between the goals, the cube, and dozens of possibilities for prevention in every cell of this cube there are thousands of alternatives that could be explored.

This chapter talks about creating ideas for prevention programs, but whatever we plan, the next step must be to make those programs effective. The best plan has no value unless it has a powerful and positive effect. The other chapters in this book that deal with persuasion, how to change attitudes, beliefs, and behaviors, take us to that next stage of prevention planning.

REFERENCES

Beauvais, F., & Oetting, E. R. (1986). Drug use in an alternative high school. *Journal of Drug Education, 16*(1), 43–50.

Beauvais, F., & Oetting, E. R. (1989). *Adolescent drug use: National and local epidemiology.* Manuscript submitted for publication.

Bronfenbrenner, U. (1979). *The ecology of human development.* Cambridge, MA: Harvard University Press.

Caplan, G. (1964). *Principles of preventive psychiatry.* New York: Basic Books.

Green, M. G., Blake, B. F., & Zehaysern, R. T. (1973). Some implications of marijuana usage by middle-class high school students. *Proceedings of the 81st Annual Convention of the American Psychological Association, 8,* 679–680.

Jones, A. P. (1973). Personality and value differences related to use of LSD-25. *International Journal of the Addictions, 8,* 549–557.

Miranne, A. C. (1981). Marijuana use and alienation: A multivariate analysis. *International Journal of the Addictions, 16,* 697–707.

Moos, R. (1974). Systems for the assessment and classification of human environments: An overview. In R. Moos & P. Insel (Eds.), *Issues in social ecology* (p. 6). Palo Alto, CA: National Press Books.

Morrill, W. H., Hurst, J. C., & Oetting, E. R. (1980). *Dimensions of intervention for student development.* New York: Wiley.

Morrill, W. H., Oetting, E. R., & Hurst, J. C. (1974). Dimensions of counselor functioning. *The Personnel and Guidance Journal, 6,* 354–359.

Oetting, E., & Beauvais, F. (1986a). Peer cluster theory: Drugs and the adolescent. *Journal of Counseling and Development, 65*(1), 17–22.

Oetting, E. R., & Beauvais, F. (1986b). Clarification of peer cluster theory: A response to Peele, Cohen and Shaffer. *Journal of Counseling and Development, 65*(1), 29–30.

Oetting, E. R., & Beauvais, F. (1987a). Common elements in youth drug abuse: Peer clusters and other psychosocial factors. *Journal of Drug Issues, 17*(1 & 2), 133–151.

Oetting, E. R., & Beauvais, F. (1987b). Peer cluster theory, socialization characteristics and adolescent drug use: A path analysis. *Journal of Counseling Psychology, 34*(2), 205–213.

Oetting, E. R., & Beauvais, F. (1989). *Orthogonal cultural identification theory: The cultural identification of minority adolescents.* Manuscript submitted for publication.

Oetting, E. R., Edwards, R. W., & Beauvais, F. (1989). Drugs and Native-American youth. *Drugs and Society, 3*(1/2), 6–38.

Oetting, E. R., Swaim, R. C., Edwards, R. W., & Beauvais, F. (1989). Indian and Anglo adolescent alcohol use and emotional distress: Path models. *American Journal of Alcohol and Drug Abuse, 15*(2), 153–172.

O'Malley, P. M. (1975). Correlates and consequences of illicit drug use. *Dissertation Abstracts International, 36*, 3011B. (University Microfilms No. 75-29, 302).

Review of prevention research by the National Academy of Sciences. (1989). *Prevention Pipeline, 2*(1), 2.

Schooler, J. C., White, E. H., & Cohen, C. P. (1972). Drug abusers and their clinic-patient counterparts: Comparison of personality dimensions. *Journal of Consulting and Clinical Psychology, 39*, 9–14.

Simon, W. E., Primavera, L. H., Simon, M. G., & Orndoff, R. K. (1974). A comparison of marijuana users and nonusers on a number of personality variables. *Journal of Consulting and Clinical Psychology, 42*, 917–918.

Spevack, M., & Pihl, R. O. (1976). Nonmedical drug use by high school students: A three-year survey study. *International Journal of the Addictions, 11*, 755–792.

Swaim, R. C., Oetting, E. R., Edwards, R. W., & Beauvais, F. (1989). The links from emotional distress to adolescent drug use: A path model. *Journal of Consulting and Clinical Psychology, 57*(2), 128–136.

13

School-Based Social and Personal Coping Skills Training

Susan G. Forman
Jean Ann Linney
University of South Carolina

RATIONALE FOR SCHOOL-BASED PROGRAMS

The schools have been among the most common settings for programs to prevent alcohol and drug abuse among adolescents. Several factors make the school an attractive setting for prevention efforts. The schools offer an existing structure with almost ideal characteristics for implementation of a variety of curricula. Almost all children and adolescents can be reached via the school setting. Because of the age range served by the schools and the use of age grouping, repeated, age-appropriate interventions can be implemented. School personnel already trained in general teaching, intervention, assessment and evaluation procedures further contribute to the attractiveness of the school as an intervention site. Finally, children and youth spend a large portion of their waking hours in the school setting, and peers and adults in this setting can be important sources of social influence.

RATIONALE FOR COPING SKILLS TRAINING

In the past few years, substance abuse prevention programs aimed at helping the adolescent develop personal and social coping skills have received empirical support. Most of these programs were initially developed to prevent cigarette smoking. Recently, however, the effectiveness of some of them in preventing alcohol and drug abuse has been evaluated. Researchers in the substance abuse area have noted that there is an association between the factors that underlie various types of substance use and other health-compromising behaviors, and therefore have contended that similar approaches may be effective in preventing various forms of substance use.

These programs teach adolescents personal and social skills in an attempt to counter one or more variables related to substance abuse. The programs are based on social learning theory (Bandura, 1977) and problem behavior theory (Jessor & Jessor, 1977). These theories view substance use as a socially learned behavior having both purpose and function, that is the result of both personal and social/environmental factors.

Factors Related to Substance Use

A wide variety of social, psychological, and behavioral factors have been found to be associated with substance abuse in adolescents. In addition, knowledge, attitudes, and beliefs about drugs and alcohol have a significant effect on their levels of use.

Social Factors. Among the social factors affecting substance use, research has shown the attitudes and behavior of family and friends to be significant influences. Adolescents whose parents or older siblings use substances tend to engage in substance use (Baumrind, 1985; Department of Health, Education and Welfare, 1976; Kandel, 1973; Tolone & Dermott, 1975). Positive relationships have been found between adolescent substance use and parent permissiveness or parental approval regarding the substance (Hunt, 1974; McRae & Nelson, 1971).

Other family factors that have been found to be related to substance abuse include parenting style and family communication patterns. Low levels of parental support and control, and an authoritarian or laissez-faire discipline style have been related to substance use (Jessor, 1976; Jurich, Polson, Jurich, & Bates, 1985; Smart, Gray, & Bennett, 1978). Poor family communication and high family conflict have also been significantly correlated with higher levels of substance use (Barnes, 1984; Wechsler & Thurn, 1973).

Peers are a major influence on adolescent substance use habits. Numerous studies have indicated that adolescents with friends who use substances are likely to be substance users themselves (Brook, Lukoff, & Whiteman, 1977; Kandel, 1976; Kaplan, Martin, & Robbins, 1982). Real or perceived support or approval of peers regarding substance use has also been related to increased substance involvement (Wechsler & Thurn, 1973). Although peers are perhaps the most powerful force in influencing an adolescent to initiate substance use, lack of close peer relationships has been found to be related to higher levels of use (Brook et al., 1977).

Psychological Factors. Several personality factors have been found to be related to substance use. Adolescents who use substances have repeatedly been found to fall on the external end of the locus of control continuum (Brook et al., 1977; Wright, 1985). Users have also been found to have lower self-esteem than non-users (Smith & Fogg, 1976). Impulsivity (Smith & Fogg, 1976), depressive feelings (Kandel, 1976), low assertiveness (Horan, D'Amico, & Williams, 1975), high anxiety (Kilpatrick, Sutker, Roitzsch, & Miller, 1976), and high need for social approval (Khavari, Mabry, & Humes, 1977) have also been found to be related to substance use.

Stress and coping skills are additional psychological factors that have been associated with substance abuse among adolescents. Stress is a process that typically includes: (a) an environmental event; (b) intervening characteristics of the individual, such as perceptions or coping skills; and (c) a stress reaction. Studies of stress and substance use have focused on the occurrence of life events and a number of investigations have found that adolescent substance users report experiencing a greater number of life events, especially negative ones, than non-users (Bruns & Geist, 1984; Duncan, 1978; Headlam, Goldsmith, Hanenson, & Rauh, 1979; Huba, Newcomb, & Bentler, 1986).

Recently, investigators have begun to explore the relationship between stressful events, substance use, and coping skills. Coping skills are cognitive and behavioral strategies to manage demands that are appraised as taxing or stressful. A number of studies have found that adolescents report that they use substances as a way of helping them deal with problems, negative feelings, and stressful situations (Carmen, 1979; Carmen, Fitzgerald, & Holmgren, 1983; Johnston & O'Malley, 1986; Jurich et al., 1985; Shibuya, 1974). Three studies have directly examined the relationship of stress, coping, and substance use. Wills (1985), and McCubbin, Needle, and Wilson (1985) found coping styles and strategies as well as stress levels to have an effect on substance use. Stress was found to be a positive predictor of substance use, as was peer support, aggression and ventilating feelings (e.g., complaining, blaming others). Behavioral and cognitive coping strategies such as information seeking, focusing on the positive, problem solving, and relaxation were inversely related to substance use.

Behavioral Factors. Behavioral factors related to substance use include academic performance and antisocial and deviant acts. Substance users have been found to have lower grades than non-users (Donovan & Jessor, 1978; Jessor, 1976; Smith & Fogg, 1976), have more negative attitudes toward school, have lower academic expectations, and place lower value on academic achievement (Dembo, Farrow, Burgos, & Schmeidler, 1981; Wechsler & Thurn, 1973). Substance users are more likely to be absent from school and cut classes as well (Brook et al., 1977).

Disruptive behavior in school has been shown to be related to substance use (Hendin, Pollinger, Ulman, & Carr, 1981). Other antisocial behaviors linked to substance abuse include legal offenses (Dawkins & Dawkins, 1983), delinquent activities such as shoplifting and vandalism (Wechsler & Thurn, 1973), running away from home, assault, driving under the influence of alcohol (Barnes, 1984), lying, cheating, and stealing (Wechsler & Thurn, 1973).

Knowledge and Attitudes. Although it would seem that individuals who are aware of the hazards of substance use would be less likely to engage in such use, studies have shown that adolescents who use substances are cognizant of substance information (DHEW, 1976; Swisher, Crawford, & Goldstein, & Yura, 1971) and programs attempting to decrease drug use by increasing knowledge have not been effective (Schaps, DiBartolo, Moskowitz, Palley, & Churgin, 1981). In general, however, a direct relationship has been found between attitudes toward a substance and its use, with those having positive attitudes being more likely to initiate and continue use (Downey & O'Rourke, 1976; Jessor, Jessor, & Finey, 1973).

COPING SKILLS PROGRAMS: PRIMARY PREVENTION

Two major types of skills training programs that have evidence of effectiveness can be found in the substance abuse prevention literature. The first type teaches adolescents skills that can be used to deal with social influence and pressure. A second type of skills program focuses on interpersonal and intrapersonal coping skills that can be used to deal with the wide variety of factors, both social/environmental and personal, which may influence substance use.

Social Influence Programs

Evans (1976) developed the first of a number of social psychological programs based on the principle of social inoculation. Given the fact that social variables are of major importance in the decision to use substances, the social inoculation model assumes that resistance to these social pressures for substance use will be greater if the individual has been given experience in a controlled setting dealing with social pressure.

Evans' initial social influence program used nonsmoking peers on film to present information on social influences on smoking. Film presentation was followed by knowledge tests that emphasized the immediate consequences of smoking, discussion of resistance to persuasion, and school posters to serve as reminders. Junior high school students who participated in the program had lower smoking onset rates than those who did not (Evans et al., 1978).

A program that built on this approach, Counseling Leadership Against Smoking Project (project CLASP, McAlister, Perry, Killen, Slinkard, & Maccoby, 1980; McAlister, Perry, & Maccoby, 1979) consisted of three sessions presented on consecutive days and four booster sessions spaced over the remainder of the school year. Older student peer leaders implemented this program that included videotapes on the three sources of social pressure to smoke (peers, parents, media) and specific techniques for resisting these pressures, demonstrations of the immediate physiological effects of smoking, role-playing to practice resistance skills, and activities designed to elicit social commitment not to smoke. During the booster sessions students discussed pressures they encountered to smoke and the methods they used to resist them. Project CLASP resulted in reductions in self-reported cigarette smoking, as well as other drug and alcohol use among seventh-grade participants.

The Robbinsdale Anti-Smoking Project (RASP, Hurd, Johnson, & Luepker, 1978; Hurd et al., 1980; Murray et al., 1978) used procedures similar to CLASP. This program involved peers as actors in the videotapes on social pressure. The program included information about peers, family, and advertising influences and the immediate physiological consequences of smoking. Training in resistance skills was given and the seventh-grade student participants were encouraged to make public commitments of their intention not to smoke. After participation in this program, smoking prevalence increased at a lower rate than would have been expected.

The Prevention of Cigarette Smoking in Children Project (PCSC, Murray, Johnson, Luepker, Pechacek, & Jacobs, 1980) has provided further evidence of the effectiveness of these "Saying No" programs by exploring use of peer-led programs, as well as adult-led ones. Both resulted in decreases in smoking onset for seventh-grade students.

The Waterloo Smoking Prevention Program (Flay, d'Avernas, Best, Kersell, & Ryan, 1983) followed the basic approach of the social influences of "Saying No" programs, but added a component on decision making that was specific to the smoking decision. The program consisted of six 1-hour weekly sessions delivered to sixth graders by health educators at the beginning of the school year, two booster sessions at the end of Grade 6, two booster sessions at the beginning of Grade 7, and one booster session at the beginning of Grade 8.

The program had three major components. The first provided information about the consequences of smoking and the reasons for smoking through activities that elicited the information from the children rather than providing it for them. The information was repeated via videotapes, postermaking, role-playing, and class discussion. The second component focused on the social influences that encourage smoking and on skills to resist those pressures. Social coping skills were taught, role-played, and practiced. The third component focused on decision making and public commitment. An evaluation of use of this program was conducted with 697 children in 22 schools. Results indicated reduced onset of smoking, as well as increases in the number of smoking quitters.

Using a somewhat different approach, but still emphasizing the importance of social influence as a factor in substance use, Pentz (1985) developed a prevention program that focused on social assertiveness skills. The program consisted of seven 55-minute sessions and taught students assertiveness skills that they could use in everyday situations with teachers, parents, and peers. After participation in this training, sixth- through ninth-grade students were found to increase in social competence, self-efficacy, and grade-point average, while decreasing in onset rates for alcohol use.

Similarly, Horan and Williams (1982) used assertion training as a drug and alcohol abuse prevention strategy. Nonassertive junior high school students participated in groups run by counselors that met for five 45-minute sessions over 2 weeks. One third of the training stimuli situation involved peer pressure to use drugs or alcohol. Students who participated in this program showed gains on behavioral and psychometric measures of assertiveness, as well as decreased willingness to use alcohol and marijuana. At 3-year follow-up, the students continued to display higher levels of assertiveness and less self-reported drug use.

Personal and Social Coping Skills Programs

Two major personal and social coping skills programs are described in the literature. Cognitive-Behavioral Skills Training (Schinke, 1982; Schinke & Gilchrist, 1977) is a coping skills program that focuses on smoking prevention and provides students with both general personal and social coping strategies as well as specific techniques that can be used in situations related to smoking. The program consists of eight 1-hour sessions and covers a variety of topics. Students are provided with health information concerning the advantages and disadvantages of smoking. They are trained in decision-making and problem-solving skills that can be used in dealing with peer pressure to smoke. Self-instructional techniques that can be used to guide behavior in difficult situations are also taught. In addition, assertive communication skills (eye contact, appropriate facial expressions, hand gestures, loudness of voice, assertive statements) are addressed.

A number of studies (Schinke & Blythe, 1981; Schinke & Gilchrist, 1984) have demonstrated that this program can provide an effective approach to smoking prevention. When used with sixth graders, improvements have been found on measures of problem solving, decision-making skills, smoking knowledge and attitudes, assertiveness skills, and intentions to smoke in the future.

The personal and social coping skills program having the most empirical support with respect to both smoking prevention and drug and alcohol abuse prevention is Life Skills Training (LST, Botvin, 1983). Life Skills Training teaches general life skills as well as skills and knowledge specifically related to substance use.

The training is typically conducted in 10 weekly sessions. It consists of five major components. The first is a cognitive component with information concerning short- and long-term consequences of substance use, prevalence rates, social acceptability, and the process of becoming dependent on tobacco, alcohol, or marijuana. The second is a decision-making component that addresses the process of critical thinking and decision making. An anxiety management component provides students with cognitive and behavioral techniques such as imagery and physical relaxation that can be used to cope with anxiety. A social skills training component includes general social and communication skills as well as assertiveness techniques that can be used to resist peer pressure to smoke, drink, or use drugs. Finally, a self-improvement component provides students with the principles of behavioral self-management and is designed to improve self-esteem.

Life Skills Training was initially evaluated with respect to prevention of cigarette smoking (Botvin & Eng, 1982; Botvin, Eng, & Williams, 1980; Botvin, Renick, & Baker, 1983). These studies indicated that after LST training conducted either by project staff, peer leaders, or teachers, secondary school students had lower rates of smoking onset and made more positive changes on cognitive, attitudinal, affective, and social measures than did no-treatment control group students. These changes were found to maintain at 1-year follow-up. Botvin, Baker, Renick, Filazzola, and Botvin (1984) have also examined the impact of LST on alcohol and marijuana use. In a study of over 1,300 seventh-grade White middle-class students from suburban New York City schools, significant treatment effects were found for substance use, substance knowledge, substance attitudes, locus of control, and influenceability.

The final report of a 5-year investigation of LST funded by the National Institute on Drug Abuse (Botvin, 1987) indicated that at initial posttest students participating in a peer-led LST group were significantly different from control group students with regard to tobacco, alcohol, and marijuana use, as well as several mediating variables. Students participating in a teacher-led intervention, however, did not differ significantly from those in the control group. The ineffectiveness of the teacher-led groups was attributed to possible problems with teacher training. Results were maintained at 1- and 2-year follow-up while booster sessions were implemented. After the 2-year follow-up, booster sessions were terminated. One year after termination no effects were present. This finding can be interpreted in a number of ways. Some might see it as showing coping skills training to be ineffective. However, it can also be viewed as an indication of the importance of continued intervention through booster sessions and the necessity of continuous efforts to maintain behavior change when environmental conditions are not conducive to maintenance of the behavior. Prevention of substance use by adolescents in a social environment that still encourages use is not likely to occur without continuous effort.

Summary

In a meta-analysis of the outcome results of 143 adolescent drug prevention programs, Tobler (1986) identified five different types of programs: knowledge only, affective only, peer programs, knowledge plus affective, and alternatives. Peer programs included those that taught refusal skills as well as those that taught social and personal coping skills. These programs were found to be superior for the magnitude of the effect size obtained on all outcome measures for the average school-based population.

Examination of the literature on primary prevention coping skills training programs shows some evidence of success. However, definitive conclusions cannot be drawn about the effectiveness of these programs because of methodological problems of existing studies including overreliance on self-report measures, lack of follow-up data indicating maintenance of effects, and use of predominantly White middle-class students.

COPING SKILLS PROGRAMS:
SECONDARY PREVENTION

Surprisingly, little research has been conducted on secondary prevention programs. These are programs for students most at risk for substance abuse. Such students have social, behavioral, or personality characteristics that have been shown to be predictive of later substance abuse, or have actually begun experimental substance use.

Project SCCOPE—The South Carolina Coping Skills Project (Forman & Linney, 1988) has focused on use of broad-based personal and social coping skills training with high-risk youth. In the development of this intervention, the need to intensify the training experience for high-risk youth through use of multiple sources of communication and multiple communication settings was recognized. Behavioral psychology literature, on which personal and social coping skills training is based, indicates that provision of the training stimuli or messages by multiple communicators in multiple settings can enhance the effectiveness of training with regard to generalization and maintenance of behavior change. Project SCCOPE provided an intensive coping skills training format through use of four sources of communication (group leaders, peers, teachers, and parents) in two communication settings (home and school).

Project SCCOPE

Student Training Component. The student training component of this intervention was a broad spectrum program based on Botvin's (1983) Life Skills Training. It consisted of a 10-session small group training experience conducted once a week, 2 hours per session during the school day in the school setting. The training was based on behavioral and cognitive-behavioral procedures with the overall goal of teaching constructive methods of dealing with problems and stress, so that group participants would learn to resist peer pressure to use substances and would not turn to substance use as an inappropriate avoidant coping response.

During the 10 training sessions, students learned coping skills in four major areas: behavioral self-management, emotional self-management, decision making, and interpersonal communication. In addition, substance information was addressed. During the first session, participants were provided with a student handbook that contained summaries of concepts, facts and skills discussed during group sessions, printed materials for group exercises and activities, and directions for completing homework assignments given at the end of each session. Instructional methods used during the sessions included didactic instruction, modeling, role-play, discussion, rehearsal through homework assignments and feedback. The coping skills were presented within the context of substance use problem situations as well as a variety of other problem situations that adolescents encounter. Thus, students learned how to cope with substance specific problems, as well as how to deal with a range of other potential stressors.

The first session was an introductory session during which the purpose of the group was explained and ground rules for group behavior were established. The participants engaged in a number of group exercises aimed at helping them get to know each other and establishing expectations for participation and comfort in it.

During Session 2, behavioral self-management skills were presented as a means of improving self-image. Students learned what self-image is, how it is formed, how it relates to behavior, and how it can be changed through behavioral self-management strategies. Students were taught that our feelings about ourselves can improve if we learn to do better in situations that are difficult for us. Strategies discussed during this session included: goal-setting, specifying behaviors, use of reinforcers, stimulus control, and charting progress. With these strategies students formulated individual self-change projects that were implemented throughout the remainder of the training period.

Substance use information was addressed during the third session, with a focus on tobacco, alcohol, and marijuana. Incidence rates and reasons for substance use were explored, as well as short- and long-term consequences of substance use.

Emotional self-management skills were addressed in the fourth and fifth sessions and included relaxation, cognitive restructuring, and self-instructional techniques. Three relaxation skills were taught as methods of coping with anxiety: deep muscle relaxation, deep breathing, and mental rehearsal. During the session on cognitive techniques, students were taught that their thoughts influence their feelings and that negative emotions can be reduced by changing thoughts. Using a framework derived from Rational-Emotive Therapy (Ellis, 1962) students discussed common irrational beliefs of adolescents and their rational alternatives. For example, a rational alternative to "It would be awful if other kids didn't like me" is "I can't please everyone all of the time. I don't need and can live without everyone's approval". Students were also taught a self-instructional sequence that could be used in potentially stressful situations (Meichenbaum, 1985). The sequence involves thinking calming, constructive, rational thoughts at four points: (a) preparing for the situation (before the situation occurs; (b) confronting the situation (during the situation); (c) coping with the situation (when upsetting feelings start); and (d) reflecting on the situation (after the situation).

During the next session, decision-making skills were addressed. Students were taught what decisions are, how others attempt to influence their decisions, and how good decisions can be made through a series of decision-making steps. These steps included problem definition, identification of personal goals and values, obtaining information, consideration of alternatives and consequences, and making a commitment.

The interpersonal communication component of the program was addressed during Sessions 7, 8, and 9, and included training in assertiveness and peer resistance skills, communication skills, and social skills. During the segment on assertiveness, students learned to differentiate passive, aggressive, and assertive behavior and learned to use verbal and nonverbal assertive behaviors. The communication skills segment included training in active listening and avoiding misunderstandings. The social skills segment focused on conversational skills that can be used to make and maintain friendships, including how to initiate, maintain, and terminate a conversation.

The last session of the training program focused on integration and application of the coping skills taught in previous sessions. Participants did a final review of their self-change projects and participated in role-play activities during which they suggested use of various coping skills and taught them to each other.

One year after termination of the coping skills groups, students participated in two 2-hour booster sessions, conducted in consecutive weeks during the school day, in the school setting. During the booster sessions each coping skill was reviewed and students participated in role-play activities.

School Staff Training Component. The objective of the school staff training component of the intervention was to enhance generalization of behavior change by teaching school personnel to encourage use of coping skills in the classroom and school setting on a daily basis. This training component consisted of a half-day inservice program provided for all professional staff in project schools. During the program each coping skill was presented along with information on how each skill could be encouraged through three methods: modeling, cueing, and reinforcing. Instructional methods for this component included didactic instruction, discussion, and videotape modeling. Participants were provided with a take-home handbook that reviewed the coping skills and specific school staff behaviors that would encourage use of coping skills in students. As an additional cueing device, wall posters, illustrating each coping skill with cartoon-like characters, were provided to school staff for classroom and school corridor display.

Parent Training Component. A parent training component was developed to parallel the student intervention. The parent training program consisted of five weekly 2-hour sessions and had three objectives. The first was to teach parents about the coping skills their children were learning in the student groups. Each skill was presented and parents were taught that they could complement the student groups and become ''trainers at home'' by modeling, cueing, and reinforcing the coping skills. In addition, parents were encouraged to use the skills to deal with their own problems and stress. The second objective was to teach the parents some behavior management skills, because a number of studies have indicated family management problems to be a correlate of adolescent substance use (Hawkins, Lishner, & Catalano, 1985). The third objective was to develop a small group support system for the parents so that they could encourage each other to take positive, constructive action regarding their adolescents.

Instructional methods used during the group sessions included didactic presentation, discussion, modeling, role-play, feedback, and additional rehearsal through homework assignments. After each skill was presented, specific suggestions were given concerning how the parent could be a "trainer at home" through modeling, cueing, and reinforcement procedures. At the first session, each parent was given a parent handbook that included a summary of each skill and procedure presented, and specific methods that could be used to model, cue, and reinforce each coping skill.

During the first session, the purpose and content of the student and parent groups was explained, and the three main parent methods of encouraging adolescent use of coping skills (modeling, cueing, and reinforcing) were presented. Behavioral self-management techniques were presented as a means of helping adolescents change their behavior and self-image. Finally, contingency contracting procedures were presented as a method that parents could use in dealing with parent–child conflicts.

During the second session relaxation approaches to dealing with anxiety were presented. In addition, parents learned about rational thinking techniques and use of self-instruction as methods of managing emotions.

The third session focused on decision making and assertiveness. Decision steps, as well as verbal and nonverbal assertiveness skills, were presented.

During Session 4, parents learned about communication and social skills. This session covered active listening, avoiding misunderstandings, and conversational skills.

The fifth and final session focused on provision of substance information and a summary of previous sessions. Information concerning incidence, symptoms, causes, effects, and treatment options was presented. Parents also engaged in a final discussion and evaluation of previous group sessions.

Project SCCOPE Student Outcomes. The effectiveness of Project SCCOPE and its components was examined in a three-group repeated measures design. Thirty secondary schools were matched in groups of three on the basis of secondary level (middle vs. high school), racial composition, percentage of students receiving free lunch, and school size. Within each matched cluster, schools were randomly assigned to one of three treatment conditions: (a) school intervention consisting of student training in coping skills plus training for all professional staff at the school; (b) school plus parent intervention, which is student training in coping skills, school staff training, and parent training; and (c) comparison control, in which students attended a structured group that provided attention and focused on self-awareness and building a cohesive support group. Students in the comparison control also participated in 10 small group sessions and two

2-hour booster sessions in the following year. All student and parent groups were led by nonschool personnel experienced in working with youth groups and trained by the Project SCCOPE principal investigators in a 2-day workshop. Training included role-play and practice as a group leader with feedback from workshop participants.

Students participating in Project SCCOPE were initially referred by school staff on the basis of observation of two or more of the following risk indicators:

1. high number of disciplinary incidents,
2. low grades,
3. high number of unexcused absences,
4. drug or alcohol use by most friends,
5. drug or alcohol abuse by family members,
6. low self-esteem,
7. social withdrawal, and
8. experimental alcohol or drug use.

All participants were assessed prior to the intervention, immediately after the training, and at 1-year follow-up. The assessments included self-report of substance use, attitudes toward substance use, knowledge of substances, self-concept, assertiveness, locus of control, social anxiety, influenceability, rebelliousness, and attitudes toward school and teachers. Grades, attendance, and disciplinary actions for each student were gathered from school records. A classroom teacher completed a behavior rating scale for each student. Acquisition of the coping skills was assessed with the use of videotaped vignettes of problem situations followed by a structured sequence of questions designed to elicit coping responses. To enhance the validity of the self-reports of substance use a bogus pipeline procedure with saliva samples was employed.

There were 279 students who completed the 20 1-hour groups and pre- and postassessment. There were 201 students who completed booster sessions and a 1-year follow-up assessment. Demographically, 64% of the sample was male, 74% White and 26% Black. The average age of the sample at pretest was 14.4 years. Information from the referring teachers indicated that on average, the students presented four of the risk characteristics. The most commonly cited risk factors were poor academic performance, low self-esteem, involvement with peers suspected of substance use, and impulsivity. The mean grade-point average of this sample was 1.47 on a 4-point scale. Reported levels of substance use are further evidence of the high-risk nature of this sample. The Project SCCOPE sample reported lifetime incidence rates for alcohol and other drugs that are twice that of the

1985 NIDA Survey of Households sample. Monthly incidence of marijuana and alcohol use were about 50% higher than those in the NIDA
sample.

Analyses of the Project SCCOPE intervention effects indicate that from
pretest to follow-up, students in the coping skills conditions made significant gains on measures of coping skills acquisition, whereas those in the
comparison control did not. Furthermore, those in the coping skills training conditions generated coping responses rated more effective and higher
in specificity at follow-up. These effects were strongest for the coping skills
of assertiveness and anxiety management. At the follow-up assessment,
students in the school intervention condition were rated significantly higher
in overall coping skills than the students in either the comparison control
or the school intervention plus parent groups.

Students in all conditions made positive changes on a number of personality measures including self-esteem, self-confidence, social anxiety, social assertiveness, and influenceability. Subjects in all conditions increased
in substance knowledge, although attitudes toward substance use did not
change over time. The value that the students placed on school increased
over time and the rate of tardiness decreased for all conditions. Marijuana
use frequency showed a slight increase and cigarette smoking showed no
change for any condition. Drinking quantity per occasion decreased for
students in the school intervention condition.

These data suggest that preventive intervention may contribute to positive changes in high-risk youth, although significant differences in the effects of the three intervention conditions were not found. It is possible that
the coping skills groups were not effective, as changes in these groups did
not differ significantly from the comparison control, or, more likely, that
the control was actually a more powerful intervention than had been anticipated, as this intervention provided attention, substance information
and activities designed to increase self-awareness and build a cohesive peer-
support group. Lack of large increases in substance use over a 1-year period can be viewed as a positive outcome given the increases that would
normally be expected for adolescents over such a period.

Examination of group means over time suggested that somewhat
more positive changes were evident for the students whose parents were
not involved in the intervention. On some variables (e.g., self-esteem,
teacher ratings of girls' delinquency, and aggression) the students in the
parent-training condition tended to deteriorate or showed the smallest increases. From these data, parent intervention does not appear to enhance
the student coping skills intervention, but instead may be counterproduc-
tive. With this age group and risk status, involving parents in the manner
described may exacerbate the teen's rebelliousness and add to family
conflict.

CONCLUSIONS

Most coping skills programs have been implemented in school settings and have shown limited success. Although the schools provide a convenient setting, they may not be the only or even the best setting for adolescent substance abuse prevention programs.

There are several reasons for this. First, many of the adolescents most at risk are frequently absent from or have dropped out of school. Second, the school may represent traditional adult authority for many adolescents. During this developmental phase rebelliousness and rejections of adult authority become salient personality and behavioral characteristics. These characteristics have also consistently been found to be associated with adolescent substance use (Hawkins et al., 1985). Thus, those most at risk for substance use are most likely to resist adult authority. The image of the schools as authority focused institutions may reduce the effectiveness of programs that advocate behavior that is counter to current norms of the adolescent peer group. Information transmitted by adults or provided in the school, and thereby apparently sanctioned by it, may be discounted or disregarded by the adolescent. Surveys showed that adolescents are very unlikely to seek information about illegal substances or support regarding them in the school setting (Silverman & Silverman, 1986; Silverman, Watson, & Silverman, 1985). The differential effects found by Botvin (1987) for peer led versus teacher-led LST groups may be further evidence of the less than optimal effect of the school setting.

A recent review of policy on adolescent substance abuse prevention efforts questioned reliance on school-based programs (Lohrmann & Fors, 1986). The authors contend that school based programs can be effective only if strategies for reinforcing the goals of such programs are developed and implemented by other social institutions, so that school-based programs are conducted in a social environment that promotes and reinforces their goals. They concluded that some important substance use variables may be influenced by schools, but that major influences occur during the 18 hours per day spent away from school.

In order to enhance the effects of coping skills training with respect to maintenance of effects on behavior and individuals most at risk for substance abuse, additional communication sources and settings should be explored. Project SCCOPE included parents as an additional communication source. However, the student outcomes from this intervention do not support the efficacy of this approach for high-risk adolescents. Alternatively, the mass media have been identified as major sources of influence for adolescents and television has been recognized as the most influential type of media. American adolescents spend more time watching television than in any other activity including going to school or interacting with friends (Liebert, Sprafkin, & Davidson, 1982). A substantial body of research indicates that behavioral learning occurs during television viewing and that both aggressive and prosocial behavior can be learned through this medium (Pearl, Bouthilet, & Lazar, 1982; Roberts, 1983).

Television is an important source of social influence for adolescents that is not typically associated with adult authority as are parents and the school. Messages and images provided through this medium therefore may be more readily assimilated by the general adolescent population, and by those who are highly rebellious against traditional authority and therefore at highest risk for substance abuse. Thus, it appears logical to consider television as an alternative vehicle for adolescent substance abuse prevention programs.

A number of attempts have been made to use television as a medium for adolescent substance abuse prevention. Unfortunately, most of these programs have not shown evidence of effectiveness. As with most of the early school-based interventions, the focus of the media effort has been on substance information, health appeals, and fear messages (Flay & Sobel, 1983). Surprisingly, even the most recent media programs continue to focus on substance information and fear messages, although newer, more successful psychosocial approaches have been developed and have shown to be more effective.

Thus, use of mass media as a communication vehicle should provide a focus of future research for those interested in expanding knowledge about the potential role of coping skills training in substance abuse prevention. In addition, use of other communication settings in the community and sources of communication such as peers should be targets of further investigation.

ACKNOWLEDGMENT

This work was supported in part by grant #DAO4022 from the National Institute on Drug Abuse.

REFERENCES

Bandura, A. (1977). *Social learning theory*. Englewood Cliffs, NJ: Prentice-Hall.

Barnes, G. M. (1984). Adolescent alcohol abuse and other problem behaviors: Their relationship and common parental influences. *Journal of Youth and Adolescence, 13*, 329–348.

Baumrind, D. (1985). Familial antecedents of adolescent drug use: A developmental perspective. In *Etiology of drug abuse* (DHHS Publication No. ADM 85-1335). Washington, DC: U.S. Government Printing Office.

Botvin, G. J. (1983). *Life skills training: A self-improvement approach to substance abuse prevention*. New York: Smithfield Press.

Botvin, G. J. (1987). *Factors inhibiting drug use: Teacher and peer effects.* Report presented to the National Institute on Drug Abuse, Rockville, MD.

Botvin, G. J., Baker, E., Renick, N., Filazzola, A. D., & Botvin, E. M. (1984). A cognitive-behavioral approach to substance abuse prevention. *Addictive Behaviors, 9,* 137–147.

Botvin, G., & Eng, A. (1982). The efficacy of a multi-component approach to the prevention of cigarette smoking. *Preventive Medicine, 11,* 199–211.

Botvin, G., Eng, A., & Williams, C. (1980). Preventing the onset of smoking through life skills training. *Preventive Medicine, 9,* 135–143.

Botvin, G., Renick, N., & Baker, E. (1983, November). *Life skills training and smoking prevention: A one year follow-up.* Paper presented at the meeting of the American Public Health Association, Los Angeles, CA.

Brook, J. S., Lukoff, I. F., & Whiteman, M. (1977). Peer, family, and personality domains as related to adolescents' drug behavior. *Psychological Reports, 41,* 1095–1102.

Bruns, C., & Geist, C. S. (1984). Stressful life events and drug use among adolescents. *Journal of Human Stress, 10,* 135–139.

Carmen, R. S. (1979). Motivations for drug use and problematic outcomes among rural junior high school students. *Addictive Behaviors, 4,* 91–93.

Carmen, R. S., Fitzgerald, B. J., & Holmgren, C. (1983). Drinking motivations and alcohol consumption among adolescent females. *Journal of Psychology, 114,* 79–82.

Dawkins, R. L., & Dawkins, M. P. (1983). Alcohol use and delinquency among White, Black and Hispanic adolescent offenders. *Adolescence, 17(72),* 799–809.

Dembo, R., Farrow, D., Burgos, W., & Schmeidler, J. (1981). Examining a causal model of early drug involvement among inner city junior high school students. *Human Relations, 34,* 169–193.

Department of Health, Education & Welfare. (1976). *Teenage smoking: National Patterns of Cigarette Smoking, Ages 12 through 18, in 1972 and 1974* (DHEW Publication No. NIH pp. 76–931). Washington, DC: U.S. Government Printing Office.

Donovan, J. E., & Jessor, R. (1978). Adolescent problem drinking: Psychosocial correlations in a national sample study. *Journal of Studies on Alcohol, 39,* 1506–1524.

Downey, A., & O'Rourke, R. (1976). The utilization of attitudes and beliefs as indicators of future smoking behavior. *Journal of Drug Education, 6,* 283–295.

Duncan, D. (1978). Family stress and the initiation of adolescent drug abuse: A retrospective study. *Corrective and Social Psychiatry and Journal of Behavioral Technology, Methods and Therapy, 24,* 111–114.

Ellis, A. (1962). *Reason and emotion in psychotherapy.* New York: Stuart.

Evans, R. I. (1976). Smoking in children: Developing a social psychological strategy of deterrence. *Journal of Preventive Medicine, 5,* 122–127.

Flay, B. R., d'Avernas, J. R., Best, J. A., Kersell, M. W., & Ryan, K. B. (1983). Cigarette smoking: Why young people do it and ways of preventing it. In P. J. McGrath & P. Firestone (Eds.), *Pediatric and behavioral medicine* (pp. 132–183). New York: Springer.

Flay, B. R., & Sobel, J. L. (1983). The role of mass media in preventing adolescent substance abuse. In T. J. Glynn, C. G. Leukefeld, & J. P. Ludford (Eds.), *Preventing adolescent drug abuse: Intervention strategies* (NIDA Research Monograph No. 47, pp. 5–36). Rockville, MD: National Institute on Drug Abuse.

Forman, S. G., & Linney, J. A. (1988). School-based prevention of adolescent substance abuse: Programs, implementation and future directions. *School Psychology Review, 17,* 550–558.

Hawkins, J. D., Lishner, D. M., & Catalano, R. F. (1985). Childhood predictors and the prevention of adolescent substance abuse. In C. L. Jones & R. J. Battjes (Eds.), *Etiology of drug abuse: Implications for prevention* (pp. 75–126). Rockville, MD: National Institute on Drug Abuse.

Headlam, H., Goldsmith, R., Hanenson, I., & Rauh, J. (1979). Demographic characteristics of adolescent with self-poisoning: A survey of 235 instances in Cincinnati, Ohio. *Clinical Pediatrics, 18,* 147–154.

Hendin, H., Pollinger, A., Ulman, R., & Carr, A. (1981). *Adolescent marijuana abusers and their families* (NIDA Research Monograph No. 41). Rockville, MD: National Institute on Drug Abuse.

Horan, J. J., D'Amico, M. M., & Williams, J. M. (1975). Assertiveness and patterns of drug use: A pilot study. *Journal of Drug Education, 5,* 217–221.

Horan, J. J., & Williams, J. M. (1982). Longitudinal study of assertion training as a drug abuse prevention strategy. *American Educational Research Journal, 19,* 341–351.

Huba, G., Newcomb, D., & Bentler, P. (1986). Adverse experiences and drug use behaviors: A one year longitudinal study of adolescents. *Journal of Pediatric Psychology, 11,* 203–219.

Hunt, D. G. (1974). Parental permissiveness as perceived by the offspring and the degree of marijuana usage among offspring. *Human Relations, 27,* 267–285.

Hurd, P. D., Johnson, C. A., & Luepker, R. L. (1978). *A description of the intervention strategies of an anti-smoking project conducted for junior high school students.* Unpublished manuscript, University of Minnesota, Minneapolis, MN.

Hurd, P. D., Johnson, C. A., Pechacek, T., Bast, L. P., Jacobs, D. R., & Luepker, R. V. (1980). Prevention of cigarette smoking in seventh grade students. *Journal of Behavioral Medicine, 3,* 15–28.

Jessor, R. (1976). Predicting time of onset of marijuana use: A developmental study of high school youth. In D. Lettieri (Ed.), *Predicting adolescent drug abuse: A review of issues, methods and correlates* (DHEW Publication No. ADM 76–299). Washington, DC: U.S. Government Printing Office.

Jessor, R., & Jessor, S. L. (1977). *Problem behavior and psycho-social development: A longitudinal study of youth.* New York: Academic Press.

Jessor, R., Jessor, S. L., & Finney, J. (1973). A social psychology of marijuana use: Longitudinal studies of high school and college youth. *Journal of Personality and Social Psychology, 26,* 1–15.

Johnston, L. D., & O'Malley, P. (1986). Why do the nation's students use drugs and alcohol? Self-report reasons from nine national surveys. *Journal of Drug Issues, 16,* 29–66.

Jurich, A., Polson, C., Jurich, J., & Bates, R. (1985). Family factors in the lives of drug users and abusers. *Adolescence, 20*(77), 143–159.

Kandel, D. (1973). Adolescent marijuana use: Role of parents and peers. *Science, 181,* 1067–1081.

Kandel, D. (1976). Some comments on the relationship of selected variables to adolescent drug use. In D. Lettieri (Ed.), *Predicting adolescent drug abuse: A review of issues, methods and correlates* (DHEW Publication No. ADM 76–299). Washington, DC: U.S. Government Printing Office.

Kaplan, H., Martin, S., & Robbins, C. (1982). Applications of a general theory of deviant behavior: Self-derogation and adolescent drug use. *Journal of Health and Social Behavior, 23,* 274–294.

Khavari, K. A., Mabry, E., & Humes, M. (1977). Personality correlates of hallucinogen use. *Journal of Abnormal Psychology, 86,* 172–178.

Kilpatrick, D. G., Sutker, P. B., Roitzsch, J. C., & Miller, W. C. (1976). Personality correlates of poly-drug abuse. *Psychological Reports, 38,* 311–317.

Liebert, R. M., Sprafkin, J. N., & Davidson, E. S. (1982). *The early window.* New York: Pergamon.

Lohrmann, D. K., & Fors, S. W. (1986). Can school-based educational programs really be expected to solve the adolescent drug abuse problem? *Journal of Drug Education, 16,* 327–339.

McAlister, A., Perry, C. L., Killen, J., Slinkard, L. A., & Maccoby, N. (1980). Pilot study of smoking, alcohol and drug abuse prevention. *American Journal of Public Health, 70,* 719–721.

McAlister, A., Perry, C., & Maccoby, N. (1979). Adolescent smoking: Onset and prevention. *Pediatrics, 63,* 650–658.

McCubbin, H., Needle, R., & Wilson, M. (1985). Adolescent health risk behaviors: Family stress and adolescent coping as critical factors. *Family Relations, 34,* 51–62.

McRae, C. F., & Nelson, D. M. (1971). Youth to youth communication on smoking and health. *Journal of School Health, 41,* 445–447.

Meichenbaum, D. (1985). *Stress inoculation training.* New York: Pergamon.

Murray, D. M., Johnson, C. A., Leupker, R. V., Pechacek, T. F., & Jacobs, D. R. (1980). *Issues in smoking prevention research.* Paper presented at the annual conference of the American Psychological Association, Montreal, Canada.

Murray, D. M., Johnson, C. A., Leupker, R. V., Pechacek, T. F., Jacobs, D. R., & Hurd, P. D. (1978). *Social factors in the prevention of smoking in seventh grade students: A followup experience of 1 year.* Unpublished manuscript, University of Minnesota, Minneapolis, MN.

Pearl, D., Bouthilet, L., & Lazar, J. (1982). *Television and behavior: Ten years of scientific progress and implications for the eighties: Vol. II: Technical Reviews* (DHHS Publication No. ADM 82-1195). Washington, DC: U.S. Government Printing Office.

Pentz, M. A. (1985). Social competence skills and self efficacy as determinants of substance use in adolescence. In S. Shiffman & T. A. Wills (Eds.), *Coping and substance use.* New York: Academic Press.

Roberts, D. F. (1983). Children and commercials: Issues, evidence, intervention. In J. Sprafkin, C. Swift, & R. Hess (Eds.), *Rx television: Enhancing the prevention impact of TV.* New York: Haworth Press.

Schaps, E., DiBartolo, R., Moskowitz, J., Palley, C. S., & Churgin, S. (1981). A review of 127 drug abuse prevention program evaluations. *Journal of Drug Issues, 11,* 17–43.

Schinke, S. P. (1982). A school-based model for teenage pregnancy prevention. *Social Work in Education, 4,* 34–42.

Schinke, S. P., & Blythe, B. J. (1981). Cognitive-behavioral prevention of children's smoking. *Child Behavior Therapy, 3,* 25–42.

Schinke, S. P., & Gilchrist, L. D. (1977). Adolescent pregnancy: An interpersonal skill training approach to prevention. *Social Work in Health Care, 3,* 159–167.

Schinke, S. P., & Gilchrist, L. D. (1984). Preventing cigarette smoking with youth. *Journal of Primary Prevention, 5*(1), 48–53.

Shibuya, R. R. (1974). Categorizing drug users and nonusers on selected social and personality variables. *Journal of School Health, 44,* 442–444.

Silverman, S. H., Watson, D., & Silverman, M. (1985). Community-owned primary prevention for adolescent substance abuse. *Bulletin of Society of Psychologists in Addictive Behaviors, 5,* 75–86.

Silverman, W. H., & Silverman, M. (1986, October). *Using demographic data for planning primary prevention substance abuse programs.* Paper presented at the annual meeting of the Evaluation Research Society, Toronto, Canada.

Smart, R., Gray, T., & Bennett, S. (1978). Predictors of drinking and signs of heavy drinking among high school students. *International Journal of the Addictions, 13,* 1079–1094.

Smith, G., & Fogg, C. (1976). Teenage drug use: A search for causes and consequences. In D. Lettieri (Ed.), *Predicting adolescent drug use: A review of issues, methods, and correlates* (DHEW Publication No. ADM 76-299). Washington, DC: U.S. Government Printing Office.

Swisher, J. D., Crawford, J., Goldstein, R., & Yura, M. (1971). Drug education: Pushing or preventing? *Peabody Journal of Education, 49,* 68–75.

Tobler, N. S. (1986). Meta-analysis of 143 adolescent drug prevention programs: Quantitative outcome results of program participants compared to a control or comparison group. *Journal of Drug Issues, 16,* 537–567.

Tolone, W. L., & Dermott, D. (1975). Some correlates of drug use among high school youth in a midwestern rural community. *International Journal of the Addictions, 10,* 761–766.

Wechsler, H., & Thurn, D. (1973). Alcohol and drug use among teenagers: a questionnaire study. In M. Chafetz (Ed.), *Proceedings of the Second Annual Alcoholism Conference* (DHEW Publication No. HSM 73-9083). Washington, DC: U.S. Government Printing Office.

Wills, T. (1985). Stress, coping and tobacco and alcohol use in early adolescence. In S. Shiffman & T. Wills, *Coping and substance use*. Orlando, FL: Academic Press.

Wright, L. (1985). High school polydrug users and abusers. *Adolescence, 20*(80), 853–861.

14

Combining Broadcast Media and Parent Education to Prevent Teenage Drug Abuse

J. David Hawkins
Richard F. Catalano
University of Washington

Lori A. Kent
The Leonhardt Group, Seattle

Public health researchers have reduced illness and death due to heart disease by focusing preventive interventions on risk factors for such diseases (Puska, Vartianen, & Pallonen, 1982). This strategy can be applied to drug abuse prevention. Risk-focused drug abuse prevention seeks to reduce identified risk factors for drug abuse. Analyses have revealed a number of drug abuse risk factors that can be reduced by parental action. These include poor family management practices, permissive parental attitudes toward adolescent drug use, parental drug-using behaviors, high levels of family conflict, low levels of family bonding, peer influences to begin drug use, and early first use of drugs (Hawkins, Jenson, Catalano, & Lishner, 1988).

The identification of a set of risk factors for drug abuse that can be addressed by family action has increased interest in parenting skills training as a drug abuse prevention strategy (Cavazos, 1989). Unfortunately, although parenting skills training has been shown to be effective in increasing the family management skills of parents (Patterson, Chamberlain, & Reid, 1982), parent education programs have faced major problems in recruiting and retaining parents in parenting skills workshops (Perry, Crockett, & Pirie, 1987). School-based parenting prevention programs report recruiting between 40% and 50% of eligible parents (Grady, Kelin, & Boratynski, 1985; Hawkins, Catalano, Jones, & Fine, 1987). In programs for parents of conduct-disordered children, dropout rates in excess of 40%

are not uncommon (Eyeberg & Johnson, 1974; Firestone, Kelly, & Fike, 1980; Weathers & Lieberman, 1975). In spite of the evidence that parents are well positioned to address drug abuse risk factors in their own families, participating in parent workshops has not yet become expected or normative behavior for the majority of American families.

Prevention researchers have sought alternative vehicles for communicating information and skills to parents. One has been to involve parents in completing homework assignments sent home from school with their children. In seeking to educate parents regarding good nutrition, Perry (1986) and Perry, Klepp, and Shultz (1988) developed and tested a homework-based program for third-grade students and their parents that included an incentive system for parents to complete homework assignments with their children. Overall, 86% of the eligible families participated and 71% completed the program. Pentz et al. (1989) also included a family homework component in their comprehensive drug abuse prevention program and reported that over 80% of parents completed homework assignments with their children. The effects of these programs on the acquisition of parenting skills are unknown, but they have shown promise in producing parental involvement in the intervention. Moreover, Perry et al. (1988), found that subjects in the homework condition involving parents made more behavioral change in dietary habits than students in an exclusively school-based program.

Others have used print and video to reach parents (McMahon & Forehand, 1978; Webster-Stratton, Kolpacoff, & Hollinsworth, 1988). However, although books, pamphlets, and videotapes offer a low-cost alternative to parent training by professionals, there are indications that partial understanding and misunderstanding may result from exclusive reliance on such materials (Christensen, Johnson, Phillips, & Glasgow, 1980).

In our own work, we have begun to explore several approaches to broadening the involvement of parents in learning skills to prevent drug abuse in their families. We have asked: How can we convince large proportions of the parenting population that learning and using parenting skills to reduce their childrens' health risks is desirable, normative behavior? How can we make it popular to participate in learning and practicing good parenting? One direction of our research has been to explore the use of broadcast media as a tool for recruiting parents to participate in parent education. This chapter reports on an intervention of this type.

The research objectives of the intervention test were twofold: (a) to determine the extent to which broadcast media can be used to legitimate and stimulate attendance at parenting education workshops, and (b) to determine the extent to which a skills training parenting curriculum can be delivered by volunteer workshop leaders to large numbers of parents with sufficient fidelity to create desired behavioral and attitude changes.

PROJECT DESCRIPTION

In 1987, in collaboration with KING Broadcasting Company, Seattle's NBC affiliate television station, the authors designed and conducted a television-assisted parent training campaign consisting of a 1-hour television special aired at 9 p.m. on a Tuesday evening, a series of four 2-hour parenting workshops conducted at weekly intervals and offered simultaneously in 87 sites across KING's Channel 5 western Washington viewing area, and television public service announcements and additional written promotional materials distributed by schools, pharmacies, and community organizations to publicize the parent workshops.

The parent workshops were from the "Preparing for the Drug (Free) Years" parenting curriculum that is being tested in our NIDA-funded study on preventing teenage drug abuse. "Preparing for the Drug (Free) Years" is a risk-focused, workshop-format, skills training curriculum for parents of children aged 8–14. The content and learning format of the program are designed to generate motivation and behavioral skills to implement risk-reduction strategies in the family. The actions sought are as follows: establish a family position or policy on drugs on which all family members agree, teach the children social influence resistance skills to stay out of trouble while maintaining peer friendships, practice self-control skills to reduce family conflict, and create new opportunities for children entering adolescence to contribute and learn through active involvement in new roles in the family.

These changes in the family should reduce the following drug abuse risk factors: poor family management, favorable parental attitudes toward teen drug use, friends who use drugs, low family bonding, high family conflict, and early first use of drugs (Hawkins, Lishner, Catalano, & Howard, 1986). The program seeks to increase protective factors against drug abuse by strengthening bonding to the family and by establishing clear family norms against drug use by teenagers.

In the television-assisted campaign, the curriculum was split into two components. One was the hour-long television special that dramatized the family consequences of teenage drug abuse, reviewed risk factors for drug abuse, and presented family risk-reduction strategies for preventing drug abuse through a series of vignettes modeling effective behavior. The other component was a set of four community workshops in which all skills in the curriculum were taught. The first workshop "Setting Clear Family Expectations on Drugs," taught parents the importance of developing a clear family policy on alcohol and other drug use and trained them to clarify their own expectations and communicate them in a family meeting. The second workshop, "Avoiding Trouble, Teaching Children to Say 'NO' " trained parents and children to use a five-step procedure to resist social pressure to use drugs. The third workshop, "Managing Family Conflict", trained parents how to control and express anger without damaging family bonds. The fourth workshop, "Strengthening Family Bonds," trained parents in ways to increase children's participation in the family and contribution to it, taught skills to express positive feelings and love to teenagers, and provided a process for developing an ongoing parent support network beyond the "Preparing for the Drug (Free) Years" sessions. In each workshop, parents were trained to set aside family time to introduce program content into family life and practice skills learned in workshops.

To ensure the availability of workshops to parents throughout the broadcast market, letters with applications to serve as a workshop site were sent to over 3,000 school principals and community leaders in western Washington. The letters, printed on KING 5 letterhead and signed by the President of the Washington State Substance Abuse Coalition, KING 5's public affairs director, and one of the investigators, outlined the program and requirements for serving as a workshop site. The requirements included the stipulation that the school principal attend the first workshop session to welcome attending parents, the nomination of two co-leaders from the school community to be trained and conduct the series of four parenting workshops, and the designation of a site coordinator to open building space and handle logistics. There were 87 organizations, mostly public and private schools, chosen to hold parent workshops following this solicitation.

To increase the reliability and fidelity of the intervention, a 3-day workshop leaders' training program was provided to the 174 workshop co-leaders nominated by host sites. The training program was a single large group event conducted 3 weeks before the parenting workshops were offered. Over 75% of the volunteer workshop leaders were women and 47% were themselves parents.

Method

A sample of 20 workshop sites, stratified for rural, suburban, and urban locations, was selected to participate in evaluation activities related to the research objectives. Workshop participants in these evaluation sites completed questionnaires before and after each workshop session to assess recruitment sources, demographic characteristics, attitudes toward adolescent drug use, knowledge and skills of program prevention practices, application of prevention methods with their families, and reactions to workshop sessions.

Implementation

A project with this degree of visibility requires broad sponsorship, support, and endorsement. The Washington State Substance Abuse Coalition, the Washington State Bureau of Alcohol and Drug Abuse, the Washington State Principals Association, the Washington State Pharmacists Association, and the Washington State Parent Teachers Students Association all reviewed, approved, and supported the project. In addition, the project was reviewed periodically by a standing community advisory board to KING Broadcasting's "Getting To NO!" drug abuse prevention project, of which the "Preparing for the Drug (Free) Years" campaign was a part. Members represented community drug abuse prevention coalitions, education, civic and business groups, law enforcement, health and human service agencies, and local and state government. In designing the campaign, the authors viewed awareness and approval of the project by community opinion leaders concerned about the drug abuse issue to be essential given the campaign's sensitive content. Several of the collaborating organizations provided major support for the project by communicating with their memberships regarding the project and encouraging participation.

A second concern was the fidelity of the intervention, given the decision to use volunteer co-leaders to present the workshops. To ensure that workshop leaders covered the designated content, and to ensure that skills were modeled as desired, videotapes were developed for each of the workshops. The videotapes were hosted by Betty Thomas, host of the TV special. They presented key information, modeled skills using professional actors, and provided feedback from the experiences of actual parents who had previously participated in the workshops. The videotaped segments were interspersed throughout the 2-hour workshop. Workshop leaders were also provided with a workshop leader's guide with activity-by-activity instructions for leading the workshops. The guide instructed leaders to show designated video segments at specified points in the session, thereby encouraging leaders to follow the curriculum and maintain the schedule of the program.

To increase the likelihood that participating parents should acquire and use the information and skills presented in the workshops, a 142-page family activity book was developed. It contained all content presented in the workshops as well as worksheets, instructions, and agendas for family meetings and other activities to be carried out at home. Funding from the Stewardship Foundation, the Safeco Insurance Companies, the Medina Foundation, and the Comprehensive Health Education Foundation provided each participating family with a copy of the *Preparing for the Drug (Free) Years Family Activity Book* at no charge.

To increase the accessibility and visibility of the campaign, the TV special was aired on a Tuesday evening at 9 p.m., and 10-, 15-, and 30-second PSAs announcing the existence and locations of workshops were aired throughout the day and evening for 2 weeks prior to the campaign with heavy exposure during news broadcasts.

Results

The television special earned a 13 share in the market. Approximately 98,000 households viewed the program, indicating adequate market coverage to assess the question of whether exposure to the TV campaign would yield participation in parenting workshops.

Parent attendance records were available from 79 of the 87 participating workshop sites. Attendance at Session 1 ranged from 5 to 50 participants per workshop site and averaged 26.2 per site; attendance at Session 2, to which parents were encouraged to bring a child, ranged from 4 to 98 participants per workshop site and averaged 29.7 per site; attendance at Session 3 ranged from 3 to 45 parents per site and averaged 19.8 per site; attendance at Session 4 ranged from 3 to 43 parents per site and averaged 18.2 per site. Using the most conservative estimate to avoid duplicated counts of parents attending multiple sessions, 2,497 parents participated in the workshops. In the sample of 20 evaluation sites, 65% of participants attending the first workshop session reported that they had never attend-

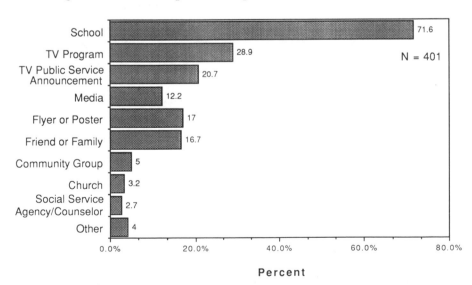

FIG. 14.1. Sources from which program participants learned of workshops (more than one response possible).

cd a workshop on parenting before. In these sites, 90% of the participants were White and 70% were female.

Workshop leaders were trained in risk factors for adolescent substance abuse (Hawkins et al., 1986). At the conclusion of the workshop series, workshop leaders were asked to identify participating families whose children were at risk for drug abuse because of exposure to multiple risk factors. Using these clinical ratings, 16% of the participating families were judged to have a child at high risk for drug abuse.

Data from the 20 evaluation sites indicate that the combination of broadcast media and local site recruitment efforts was responsible for recruiting the large majority of participants, as shown in Fig. 14.1. Of the participants, 53% had viewed the television special, and 28.9% said that the special was the way they had learned about the workshop program. Nearly 72% of participants learned of the workshops through the school hosting the workshop (citations of multiple sources were allowed). Only 20.7% of the participants reported learning of the program through televised public service announcements.

As shown in Fig. 14.2, the preponderance of participating parents had children in Grades 4 through 7, the target group for this parenting program that focuses on preventing the early initiation of alcohol and other drug use because it increases risk of drug problems. Over 57% of participants had children in Grades 4 and 5 and 42.6% had children in Grades 6 and 7.

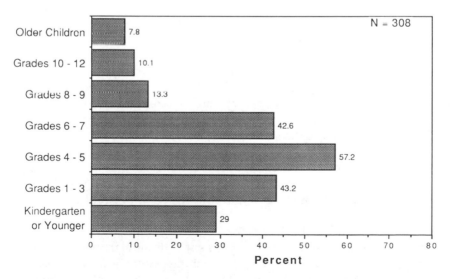

FIG. 14.2. Percentage of program participants with children in different groups. Means for sessions 1–4 (more than one response possible).

Linked pretests and posttests from the 20 evaluation sites were analyzed using dependent *t* tests to determine short-term knowledge, attitude, and behavior impacts on participants. Significant changes in the desired direction were found for 23 of the 30 planned comparisons.

Following the session on setting clear family expectations about drugs, significant pre- to posttest increases were observed in the degree of endorsement of the statement that before parents can develop a clear family position on drug use, they must be clear about their own views ($t = -3.77$, $df = 354$, $p < .001$). Significant decreases were observed in the degree to which parents agreed that "kids can tell what their parents think about the use of alcohol and drugs even if their parents never say so directly" ($t = 7.5$, $df = 353$, $p < .001$) indicating increased understanding of the importance of explicitly communicating a family position on drugs to children. At the end of the session, parents were also more likely to agree that parental involvement is important in preventing drug abuse ($t = 2.8$, $df = 359$, $p < .01$) and that good family management reduces the risk of drug abuse ($t = 7.4$, $df = 355$, $p < .001$).

Following the session in which parents and children learned refusal skills together, parents were significantly more likely to recognize that "most children are first offered drugs by friends or family members" ($t = 5.9$, $df = 291$, $p < .001$) and less likely to believe that "teenagers who refuse to try alcohol and other drugs should be prepared to lose popularity" ($t = 3.1$, $df = 291$, $p < .01$). The latter finding indicates an increased understanding of the importance of peer friendships to teenagers. This understanding is hypothesized to be an important motivator for parents to help their children learn refusal skills that allow them to keep friends while refusing drug offers. Consistent with this perspective, following the session, parents were significantly less likely to support the view that "say 'No' and walk away" is the way to stay out of trouble with drugs ($t = 5.9$, $df = 294$, $p < .001$) and significantly more likely to endorse the importance of suggesting an alternative activity when confronted by friends with an opportunity to use drugs ($t = 7.9$, $df = 292$, $p < .001$). Further, they were more likely to subscribe to the statement: "It's important for family members to practice new skills together even if it makes them uncomfortable at first" ($t = 4.9$, $df = 289$, $p < .001$). This finding indicates that workshop participation increased parental motivation to actually teach and practice refusal skills with their children, an important behavioral goal of the parenting program.

At the conclusion of the session on family conflict management, parents expressed significantly less agreement with the statement that "everyone gets angry in their own way, so teaching people how to express anger is a waste of time" ($t = 4.6$, $df = 245$, $p < .001$), and with the statement: "Yelling at teenagers when you're angry with them gets the best results"

$(t = 3.3, df = 249, p < 001)$. They were also less likely to think that "when parents are angry with their children, they should keep the specific reasons for their anger to themselves" $(t = 2.3, df = 247, p < .02)$. These findings indicate that participating parents became more convinced of the importance of expressing anger constructively so as not to weaken family bonding. Following the session, participants also evidenced greater endorsement of statements regarding the importance of controlling anger toward family members. They were more likely to agree that "there are times when it's important to control your anger and not express it right away" $(t = 3.6, df = 249, p < .001)$ and less likely to agree that "when you are angry with your child, it is always best to tell him/her immediately $(t = 6.8, df = 249, p < .001)$. At the conclusion of the session parents again appeared motivated to practice the conflict management skills with their families, as evidenced by significantly greater endorsement of the statement: "It's important for family members to practice conflict management skills even if it makes them uncomfortable at first" $(t = -5.8, df = 244, p < .001)$.

At the conclusion of the session on strengthening family bonds by increasing children's contributing roles in the family, participants evidenced significantly greater understanding of the importance of involving adolescent children in new family roles. Parents expressed greater agreement with the idea that children should participate in family management by involving them in "deciding what the family rules should be" $(t - -7.5, df - 242, p < .001)$. They also were significantly more supportive of the idea that adolescents can be involved in family financial management. At the conclusion of the session they expressed less agreement with the statement "Discussions about family finances are private, and teenagers should not be involved" $(t = -4.7, df = 242, p < .001)$. Also, after participating in the session, parents appeared less inclined to allow their adolescent children to avoid actively contributing to the family. They expressed less agreement with the statement "asking teenagers to do chores for the family only increases their resentment" $(t = 2.0, df = 242, p < .05)$

The "Preparing for the Drug (Free) Years" program seeks to generate behavioral change in parents by motivating them and giving them skills to conduct meetings with their families following each workshop session. The content of the session is to be taken home and introduced to the family through a family meeting. At pretest in the evaluation sites, 71% of the participants reported that they did not hold periodic family meetings, whereas 12% of the participants reported that they already conducted family meetings every few months and 17% reported that they held family meetings several times per month. At each session, returning participants were asked whether they had conducted a meeting with their families on the topic of the previous session. Of the participants, 59% reported that they held a family meeting to develop a family position on drugs; 58% reported that they met with their families to teach and practice refusal skills, and 40% reported that they met with their families to practice and teach skills for reducing family conflict. These self-report data may be biased, in that they are from a sample of returning participants. However, they suggest that a majority of participating parents in the evaluation sites put the "Preparing for the Drug (Free) Years" program content and skills into practice with their families within the week following workshop sessions.

Finally, as shown in Table 14.1, participants in the evaluation sites were very favorable to the program, rating the workshop content, process, and leaders highly.

DISCUSSION

These results support the combined use of broadcast media and parent skills training in a workshop format to reach and train relatively large numbers of parents to reduce drug abuse risk factors in their families. Both media and local school efforts contributed to recruitment success, suggesting that mass media may effectively reinforce and legitimate local site recruitment efforts, but should not be expected to replace local site recruitment activities. It is likely that the media's contribution was, as hypothesized, to create public awareness and acceptance for this parenting prevention campaign.

It is instructive to note that only 53% of the workshop participants had viewed the TV special. Campaigns combining broadcast media and work-

TABLE 14.1
Program Participants' (Mean) Evaluation of Parent Workshops

	Session 1 (N = 401)	Session 2 (N = 329)	Session 3 (N = 259)	Session 4 (N = 250)	Overall (N = 250)
How worthwhile (1 = not; 6 = very) was:					
Overall session	5.3	5.4	5.4	5.4	—
Video segments	5.3	5.2	5.1	4.9	—
Activities/Exercises	4.9	5.3	4.8	5.1	—
Family activity book[a]	—	5.3	5.3	5.4	—
How good (1 = poor; 6 = excellent) was:					
Workshop content	5.2	5.4	5.4	5.4	5.6
Workshop process	5.0	5.3	5.1	5.3	5.4
Workshop leaders'	5.2	5.4	5.3	5.6	5.5

[a]Family Activity Book was distributed during first session.

shop sessions should not be structured on an assumption that workshop participants all have been exposed to the broadcast material. Broadcast material that is key to knowledge, attitude, or skills development should be repeated in workshop sessions in future campaigns of this type.

Further, it may be useful to reinforce workshop participation using broadcast and other media over the course of the workshop series. Mean attendance per site declined from over 25 participants in the first two sessions to under 20 in the last two sessions. It is possible that broadcast news coverage and print media coverage of the workshops as well as ongoing PSAs about the program could enhance motivation to continue participation in the workshops, although this suggestion is purely speculative.

The data also suggest that workshops led by trained volunteers were effective in generating significant knowledge, attitude, and behavior change in the majority of participants. Significant changes in participants' knowledge and attitudes regarding parenting practices to reduce drug abuse risk factors in the family were observed on 23 of 30 planned comparisons. All changes were in the desired direction. Moreover, a majority of participants reported conducting family meetings to set a family position on drugs and to teach their children refusal skills within the week following the introduction of that topic in the workshop. It appears that volunteers can be trained to lead parenting workshops with fidelity to the "Preparing for the Drug (Free) Years" program using the video and print materials provided.

These results suggest a sufficient degree of implementation using this media/workshop approach to justify a rigorous evaluation of this combined strategy.

REFERENCES

Cavazos, L. F. (1989). *Keynote address: Third annual conference on drug-free schools and communities.* Baltimore, MD.

Christensen, A., Johnson, S. M., Phillips, S., & Glasgow, R. E. (1980). Cost effectiveness in behavioral family therapy. *Behavior Therapy, 11,* 208–226.

Eyeberg, S. M., & Johnson, S. M. (1974). Multiple assessment of behavior modification with families: Effects on contingency contracting and order of treated problems. *Journal of Consulting and Clinical Psychology, 42,* 44–47.

Firestone, P., Kelley, M. J., & Fike, S. (1980). Are fathers necessary in parent training groups? *Journal of Clinical Child Psychology, 9,* 44–47.

Grady, K., Kelin, E. G., & Boratynski, M. (1985). Preparing parents for teenagers: A step in the prevention of adolescent substance abuse. *Family Relations, 34,* 541–549.

Hawkins, J. D., Catalano, R. F., Jones, G., & Fine, D. N. (1987). Delinquency prevention through parent training: Results and issues from work in progress. In J. G. Wilson, & G. C. Loury (Eds.), *From children to citizens: Families, schools, and delinquency prevention* (Vol. 3, pp. 186–204). New York: Springer-Verlag.

Hawkins, J. D., Jenson, J. M., Catalano, R. F., & Lishner, D. M. (1988). Delinquency and drug abuse: Implications for social services. *Social Service Review, 62*, 258–284.

Hawkins, J. D., Lishner, D. M., Catalano, R. F., & Howard, M. O. (1986). Childhood predictors of adolescent substance abuse: Toward an empirically grounded theory. *Journal of Children in Contemporary Society, 18*, 1–65.

McMahon, R. J., & Forehand, R. (1978). Nonprescription behavior therapy: Effectiveness of a brochure in teaching mothers to correct their children's inappropriate mealtime behaviors. *Behavior Therapy, 9*, 814–820.

Patterson, G. R., Chamberlain, P., & Reid, J. B. (1982), A comparative evaluation of a parent training program. *Behavior Therapy, 13*, 638–650.

Pentz, M. A., Dwyer, J. H., MacKinnon, D. P., Flay, W. B., Wang, E. Y. I., & Johnson, C. A. (1989). A multi-community trial for primary prevention of adolescent drug abuse: Effects on drug use prevalence. *Journal of the American Medical Association, 261*, 3259–3266.

Perry, C. L. (1986). Community-wide health promotion and drug abuse prevention. *Journal of School Health, 56*, 359–363.

Perry, C. L., Crockett, S. J., & Pirie, P. (1987). Influencing parental health behavior: Implications of community assessments. *Health Education, 18*(5), 68–77.

Perry, C. L., Klepp, K. I., & Shultz, J. M. (1988). Primary prevention of cardiovascular disease: Communitywide strategies for youth. *Journal of Consulting and Clinical Psychology, 56*, 358–364.

Puska, P., Vartiainen, E., & Pallonen, U. (1982). The North Karelia Youth Project: Evaluation of two years of intervention on health behavior and CVD risk factors among 13 to 15-year old children. *Preventative Medicine, 11*, 550–570.

Weathers, L., & Lieberman, R. P. (1975). Contingency contracting with families of delinquent adolescents. *Behavior Therapy, 6*, 356–366.

Webster-Stratton, C., Kolpacoff, M., & Hollinsworth, T. (1988). Self-administered videotape therapy for families with conduct-problem children: Comparison with two cost effective treatments and a control group. *Journal of Consulting and Clinical Psychology, 56*, 558–566.

Persuasive Communication and Drug Prevention: An Evaluation of the DARE Program

Richard R. Clayton
Anne Cattarello
L. Edward Day
Katherine P. Walden
University of Kentucky

Much of our nation's effort to deal with the use and abuse of drugs among youth involves school-based prevention programming. The rationale for conducting prevention programs in schools is one of coverage; it is the best site for reaching the most children. The goal is simple: to influence children and youth to never initiate use of drugs, or at least to "delay" the onset of use. If onset is inhibited or at least delayed, then ultimately, there may be a significant reduction in the negative consequences of drug use, both acute and chronic.

Many early prevention efforts used fear tactics that have been found ineffective in either inhibiting or delaying onset. More recent programs, founded on a more accurate understanding of the primary risk and protective factors for initiation of drug use, have been somewhat successful in inhibiting and delaying onset of use.

Drug abuse prevention programs are usually classified according to the central thrust of the curriculum: (a) information only, (b) values clarification or affective education, (c) skills training, (d) peer resistance. This is an understandable way to organize the field. However, a key element in all programs and one that is given minimal attention is the person and the process of communicating the curriculum.

Persuasive communication is, of necessity, an integral part of school-based drug prevention efforts. As Holder (1972) stated, "communications comprise the fundamental element in the influence-learning process" (p. 343). Although prevention programs tend to employ standard curricula, they are implemented by people through the process of communication. Therefore, the effects of a curriculum on relevant outcome measures can be conceptualized as being mediated through the person delivering or communicating the program. The significance of this is usually found in reports of process evaluations, although process evaluations are often limited or even missing in most evaluation studies of prevention interventions.

PURPOSE

In this chapter, data are presented from an evaluation of the short-term effectiveness of project DARE (Drug Abuse Resistance Education). DARE is a school-based, primary prevention program aimed at elementary school-aged children in either the fifth or sixth grades. The curriculum is taught by police officers who have completed an 80-hour training course designed to prepare them for working with elementary-aged children in the classroom and for delivering a specific curriculum. This report focuses on short-term results in that it examines changes from the pre- to posttest period, a time span of 17 to 19 weeks. The focus of the evaluation is twofold. First, the effects of the DARE curriculum on students' attitudes toward drug use (both general and substance specific), peer-related factors, self-esteem, and self-reported substance use are examined. Second, in viewing the program from a persuasive communications standpoint, the results are examined separately for each of the four police officers delivering the DARE curriculum.

THE SCHOOL-BASED PREVENTION LITERATURE

Outcome evaluations of drug prevention programs conducted prior to the early 1980s presented a rather dim picture regarding the efficacy of such efforts (see Braucht, Follingstadt, Brakarsh, & Berry, 1973; Durell & Bukoski, 1984; Kinder, Pope, & Walfish, 1980; Schaps, DiBartolo, Moskowitz, Polley, & Churgin, 1981, for reviews of this research). Most early programs tended to provide information only. Although research indicated that this approach was somewhat effective in increasing knowledge about drugs, corresponding desired changes in attitudes and behavior did not occur. In some instances, it appeared that the prevention programs may have had effects in the wrong direction. In addition, the lack of methodological rigor was pervasive leading to serious questions about the validity of the results.

Fortunately, in recent years significant progress has been made in the prevention field, both theoretically and methodologically. Knowledge about the risk factors for drug use informs the curriculum of many prevention programs. Methodologically, although we still have a long way to go, emphasis is on designing studies to insure reasonable levels of external and internal validity.

The prevention programs currently exhibiting effectiveness focus either exclusively or to a large degree on helping children to recognize and respond appropriately to the social pressure they experience to use drugs. *Psychosocial approaches*, as they are termed, were first implemented with regard to cigarette smoking (see Battjes, 1985; Botvin, 1986; Flay, 1985; Flay et al., 1985). The success of these programs led them to be applied to the use of other substances.

Hansen, Johnson, Flay, Graham, and Sobel (1988) compared the effectiveness of social and affective curricula with a control group in their evaluation of Project SMART. Affective curricula are targeted at the psychological reasons for drug use and emphasize the clarification of values as a key element in preventing drug use. The study involved seventh-grade students from eight randomly assigned schools, two of which received a social prevention curriculum, two of which received an affective-based curriculum, and four of which served as controls. The students were surveyed prior to participation in the program and 12 and 24 months later. The results indicated that the social program was far superior to the affective program. In fact, the affective curriculum seemed to have some pro-drug effects when compared to the control group. At both follow-up times, students who received the social program exhibited significantly lower rates of cigarette use and alcohol use (defined as two or more drinks in the last 30 days). With regard to marijuana use, there were significantly lower onset levels at Time 1, but not at Time 2. However, at Time 2, the differences were in the expected direction.

Another psychosocial approach to prevention, Life Skills Training (LST) was developed by Botvin and colleagues (see Botvin, 1983). LST focuses not only on social pressure, but also incorporates training in general social and psychological skills. This program has been found to be effective in terms of cigarette smoking (Botvin, 1983; Botvin & Wills, 1985), and more recently has been applied to alcohol and marijuana use. One evaluation of this program, which focused on alcohol use with seventh-grade students from two schools (one treatment and one control), found that students who received LST reported significantly lower alcohol consumption at 9-month follow-up (Botvin, Baker, Botvin, Filazzola, & Millman, 1984).

Life Skills Training has also been evaluated in terms of who delivers the program utilizing seventh graders from 10 New York City junior high schools (Botvin, Baker, Renick, Filazzola, & Botvin, 1984). Through random assignment, 4 schools received a peer-led condition, 4 a teacher-led condition, and 2 were employed as controls. The results indicated the superiority of the peer-led condition over both the teacher-led and control schools. Concerning drug use, the peer-led LST condition versus teacher-led and controls produced significantly lower proportions of cigarette, alcohol, and marijuana use on certain measures. In addition, LST as implemented by peers produced significantly greater anti-drug attitudes than the other two conditions. These results lend credence to our hypothesis that the perceived nature of the deliverer is an important overlooked variable in most evaluations of prevention programs.

The efficacy of psychosocial programs was also supported by Tobler's (1987) meta-analysis of 143 drug prevention programs. Comparisons of five of the most often implemented prevention approaches indicated that the psychosocial programs or peer programs (Tobler's designation) are superior to the others in producing anti-drug attitudes and lower levels of use. Although the studies by Hansen et al. and Botvin et al., as well as those incorporated in Tobler's meta-analysis, display methodological problems such as initial nonequivalence, in certain instances, and sample attrition in others, the consistency in results indicates the promise of psychosocial approaches to prevention.

PROJECT DARE: A PSYCHOSOCIAL PROGRAM

Project DARE is another psychosocial prevention program that is currently being implemented in over 450 cities across the nation and statewide in some cases. DARE was developed as a joint effort between the Los Angeles Police Department and the Los Angeles Unified School District. It is based, to a large degree, on the curriculum designed for SMART (Hansen et al., 1988), a curriculum that is quite similar to that being delivered in Kansas City and Indianapolis as Project STAR (see Pentz et al., 1989). The thrust of the STAR program is on teaching adolescents (primarily fifth and sixth graders) to resist peer pressure to use drugs. However, the in-school curriculum is only one element in a comprehensive, community-based intervention. Overall, Pentz and her colleagues reported significantly lower rates of use of cigarettes, alcohol, and marijuana among those who received the STAR curriculum.

In contrast to other psychosocial approaches, a unique and potentially important element of DARE is that the curriculum is delivered by uniformed police officers. The officers are, in essence, "hand-picked" to deliver the program based on possessing the social skills necessary to communicate with young people. The training received by the police officers is more extensive than that given to many others who deliver prevention programs, such as teachers or peers. For example, in one instance, in the LST program, peer leaders received only a 4-hour training program and briefing meetings and the teachers a 1-day session (see Botvin et al., 1984), compared to 2 full weeks in the DARE program.

From a persuasive communications perspective where the program deliverer "mediates" the effects of the curriculum, intensive training in the curriculum as well as other areas, should be considered of prime importance. It certainly should have a major influence on "fidelity" to the curriculum lesson plans. Further, because the DARE officer is responsible for only one course, it is unlikely he or she will cut short time spent on the prevention curriculum in favor of time spent on the academic subjects.

In addition, "source credibility" is considered to be an important element in persuasive communication (see Bostrom, 1983) and should be viewed as such in drug prevention. Bailey (1985) defined credibility as believability, including components of knowledge, experience, and expertise. Intuitively, in terms of these factors, a police officer would seem to be a credible source, particularly by adolescents.

Description of the Curriculum

The DARE curriculum, as implemented in Lexington, Kentucky is delivered 1 hour each week for 16 weeks. The primary focus is on peer-pressure resistance training. Students are taught to recognize peer pressure to use drugs and ways to say no to this pressure that are reinforced through role playing in the classroom. Assertiveness is emphasized in this process. Media pressures to engage in drug use are also discussed along with techniques to analyze and resist them.

In addition to resisting social pressure, the DARE curriculum helps students to recognize the consequences of drug use, build self-esteem, manage stress, form a support system, and make responsible decisions. In one session the children are visited by high school students as "positive" role models who discuss with them what to expect regarding pressures to use drugs as they enter junior high and high school. The DARE program culminates in a graduation ceremony, in which participants receive a diploma and are addressed by a prominent member of the community. Before the children can participate in graduation, they must complete the DARE workbook and write an essay taking a personal and public stand against drug use.

Prior Evaluations of DARE

Although the DARE program has been in existence since 1983, few evaluations of the program have been reported in the scientific literature. DeJong (1987) evaluated the program with seventh-grade students in Los Angeles.

His analyses of questionnaire data suggested that DARE students accepted significantly fewer offers to use drugs and reported significantly lower levels of substance use than control group students. However, DeJong's study was seriously flawed in at least two ways. First the students were surveyed at only one point in time; and second there was no random assignment to treatment and control conditions. In fact, DeJong's designation of treatment versus control resulted from a response to one question in which students were asked if they had participated in the DARE program when they were in the sixth grade.

Several other attempts have been made to evaluate the DARE program (Honolulu, 1986; Illinois State Police, 1987; Kokomo, Indiana, 1987; Los Angeles, 1987; Pittsburgh, 1987; Kentucky State Police, 1989; North Carolina, 1989), most of which are unpublished and most of which are at best "pilot" and/or descriptive in nature. However, two of these evaluations were reasonably rigorous methodologically and deserve mention.

The North Carolina evaluation (Ringwalt, Ennett, & Holt, 1990) focused on pre- to posttest differences for students attending 10 schools randomly assigned as DARE schools and 10 schools randomly assigned as control schools. From pre- to posttest, the DARE curriculum exhibited no significant effect on self-reported drug use or intentions to use drugs or on a measure of self-esteem. However, there were statistically significant differences in the appropriate direction between those students who received DARE and those who were in the control group on attitudes toward specific substances and drug use in general, the perception of peers' attitudes toward drug use, assertiveness, and recognizing media influences.

The Kentucky State Police evaluation (Faine & Bohlander, 1989) examined pre- to posttest differences between students who received DARE and those who did not, controlling for type of school (rural, parochial, inner-city, and suburban). Self-reported use of drugs was not examined. However, the evaluation did show a significant improvement in self-esteem comparing the treatment and control students. There were not significant differences in the changes across the four types of schools. With regard to perceived external control, there were also significant differences between treatment and control students and among types of schools. Attitudes toward police improved more among DARE than non-DARE students, but did not vary significantly among schools. Finally, the DARE curriculum did have the desired effect of producing significantly greater peer-resistance scores. Faine (1989) conducted a pre- to posttest evaluation of the effectiveness of DARE among 400 inner-city youth in Nashville. He found no support for effectiveness in changing peer resistance or positive drug attitudes. Further, the one significant difference between DARE and non-DARE students, positive police attitude, was in the opposite direction predicted. DARE students had significantly more negative attitudes toward the police than the non-DARE students.

Research Design

In the Fall of 1986 and Spring of 1987, DARE was implemented on a pilot basis in Lexington, Kentucky. Given a positive reception by school personnel, students, and the community, and the results of a pilot evaluation, the Lexington-Fayette county school board mandated the implementation of DARE in its 31 elementary schools. In September 1987, a grant was received from the National Institute on Drug Abuse (NIDA) to formally evaluate the program over a 5-year time span, beginning with the sixth-grade cohort of the 1987–1988 academic year.

For the first cohort, 23 of the schools were randomly assigned to receive the DARE curriculum and 8 schools were randomly designated as controls. The control students did not receive DARE, but did receive the drug unit in the existing science curriculum.

In this chapter, data collected during the first year of the study (Fall 1987 and Spring 1988) are presented. The data are from the pre- and posttest questionnaires provided by these students. Therefore, the results address the short-term effectiveness of the program. The sixth graders who participated in the first year of the study will be resurveyed in the 7th, 8th, 9th, and 10th grades. Subsequent to the first year of implementation, all 6th graders in the school system will be receiving DARE and will be surveyed through the 1991–1992 school year. Therefore, we are employing a cohort sequential design with randomly assigned treatment and control schools only for the first cohort.

Research Procedure

Students in the treatment and control groups completed a 154-item questionnaire prior to the exposure of the treatment group to DARE or the control group to the drug unit in the science curriculum. Passive consent was employed and the number of nonparticipants was negligible. Approximately 4 months later, shortly after the completion of the program, the posttest questionnaires were administered. Confidentiality was emphasized verbally by data collectors who were independent of the school system, and dramatized by having the students tear off the first page of their questionnaire that contained identifying information. This material was then placed by the data collector in a separate envelope. The majority of the sixth graders completed the questionnaire in 45 minutes. Students who had serious problems reading the questionnaire were interviewed or were allowed extra time to complete the questionnaire that was then mailed to the investigators. Questionnaires were left at the schools for those who were absent on the day of administration. Instructions were left concerning confidentiality and assurances given by the teachers that privacy would be provided so the students could complete the questionnaires.

Measured Variables

1. *General Attitudes Toward Drug Use (ATTGEN)*. This is a 7-item Likert-type scale measured on five points, ranging from "I agree strongly" to "I disagree strongly." Higher scores on this scale reflect negative attitudes toward drugs.

2. *Substance Specific Attitudes.* There were three eight-item scales designed to measure positive utilities (i.e., attitudes) toward use of cigarettes, alcohol, and marijuana. The positive utilities scales were measured on four points, varying from "Does not help at all" to "Helps very much." Three five-item scales were used to measure negative utilities toward these three substances. The negative utilities scales were measured on a 5-point scale, ranging from "I agree strongly" to "I disagree strongly." These six scales are labeled CIPOSUT, CINEGUT, ALPOSUT, ALNEGUT, MJPOSUT, and MJNEGUT. On all positive and negative utility scales lower scores reflect negative attitudes toward the specific substance.

3. *Self-Esteem (SELF)*. This 10-item scale was measured on five points, varying from "I agree strongly" to "I disagree strongly." Higher scores on SELF reflect higher self-esteem.

4. *Peer Relationships (PEERREL)*. This is an eight-item scale measured on five points, ranging from I agree strongly" to "I disagree strongly." The higher the score on this scale, the more popular one is among their peers.

5. *Peer-Pressure Resistance (PEERPR)*. This nine-item scale taps a tendency to resist or succumb to peer pressure to engage in various forms of deviance using a 5-point range from "Definitely not" to "Definitely will." Low scores on PEERPR reflect the ability to resist negative peer pressure.

6. *Reported Drug Use.* Questions were asked about lifetime, past year, and past month use of cigarettes, alcohol, and marijuana. Seven answer categories were provided for use of cigarettes, ranging from "None" to "31 or more cigarettes." There were also seven possible answers for use of alcohol and marijuana, ranging from "0 times" to "40 or more." The nine drug use questions are labeled CIGLIF, CIGYR, CIGMO, ALCLIF, ALCYR, ALCMO, MJLIF, MJYR, and MJMO.

The information on the reliabilities of the scales are presented in Table 15.1.

TABLE 15.1
Internal Consistency of Scales: Cronbach's Alpha
(N in Parentheses)

	T^a Alpha	T^b Alpha
Scale of general drug attitudes ATTGEN[a]	.76 (1834)	.80 (1867)
Scale of postive utilities of cigarettes CIPOSUT[b]	.91 (1819)	.88 (1857)
Scale of negative utilities for cigarettes CINEGUT[c]	.74 (1859)	.75 (1898)
Scale of positive utilities for alcohol ALPOSUT	.89 (1789)	.88 (1842)
Scale of negative utilities for alcohol ALNEGUT	.79 (1840)	.81 (1874)
Scale of positive utilities for marijuana MJPOSUT	.91 (1809)	.89 (1854)
Scale of negative utilities for marijuana MJNEGUT	.80 (1871)	.83 (1888)
Scale of peer relationships PEERREL[d]	.77 (1774)	.80 (1811)
Scale of suceptibility to negative peer pressure PEERPR[e]	.87 (1826)	.87 (1836)
Scale of self-esteem SELF[f]	.77 (1712)	.80 (1759)

Scale:

[a]Adapted from Drug and Alcohol Survey, see Moskowitz, Schaeffer, Condon, Schaps, and Malvin (1981).

[b,c]Positive and negative utility scales were taken from Drug and Alcohol Survey, see Moskowitz et al. (1981).

[d]Adapted from Drug and Alcohol Survey, see Moskowitz, Condon, Brewer, Schaps, and Malvin (1979).

[e]Adapted from Dielman, Shope, Campanelli, and Butchart (1986).

[f]Adapted from Rosenberg (1965).

As can be noted in Table 15.1, all scales exhibit acceptable degrees of internal consistency, with Cronbach's *alpha* scores ranging from .74 to .91.

Description of the Sample

There were 1,002 sixth graders pretested in the Fall of 1987 and 989 the following spring, for a sample size of 2,091. Posttest information was obtained for 1,927 of those pretested, approximately 92%. Sample attrition was virtually identical for both the treatment and control groups (i.e., 8%). The main reasons for sample attrition were: (a) students moving out of the county; (b) students changing schools; and (c) questionnaires not being returned that were left at the school for the absentees to complete when they returned.

Of the 1,927 students from whom complete information was obtained, 51% are male and the majority (i.e., 76%) are White, with Black (i.e., 21%) being the next largest racial group. Other race and ethnic groups make up slightly less than 4% of the sample. Most of the children were either 11 or 12 years old. In terms of lifetime drug use, alcohol had the highest prevalence rate; 30% of the students had used alcohol at least one or two times. Cigarettes were the next most widely used, with 28% of the students having at least tried them. Slightly over 4% of the sample had tried marijuana.

Initial Equivalence of Treatment and Control Groups

Several analyses were conducted to assess whether significant differences existed between the treatment and control groups prior to the implementation of the DARE curriculum. These tests examine key demographic variables as well as all variables and scales used in the analyses reported in the following sections. The results are shown in Table 15.2.

Both treatment and control groups have nearly identical distributions for gender, age, and the presence of siblings in the home. The treatment group has a slightly higher percentage of White students, and a correspondingly lower percentage of Blacks. The value of chi-square by condition is statistically significant. Thus, race (White, non-White) is used as a control variable in subsequent analyses.

T tests were performed to assess initial equivalence on the scaled items. There are no significant initial differences between treatment and control group students on the three positive and three negative-oriented scales for cigarettes, alcohol, and marijuana, the self-esteem scale, or the two scales that measure peer-pressure resistance and peer relationships. A significant difference was found on the scale designed to measure general attitudes toward drugs. The control group is significantly more negative toward drugs. The implications of this in light of our results are discussed here.

The last part of Table 15.2 shows the percentage of respondents who report at least some drug use. The *t* tests presented here are based on means computed from the seven ordinal categories of each variable. No significant differences emerge for any of the measures of cigarette or marijuana use. The treatment and control groups do differ, however, on each of the alcohol use measures. In each instance, it appears that the treatment group exceeds the control group in the prevalence of alcohol use prior to their exposure to DARE.

TABLE 15.2
Initial Equivalence for 23 Treatment and 8 Control Schools:
Evaluation of Project DARE in Lexington

Items and Scales for Assessing Initial Equivalence	Treatment (n = 1,438)	Control (n = 487)*	
Gender			
Male	51.3%	50.3%	
Female	48.7%	49.7%	
Race χ² = 8.66; df = 2; p. < .01)			
White	77.3%	71.0%	
Black	19.2%	25.5%	
Other	3.5%	3.5%	
Birth Cohort			
1974 or prior	8.4%	9.1%	
1975	39.2%	40.2%	
1976	51.5%	50.0%	
1977 and after	.8%	.6%	
Number of Siblings			
None	17.3%	17.9%	
One or more	82.7%	82.1%	
Scales			
ATTGEN	32.41	32.88	(.01)
CIGPOSUT	10.92	11.11	
CIGNEGUT	10.50	10.10	
ALCPOSUT	10.92	10.70	
ALCNEGUT	8.99	8.74	
MARPOSUT	10.71	10.76	
MARNEGUT	8.12	8.04	
PEERREL	30.34	30.93	
PEERPR	14.23	13.76	
SELF	39.36	39.41	
Self-Reports of Drug Use			
CIGLIF	28.3%	29.0%	
CIGYR	15.0%	13.0%	
CIGMO	4.7%	5.0%	
ALCLIF	32.0%	26.0%	(.006)
ALCYR	20.4%	15.3%	(.001)
ALCMO	10.6%	5.4%	(.001)
MJLIF	4.1%	6.1%	
MJYR	3.1%	3.1%	
MJMO	1.6%	1.3%	

*School identification on two students was missing.

Analysis

This evaluation of DARE focuses on two different types of possible effects. The analysis of "curriculum effects" compares the treatment group with the control group, asking whether exposure to the DARE program alters either attitudes or the reported patterns of substance use. The examination of "officer effects" focuses on differences within the treatment group, subdividing it on the basis of which police officer presents the curriculum. This could provide interesting information for assessing the importance of persuasive communication. Informal observations provide *prima facie* grounds for believing that there are significant differences in the communication styles of the four officers responsible for DARE instruction in Lexington. Comparing across categories within the treatment group provides evidence for whether these differences in style affect the acceptance of the principles taught in the DARE program.

Curriculum Effects

To assess changes, standardized gain scores were computed for each of the targeted variables by subtracting Time 1 scores from Time 2 scores and dividing this result by Time 1 scores. The use of simple difference scores introduces bias according to the value of the Time 1 measurement (Bornstedt, 1969). Dividing the result by the Time 1 score provides a partial correction for this bias. Analysis of variance was then performed on the standardized gain scores, controlling on race because of initial nonequivalence. An interaction between race and condition is also included in the analysis of variance results.

Analyses of the short-term curriculum effects are presented in Table 15.3. Before the data are examined, an orienting comment is appropriate. Low mean scores throughout these tables indicate that there was little average change in the scale scores between pre- and posttest. This is not an unexpected result given the amount of time that passed between the surveys. Ceiling effects could also play a part. In general, preteens already hold negative attitudes toward drugs and the majority have not yet initiated use, even of the so-called licit drugs. Interventions that target this age group are best viewed as attempts to slow the rate at which students fall away from these ceilings as they age.

Statistically significant differences in the predicted direction emerged between the DARE and non-DARE students on general attitudes toward drugs and the three scales measuring negative utilities toward cigarettes, alcohol, and marijuana. The magnitude of the differences in gain scores for the substance specific scales was somewhat unexpected given the usual problem in primary prevention programs with ceiling effects, particularly

TABLE 15.3
Analysis of Variance of Attitude Gain Scores by Experimental
Condition and Race

	$\bar{X}$,	Whites	$\bar{X}$,	Non-Whites	F, Race	F, Treatment	F, Interaction
GATTGEN							
Treatment	.019	(.155)[a]	.022	(.197)	.01	7.12***	.05
Control	−.003	(.112)	−.003	(.147)			
GALPOSUT							
Treatment	−.017	(.318)	.064	(.440)	3.49*	.30	12.10***
Control	.035	(.383)	−.036	(.368)			
GALNEGUT							
Treatment	−.030	(.454)	.003	(.533)	4.33**	22.79***	.56
Control	.082	(.473)	.159	(.591)			
GCIPOSUT							
Treatment	.002	(.359)	.059	(.431)	1.72	.24	4.76
Control	.019	(.361)	−.024	(.437)			
GCINEGUT							
Treatment	.011	(.430)	.065	(.604)	3.99**	16.26***	.21
Control	.125	(.571)	.152	(.444)			
GMJPOSUT							
Treatment	−.001	(.350)	.024	(.392)	.59	.23	.42
Control	.017	(.412)	.011	(.505)			
GMJNEGUT							
Treatment	−.020	(.452)	.007	(.587)	3.11*	14.93***	.62
Control	.073	(.511)	.148	(.706)			
GPEERREL							
Treatment	.032	(.196)	.055	(.198)	2.32	4.76**	.48
Control	.014	(.186)	.020	(.208)			
GPEERPR							
Treatment	.044	(.381)	.060	(.425)	.20	3.82*	.40
Control	.094	(.435)	.079	(.384)			
GSELF							
Treatment	.036	(.159)	.036	(.182)	.22	1.84	.67
Control	.020	(.158)	.036	(.158)			

*p is less than .10; **p is less than .05; ***p is less than .01
[a]Standard deviation is given in parentheses

on specific attitudes toward specific substances. Given the passage of close
to 19 weeks between pre- and posttest, a problem with response set is unlikely. It is interesting that no statistically significant difference emerged
for the self-esteem scale. A core etiological assumption behind the DARE
curriculum is that enhanced self-esteem is a protective factor against drug
use.

A closer examination of the results for the general attitudes scale suggests that the DARE curriculum has had a significant impact despite the
treatment group's initial less anti-drug stance. In fact, as demonstrated

by the sign of the mean gain scores, whereas the control group followed normal developmental expectations and became more positive toward drug use over time, the treatment group actually became more anti-drug.

Statistically significant differences did emerge between DARE and non-DARE students on the scale measuring peer relationships, but significance was not achieved on the more salient scale measuring peer-pressure resistance. However, in the latter instance, the results were close to the .05 criterion. Learning skills to resist peer pressure to use drugs is a clear focus of the DARE curriculum. These short-term effects are in the expected direction and may become more pronounced as larger proportions of the sample encounter situations where they can choose to employ or not employ the skills.

The ultimate criterion of DARE or any other primary prevention curriculum is whether those who received the intervention: (a) choose not to use drugs, or (b) significantly delay onset of use, or (c) have a significantly lower probability of excessive use. The data on the effect of DARE on actual substance use are presented in Table 15.4. These data show no significant differences between the DARE and nonDARE students in reported involvement with cigarettes, alcohol, or marijuana. The lack of significant differences in the gain scores here may be more a reflection of low baseline rates of substance use in this age group than evidence of lack of effect. It is possible that differences will emerge as these students enter the modal ages for initiation of drug use.

Officer Effects

The analyses of officer effects are displayed in Table 15.5. The data here are limited to those students receiving the DARE curriculum. These four officers went through the same training regimen and are approximately the same age. Officer 1 has slightly more experience having been the officer responsible for teaching during the pilot phase.

Process evaluations conducted by multiple-trained observers indicated that all of the officers followed the lesson plans and were, without exception, rated as excellent teachers on a number of criteria. They were particularly and equally good at achieving rapport and eliciting classroom participation in the DARE exercises. There was general consensus among the process evaluation observers and among the officers that Officer 4 was more "expressive" than the others in his teaching. Officers 1 through 3, although expressive, were more often than Officer 4 "instrumental" and "task oriented" in the classroom.

For the general attitudes toward drugs scale, the higher the score, the more negative students became toward drugs from pre- to posttest. With the caveat that ceiling effects are operative, the gain scores for Officers 1 through 3 are in the desired direction, whereas those for Officer 4 are not. There were statistically significant differences between the officers on this scale with most of the difference accounted for by Officer 4.

For the substance-specific scales, only those assessing positive utilities concerning the three drugs produced statistically significant results. Substantively, this means that the students became less willing to acknowledge the possibility of positive reasons for using these substances. For these scales, the lower the score the more negative the students became from pre- to posttest toward use of these substances. In each instance where

TABLE 15.4
Analysis of Variance of Substance Use Gain Scores by Experimental
Condition and Race

	$\bar{X}$,	Whites	$\bar{X}$,	Non-Whites	F, Race	F, Treatment	F, Interaction
GCIGLIF							
Treatment	.209	(.689)[a]	.154	(.519)	3.63*	.01	.51
Control	.220	(.836)	.106	(.466)			
GCIGYR							
Treatment	.114	(.634)	.055	(.510)	3.90**	1.81	.42
Control	.174	(.834)	.065	(.361)			
GCIGMO							
Treatment	.100	(.631)	.033	(.419)	6.22**	.11	.32
Control	.121	(.573)	.014	(.208)			
GALCLIF							
Treatment	.066	(.613)	.049	(.684)	.09	.99	.05
Control	.094	(.577)	.093	(.473)			
GALCYR							
Treatment	.051	(.513)	.022	(.469)	74	.07	.09
Control	.053	(.152)	.042	(.336)			
GALCMO							
Treatment	.025	(.383)	.025	(.413)	.01	.00	.02
Control	.022	(.365)	.030	(.280)			
GMJLIF							
Treatment	.051	(.470)	.091	(.477)	1.41	3.11*	.37
Control	.019	(.278)	.027	(.237)			
GMJYR							
Treatment	.028	(.393)	.052	(.367)	.69	.45	.29
Control	.021	(.274)	.022	(.203)			
GMJMO							
Treatment	.014	(.281)	.024	(.260)	.24	.06	.09
Control	.020	(.261)	.020	(.282)			

*p is less than .10; **p is less than .05; ***p is less than .01
[a]Standard deviation is given in parentheses

TABLE 15.5
Analysis of Variance of Gain Scores by Officer

	$\bar{X}$ Officer 1	$\bar{X}$ Officer 2	$\bar{X}$ Officer 3	$\bar{X}$ Officer 4	SS, Explained	SS, Residual	F
GATTGEN	.02	.03	.02	−.03	.480	42.965	5.165***
GALPOSUT	.02	−.01	−.03	.07	1.328	162.008	3.696**
GALNEGUT	−.02	−.03	−.05	.03	.886	299.393	1.334
GCIPOSUT	−.02	.01	.00	.10	1.807	191.475	4.316***
GCIGNEGUT	.02	−.01	.05	.04	.742	313.333	1.083
GMPOSUT	.01	.00	−.03	.11	2.436	176.853	6.313***
GMJNEGUT	−.04	−.03	−.01	.06	1.321	323.921	1.870
GSELF	.05	.03	.04	.00	.332	37.709	4.067***
GPEERPR	.02	.05	.02	.15	2.354	208.976	5.209***

*p is less than .10; **p is less than .05; ***p iss less than .01

significant differences emerged, the officer with the less desirable score was Officer 4. Again in each instance, there was little difference between Officers 1, 2, and 3.

For the self-esteem scale, the higher the score the greater the increase in self-esteem between pre- and posttest. The statistically significant differences here are especially important. Intuitively, it would be predicted that the more expressive and affective officer would have the most pronounced effect on self-esteem. The data suggest that this did not occur.

Finally, on the peer-pressure resistance scale, lower scores indicate less susceptibility to peer pressure to use drugs from pre- to posttest. Again, the results indicate greater effectiveness of Officers 1 through 3 than for Officer 4.

Plausible Interpretation for Officer Effects

The data on officer effects are important from a number of different perspectives, particularly persuasive communications. Persons who deliver prevention interventions to youth usually do so out of a sincere commitment to both the strategy of the intervention and the combating the problem addressed by the intervention. A particularly attractive aspect of the DARE intervention is that it is taught by police officers who are trained to "go by the book." The process evaluation observations confirm a high degree of fidelity to the curriculum and a uniformity of presentation that, from a methodological perspective, eliminates some of the "deliverer" confounds that plague many interventions. Further, the pedagogical principles embodied in the DARE curriculum and training are sound and based on a broad body of research on teaching. Finally, the officers and the DARE curriculum are not part of the school system. This, plus the symbolic value of the uniform, and the obvious commitment of the officer to his or her task, are all positive.

It would be too easy to conclude that more "instrumental" and "task" oriented DARE officers are simply more effective at persuasive communication than officers who are more "expressive" and "affective" oriented. This is a possibility, but the data presented here are merely suggestive, not conclusive.

A possible confound to these data is something not built into the research design and something so subtle that most researchers may be unaware of it. In this as in most school based interventions, neither the officers/teachers delivering the intervention nor the students are randomly assigned. In this instance, Officer 4 requested that he be assigned to the inner-city types of schools or to those schools where youth from "high-risk" neighborhoods might be more densely concentrated. Therefore, it is likely that attempting to inoculate his students against drugs was a more formidable challenge than that faced by his other three colleagues. In fact, this interpretation leads to another possibility. Because the intervention is an "educational" one requiring reading and homework, and so on, it is possible that a more "instrumental" and "task" oriented officer would have been even less effective than Officer 4 with similar students. It would behoove persons developing and evaluating prevention interventions to focus more attention on matching the curriculum and persuasive communication styles of the deliverer with the cognitive/affective demands or needs of the students. Further, there are a host of other environmental factors that are not school based (e.g., family and neighborhood factors in particular) that may affect the outcomes of an intervention. Even powerful curriculum effects may be neutralized by factors external to the individual student and the school and classroom.

DISCUSSION

This chapter has described short-term effects (pre- to posttest, covering a period of 19 weeks or less) of the DARE curriculum on general and substance specific attitudes, self-esteem, resistance to peer pressure to use drugs and peer relationships, and on reported use of cigarettes, alcohol, and marijuana. In addition, an attempt has been made to assess the differential effectiveness of those delivering the DARE curriculum.

The sample consisted of 23 schools randomly assigned to receive the DARE curriculum in the sixth grade and eight schools randomly assigned to a non-DARE condition. Data were obtained prior to receipt of any instruction for all schools in both conditions and subsequent to receipt of the DARE curriculum in the treatment schools and the drug unit in the science curriculum in the control schools.

Because initial equivalence was not achieved on race, it was included as a control variable in the analysis of variance on standardized gain scores for a number of attitudinal and self-reported drug use scales. Some significant differences in gain scores in the predicted direction emerged for the attitudes, but not for self-reported drug use. Therefore, there is some evidence of effectiveness for the curriculum, but it is neither uniform nor large. This may be a result of ceiling effects on many of the variables or measurement before exposure by a large enough percentage of the sample to opportunities to initiate use.

Interesting and consistent results emerged from a subanalysis of differences in officer effects. These results suggest that a simple focus on "outcomes" may ignore an important element in any prevention intervention. Differences in both personal and teaching styles and differential persuasive communication skills may need to be matched to the modal learning styles of students. These may vary considerably within schools by classroom and across schools by ecological types of variables that are not school based.

REFERENCES

Bailey, W. J. (1985). Message source credibility in drug education. *Journal of School Health*, 55, 385–388.

Battjes, R. J. (1985). Prevention of adolescent drug abuse. *International Journal of the Addictions*, 20, 1113–1134.

Borhnstedt, G. W. (1969). Observations on the measurement of change. In E. F. Borgatta (Ed.), *Sociological methodology* (pp. 113–136). San Francisco, CA: Josey-Bass.

Bostrom, R. N. (1983). *Persuasion*. Englewood Cliffs, NJ: Prentice-Hall.

Botvin, G. (1983). Prevention of adolescent substance abuse through the development of personal and social competence. In T. Glynn, C. Leukefeld, & J. Ludford (Eds.), *Preventing adolescent drug abuse: Intervention strategies*. Washington, DC: National Institute on Drug Abuse.

Botvin, G. J. (1986). Substance abuse prevention research: Recent developments and future directions. *Journal of School Health*, 56, 369–375.

Botvin, G. J., Baker, E., Botvin, E. M., Filazzola, A. D., & Millman, R. B. (1984). Alcohol abuse prevention through the development of personal and social competence: A pilot study. *Journal of Studies on Alcohol*, 45, 550–552.

Botvin, G. J., Baker, E., Renick, N. L., Filazzola, A. D., & Botvin, E. M. (1984). A cognitive-behavioral approach to substance abuse prevention. *Addictive Behaviors*, 9, 137–147.

Botvin, G. J., & Wills, T. A. (1985). Personal and social skills training: Cognitive-behavioral approaches to substance abuse prevention. In C. S. Bell & R. Battjes (Eds.), *Prevention research: Deterring drug abuse among children and adolescents*. Washington, DC: National Institute on Drug Abuse.

Braucht, G., Follingstadt, D., Brakarsh, D., & Berry, K. (1973). Drug education: A review of goals, approaches and effectiveness and a paradigm for evaluation. *Quarterly Journal for Studies on Alcohol*, 34, 1279–1292.

DeJong, W. (1987). A short-term evaluation of project DARE (Drug Abuse Resistance Education): Preliminary indications of effectiveness. *Journal of Drug Education, 17,* 279–294.

Dielman, T. E., Shope, J. T., Campanelli, P. C., & Butchart, A. T. (1986). *An elementary school-based, social skills approach to alcohol misuse prevention.* Paper presented at the First National Conference on alcohol and Drug Abuse Prevention, Arlington, VA.

Durell, J., & Bukoski, W. (1984). Preventing substance abuse: The state of the art. *Public Health Reports, 99,* 23–31.

Faine, J. R. (1989). *The Nashville DARE project: An evaluation of the 1988–89 Drug Abuse Resistance Education program.* Final report to the Metropolitan Public Schools, Western Kentucky University, Bowling Green, KY.

Faine, J. R., & Bohlander, E. (1989). *Drug abuse resistance education: An assessment of the 1987–88 Kentucky State Police DARE Program.* Bowling Green, KY: Western Kentucky University Social Research Laboratory.

Flay, B. R. (1985). Psychosocial approaches to smoking prevention: A review of findings. *Health Psychology, 4,* 449–488.

Flay, B. R., Ryan, K. B., Best, J. A., Brown, K. S., Kersell, M. W., d'Avernas, J. R., & Zanna, M. P. (1985). Are social psychological smoking prevention programs effective? The Waterloo study. *Journal of Behavioral Medicine, 8,* 37–59.

Hansen, W. B., Johnson, C. A., Flay, B. R., Graham, J. W., & Sobel, J. (1988). Affective and social influences approaches to the prevention of multiple substance among seventh grade students: Results from Project SMART. *Preventive Medicine, 17,* 1–20.

Holder, L. (1972). Effects of source, message, audience characteristics on health behavior compliance. *Health Services Reports, 87,* 343–350.

Kinder, B. N., Pope, N. W., & Walfish, S. (1980). Drug and alcohol education programs: A review of outcome studies. *The International Journal of the Addictions, 15,* 1035–1044.

Moskowitz, J. M., Condon, J. W., Brewer, M., Schaps, E., & Malvin, J. (1979). *Scaling of student self-report instruments.* Report submitted to the prevention branch of the National Institute on Drug Abuse, Washington, DC.

Moskowitz, J. M., Schaeffer, G. A., Condon, J. W., Schaps, E., & Malvin, J. (1981). *Psychometric properties of the "Drug and Alcohol Survey."* Report submitted to the prevention branch of the National Institute on Drug Abuse, Washington, DC.

Pentz, M. A., Dwyer, J. H., MacKinnon, D. P., Flay, B. R., Hansen, W. B., Wang, E. Y., & Johnson, C. A. (1989). A multicommunity trial for primary prevention of drug abuse. *Journal of the American Medical Association, 261,* 3259–3266.

Ringwalt, C., Ennett, S. T., & Holt, K. D. (1990). *An outcome evaluation of Project D.A.R.E. (Drug Abuse Resistance Education).* Unpublished manuscript, Center for Social Research and Policy Analysis, Research Triangle Institute, Research Triangle Park, NC.

Rosenberg, M. (1965). *Society and the adolescent self image.* Princeton University Press: Princeton, NJ.

Schaps, E., DiBartolo, R., Moskowitz, J., Polley, C. S., & Churgin, A. (1981). A review of 127 drug abuse prevention program evaluations. *Journal of Drug Issues, 11,* 17–43.

Tobler, N. S. (1987). Meta-analysis of 143 adolescent drug prevention programs: Quantitative outcome results of program participants compared to a control or comparison group. *Journal of Drug Issues, 16,* 537–567.

VI

AN OVERVIEW
OF COMMUNICATION
AND DRUG ABUSE PREVENTION

16

Muddling Through Toward Small Wins: On the Need for Requisite Variety

Teresa L. Thompson
Louis P. Cusella*
University of Dayton

The conference on Persuasive Communication and Drug Abuse generated insights that were provocative and important. On some issues, most of the researchers agreed. On other issues, there was agreement on major points but not on subtleties. And on yet other issues (e.g., the role of ''information'' alone) there was complete disagreement. At the conclusion of the conference a round-table discussion attempted to answer questions such as, ''What do we now know?'', ''What thoughts would you like people to take away from this conference?'', and ''Where do we go from here?'' These questions are also the focus of this chapter.

Let us begin by discussing some of the particularly provocative insights that came out of the presentations and papers. Sometimes these insights came directly out of various presentations; other times they were generated indirectly through discussion or deduction. We concentrate on insights and conclusions that should have some practical utility for those attempting to address the drug abuse problem. Because many of the chapters in this book have been rather lengthy, we attempt to be relatively succinct in our discussion of these conclusions. We make note of chapters within the book to which the interested reader may refer for more discussion of each topic.

NOTABLE INSIGHTS FROM THE PRESENTATIONS/PAPERS

1. The more ''risk factors'' experienced by an individual, the greater the likelihood of a drug abuse problem (Bukowski).

---

*Both authors contributed euqally to this chapter.

2. Putative risk factors for drug abuse include:
   a. parent drug use
   b. perceived adult drug use
   c. peer use of drugs
   d. poor grades in school
   e. poor relationship with parents
   f. low self-esteem, depression, and psychological distress
   g. unconventionality and tolerance for deviance
   h. high sensation seeking
   i. low social responsibility
   j. low religiosity
   k. lack of purpose in life
   l. disruptive life events
   m. early adjustment difficulties (Pickens)

3. The type of risk factor involved in drug abuse affects the type of intervention required (Pickens).

4. There is a strong link between academic performance and drug abuse. Improving educational opportunities can lessen the drug problem (Bukowski).

5. Although drug abuse programs in the school have frequently been criticized for ineffectiveness, we must remember there is a difference between school-*based* and school-*only* programs (Leukefeld; see also Forman; Hawkins). School-based programs are typically more successful than school-only programs.

6. Teacher-training approaches seem to be somewhat more effective and are easier to implement than parent-training approaches (Hawkins).

7. Substantial changes have been observed in the markets that have received *high exposure* to the Partnership for a Drug Free America ads (Black). Many times, these high exposure areas account for an apparent average change across the nation. To be effective, then, anti-drug ads need to reach a density well beyond what is typically found in public service campaigns—or even beyond the density found in many commercial campaigns.

8. Campaigns targeting siblings appear to be a promising idea. The appeal should remind message receivers of the impact of their own drug use on drug abuse in their younger siblings (Black).

9. Attitude changes affect drug use, rather than changes in drug use over the years leading to changes in attitudes (Bachman).

10. The reason you start using drugs may determine whether you will continue using them (Pickens).

11. There has long been agreement on family influence in drug use. However, we now believe that there is *specificity* in that influence. For instance, individuals with family members who have problems with alcohol are more likely to have problems with alcohol, but not necessarily more likely to have problems with other drugs (Pickens).

12. Different approaches are necessary for high-sensation seekers versus low-sensation seekers. High-sensation seekers should be encouraged to find other forms of excitement; peer pressure should be targeted toward low-sensation seekers (Donohew, Palmgreen, & Lorch).

13. Parental involvement in drug presentation programs may heighten rebelliousness in children (Forman).

14. People who are positively bonded are less likely to violate norms, associate with friends who use drugs, or use drugs themselves (Hawkins).

15. Most drug use takes place in a peer cluster (Oetting).

16. Children are not *subject to* peer pressure, they are a *part of* peer pressure (Oetting).

17. Anger is a better predictor of drug use than either depression or anxiety (Oetting).

18. Intervention does not work if you then place the child back with friends who are users (Oetting).

19. Most prevention programs seem effective at first, then people become bored with it and it loses its effectiveness (Beisecker).

20. Simple strategies are most likely to be followed (Beisecker).

21. Peer influence is stronger than parental influence (Oetting; Beisecker).

22. Programs should address the misperceptions in kids about drug use and about the drug use of and attitudes toward drugs of their peers (Beisecker).

23. We have to look at *all* the messages in the media about drugs, not just at targeted campaigns, in order to understand the impact of the media on drug use (Wartella).

24. The media work only in combination with school and interpersonal campaigns, not alone (Wartella).

25. There is a weak link between attitudes and behaviors (Wartella). Many factors influence behavior in addition to attitudes (Petty).

26. Everyone does not process messages in the same way (Petty; Donohew et al.; Wartella).

27. The same attitude may have different implications for behavior in different people (Petty).

28. Messages have to be very self-relevant to be persuasive (Petty).
29. Effective messages have to target attitudes that come to mind immediately, not those that have to be pulled out (Petty).

PROVOCATIVE SUGGESTIONS
AND FUTURE DIRECTIONS

In addition to these insights, which came out of the presentations and papers at the conference, several suggestions for future research and future campaigns were generated in both formal and informal discussion among the conference participants. Many of these came from the round-table discussion.

1. More research needs to focus on campaigns that target *significant others*. Other message-oriented research (e.g., the fear appeal research) has found that communications that talk about the effect of a behavior on one's significant others are more persuasive than are those directed toward the message receiver him or herself. This might have implications for drug abuse campaigns.

2. Although several of the researchers noted in their presentations that, in their research, information itself seemed to lessen drug use, such use remains high. Although information may help, it is not enough. Research needs to examine information/education *in combination with* other modes of communication. The research that has concluded that information alone works does not take into account other communication that may be occurring at the same time as the information campaigns (e.g., interpersonal communication prompted by the campaign or school campaigns of which the researcher is unaware).

3. Several participants mentioned that the availability issue needs to be examined in research. They believed that law enforcement *is* having an impact on the problem. However, research has yet to examine the link between availability and drug use. It is an assumed relationship, rather than an empirically established one.

4. Although we know that there is an impact related to being a family member of someone with a substance abuse problem, we do not know how close that family member has to be in order to affect others. Is a grandparent close enough? Must the person be in the immediate family? Because most extended family systems seem to have at least one member somewhere with an abuse problem, we must be careful with these conclusions.

5. Similarly, we do not know the mechanism through which the aforementioned family influence operates. The knowledge that a family mem-

ber with an abuse problem puts others in the family at risk helps us target individuals, but it does not tell us how to address that influence. Knowing how the influence works (whether it is a learned behavior, genetically determined, a spurious correlation, etc.) might help us understand how to undermine the influence.

6. We need to study individuals in families with a drug abuser who do *not* become abusers themselves. What protects them?

7. Not enough of the research has focused on characteristics of messages and the impact of different characteristics. Most of the research has been too broad (e.g., looking at the impact of ''information'' rather than the characteristics of that information).

8. More long-term measures are needed for most of the areas of study conducted to date.

9. The *attentiveness* factor has not been well researched. How much attention do people pay to various kinds of messages? A message must be attended to, before it can be persuasive.

10. Measures of variance accounted for need to be reported for much of the research. Although we know that some campaigns are making a difference, we do not know how much of a difference they are making.

11. Several of the researchers reported problems with parents' effectiveness at participating in prevention programs. What can be done about this? Do parents need to be convinced of the seriousness of the problem? Do they need to be convinced that they can have an impact? Under what conditions do parents effectively participate in such programs?

12. Does parent training really work? When parents are taught skills to address the problem, do they do what they have been taught? Do these behaviors then have an impact?

13. It was noted that the campaign against drugs is quite small in scope and budget compared to the ad budgets of the tobacco and alcohol industries. On a related note, it was mentioned that there was a coincidental drop in cigarette consumption following the removal of cigarette advertising from television. This, it turned out, was due to a drop in teens trying cigarettes. When cigarette ads in other media increased in density, however, the initiation rate in teens again increased and remains high. The fact that this is true even though many other societal factors now discourage cigarette smoking may be seen as testimony to the persuasive impact of such ads.

14. The point just cited led to a discussion of the need to examine demand reduction public policies (i.e., the reduction of ads).

15. The suggestion was made of the role of afternoon television (e.g., soap operas) to target hard to reach populations, such as those in the inner-city. This, it is hoped, may help us move from changing knowledge and attitudes to actually changing behavior.

16. It was noted that the anti-drug campaigns are occurring at the same time as other, more subtle, media messages are changing. For example, writers, producers, and performers now sometimes incorporate anti-drug messages into television shows, movies, music videos, records, and so on. This makes the impact of the campaigns themselves difficult to assess.

17. The likelihood of anti-drug messages being incorporated into television shows, and the like, increases when the show's producers know that their advertisers are anti-drug. As companies have become more involved with the Partnership for a Drug Free America, for instance, social responsibility in regard to the placement of ads has increased. This puts pressure on television producers that may have secondary positive effects for anti-drug campaigns.

18. The issue of environmental/political factors in the drug abuse problem was also raised. It was pointed out that media efforts help galvanize political opinions, which typically lag far behind public concern about the issue. It was also noted that the drug abuse problem can be minimized (although not eliminated) without addressing the core causative issues. It is easier to motivate public action to address drug abuse as a problem than it is to convince people to address the fundamental societal problems leading to drug abuse.

19. We need to incorporate the notion of a peer cluster (from Oetting's work) *into* other relevant theories and research. For instance, it was suggested that the concept was particularly relevant to the study of high risk youth. Additionally, we need to study *what goes on* in the peer cluster. What interaction variables operate to facilitate drug initiation and use?

20. Concern was raised about what will happen to the anti-drug campaign when the present drug epidemic is *perceived* as having eroded. Numerous predictions were made, including that the epidemic will decline first from the decision-makers' culture, but not the inner-city, and thus less will be done about the problem. Although there was some disagreement about whether or not this will lead to a decrease in campaigning efforts, the consensus was that the inner-city population would remain a concern.

21. To address the concern in Suggestion 20, questions were raised about risk factors particularly relevant to this population. This is especially salient because few persuasive campaigns now target this group, and those that do simply address getting people into treatment, not preventing initiation, and so forth.

22. The issue of the need to target various groups with unique appeals was made, although some data indicate similar reactions among various racial groups to the Partnership ads. Others noted that so little research has yet to really target the inner city population that it is difficult to know whether there are or are not such receiver differences.

23. Another targeting concern was raised regarding the drug abuse problem among health-care workers. This requires a different approach than when addressing messages to adolescents.

24. Building on this point, it was noted that we must address the beliefs that underlie drug use. We have to uncover these beliefs in order to target messages appropriately.

25. Denial of the problem, at all levels, must still be addressed. The data indicate denial of the problem at individual, family, school, community, and so on, levels. The role of the media in stimulating interpersonal communication to overcome this denial was emphasized. Similarly, several people mentioned the role of school or community surveys to help identify their problems and avoid denial. Although researchers may be convinced that the problem is national in scope, particular regions may need their own surveys to convince them that they have a problem.

26. The suggestion was made that the federal government begin sponsoring more anti-drug ads. Concern was expressed about this, however, because the amount of money that would likely be devoted to such a campaign would be so small as to be of little help. However, the ability of the Partnership to garner free media time would be undercut by the government's efforts.

27. A related issue was raised when it was pointed out that the act of giving resources to the anti-drug campaign increases commitment to it. If the government took over this activity, the persuasive impact of this commitment would be negated.

28. The government, however, can help more effectively through sources such as notable government officials who can command free media time (in the form of news) to send persuasive messages.

29. Some of the most persuasive messages have not been in campaigns, but have come through the news, when the drug-related deaths of famous personalities and athletes are reported.

30. Communications that take place at the time of drug use are more likely to be effective (e.g., signs in bars noting that alcohol use may be damaging to unborn fetuses).

31. It is believed that adolescents, in particular, respond to *accurate* information, as opposed to the misinformation they frequently have.

32. Preventing drug abuse is more than just testing the effectiveness of intervention programs. It also involves building a knowledge base on which new interventions are based. In light of this guideline, we offer some additional ideas on which future research and campaigns might build.

SOME ADDITIONAL ISSUES AND DIRECTIONS

Some contributors either stated or implied a central interest in the causes of drug abuse. Some authors, by implication, suggest that a lack of information regarding the nature of drug abuse can directly affect the behavior of the drug abuser. In other words, drug abuse is the result of *ignorance* about drugs and abuse problems. These authors offered data to support their claim that anti-drug messages alone, when they reach a density in market weight to a degree greater than public service ads currently reach (i.e., high exposure), diminish the level of drug abuse. Other contributors argue that although ignorance may be a problem, overcoming ignorance requires information we do not as yet possess about the *beliefs* of drug abusers. In a sense, their perspective argues that drug abuse is shaped by forces other than ignorance, ranging from "society" to internal cognitive belief structures. The question one would ask is: Do we need to take a single position on the drug abuse problem?

One of the most important challenges presented to us is precisely how to "frame" the social problem of substance abuse and, in addition, how to "frame" our role as researchers. Photographers use the term *frame* to denote what they have chosen to include in their picture, including what is figure and ground. Likewise, we must choose what definitions, concepts, variables, situations, and processes to consider and focus on to create a picture or "frame" of substance abuse as a social problem and substance abuse research and communication. One useful frame may be to consider the challenges presented by the drug abuse problem in terms of control, decision making, and communication processes. These issues are also of concern to organizational scientists (McKelvey & Aldrich, 1983). In this regard, the work of Ashby (1956), Simon (1957), Lindbloom (1959), and Weick (1979) are relevant for/to us.

Requisite Variety

Many years ago, Ashby (1956) pointed out what he called the Law of Requisite Variety (LRV), which held that, in order to cope with an uncertainly varying environment, systems need to have an equivalent amount of internal variety. Variety is another term for complexity or the number of possible states of a system. Put more succinctly, only variety can regulate (absorb) variety (Buckley, 1968). Drug abuse research has not paid much attention to this law. When applied to the drug abuse problem the implication of the law of requisite variety is that anti-drug processes (e.g., message campaigns and their creators) that are applied to a "complicated" problem (drug abuse) must themselves be "complicated." If a small portion of the "variety" constituted by the drug abuse problem is attended to because anti-drug campaigns are limited in their complexity (i.e., "simple") then most of the problem will remain untouched and will remain a puzzle to people concerned with "what is up and why they are unable to manage it" (Weick, 1979, p. 189).

As in any interdependent system (Weick, 1979), when faced with the need for requisite variety there really are only three things anti-drug researchers can do. First, they can establish a one-to-one correspondence between variety in the "controller" (researcher/campaigner) and variety in the "controlled" (campaign target). Theoretically, one drug researcher would be assigned full time to a person in a target audience noting when that person departs from the researcher's understanding of why a person uses drugs and how his or her behavior could be controlled. In a situation of one-to-one correspondence there is perfect requisite variety (Weick, 1979) where one individual researcher specializes in each particular dimension of the drug user population and who attends to nothing else. Of course, aside from the resource and motivational issues in trying to implement that solution, the solution of one-to-one correspondence makes for extraordinary problems of coordination and piecing together the highly molecular single observations into an understandable form.

The second way to deal with variety is to reduce it. This option is open to only the most powerful systems who may impose agreements, establish monopolies, for example, which can simplify environments and shrink variety. This option would require more than an effective anti-drug media campaign, however, because the capacity to impose structures on the drug-using population would require social policing measures beyond those tolerable in a democratic society.

The third option when faced with the need for requisite variety, and the one toward which we are most sympathetic, is to complicate the controller, in this case the anti-drug media campaign and the research on which the campaign is based. According to Weick (1979):

> This intentional complication increases the controller's variety relative to the variety in the inputs that the controller processes. A complicated individual embodies in one place the several sensors implied when there is one sensor assigned to each variable. This embodiment means that the complicated individual can sense variations in a larger environment, select what need *not* be attended to, what will not change imminently, what *won't* happen, and by this selection the individual is able to amplify his control variety. He solely (that is, insightfully) ignores that which will not change, concentrates on that which will, and . . . is able to anticipate significant environmental variation when and where it occurs. Complicated observers take in more. They see patterns that less complicated people miss, and they exploit these subtle patterns by concentrating on them and ignoring everything else. (p. 193)

In this regard, we might ask whether it is possible for drug campaigns to have unplanned or blind variations? It appears to us that both research and campaign processes are not so advanced as to preclude blind variations. By ''blind'' variations, we are advocating not avoiding a persuasive approach or a research approach just because we do not know what will happen. In large part, these can be considered ''unjustified'' variations (Campbell, 1974). The danger is that the more ''effective'' and adapted a campaign becomes to present conditions, the more it will reduce its ability to maintain the requisite variety necessary to adapt to the future (McKelvey & Aldrich, 1983). Weick (1977) offered a useful plan for enhancing variations that may be of interest to drug researchers and creators of anti-drug campaigns. The essence of his plan is his call for effective systems to be garrulous, clumsy, superstitious, hypocritical, monstrous, octopoid, wandering, and grouchy. Strong terms indeed, but ones that seek to create a vision for variety.

Based on this view, it is well to build into a system, like an anti-drug campaign or a line of research about drug use, some clumsiness or ''galumphing,'' defined as ''patterned voluntary elaboration or complication of process'' (Miller, 1973, p. 92) instead of designing social programs that are streamlined, finely tuned, efficient, and inflexibly focused on a *specific goal*. Galumphing is a way of elaborating campaigns and research programs and thereby introducing variations that may offer requisite variety even though they may be inefficient in the short term.

Overdetermination

How might those interested in drug abuse and persuasive campaigns designed to affect that abuse employ the LRV? First, it may be helpful to allow a number of goals to be included in any research or campaign agenda. For example, is it reasonable to expect an overdetermined system like drug abuse to be eliminated as a result of a single anti-drug media campaign, no matter how long it runs? The concept of *overdetermination* states that there are usually more factors that act to produce a single behavior (e.g., drug use and abuse) than are really necessary to have it occur (Weick, 1979). As a concept, overdetermination was first described by Freud when he tried to account for the symptoms of hysteria such that a single bit of behavior served simultaneously to reduce tensions generated by several motives. Thus, the concept of *overdetermination* says that a given bit of behavior should be regarded and analyzed as expressing a maximum number of psychological, social, informational, and communicative factors.

Elimination, Prevention, and Management

If this relationship between multiple determinants and single behaviors is reflective of the drug abuse phenomenon, then elimination is one of a number of goals a campaign could have established for it by focusing on certain behaviors at certain points in time. Elimination would concern itself with the *resolution* of the drug problem such that its "causes" are addressed *after* it has already become a problem for some people and, as a result of numerous different tactics, the "problem" disappears and people stop "doing drugs." Drug *prevention* as a goal would attempt to eliminate the myriad causes of drug abuse *before* certain target audiences abuse drugs. In this way drug abuse behaviors would never occur, because drug use would never have been initiated. Drug abuse *management* would seek to diminish the magnitude or intensity of the drug problem by *containing* its causes after the phenomenon has occurred. Here our goal would be to deter the progression of drug use. It should be clear that these three goals are not "either–or" propositions. Rather, they are each potential elements of a goal set.

When the call for increased variety is blended with the realities of overdetermination it should also be clear that more should be done to understand the numerous causes of drug abuse. When causes range from environmental (economic, racial, class) to psychological (beliefs, values) to informational (data) to social (peer clusters) factors, it must be concluded that no one persuasive campaign can address all these factors. This reality may also suggest why one campaign which focuses on one or two issues (which is probably a necessity since human beings are limited in their informational and cognitive processing capabilities) may "fail" if it does not eliminate, prevent, or manage arbitrarily designated levels of drug abuse.

Another way the Law of Requisite Variety may be applied to the drug abuse phenomenon is to "experiment" more than we currently have by initiating lots of trial and miniature ventures going on at any one time. By the time researchers and campaigners have defined what they mean by mission, goal, strategy, and objective they may have so narrowly defined the boundaries of their projects as to proscribe experimentation. Both quantitative and qualitative research studies should be conducted to determine the *why* and the *how* of drug abuse. The *why* and *how* of drug abuse may be distinct but interdependent phenomenon. They may also be multilayered. For example, environmental and psychological factors may be different phenomenological strata of the *why* of drug abuse. But what also needs to be considered is the fact that people "do drugs" because "doing drugs" is pleasurable! (Morley, 1989). The variety that stems from this reality is immense and calls for new understanding. The *how* of drug abuse can only be understood by seeing the world of the drug abuse as it is seen by him or her. This calls for field work going beyond typical survey research.

Field research into the *why* and *how* of drug abuse should make researchers and the devisers of persuasive campaigns better learners because they will have first-hand knowledge of what drives the drug abuser. Miniature ventures in standard survey research and persuasive campaigns should provide first-hand knowledge of what "works" and what does not work. These miniature ventures in research and media campaigns do not have to be excessively expensive experiments if systems are established for quickly cutting off failures and stepping up resources to the apparent successes. In essence, the LRV would call for anti-drug professionals to be better strategists who are better learners who experiment more frequently. In addition, we may need to experiment with a number of different methods and messages of persuasion in terms of different demographic groups. Although some conferees disputed the "demographics as destiny" view, a sustained, subtle, and systematic approach would probably call for some audience targeting as we work on a number of levels (multiple goals) and try a number of different things in our media campaigns. Our varied research agenda may call for different message types and different campaign strategies as they relate to the different campaign goals of prevention, elimination, and management. For example, a possible scenario may take the form presented in Fig. 16.1.

Sense Making

Issues regarding the *why* and *how* of drug abuse may also be understood more complexly when researchers understand that the drug abuser is a meaning creator or, in Weick's (1979) terms, a "sense-maker" who interprets the world around him or her, including drug abuse, by talking to him or herself and others over and over to find out what he or she is thinking.

| | TARGET AUDIENCES | | | |
	Decision Makers	Health Professionals	Middle Class	Core Users
Prevention				
GOALS Elimination				
Management				

FIG. 16.1. A possible research agenda for persuasive campaigns. These were some of the target audiences suggested by conference participants. They do not, of course, represent all possible target audiences. Different persuasive campaigns would be developed to address various goals with various groups.

Here the organism or group enacts (constructs, rearranges, singles out) drug behavior (actions and talk) and that behavior and talk is viewed by the person or group retrospectively (after it has occurred). Sense is then made of that behavior such that the actor or group selects an interpretation of the meaning of the behavior. This meaning or sense is then stored as knowledge and affects subsequent drug talk and behavior and the interpretations of those actions. Thus, sense making is made up of the components—knowing, thinking, seeing, and saying. That is, "How can I know what I think until I see what I say?" As an example for the researcher, the sense-making recipe may include different pronouns that allow for the inclusion of peer clusters or conformity as tools for understanding the why and the how of drug abuse. With this technique, the researcher can portray virtually any kind of sense making (meaning creation or interpretation) related to the drug abuser process that includes not only cognition and thinking but "feelings, actions, and desires and collective attempts to understand them" (Weick, 1979, p. 134). What unfolds may take the form of interrelated research programs. For example, the drug abuse researcher could ask: "How can I (the researcher or campaigner) know (understand) what they (drug abuser, research subject, audience member) think, want or feel about drugs and anti-drug campaigns until I see and hear what they say and do?" during the actual act of drug use or the viewing of anti-drug messages. This would apply to the reception of all drug-related information, from compliance pressure tactics by peers, to anti-drug messages over the media, to news reports of the drug-related deaths of famous persons (athletes, for example).

Small Wins

The *objective* of any particular research effort or anti-drug campaign must also be understood in the context of drug abuse as an overdetermined system as we wrestle with questions surrounding campaign success or lack thereof. In this regard the concept of small wins is particularly relevant. The work of Peters (1977, 1987) and Weick (1984) suggests that social science research has done relatively little to solve social problems (see Berger, 1976; Cook, 1979; Kohn, 1976) primarily because:

> The massive scale on which social problems are conceived often precludes innovative action because the limits of bounded rationality are exceeded and arousal is raised to dysfunctionally high levels. People often define social problems in ways that overwhelm their ability to do anything about them. (Weick, 1984, p. 40)

This view comes from the work of Peters (1987) who noted that most advances in science and technology are incremental and most "breakthroughs'' are the so-called post-hoc results of the efforts of small teams of problem solvers across time. Breakthroughs or major advances are the evolutionary and developmental product of hundreds of important developments made on a small-scale. Both Peters (1977) and Weick (1984) call these numerous incremental advances "small wins."

As a result of what was discussed in this volume, we would advocate a strategy of small wins as the scale of the social problem we call drug abuse is redefined. A strategy of small wins would consist of the following steps (Weick, 1984):

1. recast larger problems (e.g., "drug abuse") into smaller, less-arousing problems (e.g., beliefs about drug use vs. abuse; peer tactics used to persuade those yet to use drugs; attractive alternatives to drug use; the perceived costs of drug use; etc.).
2. identify a series of controlled opportunities of modest size that produce *visible* results (e.g., get a key decision maker to pay attention to drug use in a specific locale); and
3. gather these into "synoptic solutions" which simultaneously show the distribution of small wins over a wide region of the drug abuse problem at a given point in time.

In a sense, the strategy of small wins would address the social problem of drug abuse by working directly on the construction or emergence of the problem and indirectly on its resolution across time. To illustrate this approach we end our discussion of the strategy of small wins for drug abuse with a focus on alcohol abuse as a particular case.

> AA has been successful in helping alcoholics, partly because it does not insist that they become totally abstinent for the rest of their lives. Although this is the goal of the program, alcoholics are told to stay sober one day at a time, or one hour at a time if the temptation is severe. The impossibility of lifetime abstinence is scaled down to the more workable task of not taking a drink for the next 24 hours, drastically reducing the size of a win necessary to maintain sobriety. Actually gaining that small win is then aided by several other small measures such as phone calls, one-hour meetings, slogans, pamphlets, and meditations, which themselves are easy to acquire and implement. (Weick, 1984, p. 42)

The small-win strategy, in other words, is incremental (AA success is "partly" due to its temporal vision), it is cumulative (not consuming a drink for 24 hours leads to another day and another 24 hour win), it is multidimensional (other measures aid you in your win) and it can only occur across time. In other words, one line of research or one persuasive campaign cannot tackle everything related to drug abuse as a social problem nor must the research or campaign tackle the most visible source of drug abuse. The strategy of small wins calls for the identification of quick, opportunistic, tangible first steps only modestly related to a final outcome. The first steps may be driven less by a logical decision calculus, the big picture, or the "real issue" and more by actions that could be built upon other actions indicating a complex pathway toward success.

Bounded Rationality and Muddling

The strategy of small wins says as much about the decision making of researchers, campaign creators, and target audience members as decision makers as the strategy speaks to the magnitude of the social problem called drug abuse. In a real sense, researchers must decide how and what to research, persuasive campaigners must decide what messages to construct and send, and receivers decide how to respond. Put plainly, it may be dangerous to assume that we as activists in the anti-drug world or individuals in a target audience are capable of being perfectly rational when we make decisions regarding research, persuasive messages, or drug-use initiation or progression. It is clear that people (whether researchers or drug users) do not behave in the manner of purely "rational" beings. We make errors in judgments, fail to search for all alternatives, misinterpret the available information, and estimate incorrectly the likelihood of various events (Ebert & Mitchell, 1975). It was Simon (1957) who perhaps took the initial step in pointing out these problems as they relate to human decision making. His principle of bounded rationality suggests that:

> The capacity of the human mind for formulating and solving complex problems is very small compared with the size of the problems whose solution is required for objectively rational behavior in the real world—or even for a reasonable approximation to such objective rationality. (p. 198)

This reality indicates the need to consider human limitations in the decision processes of all those involved in the drug abuse problem and the mechanisms each employs for adjusting behavior within these bounds. Writing in a similar vein, Lindbloom (1959) argued that "Limits on human intellectual capacities and on available information set definite limits to man's capacity to be comprehensive" (p. 84). Lindbloom suggested that, more often than not, when faced with complex problems humans simply start "muddling through" those problems. According to Lindbloom, there are two distinct types of problem solving. The first type is characterized by a logical progression through the classical stages of problem solving, from problem definition to solution implementation with full knowledge that all relevant information has been taken into account and accurately assessed. This approach is similar to Simon's (1957) "rational man" model. The second approach tries to approximate rationality but operates on the assumption that in a complex world we must work in stages of successive comparisons and "muddle through" to the best of our ability. This second approach is similar to Simon's (1957) model of "satisficing". All elements of the drug abuse constellation (researchers, persuasive campaigners, and members of target audiences) make decisions that are intendedly rational but our decisions suffer because we have limited cognitive and problem solving capacities and limited knowledge of future events.

The reality of our own bounded rationality as we are faced with the overdetermined social problem we call drug abuse indicates the necessity to target on small wins for our research and persuasive campaigns as we deal with media campaign targets who are themselves bounded in their rationality. The complexity inherent in this problem calls for us to increase our own complexity in both our research and our persuasive campaigns. Small incremental changes are a means to cope with this complexity. The next question is, of course, how do we deal with this inefficiency and irrationality. Our thinking and research must center on methods and models of increased complexity and efficiency in order for us to win at all.

REFERENCES

Ashby, W. R. (1956). *An introduction to cybernetics.* London: Chapman & Hall.

Berger, B. M. (1976). Comments on Mel Kohn's paper. *Social Problems, 24,* 115–120.

Buckley, W. (1968). Society as a complex adaptive system. In W. Buckley (Ed.), *Modern systems research for the behavioral scientist* (pp. 490–513). Chicago: Aldine.

Campbell, D. T. (1974). Unjustified variation and selective retention in scientific discovery. In F. J. Ayala & T. Dobzhansky (Eds.), *Studies in the philosophy of biology* (pp. 139–161). New York: MacMillan.

Cook, S. W. (1979). Social science and school desegregation: Did we mislead the Supreme Court *Personality and Social Psychology Bulletin, 5,* 420–437.

Ebert, R. J., & Mitchell, T. R. (1975). *Organizational decision processes: Concepts and analysis.* New York: Crove, Russak.

Kohn, M. L. (1976). Looking back: A 25 year review and appraisal of social problems research. *Social Problems, 24,* 94–112.

Lindbloom, L. E. (1959). The science of muddling through. *Public Administration Review, 19,* 290–309.

McKelvey, B., & Aldrich, H. (1983). Populations, natural selection, and applied organizational science. *Administrative Science Quarterly, 28,* 101–128.

Miller, S. (1973). Ends, means, and galumphing: Some leitmotifs of play. *American Anthropoligist, 75,* 87–98.

Morley, J. (1989, October 2). What crack is like. *New Republic,* pp. 12–13.

Peters, T. J. (1977). *Patterns of winning and losing: Effects of approach and avoidance by friends and enemies.* Unpublished doctoral dissertation, Stanford University, Stanford, CA.

Peters, T. J. (1987). *Thriving on chaos.* New York: Harper & Row.

Simon, H. A. (1957). *Models of man*. New York: Wiley.

Weick, K. E. (1977). Re-punctuating the problem. In P. S. Goodman, J. M. Pennings, & Associates (Eds.), *New perspectives on organizational effectiveness* (pp. 193–225). San Francisco: Jossey-Bass.

Weick, K. E. (1979). *The social psychology of organizing* (2nd ed.). Reading, MA: Addison-Wesley.

Weick, K. E. (1984). Small wins: Redefining the scale of social problems. *American Psychologist, 39*, 40–49.

Author Index

335

Subject Index